Designing Information Technology
in the Postmodern Age

Designing Information Technology in the Postmodern Age

From Method to Metaphor

Richard Coyne

The MIT Press
Cambridge, Massachusetts
London, England

This book was set in Baskerville by Achorn Graphic Services Inc. and was printed and bound in the United States of America.

Library of Congress Cataloging-in-Publication Data

Coyne, Richard (Richard D.)
  Designing information technology in the postmodern age : from method to metaphor / Richard Coyne.
      p.   cm.
  Includes bibliographical references.
  ISBN 0-262-03228-7 (acid-free paper)
  1. Information technology. 2. System design. I. Title.
T58.5.C69   1995
004.2′1′01—dc20   95-8253
                                                                          CIP

To Jack, Gwen, Alan, and Betty

Contents

Contents

Preface

It is not necessary to begin a book on information technology by cataloging the triumphs and challenges of computers. Philosophy is a different matter. This book assumes three audacious propositions about philosophy as it pertains to information technology. The first proposition is that philosophy is consequential. This is not to say that people need an underlying philosophy on which to found their actions. Rather, there is a domain of action known as philosophy that interacts consequentially with other domains of action, such as computer systems design. Not everyone agrees that philosophy is consequential. Some people despair of philosophy, seeing it as a domain of esoteric argument that seems unable to resolve the problems it has set itself. Contrary to this view, in this book I show how philosophical writing weaves its way through the concerns of computer systems designers and how it is leading to different ways of talking about information technology and different ways of teaching, using, and designing it.

Some people not only question the relevance of philosophy to our day-to-day concerns, but more particularly they question contemporary philosophy—the different styles of philosophy emerging from continental Europe, notably Germany and France, and now also promoted by several key United States philosophers. The philosophy many of us were brought up with purported to teach us how to think. In many cases this was the philosophy of the analytical school. It emphasized how to construct and evaluate rational argument. The various schools of contemporary philosophy have mostly shifted from this ground. There is now philosophy that we know as "post-modern," "postrationalist," and "poststructuralist." For those who have not engaged contemporary philosophy, it can appear from the outside as a kaleidoscopic, jargon-laden world of unnecessary complication. Some reject it on these grounds. Others appropriate the superficial characteristics of its language without appreciating its substance. The result of such uncommitted philosophical reflection (a kind of "armchair postmodernism") is to indiscriminately clump all major contemporary phenomena together, as some heterogeneous array of unconnected voices: computer networking, genetic engineering, deconstructive architecture, artificial intelligence, poststructuralist literary criticism, chaos theory, the demise of communism, the stock market crash of 1987, virtual reality, quantum physics, and Martin Heidegger. There is little that is revealing in random juxtapositions of opposing thoughts and ideologies, which can end with the removal of all distinctions and can render philosophical reflection inconsequential. Contemporary philosophy trades in carefully articulated distinctions as much as philosophy ever has. This book recognizes and articulates the differences and incommensurabilities that abound in contemporary discourse and attempts to show what is at stake in these distinctions as they pertain to information technology.

The second proposition that pervades this book is that the operative philosophy of the computer world is not logical positivism, or even analytical philosophy, but liberal pragmatism. The computer systems developers and the successful executives of the computer corporations who write about what they do are more likely to enlist John Dewey than Bertrand Russell, or Marshall McLuhan than A. J. Ayer in support of their enterprises. Neither is the computer world driven by a kind of inhuman "technorationalism," materialism, a belief in the ultimate computability of all phenomena, or even systems theory—at least, no more than in any other area of endeavor. The successful computer developers and executives no longer talk approvingly (if they ever did) of formality, order, hierarchy, and rule, so much as freedom, community, and engagement. A quick perusal of some Internet news groups, of the content of World Wide

Web sites, or of *Wired* magazine, captures the dominant philosophical mood of the computer world. A kind of overt "technorationalism" exists, but that is not its intellectual driving force or even where the power seems to reside at the moment.

The third proposition that underlies this book is that it is possible to write clearly and in an explanatory manner about contemporary philosophy. To write clearly is not to resort to Aristotelian logic, nor is it to bend the knee to technorationalism or instrumental reason. To write is to enter into a particular discursive practice. Having spent several years working with and teaching the logic programming language Prolog, with which one can express and operationalize carefully formed syllogisms, I am acutely aware that it is impossible to construct a practical argument in pure logic. But then argument, whether traditional or contemporary, does not depend on the syllogism. Of course, contemporary philosophical writing often attempts to break with traditional modes of writing, to unsettle our thinking, to set up a distance, to make familiar ideas appear strange, and to break down entrenched oppositions, such as that between the form of a written work and its content. Contemporary writing seeks to open up a space rather than pronounce the definitive word or settle disputes. But the lesson of the contemporary school of philosophy known as hermeneutics (the study of interpretation) is that all successful rhetoric achieves this opening of a space, whether it recognizes it or not. For example, the force of Descartes's rhetoric is as much attributable to the opening up of a space as Derrida's masterly, provocative, and sometimes strange expositions and wordplay are. It is not essential to enter into wordplay to open up a space for knowledge.

In many cases those who have advocated "clarity of expression" have, by their incessant appeal to reason and reasonableness, served to obscure rather than clarify issues. (Derrida's debate with John Searle, recorded in *Limited Inc*, is very telling on the matter of clarity and seriousness.) Ironically, "clarity" becomes a means of concealing one's prejudices and obscuring issues. Within contemporary discourse, being "clear" is opened to redefinition. But Derrida, along with other contemporary philosophers, is often being far "clearer" than his imitators suspect, if only they understood his references and the subtlety of his reasoning. Attempting to be clear carries risks, but it is a game well understood by the audiences to whom I address this book, particularly the information technology world, whose modes of practice trade under the helpful myth of "clear and unambiguous communication."

I have written this book for the researcher, designer, practitioner, commentator, and educator working in information technology. It is for those concerned with the technical, social, and philosophical aspects of computers and electronic communications. I hope to demonstrate the strong relationship between the varieties of postmodern thinking and all aspects of information technology. I hope the book is of practical use in that regard, engaging the praxis of information technology.

I call on a range of postmodern writing, including Martin Heidegger's ideas about technology and Being, and the debates that have stemmed from this work, including those by Adorno, Benjamin, Bernstein, Caputo, Derrida, Fish, Foucault, Gadamer, Habermas, Lyotard, Marcuse, and Rorty. I make use of contemporary work in the philosophy of technology and also call on work within information technology fields, such as artificial intelligence, design theory and methods, formal theory, communications theory, computer-aided design, media studies, and studies on the social impact of information technology. The book also incorporates the studies of metaphor by Black, Richards, Ricoeur, Lakoff, Johnson, and others.

The book is unusual in that it presents both technological and philosophical issues side by side, and in some depth. I resist the temptation to oversimplify the philosophical issues, and, wherever possible, I show the counterviews to those supported by my major argument. I also avoid giving the impression that there is a uniform postmodern position on the issues I discuss. For example, one cannot simply infer support for the ubiquity and importance of metaphor from a reading of Heidegger when he made clear statements against such inferences. In arguing against intentionality and in favor of the embodied nature of thought, one cannot enlist Derrida against intentionality and yet ignore his stand against embodiment, at least not without qualification. Nor can one simply incorporate (or refute) Heidegger's lofty characterizations of how technology involves Being without also showing how other writers, important to one's argument, conform to or deviate from this position. So as not to oversimplify, it is necessary to explain some fairly intricate philosophical distinctions. The recurring "debates" presented in this book between Heidegger and Derrida about Being will tax a reader new to the ideas, but I hope the reader will be rewarded with a sense of what is at stake and how important technology, and particularly information technology, is, not only to all aspects of contemporary thought but to the history of thought.

Much of what I present has arisen from my teaching and research in computer programming, computer-aided design, multimedia, electronic communications, artificial intelligence, and virtual reality; from my studies of practitioners who use the technologies; and from the meeting of these areas with my interest in architectural design, design theory, and philosophy. I am indebted to students and colleagues in the Faculty of Architecture at the University of Sydney. I would like to make particular mention of Sally McLaughlin, who undertook a groundbreaking doctoral dissertation on the implications of Heidegger's thought on computer-aided design; my colleague Sidney Newton, who often presented these ideas with greater bravery than I could muster; and Fay Sudweeks, who remains skeptical. I have also appreciated the comments of Ivan Hybs and Steven Loo. I would also like to acknowledge the stimulation provided by various colleagues in Sydney and around the world: Aart Bijl, Alan Bridges, Tony Fry, Ray Ison, John Lansdown, Antony Radford, Paul Redding, David Week, Paul Richens, Dalibor Vesely, and Robert Woodbury, who provided opportunities to explore these ideas and debated some of them with me. Mostly I would like to acknowledge my debt to my colleague Adrian Snodgrass, with whom I have collaborated on many enjoyable educational and research projects, and who set me on this path of philosophical investigation. The best insights of this book are his.

Introduction

Being, Technology, and Design

Information technology is undeniably an important factor in contemporary life. The importance of information technology is thought by some to reside in its role as a medium for the transmission, conservation, and increase of data, information, and knowledge. Data, information, and knowledge are quantifiable entities that can be made to flow through networks and can be stored and operated on to produce more of the same. This characterization can be designated as *conservative*—in the sense that it suggests that there is something (data, information, or knowledge) to be apportioned and measured in quantity and conserved. This view provides great impetus for the development of information technology systems—to provide for faster and more ubiquitous transmission, more efficient storage, faster access, and faster and cleverer means of generating more information.

A second characterization, by no means exclusive of the first, is that the importance of information technology resides in its role as a tool. One of the common characterizations of tools is that they are extensions of the person using them. The tool becomes a part of us and we of it. Because this characterization deals in working and doing and draws attention to the person engaged in a situation, rather than to the abstract worlds of data, information, and knowledge, we will designate this characterization as *pragmatic*.

A third characterization of information technology is that its importance resides in its role in a political and social web of control.

Information technology is prone to abuse, and it promotes ways of thinking that are to be resisted, or at least treated with caution. This characterization can be designated as *critical*. It adopts a critical posture toward information technology.

A fourth characterization of information technology unsettles any claims to its importance at all by showing that any ideas we develop about the centrality of information technology turn out to demonstrate the opposite. Any sweeping change we may ascribe to the introduction of information technology into our world has already been usurped by something preexisting. This characterization can be designated as *radical*. It takes what purports to be a progressive position—namely, a recognition of the centrality and importance of information technology—and demonstrates the orthodoxy in such a position. On the other hand, it demonstrates what is radical in what we commonly take for granted.

I designate these four characterizations of thinking about information technology as four themes—conservative, pragmatic, critical, and radical. They are by no means exhaustive, but I will show how other issues cluster around them. I will show that each theme provides the focus of various discursive practices, or intellectual conversations in contemporary thinking, and how information technology is caught up in those conversations.

Notice that the four themes do not form a single spectrum or a neat set of polarities. Rather, each is part of a different spectrum. The conservative is normally pitted against the progressive, the pragmatic against the theoretical, the critical against the compliant, and the radical against the reactionary. Some of the themes also roughly correspond to philosophical movements, for example, the pragmatist movement and the critical theory school. For the time being, I wish to use the terms pragmatic and critical more loosely than is suggested by these movements and ascribe allegiances to these themes that cross philosophical boundaries.

The themes chosen are based on similar categories put forward by Shaun Gallagher in relation to education and interpretation.[1] The themes are perhaps clearest in education. The conservative view of education emphasizes conserving and maintaining knowledge. For example, one school of thought advocates a return to a corpus of "great books" as the focus of the school curriculum. It is thought that ensuring a grounding in a common culture will foster a society in which communication and debate are better. On the other hand, the pragmatic view of education emphasizes learning by doing and learning as a social activity. This is the great legacy of Deweyan educational liberalism, a view that is currently under attack from conservatives. The critical theme emphasizes education as a means of liberation from oppression and the importance in education of instilling skill in thinking critically. The schoolroom should foment political and social reform. The radical theme emphasizes that education involves a complex play between convention and the undermining of convention. It recognizes that even the critical position is subject to constraints. Freedom is elusive.

Similar themes are present in theories about the interpretation of texts. According to the conservative position, the task of interpretation is to uncover original meanings placed in the text by the author. Texts serve to conserve meaning. The pragmatic view sees interpretation as a matter of entering into the interpretive norms of a community, making judgments from within a historical context. There is no original meaning to a text. This view is pragmatic in the sense that it assumes holistic engagements beyond the exercise of some rules or principles for seeking out preexisting meanings. The critical view of interpretation seeks to challenge and unsettle claims to community and is suspicious of the power it conceals. To interpret a text is to expose the power and exploitative structures the text conceals. The radical interpretative position treats a text as an endless play of signs. Texts reveal and conceal through the play of difference and contradiction.

We can now give more concrete expression to these themes by sketching allegiance to them exhibited by some key contemporary commentators and philosophers. In education, such writers as Eric Hirsch and Allan Bloom seek to reinstate education as a means of conserving a culture. The pragmatic tradition of educational development has also been described as liberal and dates back at least as far as Rousseau in the eighteenth century. It was championed in the twentieth century by the American pragmatic philosopher John Dewey. The critical tradition of educational development has its seeds in liberalism but also in Karl Marx. One of the foremost proponents of the critical theme is the South American left-wing theorist Paulo Freire. Advocacy of radical educational theory has far less currency than that of the other three, but what exists is inspired largely by Jacques Derrida's writings on the role of the university.

In the case of interpretation, one can readily demonstrate the allegiance of theorists of structuralism to the conservation of meaning. At the beginning of the twentieth century, Ferdinand de Saussure characterized language in terms of meanings, as transmitted from one person to another through systems of reference. Sign systems conserve and transmit meaning. Structuralism also points to the idea of structures that lie behind the surface phenomenon of language. There is an attempt to uncover such constancies.[2] Allegiance to the pragmatic theme of interpretation is demonstrated by Hans-Georg Gadamer, Ludwig Wittgenstein, and other contemporary philosophers who emphasize the historical and communal situation of any interpretive act. The critical theme has allegiance from Jürgen Habermas and others of the critical theory school. Radical interpretation is promoted by Derrida, who radicalizes Saussure by showing how language does not trade in similarity and correspondence but in difference. The four views of interpretation have been articulated in a series of debates involving such writers as Gadamer, Habermas, and Derrida. The field of interpretation is known as *hermeneutics*. Hermeneutics provides a coherent focus for a consideration of many contemporary issues.

Allegiances and debates pertaining to information technology (IT) are of a different order than in education, interpretation theory, and philosophy. IT has its commentators, critics, and philosophers, but it also has its own web of intricate technical knowledge, the importance and momentum of which tends to overwhelm critique. There is a complex weaving of technological making and reflection. The four themes I have identified cut across the making of, and reflecting on, technology in complex ways, to be examined in the body of this book. Allegiance to the conservative theme is demonstrated by such writers as Herbert Simon and those in the field of artificial-intelligence research that trades in the capture and preservation of human knowledge in machine form. The pragmatic theme is advocated by much of Silicon Valley culture, which appears driven by notions of engagement between the human and technology, presented in diverse forms by researchers and developers, such as Allan Kay and Terry Winograd, but also philosophers, such as Hubert Dreyfus. The critical theme is advocated by Joseph Weizenbaum and others, who have presented scathing critiques of both the claims of information technology developers and of the technology itself. The application of the radical theme to information technology is not as well developed as the other three themes in contemporary thinking, and I examine the application of the radical theme in chapter 3. The book systematically examines each of these four themes as they pertain to information technology.

Being and Technology

It is impossible to write about technology without coming to terms with the twentieth century's most provocative philosopher, Martin Heidegger, his highly influential critique of the current technological age, and how he implicates technology in the question of Being. (Being is generally capitalized in translations of his work.) Heidegger's work is difficult and controversial, though, according to such commentators as John Caputo, its study is a necessity.[3] What is Being, and how does it relate to information technology? We will review these questions in the light of our four themes.

The origins of the question of Being are to be found within notions of conservation. Life is transient. Things come and go. They exist and they cease to exist. For Plato the flux and uncertainties of human experience, the cycles of life and death, necessitated positing a constant. For Plato true being resided in the realm of ideas, that which did not change. That realm was important for Plato as a means of accounting for the multiplicity of things and to ascribe them to a unity; to know things for what they really are beyond how they simply appear; to allow for the existence of intangible entities, such as perfect circles, justice, and abstract categories; and to provide for constancy. By this conservative reckoning, true being, what is constant and essential, resides outside of time and history. Being is conserved no matter what the vagaries of day-to-day existence. This conservative view maintains that there are constancies behind history. The way people see themselves and their world in different historical periods is subject to varying perspectives, but behind those perspectives is a constancy, a uniform thread. In essence people are the same, in whatever age, or at least they develop along a common thread. By this reckoning, being has little to do with technology or anything else. Being is ruled out of the discourse. Logical positivism was a twentieth-century philosophical movement that epitomized the quest for the conservation of truth in predicate form. Logical positivism portrayed questions of being as pure speculation, unrepresentable as unambiguous predicates, unable to be either proved or disproved, and therefore meaningless. Being was reduced to the issue of existence, in terms of truth predicates, and how we can prove or disprove the existence of an entity. Under this conservative regime, information technology can abet such "reasoning." We can designate what exists as predicates in computer databases, and we can infer facts about them.

In contrast, the pragmatic view of being recognizes that we are what we do, what we use, and what we think. Our being now is different to that of our distant ancestors. Being is historical and contingent. In any age, people take the way they see themselves to be self-evident. There are many trivial instances for illustrating this phenomenon. Middle-class, English-speaking inhabitants of urban communities take for granted the value of work, property ownership, law and order, sociability, individual freedom, and so on. In effect these and other values, norms, and practices make up our view of what it is to be. These views are total. No matter how sophisticated or how empathetic our study of other times and cultures, we judge others in our own terms. There is no escaping this. Our being is what we take to be self-evident. It is appropriate, therefore, to talk of different epochs or modes of being and to see them as incommensurate. There is no common, essential being to which we can appeal to unite all peoples and all times. This conception of being accords with Thomas Kuhn's understanding of disciplinary matrices in science or with Richard Rorty's extension of the idea of incommensurability into philosophy. We are always dealing with slippages, differences and discontinuities, rather than unities and constants. The conservative position would say that to identify epochs of being is just to identify differences in perception—people in one age see themselves differently from how people in other ages see themselves. The pragmatic position is that these differences pertain to being; they are ontological. For Heidegger, in part following Hegel, the essence of Being is time, understood historically. It is but a short step to describe Being, as does Heidegger, as revealing and concealing itself in new aspects at different times.

According to the pragmatic view, technology contributes to our understanding of who and what we are. We are shaped by our technologies as much as we fashion them. According to some commentators, the technologies of writing and print have contributed to how we see ourselves as originators and authors of ideas, as beings with minds capable of abstract thought—minds analogous to sheets of paper able to hold symbols and the results of manipulating symbols. In a preliterate age, there was a different kind of engagement between people and their world, different understandings of time, different systems of authority, different means of legitimation. The details are controversial, but the pragmatic view clearly asserts that technology is implicated in how we see ourselves and, therefore, in our being. Again, the conservative position would merely assert that such differences are perceptual and cultural. Beneath such changing perceptions is an essential constancy. From the pragmatic position, there is no underlying truth to our being beyond our seeing ourselves to be under a multiplicity of influences. Information technology is one such influence.

One variation on the notion of the autonomous, historical, and epochal nature of being is that there is a direction to its history. This accords with aspects of the critical theme within the study of being. Each epoch develops on the last, toward the liberation of our true nature and the realization of freedom. This is a Hegelian line of argument that strongly influenced Marx. Whereas the contemporary, neo-Marxist, critical-theory variation around this theme places little emphasis on notions of being, the emphasis on liberation, freedom, and one's historical situation is clear. What is the role of technology here? According to the critical view, technologies can also afford illusions of freedom while actually constraining freedom.

Technology and our obsession with it are responsible for a kind of thinking that is itself technological and instrumental—technorationality—in which we see everything, including people, in technological terms, as implements to be used and exploited. We also use the logic of the machine as a model for reason. According to critical theory, in the modern, conservative age, being is strongly dominated by technological reason. According to Heidegger, technological reason makes the issue of Being more obscure. It is as if Being has withdrawn.

The radical position on being is that there is no fundamental to which we can appeal, neither being nor any other name. Being purports to be the supercategory above which there is no other. But on investigation we find that the means by which we describe being trade in contradiction and difference. Being is yet one more concept that is in flux and play. It is forever elusive. It seems that the core of our being is indeterminacy and flux. If we want to use the word "being" as a focus of discussion, then we should at the same time strike a cross through it, either literally on the page, or metaphorically. We should write with being "under erasure." What are the implications of this radical position for technology? Technology is no great player in the matter of being. No sooner have we identified a particular technology as influential in defining our being than one can show the inherent contradictions in the demonstration. The radical conclusion is always that there is no conclusion. The role of technology is still an open question, but in the questioning we have moved on. There is a new game in play. The error is to sit on the sidelines and not take part.

Heidegger and Technology

What is Heidegger's position in relation to these four themes? Heidegger's philosophy has a conservative streak, but what he seeks to conserve is the whole, the flux, the indeterminate. So Heidegger is not a seeker and conservator of propositional structure, logical predicates, and knowledge bases. Heidegger was a conservator of early Greek and German culture and a reactionary against technology and the "Americanization" of Germany. He was also a conservator of the question of Being and, as indicated by many of his critics, to the exclusion of other questions, such as justice and human compassion. It is well known that, as a political archconservative, Heidegger was for a time one of the Nazi Party's favorite sons and never spoke against the atrocities they committed, even when they were fully known after World War II. Rather, in lofty philosophical tones, as a conservator of the grand questions of Being, Heidegger drew attention to threats and dangers beyond human suffering.

Heidegger's philosophical legacy is phenomenology. Phenomenology is one of the three great philosophical forces of the twentieth century, along with logical positivism and philosophical pragmatism. But the agreements between Heidegger and philosophical pragmatism have been identified by many American philosophers, notably by Richard Rorty and Hubert Dreyfus. Heidegger's philosophy of Being begins with the nature of the being who inquires into its own being, and how that being understands itself primarily as being-in-the-world. Being is not defined in terms of some Platonic idealism but as a grounded, involved being going about its daily practical activities. Heidegger's Being is thoroughly pragmatic. It is also thoroughly historical: "Time must be brought to light—and genuinely conceived—as the horizon for all understanding of Being and for any way of interpreting it."[4] Later in his career Heidegger emphasized the disclosive nature of Being. Being reveals and conceals itself through events focusing around great moments of thought, as when Leibniz announced the Principle of Sufficient Reason—that nothing is without ground. For Heidegger the history of thought is not about what individuals of great genius have revealed but what Being has revealed through such events. For Heidegger such pivotal events also extend to the creation of great works of art and poetry and the building of Greek temples.

For Heidegger technology does not simply make us who and what we are but is implicated in Being's mission. Technological thinking covers over Being, but this is not of our making. The disclosive entity is always Being rather than humankind: "Technology is therefore no mere means. Technology is a way of revealing."[5] This introduces the critical theme in Heidegger's thought. Technological thinking "enframes" us into particular ways of thinking. It is not simply that technologies, such as information technology, can be used for controlling or manipulating people but that the "essence" of technology traps us into the delusion that we are in control, that we can explain everything in terms of causes, and that we think information technology brings everything near. For Heidegger the "essence" of technology is to cover over the question of Being. Its way of revealing is to conceal.

What is the radical theme in Heidegger's thought? It was Heidegger (arguably following Friedrich Nietzsche) who introduced the strategy of deconstruction into philosophical discourse. Heidegger appeared to turn almost everything on its head, and—Heidegger being deconstruction's greatest exponent—no one's work has come under more minute deconstructive examination under the pen of Jacques Derrida, particularly in relation to the question of Being.

Although Heidegger wove much of his later thinking around the theme of technology, he was not in the least concerned with technology at the work face—with this or that particular technology or with discerning between technologies. He was concerned with their essence—what can be said about all technology, what technology as a whole brings to presence.

Although I appeal substantially to Heidegger's thinking on technology, in this book I examine how contemporary thinking addresses those who configure computer systems, make decisions, and read about, learn about, teach, use, and play with information technology—those for whom information technology features large in their professional and leisure practices and who are not about to dismiss it as a necessary evil. This commitment is addressed through the notion of design, which implies a level of commitment to the technology beyond critique.

Design

Our four themes conspire with the question of being to present several pictures of design. Under the conservative theme, design is an intervention, a manipulation. It is to convert an undesired situation into a desirable one. It presupposes our ability to declare needs, wants, and intentions. Artifacts are the products of creative individuals or teams of individuals. As with the conservative view of interpretation, technological artifacts conserve the intentions and meanings of their originators. The conservative view presumes that designers can control, and are in control of, what they produce. This control is realized in the activity of designing through method. A sequence of steps takes us from the undesired situation to the desired. The conservative view of design also presumes that there are principles underlying design. Design under the conservative regime follows one of two paths. There is the romantic conception of the designer as the creative individual, battling against opposition, preserving his or her creativity. On the other hand, there is the systems-theoretic view of design that seeks to enlist science and its methods to arrive at objectively valid solutions to problems.

For pragmatism design is not so much addressing needs as projecting expectations. These expectations have less to do with method and individual genius than with community. As with the pragmatic view of interpretation, designing and design evaluation are situated within communities. Notions of the individual designer and individual creativity are replaced by considerations of authority, legitimation, responsibility, and the interweaving of varying roles, practices, and technologies. For pragmatism design is a kind of "reflection in action"—needs are commonly identified in retrospect or during the development of the design rather than at the outset of the design process. Design is an exploration, but one that is already in progress prior to any particular design situation. Designers and artifacts are already caught up in a world of artifacts and practices, and their history. Within the pragmatic regime, it is but a small step to affirm with Tony Fry that being is caught up in our artifacts: "No matter who 'we' are, we are what we make, we make what we are."[6]

What is design under the critical theme? If design is a community enterprise, then the involvement of communities in design needs to be appropriated and made explicit. Design itself, insofar as it imposes the interests of a few on the many, is a subject of critical scrutiny in its own right. Under the critical theme, design is a political activity well expressed in debates within architecture, urban design, and planning. Under the critical theme, designers and planners seek to enable others—the users of a housing development, for example—to formulate and realize their own expectations, to present a voice among those of the developers, financiers, government instrumentalities, professional groups, and institutions. In the case of information technology design, the critical perspective is strong in the rhetoric of those who advocate the ubiquity of computer and communications systems and who advertise the "grassroots" origins of certain communications systems—though many critics, if not designers, are also suspicious of such claims.

What is design under the radical theme? Deconstruction features prominently in design discourse, particularly in architecture. Radical design is subversive of entrenched structures, assumptions, and oppositions. Derrida takes an established opposition in philosophical discourse, with its built-in priority, and shows how that priority is betrayed by the very texts that assert it. The "deconstructive" architectural designer identifies an oppositional priority in some orthodoxy, such as the priority given to the private over the public in standard house design, and seeks to bring the contradictions and tensions within such an opposition into the new design. Critics of this designerly application of deconstruction point out that the design has to be explained as a deconstruction in order to operate as such. Much deconstruction in design is an extension of structuralism—treating designs as texts that convey messages and that require reading and interpretation. Deconstruction also becomes a method, a creativity exercise, or a way of loosening up thinking. Whatever the merits of such exercises, they miss the radical edge of Derrida's thinking. I will show in this book how the idea of metaphor, when understood in a radical way as operating through the play of difference, provides an account of design that is also pertinent to computer systems design. I will also show how metaphor provides a counterview to method.

In this book I examine information technology in the light of four themes—the conservative, the pragmatic, the critical, and the radical—with an emphasis on design. I will keep returning to the pragmatic theme, which I argue is strong within the world of information technology systems development, though its rhetoric often carries less force than is presented from the conservative side of computing.

I argue that the idea of metaphor as a focus of design discourse belongs within the pragmatic theme. It is also pragmatically useful as a focus for discussion and enables designers to appropriate some of the more radical aspects of contemporary discourse.

The book begins with a justification of the force of pragmatism within information technology rhetoric and practice and its opposition to the tenets of Cartesian rationalism. I argue that this view accords with the highly influential writings of Marshall McLuhan. Pragmatism is optimistic about technology. I also contrast pragmatism with the tenets of critical theory. In introducing critical theory, I examine the insights of Hegel's dialectical principle that claims a basis in pre-Socratic thinking. Understanding is thought to emerge through the interaction of opposites. I contrast the way Heidegger and Herbert Marcuse apply an understanding of dialectic to criticisms of technology. Marcuse identifies technological and pretechnological thinking and advocates overthrowing the technological order. Heidegger's approach is more resigned and maintains that we are caught up in a system that is not of our making and over which we have no control. I present some of critical theory's assessments of information technology and show the strengths and shortcomings of both Marcuse's left-wing view and the Heideggerian alternative to it. I present alternative metaphors for understanding information technology that take account of the interconnected ways in which technologies are caught up in human praxis. The discussion returns to the pragmatic.

The discussion of dialectic sets the stage for considering Derrida's deconstruction and what it says about information technology. Here I make clear the distinction between the modern and the postmodern. Modernism presents a rhetoric of crisis that seeks to persuade us that its certainties are being challenged by its own product, namely technology, and particularly information technology. With its grounding in metaphysics, modernism presents a vicious circle of assertion and denial, where the only assurance is of technological progress. I show how Derrida's radical deconstruction of orthodox views of language demonstrate that any radical social, cultural, or epistemological change we may attribute to the advance of information technology is already in place. In this discussion, I also examine

Derrida's critique of Heidegger on technology and metaphysics. I return to pragmatism for other metaphors that enhance the application of Derrida's radical discourse to information technology.

I then turn to specific claims about information technology that further bring to light aspects of contemporary thinking. Commentaries on the phenomenon of cyberspace trade in various notions of world, space, place, and community. Substantial claims are made about the ability of electronic communications to make world and create space. The plausibility of these claims rests on presupposing the primacy of information. I examine these claims and the counterclaims presented by some information technology critics and then explore the phenomenological account of world, space, and place that removes the notion of information from center stage. In this discussion, I explore various concepts presented by Heidegger about how equipment discloses world and space.

I make a similar examination of claims about virtual-reality systems. This investigation brings to light different perspectives on the human-computer interface and computer-aided design. I examine the tensions between two views of perception, as a matter of data input versus mental construction. Similarly, there is a tension between pictures as representing things through their correspondence to real objects and pictures as having a place by virtue of social construction—being a part of human practices. Aspects of Heidegger's philosophy are invoked as a means of cutting through these dilemmas by challenging Cartesian notions about subject and object. In the process, truthful representation is seen as a matter of correspondence only in the light of truth as a means of disclosing a world. I argue that the disclosive nature of pictures and virtual-reality technology is well understood through a recognition of the importance of difference. This serves to introduce the nature of metaphor and its power in accounting for the workings of information technology.

From this radical perspective, I then reexamine the conservative, modern account of information technology and its grounding in systems theory. I examine the nature of methods, theories, and models in design and radicalize their best insights through the notion of metaphor. In the chapter that follows, I examine metaphor in detail. The consideration of metaphor features prominently in computer-interface design. I explore different theories of how metaphors operate in language and how metaphor can feature as a consideration in evaluating technologies. I explore the views of George Lakoff and Mark Johnson that human cognition and understanding are grounded in bodily metaphors. I also take account of the critics of metaphor theory, including Donald Davidson and Heidegger. Metaphor is also implicated in discussions of being. I look to Derrida and Paul Ricoeur for a rich account of metaphor as residing in the dialectic between literal falsehood and metaphorical disclosure. This has implications for the workings of the imagination and of design. I therefore lay out the key issues and some controversies surrounding metaphor use and how it pertains to computer systems design.

The book can be regarded as doing several things. First, it systematically examines four themes in contemporary thinking—conservative, pragmatic, critical, and radical—as they pertain to information technology. Second, it canvasses Heidegger's thinking on technology, including his pragmatism, considerations of Being, metaphysics, phenomenology of place, and notions of truth. Third, it systematically examines claims about information technology, including its presumptions of control; its claims to radicality; its ability to make worlds, as in cyberspace and virtual reality; claims about the application of systems theory; and the presumptions of artificial intelligence. Fourth, the book presents a transition from a conservative orientation (to computer systems design) in which method holds sway to a radical position sustained by the complex and contradictory workings of metaphor.

"Try as they might," digital artwork by Brad Miller.

1

Computers and Praxis

*How the Theoretical Is Giving Way to the Pragmatic
in Computer Systems Design*

Pragmatism is a school of philosophical thought that embraces the primacy of human action, the practicalities of human involvement, the materiality of the world, the interaction of the senses, and the formative power of technology. Pragmatism distinguishes itself from the analytical and theoretical orientation known as Cartesian rationalism.[1] Rationalism grants privilege to theory over practice.[2] For the pragmatist, on the other hand, theory is just another kind of practice. The current wave of popular and accessible computing seems to be attributable, whether through declared allegiance or not, largely to the pragmatic orientation. Computer systems design has been influenced by pragmatism through the philosophy of John Dewey (1859–1952). It is also sustained through the "media philosophy" of Marshall McLuhan (1911–1980) of the 1960s, and the latest revival of interest in the thought of Martin Heidegger (1889–1976), both of which readily find residence in the pragmatic mind.[3] Pragmatism is optimistic about technology and is thereby distinguishable from other traditions of thought, such as critical theory[4] and the skepticism of Derrida's radical theories.[5]

The Theoretical Orientation to Computer Systems Design

Pragmatism distinguishes itself from the analytical and theoretical orientation of Cartesian rationalism. A brief survey of rationalism is therefore appropriate before embarking on an investigation of pragmatism. Rationalism promotes the independence of reason from the material world of bodies and machines. According to rationalism, reasoning, can be considered to exist in the abstract, independently of a medium. Geometrical and mathematical proof serves as a model of reasoning.[6] Rationalism trades substantially in the currency of logic, number, and symbol. So an item of technology, such as a computer, serves as a means of storing, conveying, manipulating, and implementing information. Information is the "raw material" of reason. The rationalistic tradition originated with Plato's distinction between the realm of ideas and the world of things (or "shadows") and found full expression in Descartes's identification of the subject of reason, the thinking entity, with the object world, the extended entity. Contemporary commentators on rationalism commonly refer to "rationalism" as an orientation that also embraces Locke and Hume's empiricism.[7] Rationalism is also evident in the debates about idealism and realism—whichever side of the debate one takes. Even romanticism, with its emphasis on subjectivity—emotion, feelings, genius, and individuality—is sustained by the rationalistic tenets that began with Descartes. Rationalism is not a single philosophical position but, to use Foucault's term, a "discursive practice" we are all caught up in, and it imbues understandings of technology and of design.

There are four approaches to computer systems design that explicitly present the rationalistic orientation: cognitive modeling (or artificial intelligence); formal theory; methodology; and empirical studies.

Artificial intelligence brings the tenets of rationalism into sharp relief. The assumptions of rationalism are presented clearly in Schank's characterization of the five constituents of human intelligence.[8] According to Schank, the first constituent is the ability to communicate.[9] For artificial intelligence, communication is commonly understood in terms of passing information from one agent (or human being) to another. The second constituent of intelligence, is "internal knowledge": "We expect intelligent entities to have some knowledge about themselves. They should know when they need something; they should know what they think about something; and, they should know that they know it."[10] Third is "world knowledge." Intelligence involves knowing about the "outside world" and being able to retrieve information about it. Memory is the capacity to encode past experience and use it to guide us through new experiences. Fourth is the ability to formulate goals and plans: "Goal-driven behaviour means knowing when one wants something and knowing a plan to get what one wants."[11] Fifth is creativity. This is the ability to formulate new plans, look at things in a new way, adapt to changes in the environment, and learn from experience.

Schank's description of intelligence sits firmly within the tradition of rationalism in several ways. It highlights the rationalistic assumption that there is an inside and an outside to human cognitive experience. There is an inside world of knowledge that involves a self knowing about itself, and there is an outside world that self can also know about. Sometimes the former is called "subjective knowledge," the latter "objective knowledge." The inside world is that of the subject, the outside is that of the object. For Schank, these distinctions are unproblematic. In artificial-intelligence research, the world of the subject and that of the object are not seen merely as metaphors. Nor is their identification contingent on some particular context of discussion. There is no agonizing over the "constitution of the subject" prevalent in critical theory, for example.[12] In assuming the immutability of subject and object, communication is largely a matter of passing information from one subject to another through the medium of the "external world." Communication gives us access to each other's subjectivities.

Rationalism also assumes the priority of purposeful behavior in human affairs. The subject (the thinking self) identifies problems and goals, much like Descartes's method of reason, then sets about achieving those goals. According to Schank, intelligent action is purpose-driven. We are constantly forming and reforming goals in response to problem situations and then carrying out plans to accomplish those goals. We have ends, which are our goals, and we develop means to achieve these goals. The means are plans.

According to Schank, the ability to engage in purposeful activity involves knowledge. According to artificial intelligence, knowledge can be made explicit as procedures, rules, frames, or semantic networks.[13] The "internal" knowledge representations are often described as "cognitive models."[14] Habitual, unreflective activities, such as being engrossed in a hobby or moving about one's office or the practice of skills, do not appear to involve goals or plans explicitly. However, artificial-intelligence theorists argue that in such habitual activity, goals, plans, and knowledge are "internalized," "compiled,"[15] or handled by "default reasoning."

Behavior not readily accommodated by the idea of representable knowledge is also addressed under the rubric of "creativity." Creativity is a major preoccupation of artificial intelligence. Creativity is evident where we are not merely mapping goals and plans to situations through readily articulated knowledge. Artificial-intelligence theorists recognize that "creative knowledge" is extremely difficult to capture.

Researchers outside the area of automated intelligence are also interested in models similar to those proposed by Schank. According to some researchers, general computer systems design should consider cognitive models. A computer system embodies a representation of the goals and plans of the user. In turn, the user of the system has a model of the computer and of the situation domain he or she is working in. These researchers consider that, irrespective of whether the system is to be "intelligent," good systems design takes account of cognitive models.[16]

Schank's characterization of cognition embodies the rationalism of Descartes and Leibniz. This includes the self-evident notion of the thinking subject (*res cogitans*) set apart from an independent and measurable spatial object world (*res extensa*). The essence of thought can be described in terms of formulas, production rules, and axioms in predicate calculus, able to be processed through context-independent and unprejudiced reason. Reason can be removed from culturally situated human agency and operated on by computer. Finally, human reason and action are driven by purposes or goals. There are always ends, and we formulate means to accomplish them. These assumptions are not peculiar to Schank's work, which is strongly geared toward the explicit manipulation of "frames," "scripts," and plans as a means to automating the computerized "understanding" of stories and situations.[17] The assumptions are evident in a tradition of well-articulated researches dating back to Turing and Church, including the work of Michie, Minsky, Simon, and Dennett. They owe much to the notions of formal reasoning developed by Frege and Russell, and their theories sit comfortably within the tradition of analytic philosophy, with its emphasis on language, truth, and logic.[18]

The formalist school of design theory as articulated by March, Stiny, and Mitchell also fits within this tradition.[19] Formal theorists assume that a process like designing a building is well understood by beginning with spatial descriptions of the world in terms of points, lines, planes, and labels. From such understandings, it is possible to construct "algebras of shapes" or sets of transformation operators for creating patterns. There are also spatial or "shape grammars" by which it is possible to codify "design languages." Shape grammars are sets of rewrite rules for transforming complex configurations of lines, labels, and objects, resulting in building plans, and three-dimensional configurations of elements. Formal design theory takes to heart Descartes's model of reason as geometrical proof. The theory begins with geometrical manipulation and extends out to considerations of design function and evaluation. Mitchell is also able to demonstrate very convincing mappings between the elements of the formal theory and aspects of computer hardware and software design.[20] For example, computer screen displays are essentially point representations on a grid, drafting operations in a computer-aided design (CAD) system are transformations using shape algebras, and the hierarchical structure of a classical building facade maps onto the hierarchical structure of procedural programs. The formalist school finds support from the language theories of Carnap and Tarski and from Chomsky's use of rewrite rules for describing grammars in language.

The assumptions of rationalism are also evident in the design-methods movement, which sought to capture design expertise in process diagrams, to objectify the design process and make it explicit as an aid to collaboration and communication.[21] As with Schank's characterization of the cognitive reality of goals and plans, the design-methods movement relies substantially on the idea that design proceeds from a problem statement to a solution, which is then evaluated against the problematic situation. This formulation of the design process is closely analogous to Descartes's method of reason, by which we break a problem into parts, proceed through logical deduction to new facts (in the manner of a geometrical proof), and then iterate through the process to be sure that nothing was left out. The methodical design of a computer system therefore involves formulating a problem statement, articulating a specification of what the program should accomplish, articulating the program in terms of control flows or formulating the program in terms of general statements (often termed *pseudocode*), and then writing the program.[22] The process can then be followed by debugging (removing minor errors), testing it in use, and modifying it. Design methods also involve the numeric and symbolic formulation of design tasks to facilitate simulation (modeling how a design will perform) and optimization (generating the "best" design from a range of possible designs).

The methods approach to design is rationalistic insofar as it assumes the objective status of problem statements and to the extent that it assumes that understandings can be readily articulated as formulas, process diagrams, charts, tables, and lists—that there is a privileged relationship between these "representations of knowledge" and thought.

Finally, the rationalist tradition is evident in certain empirical approaches to the evaluation and design of computer systems.[23] The empirical method for evaluating a computer system proceeds by identifying items to be tested—such as the number of errors in using a word processor and the numbers of control devices or "buttons" on the screen. These items constitute variables to be manipulated by the experimenter (numbers of errors and numbers of buttons). The word-processing task is abstracted into a controlled situation in which extraneous factors, such as lighting levels, ergonomic comfort, and the number of distractions, can remain constant. Tests are repeated on large numbers of human subjects, and the values of the variables for each subject are recorded. Then the results are subjected to statistical analysis to determine significant correlations between variables. A simple experiment of the kind described here might conclude that there is a certain probability that typing errors will increase with the number of screen buttons presented to the computer user.

The empirical approach to the design of computer systems proceeds in a similar manner. The behaviors of large numbers of people engaged in some well-identified activity are observed under controlled conditions to discover the nature of the behaviors. The generalizations made through statistical analysis then provide information for the task of inventing or designing technologies to fit in with those behaviors. For example, knowing that the probability of typing errors increases with the number of screen buttons may prompt the systems designer to produce simple and uncluttered screen displays. As another example, empirical studies of the way people communicate face to face may provide generalizations about human behavior applicable to the design of computer systems that support collaboration. It is rare that the experimenters are also the systems designers in such situations. Experimental results generally constitute a "literature" that designers may call on (though most of those working in the field would say they rarely do). Empirical studies of the kind described here and a dependence on them are rationalistic insofar as the studies assume the validity of reducing complex human behaviors to measurement, the objective status of behavioral variables, the independence of means (technical solutions) from ends (problems demonstrated through human behavior), and the detachment of the experimenter's values from the experimental situation.

Critics and Defenders of the Theoretical Orientation

Rationalism has come under severe attack from many quarters. Some of these criticisms, particularly those by Winograd and Flores, are presented in the context of computer systems design.[24] The critics point to the difficulties in identifying what is subjective knowledge and what is objective knowledge independently of a particular situation. We are always involved in a context, even when trying to be "objective." This has led some philosophers to assert that the basic Cartesian premise of identifying a subject opposed to an object world is fundamentally flawed. Articulating human knowledge in a representational formalism is also problematic. There is never a basic, underlying formalization that accounts for everything we know in a particular situation. Formalizations are themselves artifacts, inventions of the moment to fit a particular purpose. Finally, the quest for goals appears equally elusive. We readily construct our intentions after the event. We know about planning as a tool of social mobilization, and we live and work in a culture that uses blueprints, methods, and procedures. We are so used to talking about goals that we readily identify plan formulation as a basic cognitive function. According to the critics, rationalism largely ignores the social and prejudicial nature of its own understandings. Winograd and Flores appeal to studies in language and hermeneutics to develop these and other criticisms.

These criticisms of rationalism find support from such philosophers as Nietzsche, Heidegger, and the phenomenologists, who have pointed to the inadequacy of the Cartesian focus on the *cogito* (the thinking self) rather than Being.[25] The elevation of *ontology* (the study of being) over *epistemology* (the study of knowledge) leads to a totally different line of philosophical inquiry than that offered by the tradition of rationalism. The assumptions of Schank and others regarding internal and external knowledge and the importance of representations, goals, and plans are criticized by such writers as Dreyfus, Winograd, and Flores from the perspective of phenomenology and hermeneutics.[26] Furthermore, the school of thought commonly known as critical theory presents criticisms of rationalism from the point of view of social justice. In appropriating aspects of Heidegger, along with Marx and Freud, proponents of critical theory commonly focus on the unquestioning acceptance and appropriation of reason in Cartesian and Enlightenment thought.[27] According to critical theory, rationalism pays no regard to, yet surreptitiously promotes, entrenched power structures and regimes of injustice. Weizenbaum, a computer scientist and former artificial-intelligence researcher, in railing against the "imperialism of instrumental reason," has been influential in bringing the critical perspective to the attention of the community of computer systems designers.[28]

What defences are offered against these criticisms? Some defences have been articulated in a series of reviews, by artificial-intelligence researchers, of the book by Winograd and Flores, *Understanding Computers and Cognition*. The defences have also been summarized in a reply article by Winograd and Flores.[29] One line of argument focuses on the "relativism" and "irrationalism" thought to be provoked by challenges to rationalism, a tendency identified and convincingly argued against by Bernstein.[30] Commonly, the defences of rationalism focus on the theme of misrepresentation. Both the appellation "rationalist" and the descriptions of it are regarded as attributing a particularly naive set of views to a diverse collection of schools of thought. Few people are prepared to own up to being rationalists of the kind defined by Winograd and Flores. The defenders are also quick to point to the advocacy of dissent from orthodoxy within their own literature or the literature they have appropriated. The defenders of rationalism see Gödel's proof of the undecidability of formal logic, Heisenberg's uncertainty principle in physics, Austin's and Searle's views about the situated nature of language, and Feyerabend's views of the "anarchical" basis of science as evidence of the catholic nature of their theoretical orientation. On the other hand, the critics of rationalism see these writers as providing evidence of the impoverishment of the basic tenets of rationalism.

Finally, the defenders of rationalism commonly appeal to the practical nature of such activities as artificial intelligence research in opening up new vistas. According to the defenders, the critics of rationalism are engaging in sophistry, quibbling over philosophical points that are beyond proof in any case, while the "rationalists" or theoreticians are getting on with the job of exploring new areas and developing technologies.[31] Stefik and Bobrow, for example, object to the "somewhat anti-technological stance" of Winograd and Flores. They consider the limits Winograd and Flores pose for artificial intelligence to apply only in the short term. Winograd and Flores have provided no hard evidence that what humans accomplish is ultimately impossible for a machine.[32] Even the failures of artificial intelligence (AI) are taken by its advocates as indications of the success of the endeavour. According to Suchman, "the failures of AI, in principle at least, can be as valuable as its successes. . . . [I]t can still contribute to our understanding of human intelligence, through its efforts to get closer. . . . What is crucial . . . is not so much that the current research direction should be right, but that it should be elucidating, tentative, and open always to radical redirection based not only on advances but, more importantly, on obstacles discovered in its path."[33] Suchman here reflects the common tenor of defenders of the theoretical orientation—the labels are unimportant, and the criticisms do not really impinge on the quest for workable models of cognition and useful computer systems. The rationalistic orientation claims privileged access to the practical—access the critics reading philosophy apparently do not enjoy.

Paradoxically, however, the tenets of rationalism militate *against* a deep concern with practical issues—a concern with how computers fit into human work practices or how computer technology presents itself as a practical and material concern to be analyzed, designed, and developed. Where researchers motivated and informed by rationalism are successful at the practical level, it appears to be in spite of their orientation to the primacy of theory rather than because of it. Rationalism indicates its lack of concern with the practical in at least five ways.

First, in asserting the distinction between theory and practice and the priority of the former over the latter, rationalism asserts that the practical will follow from the theoretical.[34] The practical is not, therefore, of primary concern. The distinction between theory and practice derives from Cartesian rationalism and its investment in the legacy of Plato and Aristotle. Theories are commonly taken to be abstractions, generalizations that cover a large number of specific cases and facilitate explanation, prediction, and control. The practical is what works in some context of human activity. (As I show later, philosophical pragmatism dissents from this conventional distinction between theory and practice.) From the point of view of rationalism, it makes sense, therefore, to establish such distinctions as the theoretical versus the practical and basic research versus applied research. From the point of view of rationalism, it is entirely unproblematic that the researches described above are taken as theoretical rather than practical. It is assumed that practical implementation eventually follows from sound theory. Rationalism does not promote concern about immediate practical outcome.

This lack of immediate concern with the practical is evident in the way in which some research is conducted. Although partially based in empirical studies, Schank's model is not presented in the context of working computer systems—either projected or realized. In the case of shape grammar studies, there have been many experimental computer systems for formally manipulating shapes and objects, but the theory is not presented as dependent on its usefulness or implementability. Where there are systems utilizing shape grammar theory, their design does not focus on how a person might use such a system. Design methods also appear aloof from practical concerns. Since the publication of such documents as the *Tavistock Report* into design methods in the construction industry in 1966, design methods have widely been held suspect.[35] Where design methods are now in use or even discussed at all, it is in the area of teaching and research rather than design practice. Empirical studies of the kind described above also embody an aloof posture to practicalities. They rely on transplanting a phenomenon, such as using a computer, into a rarefied context of constants and variables, rather than the world of practical situations involving people and machines and their complex interactions. In summary, rationalism supports the view that technology is a product of theoretical inquiry and is subservient to it. This is a further instance of the widely held view that technology follows scientific development—technology is applied science.

Second, the practical involves participation. The terms *work practice* and *professional practice* capture the idea that the practical is always a matter of involvement in a community. According to Dreyfus, we take over practices (such as conventions of table manners, language use, or being a business person) in a social context.[36] However, rationalism works against this participative aspect of practice. It affirms a nonparticipative, hierarchical view of knowledge.[37] In keeping with Descartes's characterization of the independence of reason and the residence of reason in the individual thinking self (*cogito*), the social group is seen as a source of errors and prejudice. The individual has to wrestle against the crowd to assert clear and independent reason. In spite of the great democratic and egalitarian legacies of the Enlightenment, rationalism favors a hierarchical and bureaucratic view of human knowledge. Knowledge can be represented, so it can be transmitted from those who know to those who are ignorant. Professional experts can reason objectively and can see their domains more clearly than nonexperts. Rationalism promotes a particular view of the clientele or end users of technological systems. Their participation in the process of inventing and designing computer systems is minimized. The experts have access to the theories and are best placed to deliver the appropriate designs. The tenets of rationalism militate against practice as participation.[38]

Third, rationalism affirms that the physical presence of a technology is subservient to what it contains or accomplishes. The rationalistic orientation supports the metaphor of technologies as containers.[39] Knowledge and information are contained and transmitted in minds, texts, electronic media, or computers. A medium/technology like television is therefore less significant and influential than its content or programs. The computer hardware sitting on a desk is less significant than its software. This emphasis plays down the *situation* in which media and technologies operate—the situation within a network of interrelated media, technologies, and practices. From the rationalistic point of view, the impact of a technology on an organization is largely a matter of how the technology delivers or hinders productivity and effectiveness in current work practices. This emphasis denies priority to a consideration of the way a new technology perturbs the organization's existing web of technologies, media, and work practices.

This orientation also suggests that how a technology presents itself in a work context is largely a matter of "interface." So distinction is made between a system and its interface. Furthermore, how the system might be used is sometimes considered after the system is designed. Most early artificial-intelligence research seemed driven by this priority. The priority was to codify the knowledge and place the rules in the system, with little regard for how one might interact with it.

Fourth, rationalism is largely indifferent to the role of the body and the engagement of the senses in our working with technology. Rationalism makes the distinction between mind and body and elevates the mind over the body.[40] In computer systems design and research this is translated as an interest in cognitive models, knowledge representations, formalized procedures, and generalizations about human behavior in terms of variables. Computer systems do not rate highly as physical objects to be touched and handled and that occupy space. Paradoxically, even virtual-reality systems deny the importance of engaging the senses in the physical world. One of the more extreme aims of virtual reality is to present sense data "directly to the brain," circumventing the body's normal engagement in the physical world.[41]

Fifth, rationalism affirms that means (such as technologies) are subservient to ends (such as human needs). In keeping with Schank's characterization of the cognitive reality of goals and plans, the rationalistic orientation suggests that technologies (means) arise and are developed in order to address needs (ends).[42] Historically, humankind has needed protection from the elements (an end) and so has invented forms of shelter (means). At the local level, a person has needs, such as to get from home to work and back again quickly and safely. That person may select the technology of the automobile to meet that need. There are ends, and technology provides the means to accomplish them. In this case, the means (technologies) are subservient to the ends (some human need). The fact of the automobile is less significant than the end, which is to move around.

Proponents of the rationalistic orientation to computer systems design are not indifferent to the issues of practice, client participation, the physical presence of technology in the workplace, the role of the senses, and the formative power of technology. However, there is very little to support these inquiries within the tenets of rationalism. The result is a devaluing of practical concerns in favor of the more certain world of theory.

But this certainty is fragile. The practical world is one in which systems have to be used by people in some context. How does rationalism fail the world of practice? First, whereas rationalism af-firms the value of theory over practice, there are strong arguments that practice does not follow from theory, or even that technologies develop from science. We commonly attribute to science great tech-nological feats, such as space travel, the creation of new drugs, and the development of the computer. But this attribution of technologi-cal success to science simply reflects our privileging of theory over practice. For example, Latour implicates technology in the scientific enterprise in a way that makes them indistinguishable.[43] Second, whereas rationalism affirms the superior position of the expert, the design and development process clearly needs to engage the experi-ences of the clientele and account for our involvement in practice as a community.

Third, whereas rationalism affirms the subservience of a technol-ogy to its content, it is apparent that technologies are more powerful than consideration of just their content would suggest. The automo-bile is not an indifferent means of getting from A to B. Even if it takes the same amount of time by bus, the activity is different. The car is implicated in a culture of values about freedom, independ-ence, and prestige. We would be indifferent to the means if this were not the case. It matters to us whether we travel by car or by bus. In a similar way, watching television is different from receiving the "same" information by reading a book, attending a lecture, or even watching a film.

Fourth, whereas the engagement of the body and its senses is a matter of indifference to the rationalistic orientation, clearly the physical form of a technology and how it presents itself to the senses matters. As will be discussed subsequently, rationalism's indifference to the senses can be seen as favoring the visual sense.

Fifth, whereas rationalism affirms the superiority of ends to means, the means (technology) must be elevated to become an ob-ject of design. It is also apparent that technologies are never just means. They also become ends in themselves. Technologies have fostered situations that ensure that they present themselves as solu-tions. An obvious example is our asserting the need to get around busy and far-flung cities. The car is there to meet that need. Of course, the cities are busy and far-flung because of the development of the automobile, or, more precisely, the car is implicated in a matrix of developments that land us with busy and far-flung cities. It is equally valid to assert that the car is the end, and the daily journey across town is the means to acquire one. In a similar way, we may assert that we need computers to cope with the vast amount of data that is being generated. The data is generated by a technological system in which computers are totally implicated. When means (technologies) and ends (something we want) are shown to be interdependent, then technologies arise as something far more important than rationalism suggests. Technologies are implicated in our whole way of being.

The Pragmatic Orientation to Computer Systems Design

The pragmatic orientation to computer systems design departs from these rationalistic tenets.[44] This orientation is primarily concerned with what works—actions and consequences. In other words, it begins with an understanding of technologies in the human context—how the technology fits within the day-to-day practical activity of people. A concern with theory (in the sense of generalizations, rules, and formulas) is therefore displaced by practice. Before considering pragmatism as a philosophical school, I will show how the pragmatic orientation is evident in the writing of several researchers in computer systems design.

Whereas rationalism is concerned with theories, the pragmatic orientation is primarily concerned with the way the computer system will be used. Weiser, a computer systems researcher at Xerox, makes this orientation clear in what he regards as the major attribute of a successful technology: "The most profound technologies are those that disappear. They weave themselves into the fabric of everyday life until they are indistinguishable from it."[45] The emphasis on the value of computer systems as a product of their relationship to practice is also evident in a heightened respect for the human-computer interface: "The user interface was once the last part of the system to be designed. Now it is the first . . . [W]hat is presented to one's senses *is* the computer."[46] This orientation is common among systems developers, such as Kay, who is one of the formative intellects behind the development of the Apple and Atari computers.[47] For some, the practical activity of computer programming is also informed by this view. According to Laurel, the functionality of computer systems "consists of the actions that are performed by people and computers working in concert, and programs are the means for creating the potential for those actions."[48] This pragmatic orientation also extends beyond the human/computer interface. For example, Mead, one of the pioneers of VLSI (very-large-scale integrated computer chips) describes how technical innovations (such as chip design) proceed from the modification of existing products. Design is a messy, ad hoc, atheoretical activity. The "analytic constructions" come into play later in the process and are constructed in hindsight. Innovations come out of this "tussle with reality."[49]

Such statements resonate with anyone concerned with computer systems design. The point is that for many of those concerned with computer systems development, the starting point is the human practices the computer is situated in. The design activity is immersed in practical concerns.

There is a further point of distinction from the rationalistic orientation. Whereas rationalism affirms the importance of the individual as an agent of independent reason, the pragmatic orientation affirms the social nature of human activity. For example, Weiser contrasts his ubiquitous computer model with those technologies that isolate the office worker as an individual working alone, epitomized in the current interest in developing virtual-reality systems: "Ubiquitous computers, in contrast, reside in the human world and pose no barriers to personal interaction."[50] Stults, another Xerox researcher directing a project on interactive video systems, focuses on "the social process of designing," in which design is conducted within "a community that maintains itself by pursuing open-ended activities."[51] He sets this view in opposition to that of "an organisation in which roles and activities have to be predetermined."[52] He asserts that he does not believe "models of physical systems constitute appropriate models for the social process of design."[53] He and his research team distinguish themselves from what they term "approaches to designing that project individual cognitive activities into the design process."[54] The approaches they reject include the problem-solving model of Herbert Simon, information-processing models, constraint-manipulation and optimization models, and grammars.

The pragmatic orientation described here is closely linked with the tenets of political and social liberalism. The ideals of human freedom and democracy are evident in the focus on human work practices; ubiquitous computing is computing for everyone, so they can interact with one another in ways of their own choosing. Computer technology is seen as potentially liberating rather than constraining, democratizing rather than enforcing rigid structures, humanistic rather than machine and theory oriented. This liberal orientation is evident in the interest among some computer systems designers in education. Since Rousseau, education has been understood as a major force for liberation. One of the foremost proponents of liberalism this century has been Dewey, a theorist of educational practice. Education is also an endeavor in which the contrasts between a rationalist or theory orientation and the liberal or pragmatic are brought into sharp relief. For example, in an article on computers and education, Kay contrasts the use of the computer as a "delivery vehicle" (the old, rationalistic idea of education condemned by such educationists as Dewey, Freire, and Illich[55]) with the computer as a means of enabling students to model their own ideas.[56] This orientation carries through into systems design, which engages client groups (particularly children) in testing prototypical systems at an early stage.[57] The intention is also to remove the idea of the expert from computer systems design. According to Kay, the objective is to achieve a level of computer systems design where "end users can change their tools and build new ones without having to become professional-level programmers."[58]

Political and social liberalism rejects autocratic structures and embraces free enterprise. Its chief tool is persuasion rather than legislation, bureaucratic control, or appeal to the inevitability of "logical argument." It comes as no surprise therefore that pragmatically oriented writing about computer systems design, including technical writing, is commonly optimistic, enthusiastic, utopian, and presented as though intended to "sell" a set of ideas. In this and other ways, the pragmatic orientation is supportive of, and enters into, "popular culture." In contrast to other intellectual traditions, such as critical theory, pragmatism unambiguously favors "mass culture."

As a further distinction from the rationalistic orientation, rationalism affirms the subservience of a technology to its content, whereas pragmatism is oriented toward an engagement with materials and technologies. Kay describes how the task of software design has been taken over from mathematicians and logicians by a "new class of artisans . . . deeply engaged in a romance with the material."[59] As indicated by Weiser and others, the configuration of computer hardware and its physical presence is part of the work environment. This orientation has led to experiments in different arrangements of hardware, such as the use of "electronic whiteboards," interesting combinations of drawing boards, video cameras, and video projectors to create novel work environments.[60] The hand-held computer by Apple (the Newton) and other manufacturers is not just a scaled-down version of the personal computer but a new device with capabilities that have been incorporated by its inventors as a response to its physicality as a portable object. Such capabilities include radio-controlled data transmission from one hand-held computer to another, and the use of a data pen and automated handwriting translation software to input text and drawings. This concern with the physical nature of technology is further reflected in Kay's advocacy of the merging of the disciplines of hardware and software design.[61]

Whereas the engagement of the body and its senses is a matter of indifference in the rationalist orientation, pragmatic computer systems design is characterized by an intrigue with the nature and influence of the senses. For example, Laurel draws parallels between the experience of theater and that of the computer: "Both have the capacity to represent actions and situations . . . in ways that invite us to extend our minds, feelings, and sensations."[62] An interest in the senses is also characterized as a concern with the human capacity to be totally engaged in a task, especially in relation to computer games.[63] According to Laurel and Kay, this engagement is at the heart of cognitive experience and its consideration should guide computer systems design. Kay calls on the psychological studies of Piaget and Bruner to illustrate the bodily and sensate nature of the learning experience that informed the design of the object-oriented graphic interface for the Macintosh computer.[64] Working with images leads to more advanced problem solving using symbols. According to Davidson, this translates into the view that "grounding the user in physical activity, linked to a visual environment where the human powers of recognition and interpretation could be harnessed, would lead naturally into abstract reasoning about how to solve problems on the computer."[65]

The sensory promise of virtual reality is intriguing to the pragmatist, though there is a suspicion of its threat to cut the human off from the material world and present an artificial and electronically mediated experience.[66] Laurel identifies the various models of human-computer interaction design in which the interface is conceived in terms of input and output devices or in terms of mental models.[67] She contrasts these views with her own preferred metaphor of close coupling and engagement, demonstrated in the relationship between the audience and the performance in theater.

The pragmatic orientation is also distinguished from the rationalistic orientation in that it exhibits and promotes a sense of awe of the formative power of technology. Rationalism affirms the superiority of ends (needs) to means (technologies), whereas, Turkle asserts, "Technology catalyzes changes not only in what we do but in how we think. It changes people's awareness of themselves, of one another, of their relationship with the world."[68] Turkle begins her book *The Second Self* with a description of the child who was believed to have had no contact with human society, up until his discovery in the woods of southern France in 1800. The Wild Child became the object of the "forbidden experiment" by which we discover the essential human, the natural person unimpeded by culture. The discovery promised access to true human nature. According to Turkle, the computer fulfills a similar function in telling us about ourselves. The Wild Child's discovery did not produce a definitive conclusion about human nature but nonetheless provided a focus of inquiry. Turkle is interested in the computer as it affects the way we think, especially about ourselves. She attempts to uncover the unstated question behind our preoccupation with the computer's capabilities. "That question is not what will the computer be like in the future, but instead, what will *we* be like? What kind of people are we becoming?"[69] According to Turkle, the computer also serves as a Rorschach inkblot. It presents ambiguous images into which we read or project different forms. This projection speaks of our larger concerns and reveals more about us than the computer.

As a further example of this conviction about the formative power of technology, Rheingold and others make strong claims for how virtual reality will affect the way we understand ourselves and the world. According to Helsel and Roth, virtual reality is a topic "that will raise more (and perhaps more significant) questions concerning the nature of reality than the human race has faced to date."[70]

These interests in the practical, the social nature of design, the physicality of technology, bodily engagement, and the formative power of technology indicate a pragmatic orientation to computer technology. These interests do not merely indicate a romantic or social orientation as opposed to a theoretical one. Nor do they arise merely when one adopts a personable, nontechnical means of describing research and development work. Pragmatism is a tradition of thought that distinguishes itself from the tenets of rationalism and presents a different view on knowledge and human involvement in the world.

The Influence of Dewey and McLuhan

Pragmatism is a philosophical school of thought dating back to the latter part of the nineteenth century with the work of the logician and philosopher C. S. Peirce (1839–1914) and the pioneer of modern psychology, William James (1842–1910).[71] Pragmatism's most influential exponent was John Dewey (1859–1952), who is best known for advancing the cause of liberalism in education.[72] The pragmatists took to task Descartes's assertion of the independence of reason and the skepticism by which it comes about. According to Peirce, we "cannot begin with complete doubt. We must begin with all the prejudices which we actually have when we enter upon the study of philosophy."[73]

There is a strong correlation between the assertions of philosophical pragmatism and the account of the pragmatic orientation to computer systems design described above. Pragmatism advances the thesis that theory is a kind of practice.[74] Pragmatism also embraces liberalism. In contrast to the Cartesian tradition, it also affirms embodiment and the engagement of the senses in human experience. It also asserts the formative power of technology in human affairs. The pragmatic attitude clearly resonates with the craft orientation of computer systems designers.

How does Dewey arrive at the conclusion that theory is a kind of practice? According to Dewey, there have been three major epochs in the development of thinking. These epochs are characterized by differing attitudes to the relationship between means (technologies) and ends (goals). The first epoch, that of primitive society, is characterized by a simple technology and an integration of means with ends. In primitive life, there were only short-term goals understood as concrete outcomes. Such things as tools did not generally point beyond themselves or signify other things. They were there to do a job.

There are no intermediate appliances, no adjustment of means to remote ends, no postponements of satisfaction, no transfer of interest and attention over to a complex system of acts and objects. Want, effort, skill and satisfaction stand in the closest relations to one another. . . . [T]ools, implements, weapons are not part of the mechanical and objective means, but are part of the present activity, organic parts of personal skill and effort.[75]

The second epoch is represented by the thought of Plato and Aristotle. In this epoch means and ends are separated, with a priority of ends (needs or outcomes) over means (the employment of tools and technologies): "Means are menial, subservient, slavish; and ends liberal and final; things as means testify to inherent defect, to dependence, while ends testify to independent and intrinsically self-sufficing being."[76] Furthermore, in this epoch, tools served to point beyond themselves. According to Dewey, a tool is more than a particular thing in Greek thought: "It is a thing in which a connection, a sequential bond of nature is embodied. . . . Its perception as well as its actual use takes the mind to other things. . . . A tool denotes a perception and acknowledgment of sequential bonds in nature."[77] According to Dewey, this view provided one of the great impediments to science. (Unlike many twentieth-century philosophers, Dewey was not skeptical of the value of science.) It developed abstractions of things and events. But because of the poor status it accorded technologies, it failed to foster an interest in instrumentation, the technological environment that enabled science. The Greeks talked about science but did not practice it. The legacy of Plato is the notion of abstraction, essence, idea, or form. Things pointed beyond themselves to ends—the forms, of which things were the mere shadow, or were in the process of becoming. Rather than getting involved with things, as in craft or the use of instruments, the highest good was the contemplation of ends.

This epoch left us with the confused legacy of the dualisms of which Dewey was so contemptuous, and which are still with us. Dewey was opposed to the tradition of oppositional thinking: ideal versus real, theory versus practice, mind versus body, means versus ends, and subject versus object.

According to Dewey, the third epoch partially reunited means with ends. During the scientific revolution of the sixteenth and seventeenth centuries, means and ends interpenetrated by alternating with one another. During this period, objects and events were taken instrumentally as data for developing further meaning and significance.[78] It was not until empirical science became technological that it got past the level of intellectual abstraction. Now the production and use of tools serves to enlarge the significance of other objects and events. In spite of any account given by rationalism, modern science has adopted this practical outlook. According to Hickman, "theory became a tool of practice and practice a means to the production of new effects. Theory no longer had to do with final certainty but instead, as working hypothesis, with the tentative and unresolved."[79] This is the key to understanding Dewey's pragmatism: facts, ideas, and concepts are tools. The scholar and the researcher have access to a workshop of many tools. In our practices surrounding these tools, we see them as interconnected. Theoreticians have no special access to the essence of things. It is simply that they use specialized tools within a particular set of practices. Hopefully these practices extend beyond the laboratory or the world of speculative theory building to impinge on the wider sphere of human engagement in practical problems.

All inquiry begins with engagement. Tensions and irresolutions require a response. Reflection can be defined as the process of going outside the immediate situation—"to something else to get a leverage for understanding it"[80]—and involves the search for an appropriate tool. The tool is part of the active productive skill brought to bear on the situation. The tools that feature in the reorganization of the experience include theories, proposals, recommended methods, and courses of action. The applicability of the tool is worked out in the situation.

A theory, or a term in a theory such as "inertia," is therefore a tool within a situation. The difference between Dewey's position and that of Plato or Descartes is that inertia does not exist as an independent property of matter but features as a tool. It is instrumental to reducing and manipulating objects and events so as to generate new meanings, such as a prediction about a future state of affairs—where a moving object will be located after a certain period of time.

Dewey accords no privilege to reason, thinking, or inference beyond that enjoyed by any other practice.

. . . [T]hinking is no different in kind from the use of natural materials and energies, say fire and tools, to refine, re-order, and shape other natural materials, say ore. . . . Thought and reason are not specific powers. They consist of the procedures intentionally employed in the application to each other of the unsatisfactorily confused and indeterminate on one side and the regular and stable on the other.[81]

In all this Dewey is anxious to unseat the power of philosophical idealism and to reinvest humankind with a sense of involvement in nature rather than being a god above it: "[T]hinking is a continuous process of temporal re-organization within one and the same world of experienced things, not a jump from the latter world into one of objects constituted once for all by thought."[82] In the light of Dewey's instrumental view of theory and experimentation, science appears as a mode of social practice that is so specialized we do not recognize it as a practice.

Dewey's pragmatism is an attempt to dislodge humankind from its fixation on some realm of "knowledge or contemplation," where we are "outside of and detached from the ongoing sweep of interacting and changing events"—where, godlike, we are responsible only to ourselves.[83] Once this fixation is released, humankind's new posture enables a new sense of responsibility toward, and involvement in, the world: "When he perceives clearly and adequately that he is within nature, a part of its interactions, he sees that the line to be drawn is not between action and thought, . . . but between blind, slavish, meaningless action and the action that is free, significant, directed and responsible."[84]

Whereas rationalism affirms a nonparticipative, hierarchical view of knowledge, Dewey's pragmatism leads to a view that is egalitarian and liberal. The influence of Dewey's work has largely been through the dissemination of his thoughts on education.[85] Dewey was clearly against rigidly applying method, against rote learning, and, calling on the writings of Rousseau, in favor of an open disposition to new experiences and the cultivation of the natural spirit. Practice is essential for Dewey, and theory is subservient to practice: "[T]here is no such thing as genuine knowledge and fruitful understanding except as the offspring of *doing*."[86] Thinking and doing are inseparable: "Only by wrestling with the conditions of the problem at first hand, seeking and finding his own way out, does he think."[87]

Through his liberalism and his acknowledgment of the ubiquity of the aesthetic in human experience, Dewey's pragmatism embraces an appreciation of popular culture and its media. For example, Dewey denounces the elitism by which the art object is differentiated from the rest of experience. What we now designate as art objects were once part of everyday life. In classical and Medieval culture, "the arts of the drama, music, painting, and architecture thus exemplified had no particular connection with theaters, galleries, museums. They were part of the significant life of an organized community."[88] The real arts of today are within the subversive but genuine realm of popular culture. For Dewey, writing in the 1930s, "The arts which today have most vitality for the average person are things he does not take to be arts: for instance, the movie, jazzed music, the comic strip, and, too frequently, newspaper accounts of love nests, murders and exploits of bandits."[89]

Rationalism affirms the subservience of a technology to its content. Dewey's counterunderstanding is most clearly indicated in his discussion of media (i.e., materials) in art. Some (the idealists) maintain that an artwork has an essence beyond its mere realization in materials. Contrary to this view, successful artists obviously embrace their medium. Dewey refers to Delacroix's observation that there is a difference between *applying* color to objects in a painting and *making* them out of color. In the former case: "Means and end did not coalesce."[90] In the latter case, there is little distinction between the means of painting (the tools, the paints, the colors) and an end (some "illusion" or a reference). At every turn in his analysis of a situation, Dewey embraces the physicality of the experience and the involved nature of human action rather than its distance from things.

The use of a particular medium, a special language having its own characteristics, is the source of every art, philosophic, scientific, technological and esthetic. The arts of science, of politics, of history, and of painting and poetry all have finally the same *material;* that which is constituted by the interaction of the live creature with his surroundings.[91]

Whereas the engagement of the body and its senses is a matter of indifference to the rationalistic orientation, Dewey's pragmatism is characterized by an intrigue with the nature and influence of the senses. For Dewey, the starting point for his inquiry into the nature of human understanding and involvement in the world is where we are prereflectively engaged in the activity of *doing*.[92] As for pragmatically oriented computer systems designers, an understanding of acting and working begins with the notion of engagement. For Dewey, a moment of engagement is an "experience," but experiences do not exist as discrete entities. Nor are they amenable to ready identification. Experiences have a "pervasive" quality. They are immediate and also aesthetic. Our immediate responses to experiences are not reflection, articulation, or analysis, but enjoyment, boredom, satisfaction, frustration, or other emotions. Experiences do not demand active reflection and responsive attention. Dewey's ideas about tool use are to be understood in the context of this involvement. When situations become tense and unresolved, we bring tools to bear as a means to operate on the unsettled situation.

For Dewey, engagement in experience is clearly not a matter of receiving and interpreting sense data.[93] The senses are active, roving, exploring, tool-like. But the senses of hearing and vision are not coequal in this regard. It is the aural sense that is the most probing. Dewey points this out in reference to how printed publications (appealing to the visual sense) and the communications of the local community (the aural sense) afford different contributions to how we are kept informed: "The connections of the ear with vital and out-going thought and emotion are immensely closer and more varied than those of the eye. Vision is a spectator; hearing is a participator."[94] The primacy of the visual sense is evident in Greek thought when we consider the priority given to a thing's shape or form. Shape made it possible to classify things with ease. But then form became "something intrinsic, as the very essence of a thing in virtue of the metaphysical structure of the universe."[95] Hence Greek thought arrived at the dualism of form and matter, the ideal and the world of shadows.

Whereas rationalism affirms the superiority of ends (needs) to means (technologies), Dewey's pragmatism clearly instills a sense of respect for the formative power of technology: "Steam and electricity have done more to alter the conditions under which men associate together than all the agencies which affected human relationships before our time."[96] This theme is developed with great pursuasive force by McLuhan.

In summary, the pragmatic orientation of certain computer systems researchers finds support in Dewey's elevation of the practical over the theoretical—where theory appears as a kind of practice. Dewey's liberalism supports the elevation of the social nature of design and the breaking down of cliques of theoretical expertise. Dewey's concern with materiality supports the computer systems designer's romance with the materials of technology. Dewey's emphasis on the primacy of engagement in experience rather than reflection supports the elevation of the importance of the body and the senses.

The "media philosophy" of McLuhan has exerted a substantial influence, through his popular writings of the 1960s.[97] This influence is evident among some computer systems designers and developers in particular. Kay and other systems developers have been strongly influenced by McLuhan in understanding the computer as a medium and in other ways.[98]

The pragmatic orientation to theory as a kind of practice is echoed in McLuhan's presentation of the subservience of theory to the technologies of writing and print. Dewey situates effective science in a post-Platonic era, in which the components of theory do not merely refer to other things but are instruments within scientific practice. For McLuhan, such artifacts as theories are objects in the world of print. Such writers as Ong, Havelock, Heim, and Illich have developed this theme further.[99]

Whereas the age of print promotes a hierarchical and bureaucratic view of human knowledge (rationalism), the electronic age, McLuhan indicates with approval, promotes a liberal orientation to knowledge. In keeping with the spirit of this age, McLuhan was a popularizer and an apologist for mass culture. For McLuhan the electronic age presents a return to "tribal culture." The world is becoming a "global village," characterized by immediacy, involvement, and even a strong sense of social cohesion. According to McLuhan: "In the electronic age we wear all mankind as our skin."[100]

Rationalism suggests that the content of a technology is more important than its physical realization. McLuhan's famous overstatement, "the medium is the message" clearly asserts the opposite. According to McLuhan, "nobody has been willing to study the personal and social effects of media apart from their 'content.'"[101] McLuhan's studies are clearly aimed at addressing this lack.

Whereas the rationalistic orientation is indifferent to bodily engagement, McLuhan echoes Dewey's assertion of the primacy of engagement and the role of the senses. This introduces the final point where McLuhan's view differs from rationalism. He sees technology not merely as a means to an end but as formative in who we are and how we see ourselves.

The starting point of McLuhan's provocative understanding of the formative power of technology is the role of the senses. McLuhan coins the term "ratio of the senses" to indicate how all the senses are in play with one another, and to differing degrees. An extreme example of altering the sense ratio, in this case *breaking* the sense ratio, is to focus on one sense to the exclusion of the others. McLuhan cites psychological evidence, including that of hypnotic pain-relief experiments, to show that this alteration has a numbing effect. In attending to just one of the senses, particularly the audial sense, we assume a kind of a trance. McLuhan extends the effects of this trance experience to the whole of human society. Like Dewey, he uses an account of history to make his point.

McLuhan divides human history into three epochs. For Dewey, primitive society was characterized by a sense of involvement and an unreflective intimacy between ends (needs and goals) and means (tools). According to McLuhan, tribal society was under a trance from a surfeit of audial sensation. Social intercourse was entirely driven by speech and chatter. The culture was oral-aural, characterized by involvement and a captivation with the "magical resonances of the spoken word."[102] There was a "Wholeness, empathy and depth of awareness."[103] Unlike the objects of the sense of sight, sound is, as indicated by Dewey, ubiquitous, nonsequential, nonspatial, and all-enveloping. There are no organic physical accoutrements for shutting out sound. For McLuhan, as for Dewey, the aural sense also implies tactility. In listening we seek out and explore. It is an active sense. McLuhan equates "ear man" with "tactile man." The simplicity of primitive modes of expression brings in all the senses. Similarly, in inspecting simple geometries, such as the boundary line of a cave painting, we are in an area of the interplay of the senses. Line drawings hence have a strong tactile character: "[T]he art of the draughtsman . . . is a strongly tactile and tangible art. And even Euclidean geometry is by modern standards very tactile."[104]

Eventually the primitive epoch gave way to a stronger influence. In the case of Dewey, it was identifying tools as pointing beyond themselves, and getting caught up in what we now call intellectual abstraction. For McLuhan, the second epoch was characterized by new technologies, those of literacy. The third epoch represents a return to the aural world.

McLuhan's understanding of the formative power of technology is his major and most provocative contribution to understanding technology, and in this he goes further than Dewey. For McLuhan, new technologies alter sense ratios, and they do so "steadily and without any resistance."[105] "When technology extends *one* of our senses, a new translation of culture occurs as swiftly as the new technology is interiorized."[106] So the second epoch is characterized by the dominance of the visual sense. The main technology of this age was the printing press, with the invention of the alphabet and the manuscript culture leading up to it. McLuhan is adamant that the transition from the "tribal web" was not brought about by the *content* of those early manuscripts. It was the impact of that technology on the alteration of the sense ratio from audial to visual experience: "Only the phonetic alphabet makes such a sharp division in experience, giving to its user an eye for an ear, and freeing him [the human] from the tribal trance of resonating word magic and the web of kinship."[107] There were other technologies, such as the clock, that entered the picture, but literacy technology was primary over all others: "It was not the clock, but literacy technology, reinforced by the clock, that created abstract time and led men to eat, not when they were hungry, but when it was '*time* to eat.' "[108] According to McLuhan, the mechanical, print era, traded on the notion of change and yet blinded the world to a real understanding of change: "The paradox of mechanization is that although it is itself the cause of maximal growth and change, the principle of mechanization excludes the very possibility of growth or the understanding of change."[109]

What of the modern era? For Dewey it began with the scientific revolution, in which objects and events were treated instrumentally and empirical science went beyond intellectual abstraction. For McLuhan, the most significant development was when we moved into the era of mass electronic communication. For Dewey, the modern era ushered in a "return" to an integration of ends and means. The electronic era is also characterized as a "return." For McLuhan, in the electronic era "the action and the reaction occur almost at the same time."[110] Electricity produced a great historical reversal in making things instant again.[111] The alphabet and print "made possible the spread of the power that is knowledge, and shattered the bonds of tribal man, thus exploding him into agglomeration of individuals. Electric writing and speed pour upon him, instantaneously and continuously, the concerns of all other men. He becomes tribal once more. The human family becomes one tribe again."[112] As an apologist of popular culture writing in the 1960s, McLuhan drew on this view to advance an explanation for the seeming irrationality of the younger generation: " 'Rational,' of course, has for the West long meant 'uniform and continuous and sequential.' In other words, we have confused reason with literacy, and rationalism with a single technology."[113]

The electronic era has the characteristics of the primitive aural culture in which all the senses were activated through the primacy of sound.[114] Electricity reconfers the mythic dimension to life. Print was too specialized and so "detribalized." The "nonspecialist electronic technology retribalizes."[115] According to McLuhan, myth is the contraction or implosion of any process. Contrary to the common opinion that electronic culture is producing a diverse, fragmented, and pluralistic world, the instant speed of electricity is contracting the world. Electronic communications confer the "mythic dimension" onto society. In *Understanding Media,* McLuhan identifies the key technologies and media of the electronic age: transportation, comics, telegraph, typewriters, telephones, phonographs, film, radio, television, and armaments. Each is discussed in the light of its contribution to an "imploding" world, how it implicates the senses, and its relationship to the influential technologies of print and electronics. In his analysis, McLuhan distinguishes between what he terms "hot media" and "cool media." A hot medium "extends one single sense in high definition."[116] It requires minimal engagement, that is, low participation from the audience. An example of a hot medium is film. The high-resolution image emphasizes the visual sense. In contrast, television is a cool medium. Considerable engagement is required on the part of the audience in order to make sense of the low resolution matrix of dots on the screen. As with cool media, television is much more engaging of all the senses, including the kinesthetic and tactile sense. Television is "audile-tactile:" "That is why it is emphatic, and why the optimal mode of TV image is the cartoon. . . . [I]t is a world in which the visual component is so small that the viewer has as much to do as in a crossword puzzle."[117] The hot/cool distinction enables McLuhan to make comparisons between different media and compare their effects on audiences and on society. He compares the photograph (hot) with the cartoon (cool), radio (hot) with the telephone (cool), the phonetic alphabet (hot) with hieroglyphic or ideogrammatic writing (cool), a book (hot) with a dialogue (cool), lecture (hot) with a seminar (cool). A society imbued with print technology is hot, while oral, tribal society is cool. McLuhan's use of the terms "hot" and "cool" is partly a play on the vernacular use of those terms, but it also reflects observations about behavioral patterns in response to media. People who are engaged are less restless than those for whom a single sense, particularly the visual sense, is operative in heightened mode. McLuhan articulates the power of media to incite in these terms. Radio has much more power to incite enthusiasm, agitate, and arouse in a cool, tribal culture. Intense, sharp-edged, precise (hot) public figures appear less engaging on the cool television medium than "blurry," "shaggy" personalities.[118] These and similar observations led McLuhan to the conclusion that the medium *is* the message rather than merely the carrier.[119]

To summarize, in keeping with the tenets of pragmatically oriented computer systems design and Dewey's philosophical pragmatism, McLuhan affirms the primacy of practice. Theory does not grant us privileged access to the essential nature of things but is a product of an era imbued with the effects of a particular technology—print. The modern electronic age is presented favorably as breaking down the social hierarchies. Technology has a presence that exceeds the mere consideration of its content. The senses and their amplification through particular technologies are implicated in the development of historical epochs. Technology is formative to the extent that we become unavoidably engaged by its power and numbed to its effects.

McLuhan's positive media philosophy points away from rationalism toward pragmatism—from a theory orientation to the elevation of social engagement in practice. The influence of this philosophy is bound to increase as the conception of the computer changes more toward media and McLuhan's ideas are translated even more widely into the area of computer systems design. Increasingly, computers are being seen as "multimedia" devices. The distinction between computers and other information technologies is therefore blurring. Computers are also becoming more interactive, more interconnected, and more engaging. McLuhan's media philosophy is gaining an even wider sphere of applicability.

The Pragmatic Turn in Design Research

The strong contention of pragmatism is that our inquiries are imbued with the practical all the way through. It is not that the theoretical and the practical are simply two ways of looking at something, or two activities—intellectual inquiry, which is theoretical, and application, which is practical. There is only the practical. What we commonly refer to as theory is just a kind of practice, in the manner outlined by Dewey. When computer systems designers call on the theories of logic or physics or invent new theories, they are not bending the knee to rationalism as long as we regard these theories as tools developed in practice situations and for practice. The collapse of the theory-practice distinction is well expressed in the thought of hermeneutical philosophers, such as Gadamer, Fish, and Dreyfus.[120] As a generalization, a theory is a rule or law that has to be applied in some situation. We seldom see theories about how theory is to be applied, and when we do see one, there is no theory about how *that* theory is to be applied. If we believe in underpinning practice by theory, then it is a foundation that involves an infinite regress of theories. According to the hermeneutical thesis, we are not beholden to theories (*theoria*) but to *phronesis,* the "intellectual virtue" of practical judgment indicated by Aristotle. According to hermeneutics, all understanding and knowledge is of this kind. Many artificial-intelligence researchers, such as Schank, acknowledge that there are other ways of knowing than those that can be made explicit as rules. For some researchers, this is "creative knowledge" or skill. Many researchers have appropriated Polanyi's concept of "tacit knowledge."[121] For hermeneutics, as for pragmatic philosophy, that is the only kind of knowing. Rules, formulas, frames, plans, scripts, and semantic networks are not forms of knowledge but tools for research.

In some quarters, the language of practice is considered to lack the sophistication of "theory talk."[122] So people revert readily to "theory talk" to justify their practices. We pay lip service to the importance of theory, while our research or design betrays our commitment to practice.[123] This quiet victory of pragmatism is evident in the "pragmatic turn" taken in design methods. Design methods began as rigorous prescriptions of how design should proceed. As accurate explanations of what happens in design, methods carried the force of the theories of rationalism. As such, methods were also prescriptive. They were a means of telling novice designers how to design. They also had the potential to be put into computers to automate design. Very rapidly researchers in design methods saw the poor utility of this view. Design methods moved on to become *guides* for practices rather than prescriptions, such that there was a plurality of methods, and theorists like Jones saw fit to offer advice about how to select from among methods. The pragmatic turn is also evident in Broadbent's comprehensive summary of design methods and in his softening of a dependence on theory. In favoring an empirical view of design, Broadbent declares, "the design of architecture finally can never be a matter of completely automated decision. It is doubtful whether design in any field can ever quite be that."[124] Alexander, one of the founders of design methods moved on from his analytic/synthetic model of the design process to one that applied a pattern language, a guidebook of loosely formed rules, the application of which required a sensitivity to context.[125]

Artificial intelligence has also undergone its own pragmatic renaissance. It is widely recognized that artificial-intelligence researchers fall into two camps. The "neats" are concerned with the careful development of theory; the "scruffs" appropriate theories from anywhere or simply try things out with only the loosest theoretical justification.[126] Artificial intelligence has been accused by some of not being theoretical enough. It is a kind of alchemy. Needless to say, the language of the "scruffs" has not yet caught up with their practices. They pay lip service to theory.

In the article by Winograd and Flores, replying to critics of their book, they observe that the one reviewer who was most sympathetic to their critique was the one who was most concerned with the practical design of expert systems. Clancy was obviously of the rationalistic tradition, believing fervently in the value and possibility of codifying expert knowledge into computer systems. Winograd's and Flores's rival accounts of understanding served to explain "what is so patently obvious when you work with experts, namely that they have so much difficulty laying out consistent networks and describing relations among concepts in a principled way."[127] The closer we are to systems development and the tools, particularly through their use, the more we know their limitations—a sentiment expressed in Dreyfus's comment on artificial intelligence (AI): "Having to program computers keeps one honest. There is no room for the armchair rationalist's speculations. Thus AI research has called the Cartesian cognitivist's bluff."[128]

Further evidence for the pragmatic turn comes from McLuhan's observation that electronic culture has ushered in new modes of philosophical thought subversive of rationalism. According to McLuhan, electronic technologies are bringing about a liberal view of education: "Paradoxically, automation makes liberal education mandatory."[129] According to McLuhan we are now like nomads, gathering knowledge, and involved in the total social process.[130] We also have a new social consciousness. We are responsible for all humankind. For McLuhan, writing in the 1960s, these and others factors have produced a culture receptive to Sartre's existentialism, which borrowed from Heidegger's "antirationalist" stance. As befitted his devotion to 1960s popular culture, McLuhan was confident enough to pen the following clumsy rubric: "Heidegger surf-boards along on the electronic wave as triumphantly as Descartes rode the mechanical wave."[131] McLuhan writes approvingly of Heidegger's "nonliterate bias" toward language and technology. Descartes looked resplendent in his day for the same reasons Heidegger does in ours: "An enthusiasm for Heidegger's excellent linguistics could easily stem from naive immersion in the metaphysical organicism of our electronic milieu."[132] Heim picks up on the theme of the receptivity of electronic culture to postrationalism and postmodernism. With word processing, "all texts make up a universal hypertext. Digital text is thus quintessentially postmodern in destabilizing and making text flexible. There are no more originals."[133] If McLuhan is right, then engaging with the medium of computation is leading, or will inevitably lead, away from rationalism, especially as the computer becomes more of a cool medium, interactive and engaging all of the senses. But McLuhan did not have to be right. Because of his influence on silicon culture, his prophecies will be largely self-fulfilling. However, in the following chapter, I examine a less optimistic view of information technology.

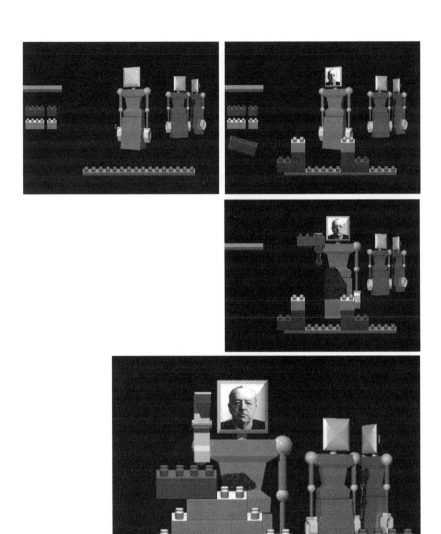

Screen display from an interactive computer system devised by Zoltan Nemes Nemeth in which the computer user builds a simple structure of blocks. The "robot" intervenes by adding blocks of its own in random locations if the user hesitates. The face on the robot is that of Ludwig Mies van der Rohe.

2

Who Is in Control?

Critical Theory and Information Technology Design

It is a commonplace to remark that advanced technologies, such as computer systems, present dangers as well as benefits to society. On one side are the benefits of gathering, processing, and disseminating information with speed, performing useful calculations, putting people in touch with one another, and providing certain freedoms—such as reducing the tedium of some routine jobs and breaking down the effects of distance in communication. On the other side are the dangers and excesses of electronic surveillance, the invasion of privacy, the suppression of diversity, and dependence. Also on the negative side, it seems that computers are powerful and can be harnessed to serve power interests. The potential benevolence of technology versus its malevolence presents a perplexity. It prompts people to ask who is in control? how do we harness or arrest the power of computers and the interests of those they serve?

According to critical theorists, arguing from a position that finds support in Hegel, Marx, and Heidegger, the matter of control is already decided in the framing of the question. According to Marcuse, it was around the fourth century B.C. that the understanding of "reason" bifurcated. One strand, "technological reason," dominated and marginalized the other, "pretechnological reason." According to critical theory (and other traditions of thought), Western societies are now irredeemably technological. We are in the grip of technology, as shown in the way we use language, structure our institutions, favor theory, and even pose such questions as "Who is in control?'' Computers are merely a recent manifestation of a human will to dominate and to see everything technologically, in terms of causes, control, and domination.

Information technology is a worthy focus for testing the arguments of critical theory. Information technology inherits the trappings of the mass media—a common focus of attack by critical theorists. Information technology is also pervasive; it relies substantially on highly developed industries, and it is ostensibly a medium for communication. It is totally implicated in the "modern condition." Information technology is also central to various discourses on language and communication, as exemplified in Shannon and Weaver's information theory.[1] Information technology is therefore implicated in ideas about reason.

Two Understandings of Reason

What are the characteristics of the pretechnological understandings of reason? Pretechnological rationality is commonly regarded as that understanding advanced by Greek philosophers prior to Socrates (469–399 B.C.) and Plato (428–348 B.C.), though there are remnants of this thinking in Plato and Aristotle (384–322 B.C.). Put simply, pretechnological, or pre-Socratic, thought understands truth as residing in the tensions, resolutions, clashes, and play between opposites. Truth and understanding are also indeterminate. Pre-Socratic thought is often termed "dialectical" (though that term is often used to indicate its converse, logic, by some writers[2]). In dialectic, truth emerges or is disclosed through the interaction between opposites, as in a dialogue between two people. The dialectical interaction may be between any oppositions we care to nominate, such as day and night, war and peace, slavery and freedom, or being and nonbeing. The pretechnological, dialectical view of reason is commonly set against the primacy of the syllogism as a model of reason—also referred to as "formal logic"—advanced by Aristotle. The basic syllogism takes this form: all *A*s are *B*; *C* is an *A*; therefore, *C* is *B*. The syllogism is a device (arguably a technology) aimed at settling matters of dispute. Reason seen as syllogistic is determinate. It closes conversation and settles the matter. The focus on the syllogism and its extensions and variations as capturing the essence of reason is here called "technological rationality." More generally, it is the imposition of any "metanarrative," metaphysical system, or appeal to principle that purports to transcend the current situation to decide matters.[3] The definition of "technological rationality" is extended even more widely within some critical theory to embrace the "irrational" and the "romantic." According to critical theory, to affirm the other side of a story (as in asserting the primacy of the irrational over the rational) is not to challenge it radically. It merely further entrenches the view that there is a rational mode of thinking to which other kinds of thinking are to be compared.

What is the character of pre-Socratic thinking or the pre-Socratic view of reason? There are two major schools of thought. Lloyd presents it as a precursor to Aristotle's understanding of logic.[4] According to Lloyd, the pre-Socratics were on the way to science. This period "is marked by notable advances in both the theory and practice of logic and scientific method."[5] On this view, the pre-Socratics fall along the early part of a historical continuum that led to science. At variance with this understanding, Heidegger advances the view that pre-Socratic writing is significant for its presentation of a primordial way of thinking,[6] which is more basic than what scientific reason offers. So, according to this view, there is a major disjunction between the pre-Socratics and what followed. According to Heidegger, the pre-Socratics were not yet philosophers, but they were the last of the great thinkers. In fact, Heidegger makes the distinction between thinking and philosophizing. Thinking is that more basic, primordial, pretechnological mode of reason that underlies all our reflections and which human society should acknowledge, return to, and appropriate. According to Heidegger, philosophizing and scientific reasoning, on the other hand, are metaphysical, in the sense that they seek all-embracing explanations of phenomena. They are also technological and determinate. They seek always to settle the matter at hand rather than leave it open for continued discussion or contemplation. According to this position, the pre-Socratics were not merely on the way to science. They were in touch with basic modes of thinking that have surfaced and resurfaced at different times in history.

According to commentators on Heidegger's writings, identification of, and respect for, pre-Socratic, pretechnological thinking resurfaced in the German mystical tradition that began with the writings of Eckhart (1260–1331). Caputo traces this influence through to the German idealists and Hegel (1770–1831), one of the most influential of German thinkers.[7] Hegel's understanding of dialectic inspired such thinkers as Marx (1818–1883), Nietzsche (1844–1900), Dewey (1859–1952), and Heidegger (1889–1976).[8] Needless to say, aspects of Eastern thought have been strongly linked with pretechnological, dialectical understanding.[9] As I will show, the assertion of the primacy of pretechnological rationality is evident in critical theory.

Oppositional Thought

Considering its profound influence on twentieth-century philosophy and the philosophy of technology, it is worth considering the nature of dialectic in some detail here.[10] There are various constructions of pretechnological rationality, but a key component is an understanding of the ubiquitous role of oppositions (oppositional thinking). In *Metaphysics,* Aristotle identified the early doctrine that "most human things go in pairs." He outlined how the Pythagoreans identified ten definitive pairs: limited and unlimited, odd and even, one and plurality, right and left, male and female, at rest and moving, straight and curved, light and dark, good and evil, square and oblong.[11] The identification of oppositions featured in the construction of argument, classification, religious understanding, and the diagnosis of medical conditions and the prescription of cures.[12]

Oppositions are simply "polar expressions."[13] Couplets, such as "mortals and immortals," "men and women," "young and old," and "land and sea," were employed by Heraclitus (one of the foremost pre-Socratic philosophers) to provide emphasis, to indicate the extensive and inclusive nature of a proposition (as in, "everyone was there, young and old alike"). They were also employed in questions about alternatives: "are you on public or on private business?" "are you some goddess or a mortal?" The oppositions were also flexible.

They sometimes permitted a middle possibility. For example, the battlefield was divided into right, left, and middle.

One of the major pre-Socratic doctrines of opposites was the assertion by Heraclitus that the opposites are in fact one: "the sea is both pure and foul"; "the way up and down is one and the same." There is unity in difference. Also, according to Heraclitus, the Pythagorean oppositions are all analogous to each other in that they embody the relation of one to many or, more precisely, the limited/unlimited. In the oppositions of rest and moving, being at rest is a limit condition or ultimate constraint on the many possible ways of movement. Being straight is the ultimate limit on being curved. One of the themes taken up in critical theory is to characterize the relationship between opposites in terms of conflict. Heraclitus refers to the interdependence of opposites but also the "constant war or strife between them."[14]

What is the relationship between opposites and logic? Aristotle uses Heraclitus to indicate the violation of the Law of Contradiction. According to Aristotle, if a person "'thinks' and 'thinks not' indifferently, what difference will there be between him and the vegetables?"[15] Lloyd interprets Heraclitus in a way that fits him within the logical framework when he says that Heraclitus simply means that opposites are the same in particular respects. There are always qualifications that remove the contradiction. The sea is both pure and foul. For fish it is pure and drinkable, for humans undrinkable and deadly. "The way up and down is one and the same."[16] To travel up the road in one direction is to travel down it in the other. For Lloyd, this is a simple case of perspective. The same object appears different from different points of view: "Writing at a period before the nature of contradiction had been explicitly analysed, Heraclitus exploits the paradoxes which result from equivocation to great effect, and his fragments illustrate particularly clearly the confusions which may arise from the use of opposite terms in unqualified and undefined senses."[17] Such logical analyses of oppositions illuminate the varied nature of oppositional thinking and the possibilities it opens up for nuance and meaning. However, from the Hegelian, mystical, and Heideggerian perspective, such an interpretation misses the identification of pre-Socratic thought as representing a fundamentally different view of the world—the dynamic, indeterminate, pretechnological view. This different view is best appreciated through an understanding of Hegel's presentation of "logic" or the "dialectical principle."

Hegel's Dialectical Principle

According to Houlgate, Hegel's dialectical principle "is the principle whereby apparently stable thoughts reveal their instability by turning into their opposites and then into new, more complex thoughts."[18] In keeping with Descartes and the project of the Enlightenment, dialectic is also, according to Hegel, a means of "thinking without presuppositions."[19] It is a way of thinking in which we are not encumbered by preconceptions about what conclusions we wish to reach.

According to Hegel, evidence of the need for such a view of thought comes from Aristotelian logic itself. It is well known that the presuppositions of logic are themselves inexplicable in terms of logic. Aristotle's principle of noncontradiction, that it is impossible for a thing to both be and not be, cannot be established by formal logic itself. We are therefore fully entitled to be skeptical about formal logic. Hegel was not opposed to Aristotelian logic, certainly not in the natural sciences, but he sought to develop a new "science of logic" in which Aristotelian logic is not presupposed.[20] Further along in the dialectical process, it may transpire that Aristotelian logic is totally vindicated by the "dialectical principle," but we do not begin with it.

If this "science of logic" cannot be reasoned through using the rules of logic, how can it be arrived at? One of Hegel's great themes is that reason has its own reason. It must follow its own path. Our role is to be attentive to reason's development. Instead of weaving a causal argument, in which one assertion depends on another, we let thinking (or reason) do its own work. This is a major theme of the pretechnological, pre-Socratic, and dialectical view of thinking. To think dialectically is to let thought carry us along. Thought is autonomous and indeterminate, and it takes nothing for granted.[21] As we shall subsequently see, this view is less ambiguously developed by Heidegger as one in which "thought" (capitalized as "Thought" in English) is accorded a mission in history. The prime example of where thought is indeterminate is in how we address the ancient question "What is all this?"[22]—how we address the issue of being.[23]

Part of the difficulty in following Hegel's inquiry about the nature of thought is that his writing is at the same time a presentation of what thought is and an example of how it proceeds. It is also a denial of the need for argument (seen as an exercise in Aristotelian logic). Hegel's "logic" is not about something as simple as "thinking through a problem" but is about thought itself and about being. Further difficulty in understanding Hegel arises from the subject matter, which requires the use of such terms as "thinking," "being," and "nothing" and uses those same terms to explain themselves and each other. Hence we find "thinking about thought," "thought is," and "to think of being is to think of nothing." All of these factors make Hegel's writing on logic difficult to follow,[24] though no less significant and influential because of that.

Houlgate provides a cogent summary of Hegel's line of inquiry. In tackling the nature of thought, Hegel supports Descartes's method of first identifying the most basic and irrefutable statement about thought. But for Hegel, instead of starting with the thinking self (the *cogito*), the least controversial statement that can be made about thought is that it *is*. This is thought that is purely indeterminate—unfixed in scope, uncertain, inconclusive. This assertion that thought *is* precedes any notion that thought is syllogistic, or that it is about objects, different from feelings, or the activity of a subject. Recognizing that thought simply *is*, is to think only of thought. What does it mean to think only of thought—thought without content? According to Hegel, to answer this question is to link thought with being. To think only about thought in this way is to think of pure being. However, according to Hegel, after pondering being in this pure way, we are led to realize that we are thinking of the possibility of there not being anything at all—or, more precisely, the thought of pure indeterminate being slides into the thought of nothing. Yet thinking of nothing is not ceasing to think. It seems to follow that just as "the thought of sheer, indeterminate being slides into the thought of nothing, therefore, so the thought of nothing slides into

the thought of being."[25] This strange behavior seems to be characteristic of thought and is typical of oppositional "logic." A thought
slides into its opposite and back again. In the case of being, to think
of pure being is to think of it disappearing into its immediate opposite. To think of being is, therefore, to think of something else, the
transition into nothing whatsoever, then back again into being. It
seems, then, that thought is about something else apart from being
and nothing. It is about transition. The dialectical process itself leads
to a new thought which emerges—the thought of becoming. According to Houlgate, summarizing Hegel, "the thought of pure being becomes the thought of pure becoming."[26]

On Hegel's view, this kind of discovery comes about by attending
to thought itself rather than by entering the investigation with presuppositions. The investigation also indicates that nothing is pure.
According to Houlgate, "the very disappearance of pure being and
pure nothing into one another undermines the pure and immediate
difference between the two, and allows us to settle into the thought
that being and nothing do not just *pass over* into one another, but
are in fact indistinguishable."[27] This thought about the indistinguish-
ability of being and nothing is settled and stable. According to
Hegel, it is, paradoxically, the first such stable thought reached by
this line of inquiry. Hegel's argument, in "letting thought speak,"
leads to the discovery that indeterminate thought leads to the
thought of becoming and then to the thought of "bare determi-
nacy"—the minimum thought that is fixed and intelligible.[28]

Part of the difficulty in Hegel's inquiry lies in his denial of the
need for deductive or inductive logic in allowing thought to chart
its course.[29] There is no appeal to premises, as in the use of the syllogism. Hegel is not arguing that A implies B (thought thinks being)
and A implies C (thought thinks becoming), therefore A implies B
and C (thought thinks determinate being). According to Houlgate,
Hegel derives or develops the categories of becoming and determinate being immanently, "from the thought of being itself."[30] According to Houlgate, "Concepts, for Hegel, are not 'tools' which we
employ to get things done. Nor, on the other hand, are they mysterious cosmic entities that 'reveal' themselves through us. They are the
intrinsic, dynamic determinations of thought which it is the task of

a fully self-critical science of logic to disclose and think through."[31] But Hegel's view of thought carries a dimension that integrates (or reintegrates) logic with the everyday existence of humankind in society. According to Hegel, ordinary thinking is syllogistic and is valid for everyday purposes. But it involves thinking about the individual.[32] It involves putting forward propositions and finding good reasons or empirical evidence to support them. But, according to Hegel, this kind of thinking takes too much for granted, and there is an arbitrariness about it. It is thinking for *oneself*. To think otherwise has the appearance of giving up our freedom. But for Hegel, to give up this kind of syllogistic thinking actually implies the reverse. Thinking that follows the dialectical principle outlined above is *free* and self-critical. What is self-critical thinking? To think self-critically is to let go. According to Houlgate, "We are being asked, therefore, to give up our self-certainty and self-assurance, to let go of everything we have held to in the past and to find true freedom of mind in the self-movement of self-determining thought."[33] This paradoxical understanding of freedom is entirely in keeping with Christian concepts of freedom, to which Hegel was deeply committed, in which true freedom is letting go and surrendering one's will to the divine. So, according to Hegel, pre-Socratic, dialectical, pretechnological thinking is intimately tied to freedom. This is a theme taken up by later writers who argue that the technological way of thinking, with its commitment to Aristotelian logic, denies or constrains personal freedom.

Hegel's view of thought and freedom is optimistic. History progresses, and this progress is evident in the area of freedom. It is not simply that people are more free now than ever but that there is a greater awareness of the issue of freedom, a greater consciousness of freedom. This awareness reveals itself in different ways among different peoples and in different epochs. Just as thought has a movement of its own, and we should attend to it, history has its own mission. Ideas develop in the context of great epochs of thought. Every age has its ways of thinking, its spirit or Zeitgeist, and one epoch may be incompatible with, and incomprehensible to, another.[34] But for Hegel, the fundamental shifts in thinking from one epoch to another have involved an increasing human self-awareness[35]—an increasing consciousness of individual freedom.[36] According to Houlgate, for Hegel, "History is thus the process whereby human beings come to new levels of awareness of their freedom, of their productive, active nature, and thereby produce new forms of social and political life."[37] So pre-Socratic, pretechnological, dialectical thinking is a basic mode of thinking, prior to what we often term "logic" (Aristotelian logic). It has its seeds in the appropriation of the movement and conflict of oppositions, the outcomes of which are indeterminate. It consists in letting thinking do its work without preconditions. It is indeterminate and unresolved, and it is free. To give ourselves up to this thinking has the appearance of denying our individuality and freedom, but only superficially. Free and critical thinking is dialectical thinking. Furthermore, the whole of history is implicated in the revelation of the consciousness of freedom by thought.

It appears that Hegel is far more accepting of the legitimacy of Aristotelian logic as a model of reason in the course of everyday affairs than his intellectual descendants. If Hegel set the pattern for radical thinking about thought, then it falls on others to turn the dialectical principle into a scathing critique of the nature of technology and technological society. More than any other writer this century, Heidegger seems to have taken on "the question of technology" as a great and heavy burden that speaks ponderously of "thought," "being," and "nothing."

Heidegger's "Thought"

Heidegger, in his later writing, amplifies Hegel's interest by distinguishing a more primordial logic, which he recognizes as Thought, from science, sociology, history, psychology, theology, and everything else, which he regards as "philosophy."[38] Like Hegel, Heidegger develops the theme of the self-revelatory and autonomous nature of thinking.[39] According to Heidegger, we have to attend to thinking and let it speak rather than search always for reasons. Thought has a history. But for Heidegger this history is also the history of Being. Heidegger's use of the capitalized word "Being" is difficult to appreciate, but it is important for an understanding of his view of technology. So we will dwell on it at some length here.

In his earlier work, *Being and Time,* Heidegger indicates how conventional attempts to address the issue of Being have foundered. Being is the most universal concept, though it is clearly not a category. In keeping with its universal nature, it defies definition. Being is also self-evident to the extent that we are capable of saying what *is* and what *is not,* yet "Being is still veiled in darkness."[40] In *Being and Time,* Heidegger systematically develops a characterization of the entity (which Heidegger identifies as *Dasein*) that is inquiring into the "possibilities of its Being."[41] Heidegger's own thinking on Being has developed since *Being and Time.* According to Caputo, the "Being" of the later Heidegger is best understood through an analogy with religious thinking, particularly that of the mystical writers and poets.[42] The autonomy of Being and its relationship to a being (or an entity) is analogous to the relationship between God and the soul. Certainly the elevated autonomy of Being and Thought (by both Heidegger and Hegel—as well as the Absolute and Spirit by Hegel and the idealists) is in keeping with the German Christian tradition.

Whereas, for Hegel, history progressively discloses consciousness of freedom, in the history of Being, according to Heidegger, Being reveals itself. Whereas philosophy would readily assert that historically philosophers and others have explored the issue of Being in different ways, for Heidegger, this process of history is more accurately described as one in which Being reveals and conceals itself. Being has "autonomy" for Heidegger. We see Being at work when we let thinking run its course. The revelation of Being is apparent when we let certain statements recorded in history, or even questions we pose, speak. Of course, what philosophers have said and the way Being speaks are not necessarily the same. When we let such statements speak, then it becomes apparent that Being has tantalizingly revealed itself, only to be covered over again. For Heidegger, there is a mission of Being. Occasionally Being breaks through and reveals itself. Whereas for Hegel history is a progressive unfolding of consciousness of freedom, for Heidegger history is a successive concealing of Being, with occasional lapses when Being is able to reveal itself.[43] Like Hegel, Heidegger calls on the thinking of the pre-Socratics for support. The insight of Heraclitus is one such occasion when Being momentarily revealed itself and on which Heidegger places great store.

For Hegel, the progress of thought is such that thought of being leads to thought of nothing. Being and nothing are intertwined. What emerges is a third thought, that of becoming. Heidegger develops a similar argument with his deep analysis of (or rather meditation on) Leibniz's (1646–1716) principle that "nothing is without reason," translated by Heidegger as "nothing is without (sufficient) *ground*." For Heidegger, this statement by Leibniz is a key moment in history when Being revealed itself in a particular way. Heidegger's process of thinking is, therefore, to take a simple, but historically significant statement, such as Leibniz's principle of reason, to look at its ontic,[44] or limited, meaning, and then to argue through to what it says about Being itself. In Heidegger's terms, this is to let Being speak through the statement.

The first and obvious reading of "nothing is without ground" is to think of everything, all beings, and how they are built on something. Every idea, concept, or entity is founded on another idea, concept, or entity. Heidegger's rereading is to indicate that "nothing is without ground" is a statement about being in general (Being) and its ground. Caputo explains this interpretation as placing the emphasis on different parts of the sentence—changing the intonation of the sentence. The statement is thereby taken as equating Being and ground: Being is the ground. But "nothing is without ground" also states the converse: Being is without ground. What does it mean to be without ground? Whatever lacks a ground is above a chasm, or an abyss. This progression of thought leads Heidegger to assert that Being is an abyss,[45] a statement which accords with the mystical poets and with Hegel. Before continuing with this discussion, it is worth reflecting on the processes at work in Heidegger's meditations on Being, as a demonstration of his view of what it means to think—and, ultimately, his view of technology.

Caputo offers an incisive summary of the Heideggerian approach to thinking. Heidegger's approach in his later writings is first and foremost meditative. We are *not* being invited to participate in a critical dialogue with Heidegger. The appeal is to thinking as a deeper form of reason, more basic than formal argument. We are being invited to participate in the profound experience of another thinker (namely, Heidegger). Further, the steps in thinking are discontinuous. Each step is characterized as a preparation for the next. Then there is a leap to the next stage, sometimes characterized by Heidegger as a "change in key." Furthermore, thinking is not about solving an everyday problem but about the profound but simple issues of Being. Thinking is getting to the essence of things, the place of Being in things. Finally, we are brought to the recognition that the whole of history is implicated in thought. Being undertakes to reveal and conceal itself throughout history. At times Being is dormant. How is this process revealed in Heidegger's analysis of Leibniz's principle? Caputo explains the process with four steps.

The first step: For Heidegger, the principle "nothing is without ground" says something about Being, or, rather, Being is disclosing itself through the principle. According to Heidegger, the principle was revealed in a momentary disclosure of Being in the writing of Heraclitus: "If you have heard not me, but the *logos,* then it is wise to say accordingly, all is one."[46] According to Heidegger the word "logos" has since changed its meaning and significance. For Heraclitus, it was something to be listened to, and it spoke of the unity of Being and ground. Being has since withdrawn itself as Being. Subsequent history developed the *logos* as logic, a concern with causes: "[T]he search is to find the ground of one being in another."[47] Logic is now the rational inquiry into the cause of beings. So the solid ground of Leibniz's principle is causal explanation.

According to Heidegger, philosophy has turned into a tyranny over things: "[I]t insists that nothing is unless human reason has certified its existence."[48] It should be added that this fallen state of philosophy is not a human error. Being has withdrawn itself. In this light we are at the mercy of Being. The play of Being is an earnest game.

The second step: In this telling of the history of Being in Leibniz's principle ("nothing is without ground"), Being is reawakened with the announcing of the principle. But it is revealed as a fundamental or first principle. According to Heidegger, establishing a principle serves to conceal Being even further. Being now conceals itself under the guise of objectivity and as a concern with objects or beings.[49] In the principle, Being calls for thinking to supply reasons.

The third step: Listen elsewhere for the voice of Being. For Heidegger, this is to listen to the mystical poets, such as Angelus Silesius. One of Silesius's poems, which so impresses Heidegger, includes a statement about the blooming of a rose. According to the poem, the rose is grounded in itself and is "without why." For Heidegger, this is a major rediscovery. It treats a being, a rose, "not as an 'object' but as 'grounded in itself.' "[50] This discovery tells us that Being and ground belong together.

The fourth step: "Generalize" this discovery. Being and ground belong together. Beings stand on their Being, their own grounds. There is no necessity for us to supply grounds (reasons) in order to legitimate things.[51]

Heidegger's Technology

On the face of it, this meditation on thought and Being seems far removed from a concern with technology, yet, according to Heidegger, technology is implicated in the whole enterprise. What does the discussion so far say about technology? According to Heidegger, the technological age can be characterized in several ways.[52] First, there is a denial in the technological age of thought in favor of philosophizing. Philosophizing is that ontic mode of "thinking" in which we are always looking for reasons for things. (For Hegel, this is exemplified in the logic of Aristotle.) This mode of thinking is *correct* according to Heidegger, but it does not uncover what is *true*.[53] Technology is implicated in this transition from thought to ontic reason. It is not just that we now see thought instrumentally as if it were an object in technology to be crafted (*techne*) and manipulated. Rather there has been a corruption in our understanding of the craftsperson's art (*techne*) itself. According to Heidegger, to craft something (*techne*), originally meant to let a thing disclose itself, for it to be revealed or "brought forth." But to craft something soon came to mean to produce or manufacture an object: "Thus what is decisive in *techne* does not lie at all in making and manipulating nor in the using of means, but rather in the aforementioned revealing. It is as revealing, and not as manufacturing, that *techne* is a bringing-forth."[54] The roots of this transformation of the meaning of *techne* are allied to various transitions in early Greek thinking outlined by Heidegger. This "productionist metaphysic" of making and manipulating came to dominate all thought, such that we now see all artifacts, thoughts, and ideas as produced. They are produced by subjects—craftspersons, artists, and thinkers—and the process is causal. Artifacts, thoughts, and ideas are derived from other artifacts, thoughts, and ideas in a series of causal links. This is what it means to ask "why?" of any phenomenon. It means to look for causes. According to Heidegger, this is scientific, philosophical, and hence technological thinking.

Second, technological thinking has imposed a "frame" over everything, such that everything is now seen as produced or caused. Technological thinking has imposed a totalizing, metaphysical orientation to everything. Everything fits within a grand and unified system. Everything can ultimately be explained. This explanatory system is homogeneous (or it seeks to be so), and the system assumes that it will ultimately show how everything is dependent on certain laws. Technological thinking assumes that the uniquely valid kind of thought is that offered by logic and mathematics.

A variation on the notion of "enframing" is to see that it treats everything as a potential to be used and exploited. To see everything as a potential is to bring it to the same level and to dispense with valuable distinctions. The relationship between technological thought and its objects is analogous to the relationship between a hydroelectric dam and its river.[55] The river becomes a potential for energy and is no different from coal dug up from the ground, which also yields suitable energy. For Heidegger, this enframing is the "essence" of technology—the way that technology discloses things to us in the modern era.

Third, Being is concealed in the technological age. This identification of the relationship between technology and Being is Heidegger's most provocative and difficult insight in the matter of technology. In summarizing Heidegger, Caputo says that in the technological age Being "has become a vapor, a vacuous abstraction."[56]

The difficulty we have in understanding and coming to terms with Being in this age is due to our concern with beings, or entities, and their causal connections, rather than with Being itself. In the technological age, there is a darkening of the essence of truth, the disclosive nature of Being.

Fourth, it is not technology that conceals Being, but rather Being conceals itself. Technology is part of Being's mission by which it conceals itself. Strangely, Heidegger concludes that the distortions to the essence of truth and of humanity are of Being's doing. The current state of the world and the various demises implied by the fall from pre-Socratic thought are not therefore "anyone's fault."[57] Heidegger's resignation toward technology is one of his most controversial points and possibly also one of his most incisive. Having dispensed with causality in thinking, Heidegger is not now in a position to say that humanity (as subject) has *caused* this takeover of technological thinking. Nor can he say that technology itself has *caused* our "enframing" of everything. Nor can we *cause* a change away from this enframing. Rather the language is that of revealing and concealing, and the ultimate "subject" and "object" of this disclosure is Being.

So Heidegger's difficult inquiry radically implicates thought, being, the opposition of being and nonbeing, and technology. Heidegger borrows Hegel's reverence for the grand sweep of history in which these things reveal themselves and are revealed. But, contrary to Hegel, the grand "message" of history is not freedom but Being's concealment through technological enframing.

Dialectic and Critical Theory

The Hegelian tradition of dialectical thinking turns in a different direction from Heidegger's with the work of critical theorists, who appropriate the rhetoric of freedom and adapt it to a rhetoric of revolution—freedom from domination. The relationship of critical theory to causation is far more ambiguous than in the difficult, though carefully crafted, story Heidegger presents. (We will consider a Heideggerian response to critical theory subsequently.) Critical theory sees itself as continuing the Enlightenment tradition of liberating people from fear and establishing their sovereignty.[58] Heidegger's philosophy is too passive for the critical theorist. The critical-theory school started in Frankfurt in 1929. It is also known as the Frankfurt school. The school owes a considerable debt to Heidegger's early writing, but critical theorists are mostly concerned with reviving Marxism—from its entanglement with economic materialism, its telling of history in terms of forms of production, and its dogmatism. Critical theory is so named because it seeks to maintain an open-ended and continuously self-critical approach to social transformation. Critical theory owes a considerable debt to Hegel. But the Frankfurt school is often highly critical of aspects of Heidegger. Heidegger's personal involvement with National Socialism is a particular issue. The Frankfurt school took exile in New York City during the era of National Socialism in Germany and returned to Germany in 1949. Among the best-known exponents of critical theory are Walter Benjamin (1892–1940), Theodor Adorno (1903–1969), Max Horkheimer (1895–1973), Herbert Marcuse (1898–1979), and Jürgen Habermas (b. 1929).[59]

Marcuse is a worthy representative of critical theory. He articulates the difference between technological and pretechnological thinking, and his eminently quotable rhetoric captures the radical flavor of critical theory's appeal in the 1960s. Marcuse makes clear the debt of critical thinking to the dialectical tradition that runs through Hegel and Heidegger—the autonomous and indeterminate nature of thought seen in terms of oppositions. Marcuse describes dialectical thinking as pretechnological. In contrast, he sees Aristotelian logic as technological. According to Marcuse, Aristotelian logic is also the logic of domination, and it removes the ethical dimension from thinking. Critical theory seizes on metaphors of oppositions in conflict and promotes a rhetoric of conflict. Furthermore, the struggle between certain oppositions is a class struggle. Reason itself needs to be rehabilitated to curtail domination of one class over another (hegemony) and to bring about social transformation.

How does Marcuse present these issues? He does so through asserting the primacy of oppositional thinking, showing how this is tied to freedom and ethics, and demonstrating the alienation brought about by technology and technological thinking.

For Marcuse, oppositional thinking is represented in Plato's dialectical, indeterminate logic of question and answer.[60] According to Marcuse, prior to Aristotle's logic "the experience of the divided world finds its logic in the Platonic dialectic."[61] Within this dialectic, oppositional terms are kept open and are not fully defined.

> They have an open horizon, an entire universe of meaning which is gradually structured in the process of conversation itself, but which is never closed. The propositions are submitted, developed, and tested in a dialogue, in which the partner is led to question the normally unquestioned universe of experience and speech, and to enter a new dimension of discourse.[62]

But the dialectical tension is also evident in Plato's two-storied universe consisting of the ephemeral world of appearances and the immutable world of ideas (the forms). Picking up on the Heraclitean and Hegelian strife of opposites, Marcuse characterizes dialectical logic as a recognition of a world of "two dimensions." The world is antagonistic in itself. For example, on the one hand, the world is constantly threatened with destruction and chaos; on the other hand, we structure it with final causes and purpose. Other antagonisms are appearance versus reality, untruth versus truth, slavery versus freedom, and the essential things versus the distorted things, in which the essential nature of things is denied. According to Marcuse, these are basic, ontological conditions. It is the task of thought (philosophy) to overcome the negative condition: "[I]ts universe of discourse responds to the facts of an antagonistic reality."[63]

How do we overcome the negative condition, respond to an antagonistic reality? According to Marcuse, it is by intuition (in the Greek sense). (The appeal to intuition here is analogous to Hegel's appeal to letting thought run its course without presuppositions and to Heidegger's autonomy of thinking.) According to Marcuse, intuition is not mysterious but is the outcome of a dialogue between the phenomenon in its essence and the phenomenon "in antagonistic relation to its contingent, immediate situation":[64] that is, between the thing itself and the situation.[65] For example, in the case of the study of the essence of humankind, we find a capacity to lead the "good life," free from toil, dependence, and ugliness. However, we have to make do with the "best life" possible under the circumstances in which we find ourselves. The "best life" is that in which we make do with our essence *in the situation*. The notion of the "best life" emerges through the antagonism between the "good life" and the situation life presents to us.

Marcuse also implicates oppositional thinking in the development of freedom. In testing propositions through dialectic, the interlocutors question the normally unquestioned universe of experience and speech. They enter a new dimension of discourse, in which they are free and "the discourse is addressed to [their] freedom."[66] Freedom emerges in the transition from potentiality to actuality: "The philosophic quest proceeds from the finite world to the construction of a reality which is not subject to the painful difference between potentiality and actuality, which has mastered its negativity and is complete and independent in itself—free."[67] This transition from potentiality to actuality is the work of both reason and eros, the attraction of the world to the realm of ideas or forms. Under this regime, reason and freedom become one: "Logos and Eros are in themselves the unity of the positive and the negative, creation and destruction. In the exigencies of thought and in the madness of love is the destructive refusal of the established ways of life. Truth transforms the modes of thought and existence. Reason and freedom converge."[68] However, according to Marcuse some modes of existence are denied this joy of being. Throughout history, the laboring classes have been denied this freedom. They are totally preoccupied with survival: "In the human reality, all existence that spends itself in procuring the prerequisites of existence is thus an 'untrue' and unfree existence."[69] In most human societies, it is considered acceptable for there to be an unfree class of people whose role it is to procure the necessities of life. This was the case with pretechnological society as it is in ours, but the way this subordination is organized differs: "The dividing line between the pre-technological and the technological project . . . is in the manner in which the subordination to the necessities of life—to 'earning a living'—is organized and, in the new modes of freedom and unfreedom, truth and falsehood which correspond to this organization."[70] There is a sense in which traditional philosophy denies freedom. In the classical understanding of philosophy, the one who comprehends the ontological condition of truth and untruth is the master of pure contemplation—the philosopher-statesman, beholden to *theoria*. The prime example is in Plato's *Meno*, which consists of a dialogue between the philosopher and the slave: "Philosophy envisages the *equality* of man but, at the same time, it submits to the factual denial of equality. For in the given reality, procurement of the necessities is the life-long job of the majority, and the necessities have to be procured and served so that truth (which is freedom from material necessities) can be."[71] This chauvinism of philosophical truth over the procurement of necessities "leaves history behind, unmastered, and elevates truth safely above the historical reality."[72]

According to Marcuse, this rarefied philosophical view of truth is carried over into technological thinking. In technological thinking, *ethics* and truth are separated. On the other hand, within dialectical logic the ethical is totally integrated. Dialectical logic reveals a tension between what really is (the world of forms) and what appears to be. According to Marcuse, such oppositions always involve the ethical. One side of an opposition is always judged to be better than the other. For example, Being is better than Nothing (Nothing is a threat to Being, destruction): "The struggle for truth is a struggle against destruction."[73] This is the essentially human project. The struggle for truth is an ethical pursuit. The operative process in this struggle is contradiction rather than correspondence. Truth emerges through subversion: "[T]he subversive character of truth inflicts upon thought an imperative quality. Logic centers on judgments which are, as demonstrative propositions, imperatives—the predicative 'is' implies an 'ought.'"[74] According to this way of thinking, to assert something is also to deny it: as is the case with "virtue is knowledge" or "man is free." If these propositions are to be true, then "is" states an "ought"—what is desirable. In other words the statements imply a process. The thing must become what it is. The copula (*is*) implicates the ethical. The ethical is caught up in being: "Dialectical thought understands the critical tension between 'is' and 'ought' first as an ontological condition, pertaining to the structure of Being itself."[75]

Marcuse's Technological Thinking

How does Marcuse characterize technological thinking? First, technological thinking identifies, isolates, and then marginalizes the ethical—*is* and *ought* no longer interfere. Propositions settle the matter.

The two dimensions of thought—that of the essential and that of the apparent truths—no longer interfere with each other, and their concrete dialectical relation becomes an abstract epistemological or ontological relation. The judgments passed on the given reality are replaced by propositions defining the general forms of thought, objects of thought, and relations between thought and its objects.[76]

According to Marcuse, the quantification of nature in technological thinking led to the separation of the true from the good.[77] When the ethical is removed from the pursuit of truth, it is relegated to the realm of the subjective:[78] "Outside this rationality, one lives in a world of values, and values separated out from the objective reality become subjective."[79]

Second, technological thinking trades in abstractions, indifference, and decontextualization. With technological thinking, we are alienated from the world.

In this formal logic, thought is indifferent toward its objects. Whether they are mental or physical, whether they pertain to society or to nature, they become subject to the same general laws of organization, calculation, and conclusion—but they do so as fungible signs or symbols, in abstraction from their particular "substance." This general quality (quantitative quality) is the precondition of law and order—in logic as well as in society—the price of universal control.[80]

This appeal by Marcuse to the universalizing nature of technological abstraction closely parallels Heidegger's notion of enframing.

Third, as is evident from the above quotation, technological thinking trades in domination. Identifying the various means of domination is basic to critical theory. According to Horkheimer and Adorno, "The general concept which discursive logic has developed has its foundation in the reality of domination."[81] According to Marcuse, "history is . . . the history of domination, and the logic of thought remains the logic of domination."[82] How is technological thinking the logic of domination? For one thing, it subjugates dialectical thinking. In technological thinking, the conflict between essence and appearance is rendered expendable and meaningless. The material content of experience is neutralized. Identity and contradiction are separated. Contradictions are thought to be the fault of incorrect thinking rather than harbingers of new thoughts. Concepts become instruments of prediction and control.

How does technological thinking support the domination by one group over another? According to Marcuse, such domination has always been a feature of society. But in the technological age, the pattern of dependence changes from slave depending on master and serf on lord to a dependence on the "objective order of things."[83] We are dominated by economic laws and the market: "[T]he progressive enslavement of man by a productive apparatus which perpetuates the struggle for existence and extends it to a total international struggle which ruins the lives of those who build and use this apparatus."[84]

Fourth (and most importantly from the point of view of the study of technology), technology itself (its objects and systems) embodies and reproduces this domination: "[T]his false consciousness [technological reason] has become embodied in the prevailing technical apparatus which in turn reproduces it."[85] It accomplishes this domination by virtue of its pervasive, totalizing presence. Whereas Marx saw production and the social system that supports it as the basic factor in understanding history, according to Marcuse, technology has taken over this role. Technology projects a totality: "[W]hen technics becomes the universal form of material production, it circumscribes the entire culture; it projects a historical totality—a 'world.' "[86] This all-enveloping hold perpetuates the power of those who are already most powerful: "Today, domination perpetuates and extends itself not only through technology but as technology, and the latter provides the great legitimation of the expanding political power, which absorbs all spheres of culture."[87]

Critical theory sets itself the task of generally bringing this picture to light. According to critical theory, one of the major perpetrators of domination is the mode of technological production itself—mass production and the mass culture it produces. According to Adorno and Horkheimer, one of the greatest delusions of the modern age is the illusion of differentiation and individuality perpetrated by mass production: "[T]he mechanically differentiated products prove to be all alike in the end. That the difference between the Chrysler range and General Motors products is basically illusory strikes every child with a keen interest in varieties."[88] Mass media is similarly implicated in promoting conformity, with the delusion of difference: "Pseudo individuality is rife: from the standardized jazz improvisation to the exceptional film star."[89] One of the major culprits is television. Television can present a veneer of the critical, radical and antiauthoritarian while concealing its tendency to promote conformity: "[T]he majority of television shows today aim at producing or at least reproducing the very smugness, intellectual passivity, and gullibility that seem to fit in with totalitarian creeds even if the explicit surface message of the shows may be antitotalitarian."[90] Put simply, this characterization paints a picture of society in which there are three protagonists. One is the dominating group, those with the vested interests in preserving the status quo. The second group is the passive, compliant, and deluded masses. The third protagonist is technology, which plays the role of entrenching the values and wishes of the dominating class in a way that is deeply structural and that masks its own work. How is information technology implicated in this domination?

Critical Theory and Information Technology

Critical theory sets the stage for a deep critique of information technology. Other writers within other traditions are also highly critical of technology, but critical theory looks beyond the surface phenomena of the problems of technology and implicates reason itself. Three aspects of this theme are the way in which information technology can be said to marginalize the ethical, decontextualize human experience, and amplify and promote domination. What follows is a summary of a critical theory of information technology that is consistent with the mainstream of the Frankfurt school.[91] It is also consistent with the views held by certain sociologists of science and technology.[92]

How does information technology marginalize the ethical? This divorce is most evident in the common distinction made between technical issues and human-factor issues in the way information technology is designed, studied, and discussed. Technical issues pertain to the design and manufacture of components and objects, their logical configuration, how they are connected together, and their analysis, testing, measurement, and quantitative evaluation. Human factors include how such artifacts fit into human society, how they are used, how they should be designed for human use, and their qualitative evaluation. The former clearly pertains to the realm of the objective, the logical, and the measurable. The latter includes everything else. There is a clear parallel here with Marcuse's complaint about the divorce within reason, represented by Aristotelian logic, between logic and value, the objective and the subjective, the propositional and the ethical, the is and the ought. Far from sustaining a dynamic, indeterminate, dialectical tension, the opposition between the technical and human factors is thoroughly entrenched and institutionalized in the way information technology industries and practices are organized. For example, courses within most universities and colleges distinguish between technology and its application and critical evaluation. The former commonly belongs to engineering, the latter to the humanities. It is rare to find a mix between these interests. For example, few engineering students study the philosophy of technology. Not only is this distinction institutionalized, but one is clearly privileged over the other. Enormous emphasis is given within universities and colleges to training in engineering and technology. The knowledge bases in those fields are relatively clearly defined, though evolving. Not only are they relatively free of conflicting schools of thought, as are the (dialectical) humanities, but they are regarded to be ultimately profitable. The engineering and technology disciplines are thought to genuinely and unambiguously contribute to international competitiveness and societal well-being. Such distinctions are also institutionalized within information technology industries and legislative structures.

Coupled with this bifurcation of the technical and the ethical is the common assumption of the neutrality of technology. Having established the distinction between technique and value, technological rationality now impresses on us that objects are neither good nor evil, but human use makes them so. High explosives can be used either to build dams or to wage war; electronic communications can be used in distance learning for children in the Australian outback or for terrorist activity. The distinction is very convenient, as it preserves the right of those involved in developing the technology to do so unimpeded by anything other than the constraints set within their own technical problem-solving domain. The development of technology can continue under its own momentum.

The way that technological reason justifies technological development is through the rhetoric of needs. Society presents various needs, such as the need for better communication, quicker transportation, and faster calculation, and technologies are developed to meet those needs. This ignores the fact that technologies are totally implicated in the framing of those needs, but it preserves the status of technology as beyond the ethical. It is thought that the good or evil manifested in our use of technology actually resides in human intentions, expressed as needs (to go to war, to maximize profits, to exploit, etc.).

The considerations so far pertain to the rhetoric of technology rather than to its artifacts. How does the split between technique and ethics reveal itself in technological objects and systems? The answer is in the mode of production itself—mass production. Mass production further institutionalizes the separation between technique and ethics. Mass-produced objects are apparently available for all, so there is the opportunity for choice. People choose whether or not to buy, and they choose from among books, soap powders, firearms, cars, prerecorded videos, and computer games. This imperative for choice brings the ethical into sharp relief. The responsibility is with the end user or consumer to choose economically, responsibly, wisely, and ethically. The divorce of the ethical from technical production is commonly institutionalized in the practice of censorship and other forms of regulation. For example, in keeping with the value-neutral nature of technology, prerecorded video material is freely mass produced and distributed. Ethical considerations follow the process, realized as a concern with regulation and censorship.

Compare this imperative for choice and its consequences with a preindustrial society in which the "choices" are already made. Unlike highly technological, industrial societies, artifacts are integrated into cultural practices. This is evident in indigenous building. For example, constructing a Fijian *burė* involves the whole village community. There are no ethical choices to be made. Constructing and using the building fits into village practices and traditions, involving ritual, symbol, and identity. The building is not seen as a commodity, entailing ownership or status. It is difficult to identify such technologies in our own society. We still retain the remnant of the preindustrial in our use of local, craft-based technologies, such as collecting firewood, producing handicrafts, gardening, hobby activities, and other outdoor and leisure pursuits. Even here, however, these are shaped by elaborate industries, mass-media promotion, and highly sophisticated technologies (for example, modern camping equipment). Ostensibly, we are given the freedom to choose. These activities are parasitic on technological society in that they are seen as an antidote to it. For some, to appropriate such pursuits is to make an ethical statement, in which suspicion is cast on the values of technological society contrasted with those of "the environment." These pursuits also commonly entail exhibition and competition, which are implicated in technological thinking—isolating objects from context, attributing them to individual creativity, and evaluating them on the basis of technological criteria, such as consistency and precision.[93] This isolation promotes the notion of the aesthetic— value applied to art, as the ethical is value applied to conduct. It is common within critical theory to identify the elevation of the good, the true, and the beautiful as symptomatic of the removal of artifacts and practices from context, further symptoms of the demise that is technological thinking.[94]

Of course, critical theory identifies the choices presented by technology as illusionary. The choices are already made, but this fact is masked by the machinery of mass advertising, which seeks both to persuade us to choose brand *X* and to persuade us that we are agents of choice. The illusion of choice is also promoted by the array of products presented in catalogs and on display shelves. These factors contribute to the illusion that we can pick and choose from among a vast array of technologies and that the ethical dimension resides in our choosing; it does not reside in the technologies themselves or among those who promote, develop, and distribute the technologies.[95]

Information technology carries mass production a few steps further. Mass production and mass availability is extended to the idea of ubiquity. The metaphor of ubiquity implies a seamless, generally available background of technological servicing that we can plug into at any place and at any time, to make use of in whatever way we choose. The distribution of electricity through the national grid is an obvious example of a service that is on the way to ubiquity. So, too, are the telephone system, television and radio broadcasting, and computer networking. The project toward ubiquity is currently being realized through the development of rapid information exchange using broadband digital-communications channels, wireless communications, the combining of media (such as digital data, video, sound, and computer-generated imagery), miniaturization, and portability. People are able to make contact with one another relatively independently of locational constraints, to access each other's databases, and to connect to centralized data and information services. The implications for organizations, as well as individuals, are obviously immense, fueling such notions as the "virtual office," where a firm's chief capital resides in databases that can be accessed from virtually anywhere. The firm no longer needs to be located in one place. It can be on the move physically, and its structure can change as it responds to situations dynamically.

From the perspective of critical theory, such developments are to be regarded with suspicion. The notion of ubiquity further masks the divorce that is the value-free technological world isolated from its uses—the ethical. Ubiquity presents the illusion of choice on a massive scale. We need look no further than the growing concern with ethical issues pertaining to computer networks for evidence of the entrenched illusion of technological neutrality represented by the idea of ubiquity. The ethical issues are presented as problems with network security, the issue of civil rights in relation to personal records, and copyright in relation to digital media. According to critical theory, the ethical is divorced in both the rhetoric surrounding technology and in the forms of technological systems and objects.

How does information technology decontextualize human experience? The story of how information technology realizes the project of technological reason has been told many times, particularly in criticisms of artificial-intelligence research, notably by Dreyfus, Weizenbaum, and Winograd and Flores.[96] The presumption that human understanding, knowledge, and experience can ultimately be extracted from context and coded into a machine is regarded by critical theory as entirely consistent with the legacy of technological thinking promoted through Aristotelian logic, Descartes's method of objective thought, Leibniz's principle of sufficient ground, the Enlightenment project of encyclopedic knowledge, and the quest of logical positivism for empirically verifiable and value-free propositions. Irrespective of one's regard for the possibility of artificial intelligence, this legacy is also evident in the current valorization of information. Information is thought to be the essence of life, as in the DNA code. To record and break the code is to have mastery over life.[97] Modern technological society assumes that the more information we have the better, even though there is scarcely space to store and process this information. The essence of an organization is thought to lie in its information capital, as in the virtual firm. Technological society assumes that human communication is the passing of information from one person to the other, that the essence of understanding resides in the information. We accord greater value to what can be passed through the conduit and stored in databases than what is exchanged through other modes of complex human interaction: ''Real life is life on-line.'' According to critical theory, the effect of valorizing information is to universalize and homogenize human practice. This happens both in the priority given to what can be expressed informationally and in the pervasive nature of the technology itself, further amplifying the homogenizing effects of mass media and mass culture.

But critical theory directs its most savage attack toward how technology is implicated in domination. How does information technology promote domination by one group over another? The obvious means of domination include the use of computers to realize aspects of the widely discredited scientific-management project of Frederick Taylor, in which jobs are divided into their smallest components and time and motion studies of workers are used to establish standards and quotas. As indicated by Marx and Sherizen, even under Taylorism, supervision was personal and the workers were likely to know when they were being watched.[98] Now the means of surveillance include video cameras, records of key strokes on a computer console, records of key-card use, and now "smart badges" for detecting the physical location of employees. These means of monitoring have become acceptable for reasons that appear relatively benign and even in the interests of the individual worker: surveillance to reduce theft, monitoring where people are so that they can get in touch with each other, and being able to see others at their work station via video link to facilitate communication.[99] In some jobs, the medium of work itself is a series of centrally stored computer files, as is the medium of communication from one worker to another. In some cases, there is an almost complete record of every transaction and communication related to the tasks, including times and durations.[100] Outside of the workplace, it is well known that credit-card transactions and other records are employed to develop profiles of individuals so they can be targeted for marketing material.[101] People are generally prepared to give up certain freedoms for the perceived benefits.

For critical theory, these issues indicate that information technologies are prone to misuse; more than that, they perpetuate domination. They promote the illusion of differentiation, choice, and freedom, thereby masking their promotion of conformity. This is evident in the promotion of the computer as a universal machine, able to do our bidding when instructed through the medium of programming. At best the computer only calculates and so further instills the primacy of its own logic and organization, while outwardly promoting a sense of control. What it instills conveniently matches the values and requirements of conforming bureaucratic organization.[102]

Information technology also embodies an inexorable push toward total control. One example is the use of computer-aided design (CAD) in the design and construction industry. In some quarters, the development of CAD systems is aimed at the fully integrated database that enables those who control the project to accurately and unambiguously represent and convey their "intentions" from conceptual design through to construction and beyond, to the long-term management of the facility. The idea of total control of the process appeals to the technologically oriented professional groups, corporations, and government and institutional bureaucracies. The process appears bent on circumventing the autonomy of trade- and craft-based practices further down the line. It is an attempt to bring the varied and local trades, with all their idiosyncrasies and imperfections, to submission or extinction, with the final goal of on-site automation, bringing construction into line with manufacturing.

Having identified the problems of the ethical, the decontextualizing of human experience, and the promotion of domination by technology, what solutions does critical theory offer?

The project of critical theory is to sustain a critical attitude, to keep alive the suspicion of totalizing arguments, philosophies, systems, and technologies. The critical attitude thereby promotes social transformation: "Critical thought strives to define the irrational character of the established rationality (which becomes increasingly obvious) and to define the tendencies which cause this rationality to generate its own transformation."[103] A change is required in reason itself. Hitherto reason was a force for domination. This needs to be redressed so that it is concerned with "'the art of living' beyond the necessities and luxuries of domination":[104] "Such qualitative change would be transition to a higher stage of civilization if technics were designed and utilized for the pacification of the struggle for existence."[105] This would be a catastrophe to the established direction of technology. It requires the emergence of a new idea of reason, theoretical and practical.[106] "It involves a political reversal."[107]

According to Marcuse, the answer to the current order lies at the point of critical theory's greatest weakness: "its inability to demonstrate the liberating tendencies within the established society."[108] The unmistakable message is that of public protest and even revolution: "But the struggle for the solution has outgrown the traditional forms. The totalitarian tendencies of the one-dimensional society render the traditional ways and means of protest ineffective—perhaps even dangerous because they preserve the illusion of popular sovereignty."[109] The solution lies in identifying with the oppressed underclass.

They exist outside the democratic process; their life is the most immediate and the most real need for ending intolerable conditions and institutions. Thus their opposition is revolutionary even if their consciousness is not. Their opposition hits the system from without and is therefore not deflected by the system; it is an elementary force which violates the rules of the game and, in doing so, reveals it as a rigged game. . . . The fact that they start refusing to play the game may be the fact which marks the beginning of the end of a period.[110]

The Limits to a Critical Theory of Information Technology

Marcuse posits radical, global reform as the solution to the problems of technological thinking. On the one hand, this sentiment resonates with the common concern for social justice and a sense of helplessness in the face of powerful institutions and technologies. On the other hand, the solution strikes anyone with such concerns as impractical, not simply because it is too costly but because such global reform is elusive. It is not only that global social reform is unlikely to eventuate, it is imprecisely specified. It is a very blunt instrument to solve a complex array of very intricate problems. In this light, Marcuse's rhetoric appears to some writers as so much posturing.

This criticism of critical theory does not come only from conservative quarters.[111] For example, Gallagher identifies several serious inconsistencies within the critical position.[112] First, there is the elusive posture of the critical overview. The major difficulty with the critical stance is that there is no position where one can stand in order to appropriate it. Critical theory buys into the Enlightenment objectives of establishing distance, looking at situations objectively, and weighing them against inalienable rights, such as freedom, liberty, and the rights of the individual. It is not surprising that critical theory should have arisen in Germany during the period of National Socialism, one of the most duplicitous and oppressive regimes in history. Whereas critical vigilance is an appropriate preventative against such regimes, its arguments lack subtlety in the current climate of political and social developments in Europe and elsewhere. It is simply not the case that mass culture represents a deception by one class dominating over another in every sense. The matter is open to debate as to who is deluding whom, in what sense, in which situation, and for what end. The assumed objective stance of critical theory appears flawed.

Second is the problem of the relativity of emancipation. If domination is not an objective fact but a matter subject to interpretation in a situation, then emancipation from domination is an elusive quest. At best we are only emancipated from one position to another. The idea of total freedom is clearly impossible and meaningless. According to Gallagher, "we can emancipate ourselves from something but never from everything."[113] The critical position largely assumes a safe haven to which we can escape once emancipation is accomplished. But once we escape, we find ourselves in a new state of oppression. Furthermore, once we have escaped, we do not cease to be critical. Retention of the critical position suggests a perpetual state of cynicism.

Third is the problem of the concealment of power relations within the critical position itself. Power can be pernicious when cloaked in the guise of the critical overview. Gadamer is critical of the critical stance: "Inasmuch as it seeks to penetrate the masked interests which infect public opinion, it implies its own freedom from any ideology; and that means in turn that it enthrones its own norms and ideals as self-evident and absolute."[114]

Fourth, there are aspects of critical thinking that are a form of technological thinking. The presumptions of the critical position place it firmly within the Enlightenment tradition. The objective is emancipation from dogma, prejudice, empire, and slavery. As for technological thinking, critical theory is a tool to produce a better society. It is the instrument with which the critic seeks to subvert the technological position. So critical theory is laced with causal thinking, identified by Heidegger as a key ingredient of technological thinking. The critical position succumbs to technological "enframing," but without recognition of this fact.

We may add the further difficulty inherent in critical theory of the ambiguous identification of the oppressed, the oppressors, and the means of oppression. Marcuse's rhetoric is clearly targeted against a group and the overthrow of that group. Yet he avoids clearly identifying those in control. In former times, and in hindsight, it might have been acceptable to identify the controllers as white-coated technocrats, media barons, directors of multinational corporations, union bosses, senior bureaucrats, politicians, an invisible elite that controls the politicians, organized crime, or simply the wealthy. It is now recognized that the system is much more complex. Certainly people have varying degrees of power, and we see greed, malice, winners, losers, injustice, and a constant need for reform, but aspects of Marcuse's arguments lead us to conclude that there is, after all, no conspiracy. No group is deliberately fabricating the technological world to keep others under control. It is more likely that technological thinking is so deep-seated and structural that those seeking to dominate do not recognize that they are doing so. In other words, there are winners and losers, but there is a sense in which we are all "victims" of the technological imperative.

Identifying these difficulties inherent in critical theory brings us back to Heidegger's skepticism about the project of critical theory and human intervention in the problems posed by technology. According to Heidegger, release from technology's pull will not be of our making.

If the essential being of technology—the *Gestell* as the danger within Being—is Being itself, then technology can never be mastered, neither positively nor negatively, through a merely self-dependent human action. Technology, whose essential being is Being itself, can never be overcome by man. This would mean that man would be the lord of Being.[115]

But we cooperate with Being: "[T]he essential being of technology cannot be led into a transformation of its mission without the cooperation of man."[116]

But Heidegger does envisage a transformation. This cooperation with Being is a "letting be" or "releasement." Heidegger uses the archaic German word *Gelassenheit,* which he borrowed from the mystical philosopher Eckhart. Letting be is what the poet does before the rose, letting Being reveal itself. The antidote to the enframing of technology is not revolution but adopting a new attitude.

We are able to use technological objects and yet with suitable use keep ourselves so free of them that we are able to let go of them at any time. We are able to make use of technological objects as they ought to be used.

But we are also able simultaneously to let them alone as something which does not concern what is innermost in us and proper to us.[117]

Borgman presents one of the most persuasive attempts to translate Heidegger's project for letting be into terms that are meaningful to late-twentieth-century technological society.[118] Borgman translates Heidegger's identification of technological objects (mere objects manufactured and exploited through the imperative of causality) as commodities or devices. In contrast to devices there are the things, of which Heidegger wrote. Things are situated, corporeal, and involved in human practices. They provide a focus. For Borgman the archetypal example of a thing is the domestic hearth, which in earlier times provided a focus for domestic activity and a focus for thinking about the home and the family. These things are still around us in the technological age but take on new significance within the current technological context. According to Borgman, there are focal things and also practices. Examples of focal practices include preparing and serving a great meal, hiking, and jogging, not as mere leisure diversions but as totally engaging activities that unite means and ends, effort and accomplishment, labor and leisure. These practices may also involve devices (such as running shoes, camping equipment, highways, and motorized transportation), but the devices are at the service of the focal practices. The technological context is not at war with focal practices, but they are mutually enhancing. According to Borgman, radical reform within technological society will come about by attending to such focal things and practices.

However we choose to realize Heidegger's ambiguous call to letting be or letting go, the solution is not entirely illuminating for the technologist, the designer, or the decision maker interested in how this understanding of technology can impinge on their practices as designers. There appears to be no positive program for intervention. The solution for designers appears to be to remove themselves from the business or to trade a concern with advanced technology for craft.[119] Designers appear as either perpetrators or victims of domination (under critical theory) or those whose work is to be a mere adjunct to focal things and practices (according to Heidegger and Borgman).

The Limits of Dialectical Thinking

From the point of view of design, the concerns of critical theory and its legacy appear limiting. How do we account for and overcome these limitations? We can regard the identification of the primordiality of dialectical thinking by Hegel, Heidegger, Marcuse, and others as promoting a particular set of metaphors. Any metaphor is both enabling and disabling in particular ways and in particular contexts. (It reveals and conceals, as is the manner with things, as outlined by Heidegger.) The dialectical metaphor entails the notion of oppositions. It is founded on the idea of antagonism, arguably as taken up by Hegel and certainly as promoted by Marcuse. Hegel's dialectic has been taken up in both political and ideological directions.[120] The Frankfurt school, and Marx before it, represents a left-wing (radical) interpretation of the dialectical principle. The clash of opposites is inherent in the nature of things and should be appropriated. Revolution appears only natural in this schema. The violence of revolution is in the very nature of things and brings about freedom. Revolution applies as one epoch gives way to another. Critical theory promotes revolution, which brings about liberation.

On the other hand, the right-wing interpretation of Hegel takes up the conservative aspects of the dialectical principle. At the most extreme, it accepts the necessity of war as nations bend the knee to the inevitability of history and the revealing of the Zeitgeist.[121] Some see Hegel as an apologist for the Prussian state and as a contributor to the ideological lineage that led to National Socialism in Germany. Hegel did not go as far as the critical theorists in denigrating social injustice, and he seemed content to preserve the status quo.[122] According to Houlgate, for Hegel, slavery "is only an injustice when the slave recognises his right to be free. The only real guarantee against slavery, therefore, is the education of people into the consciousness of their freedom so that they will not let themselves be enslaved."[123] Hegel was also an advocate of the right to pursue self-interest, one of the tenets of capitalism.[124] Poverty is regarded as an unfortunate but inevitable by-product of this process. According to Houlgate, Hegel maintains, "It is immanent in the *logic* of bourgeois freedom that it generate poverty."[125] Hegel also endorsed the preeminent authority of the state: "The authority of the state, for Hegel, is rooted in the fact that the state is immanent in the very idea of the free will."[126]

Heidegger's appropriation of Hegel and the dialectical tradition is apparently apolitical, particularly in his later writing. There is no call for revolution, no inciting in either political direction, nor in fact the advocacy of any action at all.[127] However, it is well known that Heidegger was an unrepentant supporter of National Socialism.[128] He has therefore been identified by some with the passive Right, largely because of his silence about Hitler's fascism. Bernstein attributes Heidegger's inaction to the quest for essence. Heidegger is operating at a plane above the current situation, almost in a Platonic way. For example, according to Heidegger, the real danger of technology is not the evil that is perpetrated through it—war, pollution, mind control, concentration camps, and so on—but rather its enframing power.[129] Technology masks and distorts authentic thinking. As Bernstein points out, it is unfair to say that Heidegger was unconcerned about the problems of the moment, but he did disconnect thinking as the history of Being from a concern with political and historical events.[130] His concerns were those of the thinker, aloof from current events. According to Bernstein, this aloof posture is almost formulaic in Heidegger's writing. For example, whereas the philosophical tradition takes the ethical to be about doing the right thing, for Heidegger it is about finding a dwelling place, according to Heidegger the originary meaning of *ethos* (as used by Heraclitus). The ethical problems of the day are not primarily about social justice but recovering from our homelessness. How do we recover dwelling? According to Heidegger, this is through reflecting on the writings of the poets, who show us the essential nature of things beyond technological enframing. They show us what thinking is, how we can let things be and reveal themselves.

At one level, Heidegger's approach is illuminating and refreshing. It has generated an enormously valuable and fecund discourse about technology. But this discourse has been sustained by those who do not adopt Heidegger's style. There is no doubt that his style of presentation is one that does not entertain opposition. Meditation or thinking is beyond argument. As with Hegel, the rhetoric is about the indeterminacy of thought, thinking as a process of discovery, and yet it is a style of rhetoric that closes off discussion. The conversation is taking place at a higher plane, in the grand sweep of history, as Being reveals itself through the poets.

Bernstein also indicates the limits of Heidegger's thought in terms of where he lays emphasis in the Greek philosophical legacy. According to Bernstein, Heidegger's meditations focus on establishing the primacy of his rehabilitated understanding of *techne* and *poiesis*— two of the "intellectual virtues" identified by Aristotle. According to Heidegger, *techne* was once a bringing forth of the true into the beautiful;[131] *poiesis* was bringing forth, presencing, of the kind revealed in art and poetry. The later Heidegger shows little concern with the other "intellectual virtues" identified by Aristotle, such as *phronesis* and praxis. *Phronesis,* according to its modern rehabilitation by such writers as Gadamer, is about situated judgment taking place through dialogue in human communities. Praxis concerns action in situated human practices. According to Bernstein, "The entire rhetorical construction of 'The Question Concerning Technology' seduces us into thinking that the only alternative to the threatening danger of *Gestell* [enframing] is *poiesis*. It excludes and conceals the possible response of *phronesis* and *praxis*."[132] It is fair to say that the tradition that builds on Hegel's dialectical metaphor is powerful and informing about aspects of the technological age. It establishes categories and distinctions that enable us to talk of the pretechnological as opposed to the technological. It provides, on the one hand, a powerful rhetoric for reform, on the other, a means of looking beyond the exigencies of the moment to the wider picture. It challenges the privileged position of causality and enables us to consider the possibility that we are not after all in control.

The dialectical metaphor fails, however, to satisfy the contemporary quest to understand information technology in several important respects. First, the deeper one probes into the information technology industry, the more illusive is the villainy spoken of by critical theorists. As I have indicated in chapter 1, powerful aspects of Silicon Valley culture are strongly influenced by liberalism, philosophical pragmatism, the media philosophy of McLuhan, critical theory, and even Heideggerianism, as are the universities that support these industries. The generation of students that took to the streets in the 1960s, inspired by Marcuse's *One-Dimensional Man,* now hold positions of power. There are certainly forces that are bent on conserving a status quo, and there are injustices, but the "system" is one that entertains its own subversion. It allows Marcuse to be read.

Second, the blanket disapproval of mass media, mass communication, and mass culture by some critical theorists is betrayed by their enthusiastic use of it. It is not just a case of fighting fire with fire or being so trapped that we are forced to use advanced information technologies. The fetish for information technology within universities, which are in many cases ahead of corporations and government departments in their appropriation of the technology, is across the board.[133]

Third, in spite of the deeper understanding promoted by Heidegger that to think is to contemplate things without asking why, without looking for causes, and that we are not in control of technology, the rhetoric of our disciplines indicates an unashamed concern with intervention. It may be a delusion, but the rhetoric of the professional, the technician, the educator, and the politician is to intervene. The importance of Heidegger's inquiry may be to reinstate thinking, but there are still those caught up in the practice of "philosophy," investigating causes and interventions, by virtue of the nature of their disciplines. Does Heidegger and the tradition he represents have nothing to say to those practices?

Alternatives to a Critical Theory of Information Technology

In alleviating this impasse, it is helpful to consider metaphors other than those suggested by the dialectical principle. Such a "metaphor shift" may serve to fine-tune the tenets of the dialectical tradition so that they speak to technologists and designers. This can be accomplished through three transformations of the tenets of the dialectical principle. The first is to translate the concern with domination to power. The second is to replace dialectic with the hermeneutical notion of distanciation. The third is to transform the concern with causality to an understanding of the workings of community. Each of these transformations represents a subtle shift in emphasis. They will be considered briefly here to conclude this assessment of the contribution of critical theory to the design of information technology.

From Domination to Power

It is clear from the ambiguity in Marcuse's identification of who is dominating whom, and Heidegger's thesis of the culpability of Being in technological enframing, that the notion of domination does not do full justice to the nature of technology. In contrast, Foucault's understanding of insitutionalized power captures the ubiquity, interconnectedness, and productivity of technological society and its objects and systems.[134] According to Foucault, power is evident in all human affairs, whether they are benign or oppressive.[135] But Foucault seeks to rehabilitate power from its exclusive association with oppression: "[T]here is no face to face confrontation of power and freedom which is mutually exclusive (freedom disappears everywhere power is exercised), but a much more complicated interplay."[136] Unlike Heidegger's passive *techne* and *poeisis,* the metaphor of power embraces the role of actions, praxis. Power is implicated in actions and the way actions impinge on other actions.

It is a total structure of actions brought to bear upon possible actions; it incites, it induces, it seduces, it makes easier or more difficult; in the extreme it constrains or forbids absolutely; it is nevertheless always a way of acting upon an acting subject or acting subjects by virtue of their acting or being capable of action. A set of actions upon other actions.[137]

Contrary to the tenets of critical theory in which domination inhibits individual freedom, according to Foucault, power is productive. Power "traverses and produces things, it induces pleasure, forms knowledge, produces discourse."[138]

Foucault explains the various transformations that have occurred throughout history. The way one social order has given way to another is explicable in terms of a movement from costly, agitated, and attenuated systems of power to more economical, docile, and intense systems. On the one hand, cost appears as a purely economic matter—warring feudal hierarchies and their armies are more expensive to maintain than peaceful democracies. But cost, in terms of human lives, welfare, and the reputations of the various players in the system, is also reduced in the transformation. Docility relates to the extent to which the diversity in lifestyle and opinion of a community is shaped into some kind of order. At one extreme is war, at the other is submission to law. Intensity relates to the effectiveness with which actions are carried through to some kind of completion, how productive the community is in terms of the things it regards as important. Foucault explains some of the transformations that have taken place in society by which oppressive, ostentatious, and costly social relations, such as authoritarian feudal rule, have been transformed and pacified into state institutions and technologies, such as schools, prisons, and hospitals.

According to this picture, technologies, institutions, and social practices are intimately connected and even indistinguishable in some cases. The organization of the military and systems of discipline (schools, hospitals, and penal systems) are technologies. According to Foucault, such technologies were for the social sciences what the microscope was for the natural sciences (though historically one can equally look to the technology of the Spanish Inquisition and its indefatigable scrutiny of "facts"[139]). In this light, technologies feature within transformations from one social order to another. Marcuse acknowledges the transformation from a system of domination in which the slave depends on the master to one in which domination is masked behind dependence on universal logic, which is promoted and reinforced through technology. But for Foucault, the transformation is primarily one in which power relations are changed.

Power, according to Foucault, is to be understood as operating through an interconnected system; power is "a productive network which runs through the whole social body."[140] To focus exclusively on domination is to mask the complex play within the system and to see the process as ultimately constraining. Foucault's discourse shifts the emphasis from domination and constraint to power and productivity. This resonates with the language of the technologist. It brings to the fore such worthwhile questions as productive for whom? productive in what context?

From Dialectic to Distanciation

The metaphor of dialectic assumes the deep and primordial presence of antagonism. Contemporary hermeneutical studies place the emphasis elsewhere. Whereas dialectic presupposes antagonisms and we progress through their resolutions and transformations, hermeneutical writers place greater emphasis on the situated and contingent nature of difference, or distance. According to Gadamer, Ricoeur, and other hermeneutical writers, in any interpretive situation we are caught up in the establishment of distance—distanciation—as when trying to understand a new text, or when we encounter a culture different from our own.[141] To confront difference is to confront something as alien, unfamiliar, *other*, as though the thing resides in a distant location. According to contemporary hermeneutics, we can develop new understandings only through such encounters and a recognition of the alien and distant in the other. The interpretive act, developing an understanding, arises as we traverse this distance. The spatial metaphor of establishing and traversing distance has been developed in various ways by different writers. For example, Weinsheimer develops the idea of distanciation through the journey metaphor.[142] In the process of interpretation, we set out on a journey to appropriate the strange and unfamiliar. But it is never a linear journey. There is always a return to where we started, but when we return, we find the nature of the starting position has changed. In other words, no two interpretive moments are the same, and we are always looking at things from a new position. This process applies to reading a text, understanding history, education, and all modes of action.[143]

There are two features of this account that impinge on the notion of dialectic. First, the development of the metaphor of distanciation has invoked among hermeneutical writers a suite of metaphors that focus on dialogue, conversation, and play, rather than antagonism and the clash of opposites. This focus generates a different emphasis and a different line of inquiry, with arguably less political vitriol than critical theory. Second, hermeneutical writers consider the hermeneutical account (described above) of understanding (and its variants) to be *the* account. In other words, they recognize that no one thinks with Aristotelian logic. Formal logic is a technology—arguably, as asserted by Gadamer, to counter the argumentative style of the Sophists.[144] This raises questions about the general applicability of Hegel's appeal to a presuppositionless science of logic and Heidegger's appeal to thinking as something other than what we normally do anyway. For hermeneutical writers, all writing and talking comes under the rubric of rhetoric—a suite of persuasive strategies through which understandings are formed and reformed in a discursive context. In this light, Hegel, Heidegger, and Marcuse speak to us in different and challenging ways. But, according to hermeneutical theory, none of them in their writing is jumping out of conventional modes of discourse. There is no actual pretechnological or technological way of thinking except insofar as these terms feature in a tradition of discourse. According to the hermeneutical thesis, the radical element in these writings can be understood in terms of the distances they establish and the changes they invoke as we negotiate these distances. In the case of Heidegger (and for a society dominated by positivism), such distance is established by rendering familiar notions like thinking and existing so strange by establishing the primacy of Thought and Being. The focus on distance affirms Heidegger's exposition of truth as disclosure. The question is not whether Hegel, Heidegger, or Marcuse is correct but what is revealed in the encounter.

From Causality to Community

Hermeneutical ideas about thought and understanding embrace the reality of our situation in community. In any interpretive situation, we are caught up in the norms and expectations of a community. Even the scientist is a party to the prejudices and presuppositions of some scientific community. Rhetoric operates because of what is shared and different within a community. From the hermeneutical perspective, there is no breaking out of community. Far from enjoying some enlightened position independent of group pressure, critical theory trades in the rhetoric of its own constituency and the liberalism and conservatism against which it is reacting.[145] This is not to say that the community is always right or that its values are to be conserved—far from it—but the identification of where it is in error is entirely parasitic on what that community thinks of itself. A case in point is Marcuse's use of the term "negative thinking" to characterize the desirable pretechnological mode of thought. Identifying the negative with the desirable is provocatively at odds with the dominant view of technological society that it is the *positive* that is to be affirmed. Marcuse relies on the tacit use of the terms "positive" and "negative" within the communities he is addressing to establish distance and to provoke us out of our indifference.

To focus on community is itself to lower the status of causality as a model of human interaction. A speaker or writer does not *cause* changes in attitudes or *cause* revolutions, any more than a speaker or writer communicates "intent." Rather, according to the idea of hermeneutical communities,[146] speakers and writers participate within a discourse of changing similarities and differences. They operate within a complex community, in which people assume various roles of catalyzing, provoking, pointing out, gathering concerns, and offering resistance. The modern mass media have contributed to this realization of the interconnected nature of human activity. While they fabricate and parade their heroes (an appropriate focus of criticism from critical theory), the mass media also expose the complex dependence of the "heroes" on public opinion and the complex web of power relations within which they operate. For example, it is apparent in the 1990s, thanks to mass media and television coverage of events, that to attribute the political changes in Eastern Europe simply to the agency of political leaders misses most of what is going on.

The hermeneutical focus on community also reorients the concern with modern mass media as promoting conformity (while deluding us through the myth of individuality) to a consideration of the complex power matrix within which the media operate. According to this view the media neither simply cause change nor reflect it. It is rather as if there is a complex and dynamic web or field of interactions. Each interaction is a perturbation that impinges on other parts of the web through successive transformations.[147]

The community metaphor applies to technologies themselves. The early Heidegger writes of the interdependence of equipment within the workshop, the "equipmental whole," that precedes the individual items.

> To the Being of any equipment there always belongs a totality of equipment. . . . Equipment—in accordance with its equipmentality—always is *in terms of*. . . its belonging to other equipment: ink stand, pen, ink, paper, blotting pad, table, lamp, furniture, windows, doors, room. . . . [I]t is in this that any 'individual' item of equipment shows itself. Before it does so, a totality of equipment has already been discovered.[148]

The later Heidegger presents the notion of the thing in a similar light as a gathering.[149] To invigorate Heidegger's understanding of holistic connectivity with that of the contemporary hermeneutical emphasis on community and praxis is to reflect that technologies are always caught up in a field of community praxis. This applies to their invention, design, manufacture, and use. Part of the praxis that technologies are caught up in involves communities of designers. From the hermeneutical perspective, the most telling criticism of critical theory on information technology is not of the form or mass-produced nature of technologies but of the processes by which they have come about. To focus on designing is to focus on the design *process* rather than the form of the machined artifact. Criticism of a design is not just of what one thinks of a design but of what one thinks of the way it has come about.[150] The problems with information technology discussed above do not always lie with the design technologies themselves but with the reasoning by which they have come about. Has the technology been designed with the presumption of cause and effect from designer to user, or has its design appropriated the involvement of the community that uses it? Has the design been created assuming the technologist knows best and that users should conform to some technological model of behavior, or has it been tried and adapted within the arena of situated human praxis? Contrary to the critical-theory view that presents consumers of technology as victims, the hermeneutical account presents users as participants. It assumes trust—not in an illuminating consensus—but in the process of participation, with all its vagaries and frictions.[151]

It is significant that the most technologically sophisticated, globalizing, and enframing technologies of the age, namely, those that fall under the heading of information technology, should also be a party to powerful action at the "grassroots" level. This is not only in the use of the technologies—as in the dissemination of opinions through community broadcasting, distance education, publications, and so on—but also in the designing and forming of the technology and the practices surrounding its use. The idea of the networked computer system illustrates this point. The most sophisticated parts of such systems are the electronic components (microchips), now designed and manufactured under sophisticated, specialized industries. At the level of design for end users, the technically sophisticated part of the design is largely a matter of the configuration of components, and manufacturing is now largely a matter of assembly. This applies to computers but more significantly to information systems in total—configurations of cables, computers, monitors, displays, storage devices, cameras, connections, networks, software, and standards. Whereas participation in the design of a microchip or a compact-disk player may rely substantially on the initiative and expertise of design specialists, the design of an information *system* is becoming within the grasp of any community. It also matters to such communities. One case in point is the development and extension of the international network for communications by academics (the Internet).[152] This system is composed of many interconnected components, including satellite connections, phone lines, "gateways" to different subnetworks, mass storage, personal computers, software, communications protocols, and standards. The assembly into the current configuration has been accomplished as a grassroots enterprise. Initially the Internet was marginal to the mainstream establishment of academic infrastructures. But even more significant than the spatial and "logical" form of this particular technology is the evolving and unanticipated set of practices that has developed around it, including the uses of electronic mail, user groups, and news services.[153] I examine these phenomena critically in chapter 4, but irrespective of the plausibility of the claims made of computer networking, the Internet is a technological phenomenon that is poorly understood if analyzed according to causal "technological modes of thinking," assuming someone is in control. Nor is it well understood if approached purely from the point of view of critical theory: as either instilling uniformity concealed under the guise of individuality; or promoting privilege among those who have access. Neither is it well understood if seen only as yet another of the inexorable developments signaling the technological enframing orchestrated by Being concealing itself.

The hermeneutical view does not exclude these perspectives from consideration. But it allows us to entertain the view that information technology does not only signal a will to control but affirms the desire of humankind toward praxis and community, in the way it has been put together (in some cases) and in its application. Information technology is a technology for putting people in touch with each other; as such, aspects of its invention, design, manufacture, and use (insofar as they are situated in praxis and community) provide a model for other technologies. If the essence of technology is to conceal Being's true nature, the essence of *information* technology is a "last gasp" by Being to reveal its situation in human affairs.[154]

But critical theory and Heidegger also come under the scrutiny of the radical theories of Jacques Derrida. Derrida deconstructs conservative rationalism, McLuhan's and Dewey's epochs of altered sense ratios, the implication of information technology and the mass media in some kind of social and intellectual decline, and Heidegger's mission of Being. By beginning with the scrutiny of language and writing, deconstruction presents a different orientation from critical theory for examining the issue of information technology.

Design of solar roof panel structure for the Olympic Colosseum by Lawrence Nield
(Lawrence Nield Australia Architects) and Lucy Greagh (Department of Architecture, University of Sydney). Invention of the solar panel system is by David Mills
(Department of Applied Physics, University of Sydney). AutoCAD computer model
is by Milad Saad, and computer rendering is by Francis Kelly using Rayshade software
on a SUN computer. Both were supervised by Sidney Newton in the Key Centre of
Design Computing, Department of Architectural and Design Science, University of
Sydney. The image was then manipulated by the author using Adobe Photoshop on
a Macintosh computer. Three filters were applied: wind, twirl, and extrude. The
final image appears on the cover of this book.

3

Deconstruction and Information Technology

The Implications of Derrida's Project against Metaphysics

It is a commonplace to characterize the current age as undergoing severe disruption, or crisis. Put simply, there are two accounts of disruption. The first focuses on the observation that technology is bringing about unprecedented change. Space exploration, particle physics, genetic engineering, and advanced communications are obvious sources of this disruption. The disruption may be presented in an optimistic or a pessimistic light—we may be entering a new age of enlightened global awareness or a situation in which matters are out of control. The disruption impinges on the social arena, the physical world, and it presents intellectual and philosophical challenges. For example, according to this account, certain technological changes present dangers (ecological, social, etc.), which heighten our ethical awareness and compel us to be concerned with the whole of nature and the world. Technological change has made us more globally aware. Information technology (IT) further heightens this global awareness through rapid access to information. IT is also said to present challenges. For example, it is changing the way we think about space: people are put in touch with each other in ways that transcend conventional spatial boundaries. IT challenges what we think of the intellect: human expertise can be captured within computers and stored and replayed in the absence of the originating intellect. IT also challenges accepted notions of the reliability and authorship of information: with endless quantities of information coursing through vast global networks, how can we be certain where it comes from and how reliable it is, and do we care any longer?

This first account of disruption, this technology-driven rhetoric, has most force where we hold to the philosophical position of rationalism or Enlightenment thinking, with its valorization of the individual, principle, and reason. Another characterization of this account is to describe it as modern, continuing the Enlightenment project of applying reason instead, supposedly, of relying on authority or succumbing to prejudice. Rationalism presents us with a range of legacies, each of which appears to be somehow challenged by IT. The autonomy of the individual and the notion of originality are challenged by technologies of mass production and mechanical and electronic reproduction. Whereas the rationalist legacy suggests that truth resides in the correspondence between a sign (such as a word or gesture) and the signified (the entity we are pointing out), modern electronic communications, the mass media, and computer imagery, present us with the difficulty of discerning what is referring to what. Whereas rationalism supports the notion that human intelligence resides in individuals and is based in rule, computers are shown to manipulate rules faster and more precisely than we can. How important then is the individual? Rationalism suggests that the world can be described completely and ultimately through unified theories. Now there are computer systems that are purported to create the real virtually (with virtual-reality systems), through algorithms. What is real and what is not? It is ironic that one of twentieth-century rationalism's driving metaphors, information technology, now seems to seriously challenge the fundamentals of rationalism. From the point of view of rationalism, this disruption has several dimensions: individuality is challenged; our ethical systems have not yet caught up with the social changes brought about by modern technology; and our conceptual schemas are out of date. According to this account, the disruption is that we are ill equipped to handle the changes brought about by modern technology.

It is significant that this formulation of a disruption does not automatically lead to a shattering of Enlightenment presuppositions but in a strange way reinforces them. One way the rationalist interpretation of IT does this is to present the human intellect and the conceptual systems we set in place as flawed and prone to delusion, as though there is some independent and indisputable standard against which we can compare our schemas. Rationalism points to our susceptibility to delusion and illusion measured against some higher entity, namely reason. Another word for reason is the ancient word *logos* (word), which also suggests the presence of a grounding principle. For this and other reasons, it is appropriate to attribute this modern account of disruption to a position that holds to the values of logocentrism or metaphysics. Put simply, logocentrism is the quest for the ground, the origin, the substrate on which all knowledge, understanding, and being is built. As I will show, technology and the society that uses it are discussed in these metaphysical terms within this modern account of disruption.

The second account of disruption pays little heed to the machinations of the moderns. This is the account of Nietzsche, Heidegger, Derrida, and the *post*moderns.[1] For the postmoderns, the current disruption is the realization and working out of the end of metaphysics (logocentrism). Humankind has always been confronted with uncertainty, changing values, and accommodating new technologies. But putting an end to metaphysics is a relatively recent project in the west—arguably around one hundred years old. The project comes to light most cogently in the writings of Derrida and the poststructuralists. Derrida's main project is to detect and go beyond logocentric argumentation, especially among those who claim most fervently to have abandoned it.

If metaphysics is the quest for the ground, postmodernism does not simply deny that there is a ground (to deny ground is simply relativism) but attempts to exorcise its own rhetoric, and that of its progenitors, of the metaphysical (logocentric), the need for either ground or nonground. To assert that there is no ground is itself a metaphysical assertion. Postmodern rhetoric is therefore characterized by a restlessness—no sooner establishing foundations than removing them. There is an attempt to work out a nonmetaphysical view of the topic at hand—language, literature, art, science, culture, theology, technology, design, and so on—and as I will show here in relation to information technology.

The incommensurability of the two accounts of disruption should not be underestimated. Some modern writers operating within the first account of disruption actually seek overtly to reinstate metaphysics.[2] The challenge presented by such writers as Hawking, who asserts that science will present the answer, the unified field theory that will some day enable everyone to be a philosopher, is metaphysical. So, too, is Davies's assertion that there is a purpose to the universe that points to the hand of God in nature. Boam and Peat make similar metaphysical assertions. Apparently holistic theses, such as chaos theory, the Gaia hypothesis, complex-systems theory and the theories of self-organizing systems, are similarly implicated. So, too, to assert that we live in a changing world and that information technology is going to challenge us is not a postmodern observation. It is modern.[3]

The postmodern project against metaphysics is well represented in Derrida's strategy of *deconstruction*. Deconstruction is an argumentative strategy to unsettle and challenge metaphysics (logocentrism). It can be seen as an extension of the dialectical principle of the pre-Socratics and of Eckhart, Hegel, Nietzsche, and Heidegger though the principle is extended through the metaphor of play. The dialectical principle is to keep the interaction between opposites in play.[4] The deconstructive position has also been labeled *radical hermeneutics* by Caputo and Gallagher.[5] Deconstruction seizes on the various oppositions that are assumed within intellectual inquiry and makes devastating play of their inversion, reversal, and demolition.

In what follows, I will establish the potency of deconstruction for providing an understanding of information technology. I will primarily elaborate on the deconstructive critique of the account of disruption presented by modernism—making passing reference to McLuhan's liberal technological determinism and to critical theory—before elaborating on Derrida's engagement with metaphysics.

Modern Responses to IT

There are three major components to the current disruption presented by IT seen from the modern perspective, well illustrated in the case of Mitchell's identification of the problems presented by computer imagery.[6] First, according to Mitchell, electronic communication presents us with the prospect of endlessly reproducing texts, sounds, images, and other forms of data. In the case of electronic reproduction (with computer-image files), we lose the concept of an original: "Scholars can often trace back through a family tree of editions or manuscripts to recover an original, definitive version, but the lineage of an image file is usually untraceable, and there may be no way to determine whether it is a freshly captured, unmanipulated record or a mutation of a mutation that has passed through many unknown hands."[7] This endless trail of copies brought about by the use of computers suggests the diminution of authorial responsibility: "Notions of individual authorial responsibility for image content, authorial determination of meaning, and authorial prestige are correspondingly diminished."[8] This endless reproducibility is thought to represent a significant departure from traditional manuscript and print-based technologies and practices.

The second challenge posed by IT is the uncertainty about what the signifier (the word or picture) is signifying in any particular instance. Computer images seem to refer to other images, digital and otherwise. Digital data is about other data rather than about tangible referents, such as "real-world" objects, events, or concepts. According to Mitchell, with electronic media, "The referent has become unstuck."[9] This is particularly the case with digital photographs, which can be so manipulated, either automatically or deliberately, that we lose track of their original signification: "We are faced not with conflation of signifier and signified, but with a new uncertainty about the status and interpretation of the visual signifier."[10]

Third, there is a challenge to notions about what things mean, particularly if we take meaning as the property of a text or image tied to the intention of the author or creator. According to Scruton, a kind of spectrum is in play in the "meaning content" of images.[11] At one end is the painting, which has meaning in that it expresses the artist's intentions. At the other end is the "ideal photograph," which simply records what is there. The "ideal photograph" is not of value primarily because it means anything but because it has truth content.[12] Mitchell extends this spectrum into the realm of computer imagery and to the question of the truth of an image. There are nonalgorithmic and algorithmic images. The former relies on the artist's subjectivity, the artist's intention: "A non-algorithmic image, which is the product of many intentional acts, neither establishes that the object depicted exists nor (if that object does exist) provides much reliable evidence about it, but reveals a lot about what was in the artist's mind."[13] The algorithmic image pertains to objectivity: "An algorithmic image, which to a large extent is automatically constructed from some sort of data about the object and which therefore involves fewer or even no intentional acts, gives away much less about the artist but provides more trustworthy evidence of what was out there in front of the imaging system."[14] At one end of the spectrum resides potentially meaningful images, at the other potentially truthful images. But with electronic imagery, all data is subjected to algorithmic manipulation. In that case, what is the source of meaning, and, seeing the power of digitally enhanced images to deceive, how do we establish what constitute true and reliable images?[15]

Added to this concern, we now have the use of computer imagery to "construct realities," as in "virtual-reality" systems. We can create objects and construct relationships in computer databases: "Logical associations of images in databases and computer networks become more crucial to the construal of reality than physical relationships of objects in space. Digital imaging now constructs subjects in cyberspace."[16]

These three concerns—with reproduction, the rupture between the signifier and the signified, and the dissolution of the spectrum of meaning and truth—also echo aspects of Benjamin's concern with the status and nature of the work of art in the age of mechanical reproduction.[17] But the concern is amplified by IT. According to Mitchell, "The age of digital replication is superseding the age of mechanical reproduction."[18]

This kind of reflection on IT is grounded in the traditions of analytic philosophy and related branches of psychology. There is a focus on verification, accuracy, and truthful correspondence, supported by a technical appreciation of the nature of photographic and digital imagery, which, on the one hand, provides a model for objective evidence and, on the other hand, demonstrates how easily we are deceived. It follows then that the challenge of electronic communications should be cast in this light: how can we be sure of what is true and real in the light of the characteristics of electronic communications?

As outlined in the previous chapter, there is another tradition of reflecting on IT that is more skeptical of analytical philosophy (and the legacies of the Enlightenment). This is the tradition of critical theory, with its grounding in Marxist and Freudian theory.[19] But critical theory presents a similar account of the disruption brought about by IT. According to Baudrillard, the electronic age is characterized by the lack of distinction between the real and the imaginary. In the electronic age, everything is a simulation, as evident in the successive phases in the "decline" of the image.[20] Formerly, an image may have reflected a basic reality, as in the case of a Greek statue's reflecting ideal beauty. Or an image may have masked and perverted a basic reality, as in the case of an image that presented a monarch or benefactor in a favorable light. Or an image may have masked the *absence* of a basic reality, as in the case of some religious imagery. Now there is the image that "bears no relation to any reality whatever: it is its own pure simulacrum,"[21] as exemplified by such cities as Los Angeles, which is "a town whose mystery is precisely that it is nothing more than a network of endless, unreal circulation: a town of fabulous proportion, but without space or dimension."[22] This hierarchy of imagery permits Baudrillard the provocative insight that things we take to be unreal, such as Disneyland, serve to make us believe that the rest is real. Disneyland masks the absence of a basic reality, and Los Angeles and the rest of the United States are no longer real but a simulation. They are "hyperreal."

Seen in this light, computer imagery, virtual reality, and cyberspace do not serve as new realities, or even fake realities, but, by their obvious contrivance, mask the unreality of our existence in the information age. They delude us into thinking that when we leave the computer or remove the headset we are reentering the real world. The critical-theory line has little interest in truth and validity as an appeal to some abstract notion of reason. Neither is it strictly a modern perspective. Critical theory presents a picture of a pervasive deception promoted through hegemonic structures that preserve the status quo. The appropriate response is perpetual skepticism, emancipation, or revolution.

A further variation on this strand of thinking is presented by McLuhan.[23] McLuhan is also skeptical of Enlightenment legacies, which he sees as products of a visually oriented culture. However, as outlined in chapter 1, McLuhan presents an optimistic view of IT as ushering in a return to an egalitarian village culture, at a global scale—a global village. According to this optimistic technological determinism, we are reentering the age of tribal, aural culture. Derrida has a great deal to say that challenges this position. We will consider this challenge after presenting a Derridean critique of the modern account of disruption brought about by IT.

Derrida and the Dismantling of the Modern Critique

Derrida has so far devoted little attention explicitly to exploring the nature of electronic communications or the information age.[24] This is hardly surprising. For Derrida and other language theorists, the crisis of the endless reproduction of texts, the chase of the signifier for its signified, and the elusive quest for truth and meaning are not brought about by mass media and electronic communications but are integral to our sign systems, our languages. Derrida targets basic assumptions about language. His primary focus is structuralism, arguably a twentieth-century variant of rationalism, and a logocentric pursuit intent on discovering structures underlying language use and other human activities.[25] Lévi-Strauss makes clear the structuralist project:

First, structural linguistics shifts from the study of *conscious* linguistic phenomena to the study of their *unconscious* infrastructure; second, it does not treat *terms* as independent entities, taking instead as its basis of analysis the *relations* between terms; third, it introduces the concept of *system* . . . finally, structuralist linguistics aims at discovering general laws.[26]

Derrida disarms the modern account of disruption described above (whether this rhetoric is grounded in analytical philosophy, critical theory, or structuralism).[27] There are three main arguments. These are well articulated by Culler in his summary of Derrida's various reflections on language.[28] (We will rely substantially on Culler's commentary before considering some of Derrida's key texts.)

The first argument against the modern account of technological disruption is to observe the centrality of the notion of mimicry, mimesis, in our consideration of how language operates. We instinctually deprivilege mimicry, or copying. We say disparagingly, "it is merely a copy," "that work is plagiarized," "who did they copy that from?" Plato worked the notion of mimesis into his philosophy of the bifurcated universe with its intelligible world, the realm of ideas, of which all else is a copy, or a copy of a copy. Derrida argues that even though Plato established that copies are derivative and inessential, he contradicted that insight in his own writing, as when he described memory in mimetic terms as pictures painted in the soul.

It is a simple matter to detect the illusiveness of what might constitute an original in any literary, artistic, or design enterprise. Culler gives the example of a painting of a bed.

[I]f it [a painting] represents a bed made by a carpenter, that bed may prove in turn to be an imitation of a particular model, which can in turn be seen as the representation or imitation of an ideal bed. The distinction between a representation and what it represents may have the effect of putting in question the status of any particular bed: every supposed original may be shown to be an imitation, in a process that is arrested only by positing a divine origin, an absolute original.[29]

The quest for the original presents us with a "mimetic" chain. If pursued with Platonic conviction, this chain ends with the transcendent, the idea of the bed resident in the intelligible world.[30] The mimetic phenomenon has always been in evidence and central, whatever the medium, electronic or otherwise. The Platonic conception is of some original of which the image or text is a representation, but mimetic relations appear to assume the character of endless chains of representations of representation, or texts representing texts, rather than texts representing some nontextual original.

Mimetic relations can be regarded as intertextual: relations between one representation and another rather than between a textual imitation and a nontextual original. Texts that assert the plenitude of an origin, the uniqueness of an original, the dependency of a manifestation or derivation of an imitation, may reveal that the original is already an imitation and that everything begins with reproduction.[31]

Seen in this light, there is nothing extraordinary about mechanical or electronic reproduction. Any ontology depends on it. As we will see later, the difference made by electronic media is in the modes of practice they engender.[32]

The second argument against the modern account of technological disruption is to show that the signifier and the signified are already decoupled, prior to any consideration of electronic information storage and communication. Rationalist views of representation readily establish the idea of a hierarchy of representations, with certain representations (photographs) more privileged than others (paintings). Photographs are in the realm of the objective. Other representations are in the realm of the subjective, dependent on interpretation. So there are those (objective) cases in which the signifier (word, text, or image) is closely bound to the thing signified (some event or entity). So, according to Scruton, as signifiers, photographs are bound to the scenes they depict. Mitchell asserts that in the case of modern information technology this distinction is becoming less evident—computer images (and other data) are inevitably manipulated, changed, and combined in ways that make it very difficult to tell what is being referred to. As images and data, signifiers appear to refer more to other signifiers (other images and data), in an endless chain.

To appropriate Derrida's point here is to recognize that in language there has never been a close coupling between signifier and signified. As with the mimetic chain of representation, Derrida shows the ubiquity of the "chain of signification." This can be illustrated with a simple example of signification. The sentence "there is a tree" is a sign (signifier) that denotes or signifies a tree. But in a particular context of consideration, that particular tree may act as a signifier to something else, perhaps another tree, a painting, a legend, an event. These signifieds in turn may signify something else, and so there is the familiar chain—of signification. The signified (the tree) is therefore an artifact of the moment. It is elusive. As with the phenomenon of mimesis, if the chain is to end, it ends with the "transcendental signified"—some ideal, the ultimate tree of which all others are signifiers, or signifiers of signifiers. This possibility is rejected by Derrida and other language theorists.

Derrida does not contend that we therefore drop the idea of the signified: "[T]he distinction between what signifies and what is signified is essential to any thought whatever."[33] According to Culler, Derrida's point is that there "are no final meanings that arrest the movement of signification."[34] This endless chain of signification is not an unfortunate accident of language but "a constitutive element of its structure, an incompletion without which the sign would be incomplete."[35] Neither does this imply that it is impossible to determine meaning, or that one meaning is as good as any other: "The structural redoubling of any signified as an interpretable signifier does suggest that the realm of signifiers acquires a certain autonomy, but this does not mean signifiers without signifieds, only the failure of signifieds to produce closure."[36] Meaning is disclosed in the ongoing play of signs. But it is the play of indeterminate meanings. The stability of every meaning is undermined by the ever-changing play of signifiers. This play applies to any text or sign situation.[37] It is not a phenomenon unique to the electronic age.

The third argument against the modern account of disruption is to show how meaning emerges not so much from a bonding between signifier and signified but from the play of difference within language. The conventional view of meaning, prior to Saussure, relied on the notion of dictionary definitions, which were meanings given by past acts of communication. The system of norms and regularities of a language was regarded as the result of prior speech acts.[38] Saussure departed from this conventional view in his quest for the first structure, the originary structure, of language.[39] The first gruntings and pointings that constituted rudimentary communication presupposed a structure. The grunt signifying food was distinguished from other grunts. So food was already distinguished from non-food.[40] Therefore, according to Saussure, words are distinguishable by their difference. The word "bat" is a signifier because it contrasts with "pat," "mad," and so on. One of Saussure's great insights was to describe language as a system of differences.

Derrida points out how this emphasis on difference undermines the other aspects of the structuralist project—the attempt to found a theory of language based on entities and relations. When a word is uttered, it is inhabited by the traces of what one is not uttering.

Saussure's logocentric view of language seeks meaning as present to consciousness at the moment of speaking, reading, or listening. But this moment is inhabited by difference and is difficult to capture. If we regard the ground of meaning to reside in difference, then we fare no better. Differences are not givens but products emerging through analysis. The unstable and contradictory notion of difference seems to be the only "stable" point from which to understand the phenomenon of language. According to Derrida, "the play of differences involves syntheses and referrals that prevent there from being at any moment or in any way a simple element that is present in and of itself and refers only to itself. Whether in written or in spoken discourse, no element can function as a sign without relating to another element which itself is not simply present."[41] So there is nothing present or absent in a language event that enables it to signify something. Everywhere one looks there are only differences and traces: "Nothing, either in the element or in the system, is anywhere simply present or absent. There are only, everywhere, differences and traces of traces."[42] Derrida writes about the play of difference within the system—coining the term *différance* as a play on words (in French) to imply that meaning is always deferred along the endless chain of signs. Gallagher describes the play thus: "[E]very 'truth' that the interpreter closes in on becomes one of the plurality of fictions which constitute the play of differences within the system."[43]

As already indicated, there are several implications of the Derridean view of language that impinge directly on the modern account of technological disruption. The prospect of endless reproducibility, the decoupling of the signifier and the signified, and the various challenges to truth and meaning are not new challenges brought about by IT. Language, art, communication, and arguably science could not operate without these phenomena.

Derrida also challenges the notions of authorship, subjectivity, and intentionality on which the modern account of technological disruption gains much of its impetus. The author, as presented through the logocentric tradition, disappears in Derrida's endless chains of mimesis and signification. It is not that we no longer recognize authorship. But we see the author as contingent and constructed, as is the reader, for the moment, in a situation. Postmodern theorists, such as Zavarzadeh and Morton,[44] point out that within postmodernism we "no longer talk about the individual, but about the subject."[45] Furthermore, postmodernism "does not conceptualize the subject as a stable entity but argues that the parameters of the subject vary according to the discursive practices that are current in any historical moment."[46] Seen in this light, intentionality is also contingent. To ask what the author originally meant is to engage in interpretation. Neither the reader, the scholar, nor the author can gain access to an original intention as an indisputable truth. Thus, any identification of an original intention is contingent on a situation of interpretation.

Seen in this light, Scruton's spectrum, with subjective painting at one end and objective photography at the other, loses much of its weight as a useful classification system (as does Baudrillard's spectrum of simulations)—so too, Mitchell's extension of intentional versus algorithmic representations. Talk of intentions is taken as a dead letter in postmodern interpretive discourse. Talk of intentions leads one in fruitless pursuit of the essential and undeniable truth in a matter, an attempt to close off discussion. If we know what Shakespeare meant by *Hamlet,* then there is no need for further discussion or interpretation. In the case of data processing and computer imagery, the pursuit of intentionality leads us in several directions, including applying the conduit metaphor; seeing electronic communications as conduits for intention; attempting to convey intentions through control systems; trying to capture intentions in artificial-intelligence systems; and uncovering digital deceptions, where the author's intentions are to perpetrate a falsehood.

In challenging certain entrenched views of language, Derrida provides a clearing for new ways of considering the phenomenon of IT. These will be considered at the close of this chapter. One possibility is to consider that Mitchell's examples of computerized deception are not aberrations of photography but demonstrations of its "essence." We could equally begin with the presupposition that all photography is deception, or mimicry. The nature of an image is not a matter of truthful correspondence but of disclosure,[47] only part of which is to do with the image's role in the praxis of presenting evidence. In Heidegger's terms, the notion of correspondence is built first of all on the notion of disclosure (*aletheia*).

Deconstructive Critique of Technological Determinism

What of McLuhan's technological determinism? One of Derrida's major themes is his identification of the tendency within conventional language theories to subordinate the signifier (word or language event) to the signified (the meaning or the entity referred to). The signifier exists to give access to the signified and is subordinate to the concept or meaning it communicates. Within this regime of thinking, the task of interpretation is always to get back to what is meant in any language situation. The words are obviously important but sometimes get in the way. As indicated above, Derrida argues for a reversal of this priority. Derrida shows that any discussion of the priority of meaning (the signified) also paradoxically presents a story of the priority of the signifier.

Derrida approaches this issue of the relationship between the signifier and the signified through the common distinction made between writing and speech. According to Saussure, "A language and its written form constitute two separate systems of signs. The sole reason for the existence of the latter is to represent the former."[48] Whereas speech is a direct representation of thought, writing is artificial or oblique. Writing is a representation of a representation— it represents speech, which represents thought. This conventional wisdom appears to be uncontroversial, with ample evidence to support it. For example, there are some societies in which there is no written language, but there are none in which people only write but do not speak. Children usually learn to speak before they can write. In order to communicate urgently and potently, we generally speak rather than write. This evidence strongly supports the priority of speech over writing.

As we have seen, such writers as McLuhan and Ong further promote this priority in their differentiation between aural culture, in which there is no writing, and visual culture dominated by the printed word.[49] Primal, village culture was aural; manuscript culture was visual. For McLuhan, the aural culture was characterized by a field of incessant speech and chatter; there was also an immediacy to human experience. With writing, life became less engaging and less immediate, thought could be spatialized, and notions of objectivity could be developed. Ong integrates this transition from aural to visual culture into an understanding of the development of rationalism and the Enlightenment. For McLuhan, the electronic age represents a return to an aural culture, a retribalization. The electronic media and electronic communications reinstate speech and chatter, though we have entered this age "with our eyes open."

As indicated in chapter 1, Dewey presents a similar case.[50] The pretechnological age was characterized by an immediacy of involvement; means and ends coalesced. He attributes this to the prevalence and heightened use of the immediate aural sense. According to Dewey, later Greek thinking privileged the visual sense in developing its doctrines of detachment and its bifurcated world of theory and practice. Science developed successfully only when it took a pragmatic turn with Copernicus and others who recaptured the pre-Platonic engagement with instruments, tools, and experimentation.

According to Derrida, such observations indicate a profound prejudice against the visual and the written dating back at least to Plato. Since then, the Western tradition has regarded writing as a distorted form of speech that can lead to misunderstanding. More than speech, writing is prone to tyranny and danger. So a lot is at stake in Derrida's attempts to overturn the privilege of speech over writing.

According to Derrida, Saussure contradicts his own thesis (that writing is a derivative of speech) by explaining speech in terms of arguments reliant on an understanding of the features of writing. For example, Saussure uses features of writing, such as the differences between the *appearance* of letters, to illustrate the differences between phonetic (sound) units in speech. Writing turns out to provide the best illustration of the nature of language. This is common enough practice. We often explain the ephemeral in terms of what is easiest to grasp. For Derrida, the ubiquity and exclusivity of such illustrations amounts to a presentation of the thing explained as the thing explaining. Speech is explained as writing. When Derrida points this out, he does not mean to say simply that speech is a form of writing, or distorted writing. We cannot simply say that writing comes first, and speech is its distortion. To conclude as much would go against our basic intuitions about language use. In reversing the priority, the two terms "speech" and "writing" undergo transformation through Derrida's pen. Borrowing more from Hegel than Derrida would care to admit to, a dialectical synthesis occurs. For Derrida, what we commonly call "writing" is but an instance of a more basic entity called "protowriting," "archiwriting" (archewriting) or "original writing." Speech is also an instance of protowriting.

It is in this identification of protowriting that Derrida's arguments become most persuasive. What are the features of protowriting? First, there are signs, whether uttered, gestured, drawn, or written. Signs operate through difference, as explained above. Second, these signs are repeatable, can be reproduced: spoken word sequences can be uttered by someone else, gestures can be mimicked, drawings and written words can be copied. Third, sign sequences (speeches, texts, drawings, etc.) can be disseminated; sequences of signs can be recognized as the same, even in different circumstances. It is therefore possible to pass sign sequences on from one situation to another. Fourth, sign sequences operate in the absence of an originator. It is possible to quote the sign sequence to a third party without the presence of the originator and without knowing that person's situation or intentions. The sign sequence is capable of signifying even when uttered, stored, or presented independently of intention.

These are usually the features we associate with writing. Written texts can be copied and repeated, they can be distributed and passed from one person to another, and the originator need not be present for them to signify. But exactly the same can be said of speech. A spoken utterance can be repeated by another person. It is possible to disseminate a speech to a crowd. Utterances can be passed on by "word of mouth." The original speaker need not be present. The conveyor of the utterance does not have to understand the utterance in order for a third party to receive and make sense of the sign sequence. We commonly recite poetry we do not understand, and the poem loses nothing of its power to signify when recited. We commonly learn by rote and recite sign sequences without the mediation of intention.

These features of sign, repetition, distribution, and absence are not commonly regarded as part of language but as features of writing (understood through its study, grammatology). According to Derrida, it is not helpful simply to attribute these features to language. Language is already described as a system of signs by Saussure. Saussure distinguishes between langue, language as a system of differences, and parole, actual instantiated speech events. According to Derrida, the useful terms are "already used up." The features of sign, repetition, dissemination, and absence belong to writing, hence Derrida's formulation of the study of protowriting, or archewriting, of which writing and speech are but instances.[51] "An archewriting whose\necessity and new concept I wish to indicate and outline here; and which I continue to call writing only because it essentially communicates with the vulgar concept of writing."[52] This line of argument from Derrida, that speech and writing are instances of protowriting, further disarms complaints about the corruption of the spoken word due to electronic communications technology. The features of sign, repetition, dissemination, and absence already belong to speech, to manuscript culture, to print, and to electronic communications. Likewise, the demise of the work of art, which Benjamin placed in the age of mechanical reproduction, was already in place with the first cave paintings. So, too, the first experiments in photography already acted out the features of sign, repetition, dissemination, and absence. If there is a demise or a falsifying of photographic imagery due to digital storage and manipulation, then it was already in progress. So, too, Baudrillard's complaint that everything is now a simulation or simulacrum may well have resounded throughout every age. It was never otherwise. From the Derridean reading, the essence of communication, or more accurately protowriting, lies in those very features that lead to these complaints.[53]

What do Derrida's assertions about protowriting say about McLuhan's characterization of aural culture and its displacement by the visual? Following Derrida, we must say that the aural had all the features of the visual. They were already in place. A Derridean critique of McLuhan's or Dewey's writings would show that their illustrations of the immediacy of aural culture rely on visual metaphors. For example, Dewey remarks, "The connections of the ear with vital and

out-going thought and emotion are immensely closer and more varied than those of the eye."[54] Dewey invokes the spatial property of
proximity to explain what is different and immediate about the aural
sense. Subsequently we will see how Derrida's critique of presence
dispenses with the need to pursue this strategy of argument here.
The guiding metaphor from McLuhan and the tradition that asserts
the superiority of speech to writing is always that of proximity.
Speech is present; writing is a supplemental addition. It is less proximal. The aural is present, immediate; the visual is a supplement or
a defective version of the immediate. Derrida seizes on this doctrine
of presence to identify and deconstruct logocentrism.

Metaphysics and Presence

Derrida's most potent arguments focus around the deconstruction
of logocentrism, the metaphysical element in the philosophical tradition. Of course Derrida is not the only philosopher to direct
charges of logocentrism against other philosophers. It is worth reflecting on this tradition of critique before considering Derrida's
position. According to Ihde, there have been three great philosophical traditions in the twentieth century—positivism, pragmatism, and
phenomenology—and each shares a deep suspicion of metaphysics.[55] In the case of positivism and its descendant, analytic philosophy,[56] there is a suspicion of grand metaphysical systems of the kind
put forward by Hegel, particularly his intricate hierarchies indicating
the "movement of being." Such schemas purport to account for
everything and to provide a ground for understanding the universe—according to Ayer, "unifying our various scraps of knowledge
into a higher synthesis."[57] They attempt for philosophy what science
accomplishes in its own specialized areas. From the point of view of
analytic philosophy, there is simply no way of verifying such schemas.
Not only are they ludicrously grandiose, but they are speculative.
According to Ayer,

We may accordingly define a metaphysical sentence as a sentence which
purports to express a genuine proposition, but does, in fact, express neither
a tautology nor an empirical hypothesis. And as tautologies and empirical

hypotheses form the entire class of significant propositions, we are justified in concluding that all metaphysical assertions are nonsensical.[58]

Ayer echoes the analytic philosopher's concern with truth and validity. The difficulties with this line of criticism become apparent when we note the extreme difficulty of uttering any proposition that is empirically verifiable other than in a rigorously and restrictively scientific context. More significantly, the proposition that the only sentences that are meaningful are those that are tautologous or empirically verifiable appears not to be tautologous or empirically verifiable. Ayer's critique of metaphysics is itself metaphysical and, presumably, nonsensical, when subjected to his own criteria.[59] Needless to say, the tenets of analytic philosophy are under attack from Derrida's critique of how language operates.

For pragmatism, the metaphysical gives way to the pragmatic. Truth is what works in a situation. Metaphysics presupposes the existence of the theoretical from which praxis is thought to follow. In attacking classical notions of theory and placing theory as a particular mode of practice, pragmatism affirms metaphysics as a fact of philosophy's history, but not its claims to unveiling the Absolute.

It is the phenomenological tradition, beginning, arguably, with Nietzsche at the end of the nineteenth century and developed by Husserl, Heidegger, and Derrida, that presents the most potent struggle with metaphysics. The game is to sniff out the metaphysical among those who deny it most vehemently, not simply to destroy arguments but to demonstrate that the argument is still in play.

What is the metaphysical element within the modern account of technological disruption? Derrida renders this a relatively simple exercise by recasting the issue of metaphysics in terms of presence.

Before investigating Derrida's account of presence, it is worth reiterating his argument strategy. Derrida's strategy of deconstruction is to challenge an author's thesis by uncovering oppositions in the text that betray that thesis, that is, that show how the opposite of the thesis is the case. Deconstruction often follows very indirect paths. The structuralist project set in motion by Saussure in his *Course in General Linguistics* is challenged at a point that would, prior to Derrida, have gone unnoticed, namely, the commonsense notion of the primacy of speech over writing. Deconstruction is less an engagement with authors, and their apparent concerns, through the medium of the text, than an engagement with whatever the text reveals—hence Derrida's license to focus on the marginal, literally, as in the case of his commentary on the comment, in Nietzsche's papers, "I have forgotten my umbrella" (in *Spurs*) and his commentary on a footnote from Heidegger's *Being and Time*.[60] The peculiarities of Derrida's style is a fascinating study and is explained at length by such commentators as Culler, Norris, and Spivak.[61]

It is worth recalling Derrida's strategy here before considering his discussion of metaphysics. Derrida explains his strategy of identifying and overturning oppositions in the book *Positions*.[62] He contends that oppositions, such as speech and writing, do not simply coexist in a text, but one term is regarded as superior to the other: "To do justice to this necessity is to recognize that in a classical philosophical opposition we are not dealing with the peaceful coexistence of a *vis-à-vis*, but rather with a violent hierarchy. One of the two terms governs the other . . . or has the upper hand."[63] Derrida echoes and amplifies the long-standing Pythagorean categorization of oppositions into the limited and the unlimited, the superior and the inferior. Having identified the opposition, the task is to "deconstruct the opposition . . . to overturn the hierarchy at a given moment."[64] But this overturning is not to effect a Hegelian synthesis, according to Derrida.

To overlook this phase of overturning is to forget the conflictual and subordinating structure of opposition. Therefore one might proceed too quickly to a *neutralization* that *in practice* would leave the previous field untouched, leaving one no hold on the previous opposition, thereby preventing any means of *intervening* in the field effectively.[65]

This is a necessary phase. The objective is to keep the text in play: "The necessity of this phase is structural; it is the necessity of an interminable analysis: the hierarchy of dual oppositions always reestablishes itself. Unlike those authors whose death does not await their demise, the time for overturning is never a dead letter."[66] Unlike Hegel's dialectic, Derrida's contention is that there are certain undecidables "that can no longer be included within philosophical (binary) opposition, resisting and disorganizing it, *without ever* constituting a third term.''[67] Despite Derrida's insistence to the contrary, a "third term" does frequently emerge. Hence the primordial concept of protowriting, or trace, or *différance*.

Nietzsche and Heidegger also employed the strategy of deconstruction. For example, Nietzsche described morality as "itself a special case of immorality." He described the living as "merely a type of what is dead, and a very rare type."[68] Heidegger, too, constantly takes an accepted opposition and makes its deconstruction the main route to his thesis. For example, the essence of truth, he says, is not correspondence but the disclosive play set up by the complex flux of the moment; the primary human experience is not that of a subject disconnected from an object word (as Descartes taught) but a world of unreflective involvement; time is not primarily that which is measured by clocks but a phenomenon that presents itself in terms of the unfulfillment of roles; it is not that artworks occupy a space (locus) but that place (topos) is revealed in the artwork. In all such reversals, the terms undergo revision.

It is from within this deconstructive framework that Derrida tackles the problem of metaphysics. He does so by focusing on the metaphor of presence. Where Derrida indicates that one term of a binary opposition is privileged over another, the privileging is based on the fact that one term refers to what is present, the other to what is absent or supplemental. In fact, there are two metaphorical variants at play: present versus absent and essential versus supplemental. So, writing is commonly presented by Saussure and Rousseau as a supplement to speech. Writing is not entirely necessary. It is speech that is present, immediate, available, and essential.

Similarly, extending Derrida's examples, Dewey and McLuhan write about the immediacy of primitive tool use, of the aural sense, and of speech. These are present. In contrast, visual culture is marked by an absence of immediacy. Visual culture is an encumbrance to the presence of aural culture and a supplement to it. Scruton also promotes the presence of intention in the artwork. The photograph is detached from such presence. Baudrillard suggests the presence wherein there is a basic reality to be reflected by the image. The ultimate absence is Los Angeles, which is no longer real but a simulation, or hyperreal.

So the conventional priority of speech over writing is but an instance of the more general opposition between presence and absence/supplement. This is an interesting development on the Pythagorean binary supercategories of the limited and the unlimited—one and many (there is only one way of there being one, but many ways of there being many); straight and curved (the straight is a limit to all the possible ways of being curved); at rest and moving; and so on. The former in each case is privileged over the latter. The second term is conceived in terms of the first. There is a privileging of presence: the now, the instant is present; speech is immediate; writing is a mediation, a distancing. The term that depicts presence is superior. The second term is inferior and represents a deviation or fall. Speech, the voice, has privileged access to the mind. According to Derrida, "If, for Aristotle, for example, 'spoken words are the symbols of mental experience . . . and written words are the symbols of spoken words' . . . it is because the voice, producer of the first symbols, has a relationship of essential and immediate proximity with the mind."[69] The presence/supplement distinction also reflects the classical essential/accidental distinction. The essential is what makes the thing what it is, its defining properties. The accidental is the incidental and contingent.

The sign is similarly described by Derrida. The thing is what is present, and its sign (words) is a supplement to the thing.

> The sign is usually said to be put in the place of the thing itself, the present thing, "thing" here standing equally for meaning or referent. The sign represents the present in its absence. It takes the place of the present. When we cannot grasp or show the thing, state the present, the being-present, when the present cannot be presented, we signify, we go through the detour of the sign. We take or give signs. We signal. The sign, in this sense, is deferred presence. Whether we are concerned with the verbal or the written sign, with the monetary sign, or with electoral delegation and political representation, the circulation of signs defers the moment in which we can encounter the thing itself, make it ours, consume or expend it, touch it, see it, intuit its presence.[70]

As Derrida indicates, there is a profound paradox in play in the notion of presence, and this is its undoing. The fact that a thing can be supplemented in some way implies that the thing present is incomplete. If speech is present, and as long as it can be supplemented by writing, then it is never complete. Speech is never untouched by writing. According to Derrida, there is always an "original lack." Derrida illustrates this phenomenon in relation to Rousseau's views on education. Rousseau presents education as a supplement to nature. Nature, as what is inherent within the child, is the "essential" child. Education supplements this natural spirit. But the fact that the child's nature lends itself to this supplementation indicates that the child's nature is incomplete without education. Derrida does not mean by these observations that we cease to make such distinctions, but, as with the mimetic chain and the endless play of signification, we recognize the paradox of the endless supplementarity of presence.

What has this observation of presence/supplement to do with metaphysics—the quest for underlying structure? Derrida regards metaphysics as a quest for presence, as an origin. Once the origin is identified, we then conceive of the supplement. Metaphysics is "[t]he enterprise of returning 'strategically,' ideally, to an origin or to a 'priority' seen as simple, intact, normal, pure, standard, self-identical, in order *then* to think in terms of derivation, complication, deterioration, accident, etc."[71] According to Derrida, this is the way of all metaphysical inquiry.

All metaphysicians, from Plato to Rousseau, from Descartes to Husserl, have proceeded in this way, conceiving good to be before evil, the positive before the negative, the pure before the impure, the simple before the complex, the essential before the accidental, the imitated before the imitation, etc. And this is not just *one* metaphysical gesture among others, it is *the* metaphysical exigency, that which has been the most constant, most profound, and most potent.[72]

As already indicated, this orientation that values metaphysical inquiry is also termed "logocentrism"—a centering on the *logos,* the origin or principle (literally "word" in ancient Greek). Derrida also calls the pursuit of the *logos* the "metaphysics of presence." Derrida does not want to lead us away from this orientation. It is impossible to break out of logocentrism, which is built into language. Culler makes this clear by listing some of the concepts we take to be basic and how they depend on the metaphysics of presence.

Among the familiar concepts that depend on the value of presence are: the immediacy of sensation, the presence of ultimate truths to a divine consciousness, the effective presence of an origin in a historical development, a spontaneous or unmediated intuition, the transumption of thesis and antithesis in a dialectical synthesis, the presence in speech of logical and grammatical structures, truth as what subsists behind appearances, and the effective presence of a goal in the steps that lead to it. The authority of presence, its power of valorization, structures all our thinking. The notions of "making clear," "grasping," "demonstrating," "revealing," and "showing what is the case" all invoke presence. To claim, as in the Cartesian *cogito,* that the "I" resists radical doubt because it is present to itself in the act of thinking or doubting is one sort of appeal to presence. Another is the notion that the meaning of an utterance is what is present to the consciousness of the speaker, what he or she "has in mind" at the moment of utterance.[73]

To this list of familiar concepts that depend on presence, we could add concepts that feature in the discourse on IT: the immediacy of tool use, unmediated face-to-face communication, knowledge base, data capture, truthful representations, and so on.

As we will see subsequently, Derrida's point is not to eliminate the metaphysics of presence from language—an impossible task—but to point it out wherever it appears fixed, to shake the foundations as soon as they are established.

Emphasizing these phenomena as manifestations of "presence" is a masterstroke by Derrida, because the notion of presence constructs the problems of philosophy in certain ways that lead to the possibility of their deconstruction. Contrary to the legacy of idealism that pervades metaphysical discourse, Derrida is also appropriating a metaphor grounded in concrete, day-to-day experience. (Grounding is another metaphor within the metaphysical tradition—as used by Leibniz and deconstructed by Heidegger and Derrida.) The metaphor of presence brings certain problems of metaphysics to light. If the idea of presence makes problematic the relationship between speech and writing or nature and education, as described above, then it also reveals paradoxes about metaphysics. The problem is that the phenomenon that is present already appears as a complex product. It should be otherwise. The origin should not be contingent. According to Culler, "What is proposed as a given, an elementary constituent, proves to be a product, dependent or derived in ways that deprive it of the authority of simple or pure presence."[74] The *logos,* or founding principle, is itself revealed as a social construction, a complex phenomenon beholden to the dictates of a particular set of contexts and a history of thought.

Derrida illustrates the derivative nature of presence with the concept of time. We think of time in terms of past, present, and future. We think of the present as the "basic unit," the stable entity. The present instant seems indecomposable and absolute. So, we describe the past in terms of the present. It is the present that was. The future is the present that is still to come, the anticipated present. Within this metaphysical schema the present is simply given. The other aspects of time are less stable, marked by difference from the present. They are successions of changing presences.[75]

Derrida points out the paradox in this commonsense understanding. The idea of the present moment only serves as a foundation on which to build concepts of the past and the future if we accept that the present cannot be captured as a stable understanding: "But it turns out that the present instant can serve as ground only insofar as it is not a pure and autonomous given."[76] As in Zeno's observation about the flight of an arrow, there is no moment that captures the idea of motion without considering each moment in relation to the one before it and the one after: the future and the past of any moment. So the prototypical time event by which other time phenomena are described, namely, the present, turns out not to be prototypical after all. According to Culler, "If motion is to be present, presence must already be marked by difference and deferral."[77]

We cannot dispense with metaphysical terms, but there is a way of writing that acknowledges the provisional status of our foundational notions. This is to be a "philosopher of the erasure." In his later writings, Heidegger literally crosses out certain words in the text of his manuscripts, placing the words "under erasure." So "Being" is crossed out to indicate its provisional status as a convenient fiction in the argument. Derrida follows a similar practice, in a section of *Of Grammatology,* with the copula ("is"). But the word does not need to be crossed out for erasure to be evident. There are ways of writing, brought into currency largely by Derrida and the poststructuralists, that aim to keep the terms in play rather than fixing them. Writers show the provisional nature of any conclusions and devote considerable critical effort to dislodging their own and others' certainties. It should be added that this is far removed from the games of sophistry, flaunting convention, or neglecting scholarly rigor. Derrida's writing, as an exercise in writing under erasure, reveals a breathtaking precision and rigor.

Here we come to the main difference between the modern rhetoric of technological disruption and postmodern writing against logocentrism. The former is largely unself-reflexive regarding its assumptions and its quest for principles. The latter is aware of the provisional status of its assumptions and that the game is never complete. Others may come along who bring new aspects of the discourse to light. A conversation is in progress, and the writer is a participant.

How are the modern responses to IT described above also metaphysical? From a Derridean perspective, the concerns expressed about the diminution of authorial responsibility, the uncertainty about the connection between the signifier and the signified, and the questions hanging over the meanings of computer images are each an identification of a supplemental situation, which is a deviation from a situation of presence: the authorial origins of manuscript culture, the close binding between sign and signified of speech or painting, meaning reference as grounded in authorial intent, and truth content as stemming from the algorithmic moment of image capture. As with all discourse, these various responses to IT are imbued with talk of presence and supplement. They are also deeply and unquestioningly pervaded by the *logos*—the belief in the principle of reason that will ultimately arbitrate in matters of truth and meaning.

Derrida's Critique of Heidegger on Technology

Derrida's arguments appear to make short work of the modern account of technological disruption. But, according to Derrida, even Heidegger is not immune to logocentrism. As we found in chapter

2, Heidegger presents the case for Being as the universal, self-evident concept (that defies categorization).[78] According to Caputo, Heidegger develops, in his later writings notions of Being akin to the insights of certain mystical writers and poets: the primordial entity of Being has a relationship to *beings* (living and nonliving entities) analogous to that between the divinity and the soul. Heidegger is at pains to establish this distinction between Being and beings, a distinction all but lost in the philosophical tradition dating back to Plato. In keeping with a tradition of writing that also found expression in Hegel's notions of the Absolute and of Spirit, Being reveals and conceals itself in different ways and at different times throughout history—particularly through the writings of great thinkers. Technology comes to the fore as one of Heidegger's main concerns in that it is part of Being's mission by which Being conceals itself. We are enframed in the technological age—we see everything in technological terms, as having causes, as a potential to be exploited, and as explicable by unified theories, and we are deaf to the call of Being in favor of focusing on beings. But this technological enframing is not anyone's fault. We have not caused it, and we cannot control it. Being has brought about this enframing by concealing itself. The appropriate response to the enframing is to recognize in it the withdrawal of Being, an active resignation, which carries with it an appreciation of the wonder and mystery that is within things when considered beyond causes and beyond asking "why?"

Heidegger's writing on Being and technology is intriguing and difficult and carries enormous weight in postmodernist discourse. What does Derrida say about Heidegger's notions of Being and technology's implication in the mission of Being? This encounter is the apogee of Derrida's writing—his engagement with Heidegger. It is the most revealing of Derrida's thought, and it provides a rigorous test site for his ideas.

The lineage of argument about metaphysics within the phenomenological tradition is straightforward. Nietzsche announced the death of metaphysics and wrote in a way that challenged foundational notions of goodness, truth, virtue, and so on. But Heidegger describes Nietzsche as the last metaphysician. Heidegger thinks

Nietzsche brought about new insights but was still caught up in metaphysics in posing his questions in a metaphysical way. More recently, Derrida has said the same of Heidegger. Derrida also indicates how Heidegger misrepresents Nietzsche in describing him as a metaphysician. Subsequently, such writers as Caputo have shown how Derrida misrepresents Heidegger.

According to Heidegger, a metaphysician is one who asks the question "What is the being of the entity?"[79] rather than "What is the nature of being?" According to Heidegger, Nietzsche thinks the being of the entity is the will to power.[80] So, for Nietzsche the focus of the questioning about being is the human being (humankind) and its characteristics. Heidegger's philosophy is distinctive, and difficult, for its nonanthropological, nonhumanist focus on entities like Being and *Dasein*. The question of the nonmetaphysician, for Heidegger, is "What is it to inquire into the nature of Being?" *Dasein* is the entity that is led to inquire into its Being, and it is prior to humankind. So, Heidegger moves beyond Nietzsche and his metaphysical centering on the human being.

According to Spivak, Heidegger regards Nietzsche as a metaphysician in the sense that he is not a philosopher of the erasure: "For him, Nietzsche remains a metaphysician who asks the question of being, but does not question the question itself!"[81] According to Spivak, whether Nietzsche is a metaphysician or not, Heidegger turns him into one. Derrida takes on the challenge of demonstrating the converse—that Nietzsche *is* a philosopher of the erasure—in an article entitled *Spurs* (meaning "trace"). In this article, Derrida shows how "one consistent reading constantly erases itself and invokes its opposite, and so on indefinitely."[82]

In *Spurs*, Derrida's reading of Nietzsche is deliberately and provocatively unstraightforward, to show how Nietzsche can be appropriated in ways other than through Heidegger's straight and literal interpretation.[83] Derrida brings a series of unlikely sexual images and metaphors to bear on his reading of Nietzsche. His interpretation demonstrates all the inventiveness of creative writing: "a writing launched by the encounter with a text which itself acknowledges no limit to the free play of meaning."[84] In this interpretation, Derrida reinstates Nietzsche as a philosopher of the erasure and not a metaphysician.

We turn now to Derrida's charge of logocentrism directed at Heidegger. Derrida and Heidegger seem to pursue very similar deconstructive ends, but they differ in that Heidegger seems to hanker constantly after the presence of a primary and authentic entity—Being, *Dasein,* and so on. Heidegger locates the source and ground of authentic thought in the moment of Being or completeness that precedes articulate discourse. This Derridean identification of the metaphysical element of Heidegger's thought is summarized by Norris: "For Derrida this can only represent another classic case of the familiar metaphysical hankering after truth and origins."[85] According to Derrida, Heidegger's philosophy is founded on a notion of truth as self-presence that seeks to eliminate, or claims to precede, the indeterminate play of signification. Nietzsche is much less the metaphysician. Whereas Nietzsche appeals to the diverse and dynamic nature of thought as understood by the pre-Socratics, Heidegger appears to look "to a source of authentic truth in the unitary ground of Being."[86] The difference between Heidegger and Derrida is also clear. Heidegger does not intend "to release a multiplicity of meaning but to call meaning back to its proper, self-identical source"[87] in his "destruction" of metaphysics.

Derrida has engaged Heidegger's writing through several books and articles.[88] Whereas Heidegger elevates the primordial notion of Being,[89] Derrida posits against Being the primacy of his notion of difference, explored above in relation to meaning.

Derrida establishes the primacy of *différance,* an idiosyncratic word generated by Derrida in combining the French words for differing and deferring. The term captures Saussure's sense of meanings that emerge through difference and meanings that are constantly deferred through the endless play of signs. Difference (with Derrida's inflection of *différance*) appears in various guises throughout the philosophical tradition. In keeping with the Derrida/Saussure notion of difference as requisite in establishing meaning, Heidegger's concept of Being relies substantially on his ability to establish the difference between beings and Being. Derrida uses this simple point to establish the primacy of difference over Being; difference is prior to Being, which is imbued with notions of difference: "It is the domination of beings that *différance* everywhere comes to solicit. . . . Therefore it is the determination of Being as presence or as beingness that is interrogated by the thought of *différance*. Such a question could not emerge and be understood unless the *différance* between Being and beings were somewhere to be broached."[90]

But identifying *différance* does not invoke the same celebration as Heidegger accords to Being. According to Derrida, *différance* "governs nothing, reigns over nothing, and nowhere exercises any authority. It is not announced by any capital letter. Not only is there no kingdom of *différance*, but *différance* instigates and subverts the subversion of every kingdom."[91] Nevertheless, lest we despise *différance*, Derrida asserts that it is older than Being: "Since Being has never had a 'meaning,' has never been thought or said as such, except by dissimulating itself in beings, then *différance*, in a certain and very strange way, (is) 'older' than the ontological difference or than the truth of Being."[92] Derrida relates this assertion to his notion of trace, further undermining any suggestion of Being as a primary and basic entity.

When it has this age it can be called the play of the trace. The play of a trace which no longer belongs to the horizon of Being, but whose play transports and encloses the meaning of Being: the play of the trace, or the *différance*, which has no meaning and is not. Which does not belong. There is no maintaining, and no depth to, this bottomless chessboard on which Being is put into play.[93]

Of course, lest we then establish the primordiality of trace and difference we must also let go of such concepts. They, too, are under erasure, according to Derrida: "As rigorously as possible we must permit to appear/disappear the trace of what exceeds the truth of Being. The trace (of that) which can never be presented, the trace which itself can never be presented: that is, appear and manifest itself, as such, in its phenomenon."[94] How is difference prior to Being? According to Derrida, Heidegger asserts that the difference between Being and beings has been forgotten in the philosophical tradition: "What Heidegger wants to mark is this: the difference between Being and beings, the forgotten of metaphysics, has disappeared without leaving a trace."[95] This amounts to a disappearance of the trace of the trace: "Since the trace is not a presence but the simulacrum of a presence that dislocates itself, displaces itself, refers itself, it properly has no site—erasure belongs to its structure."[96]

Reiterating what we have already said about difference as a phenomenon of language, we see that difference is implicated in the deconstruction of presence and hence metaphysics.

The paradox of such a structure, in the language of metaphysics, is an inversion of metaphysical concepts, which produces the following effect: the present becomes the sign of the sign, the trace of the trace. It is no longer what every reference refers to in the last analysis. It becomes a function in a structure of generalized reference. It is a trace, and a trace of the erasure of the trace.[97]

And for Heidegger's pursuit of Being, "That there is not a proper essence of *différance* at this point, implies that there is neither a Being nor truth of the play of writing such as it engages *différance*."[98]

If the illusive and endless play of difference precedes Being, then what of technology, Being's latest revelation, the essence of which is the enframing? For Derrida, Heidegger's characterization of the problem of technology provides further evidence of his logocentrism. Derrida explores this in an article about the political dimensions of Heidegger's concept of *Geschlecht*, a dynamic human community pursuing freedom.[99] The decisive concept is that of the hand. In his essay "What is called thinking?" Heidegger shows that it is the hand that distinguishes the human community from the animals.[100] Of course, references to the hand feature prominently in Heidegger's writing—through his notions of readiness-to-hand and presence-at-hand, as describing two modes through which we relate to the world as things or objects, and through his elevation of craft/making, *poiesis*.

As Derrida points out, "The hand cannot be spoken about without speaking of technics."[101] So, an understanding of Heidegger on the hand provides insights into his understanding of technology.

In *Parmenides*, Heidegger presents the familiar complaint about technology, in this case, how the typewriter destroys language.[102]

Derrida summarizes Heidegger: "Typographic mechanization destroys the unity of the word, this integral identity, this proper integrity of the spoken word that writing manuscripts, at once because it
appears closer to the voice or body proper and because it ties together the letters, conserves and gathers together."[103] In "What is
called thinking?" Heidegger declares that thinking is a form of
handwork. What does this mean? This is not simply thinking with
one's hands. Derrida brings out several points. The first is that thinking is not cerebral but corporeal, a point frequently made by pragmatists and phenomenologists in countering Platonism. Second,
Heidegger distinguishes between useful service for profit (as exemplified in the professions) and the authentic handwork of the skilled
craftsperson. Making cabinets for the market is an example of a professional activity. It is concerned with tools and use value. In the craft
of joinery, the joiner is engaged with the essence of the wood rather
than with the tools and use value. Elsewhere Heidegger describes
the skill of the silversmith or the joiner in providing a clearing for
the work to disclose. Third, Heidegger equates handwork with authentic thought: "The hand thinks before being thought; it is
thought, a thought, thinking."[104] There is calculation and logic (the
ontic mode of thought, which is to thinking what cabinet making is
to joinery), and there is authentic thinking (thinking as craft).[105]

As Derrida indicates, Heidegger's writing is imbued with concern
about modes of presence and the hand. In the mode of presence-
at-hand, objects have calculable properties, potentially exploitable.
In the mode of readiness-to-hand, the available equipment of the
workshop is presented to awareness only fleetingly in the event of
breakdown, which is arguably translatable to Heidegger's later concern with things—a thing is what gathers. The hand relates to *objects*
as presence-at-hand; it relates to *things* as ready-to-hand.[106] Heidegger
is intent on rehabilitating the ancient concept of *techne* (technique)
as a kind of craft and making (*poiesis*) that lets things be and lets
truth disclose itself in the artifact, as opposed to the modern kind
of technical production, which imposes control and is governed by
concepts of causality.

In Heidegger's discussion, the hand is implicitly valorized. Au-
thenticity pertains to the degree to which the hand is implicated in

what we do and think. (Doing and thinking are indistinguishable in this pragmatic strand to Heidegger.) In this discourse, writing by hand is also presented as superior to mechanical type production. Extrapolating from Heidegger, we see a hierarchy that begins somewhere in bodily immediacy and progresses to the disabling media of modern communications, the former is present, the latter is supplemental, derivative, and encumbering. Though Heidegger is valorizing hand writing over mechanical type production, Derrida interprets Heidegger as presenting a degradation of writing in general in favor of speech.[107] For Heidegger, the hand and speech are the site of presence: "So one sees being organized around the hand and speech, with a very strong coherence, all the traits whose incessant recurrence I have elsewhere recalled under the name logocentricism."[108] According to Derrida, Heidegger's writing is imbued with logocentrism, Heidegger's writing on technology presents an example of the privileging of speech over writing, further evidence of Heidegger's logocentrism.

Derrida and Radical Hermeneutics

Heidegger scholars challenge Derrida on many points.[109] One of the most telling criticisms is from Caputo and focuses on where these various discussions about writing and Being lead us. In the case of Derrida, we are led to a point of admitting that Heidegger is, in spite of his own strategies to establish the contrary, operating within a mode of philosophical discourse that is, after all, logocentric. Heidegger has not finally resolved anything. The case is still open. We are thereby convinced of the endless play that is philosophy and language. If we read Heidegger without Derrida, however, we are led toward another conclusion: the necessity for openness to the mystery of Being, to inquire into the nature of things, including technology.

Caputo reminds us that Heidegger sees the history of metaphysics as the history of Being, in other words, the history of thinking about being: "Metaphysical thinking is a certain preoccupation with present entities to the neglect of Being itself."[110] This neglect involves a readiness to investigate beingness without thinking of Being. Even then, if we can contemplate Being, it is Being as an entity, as opposed to Being as "under erasure." Or the tradition may pursue Being and miss out on the withdrawal of Being (*Ereignis*). One of Heidegger's most controversial and difficult points is that Being has withdrawn, and metaphysics is oblivious to this withdrawal. Metaphysics is about what is *given* and is oblivious to notions of withdrawal—the withholding that makes the giving possible. The symptom of the withdrawal of Being is the technological, causal, instrumental way of looking at things that pervades all contemporary thought, the enframing—the essence of technology, according to Heidegger. We are no longer capable of contemplating the mystery within things. But this is not of our doing. Hence Heidegger's elaboration on the matter of Being. It is Being that has withdrawn. We are not, and never were, in control. The quest for control, as outlined in chapter 2, is itself a delusion of metaphysics.

For Heidegger, to overcome metaphysics is to awaken to the fact that Being has withdrawn. But Being does not cease withdrawing when we are awakened to this fact. We are caught up in this withdrawal, as in a "receding tide." Under the metaphysical tradition, we are preoccupied with entities (beings), and, as tinkerers with technological objects, we are enframed. We see everything in technological terms. We cannot overcome the withdrawal of Being. That is beyond us. However, we can overcome *obliviousness* to the withdrawal of Being. We can "know about" the withdrawal. "We stand in it and acknowledge its sway."[111] Caputo summarizes the situation thus: "Metaphysical thinking is overcome but the withdrawal of Being persists. It is recognized for what it is. We stand in it and acknowledge its sway. What has been overcome is the naïveté, the obliviousness of metaphysical thought."[112] Invoking the mystical tradition of Eckhart and others, Heidegger maintains that we are not to overcome Being's withdrawal but to participate in it in a more radical way, by seeing the depths of the abyss—the nonground. Caputo summarizes the argument thus: "The point of what Heidegger calls thought is not to overcome or lay aside this withdrawal but to enter into it in a more radical way. When Dasein is 'awakened' it is not 'enlightened,' suffused with light, but rather alerted to the bottomless depths of the darkness and the withdrawal."[113] Heidegger denotes this response to the withdrawal of Being with the ancient

German word *Gelassenheit*, which translates as "letting be." Caputo offers the following summary of the nature of letting be:

> The response of Dasein to the transcendence/withdrawal of Being is what Heidegger calls *Gelassenheit*: letting go, letting be: that movement in which Dasein [the thinking being who inquires into its own being], having let go of its own representations, releases itself into the essential movement which is at work in Western history. *Gelassenheit* is the experience of the power which overpowers Dasein, not by its violence, but by its retreat and withdrawal. That is why Heidegger calls *Gelassenheit* "openness to the mystery." It lets the mystery be *as* a mystery, experiences it *in* its mysteriousness, lets it hold sway precisely as a withdrawal.[114]

According to Caputo, the significance of this mystical notion of letting be in Heidegger's writing escapes Derrida's attention: "And it is this moment of *Gelassenheit* that I locate the most extreme divergence of Derrida from Heidegger. In *Gelassenheit*, man is de-centred in favour of a centering on Being or *Ereignis* as the gentle power which withdraws."[115] That is, for Heidegger, the transcendental signified, the ground, presence (metaphysics) is the withdrawal of Being. The response is letting be, seeing metaphysics for what it is.

To Derrida, these concepts speak of supplement and deferral; the response to these reflections on Being's withdrawal is a recognition of the violence of language. Caputo summarizes Derrida's position as follows:

> For Derrida the failure of metaphysics to keep the promise of presence means that we are left holding a kind of grammatological bag, a shell, a web of signs, a differential system. The absential dimension is not the withdrawal *of* Being but the simple failure of Being to make itself felt. Absence is not the gentle power of withdrawal, the mystery concealed within things, but the vacuity of signs, the systematic displacement of things with their place-holders, the necessity of the supplement, the substitute, writing. Derrida moves from the failure of presence, not into the transcendence and recessive mystery of things, but into the indefinite play of differential systems, of infinitely interchangeable interpretations. He proposes not the gentle openness of *Gelassenheit* which accedes to the mystery within things, but the violence of language.[116]

For Derrida, thought lacks gravity, because it does not serve anything but the transient entity of presence—hence Derrida's playful and sometimes cavalier use of language. For Heidegger, on the contrary, thought serves the mystery within things: "Heidegger has broken the spell of the metaphysics of presence precisely in order to harken to the mystery within things, the recessive, withdrawn dimension within them in virtue of which things elude every scheme which representational thought can draw up."[117] Derrida suppresses and tames this vital aspect of Heidegger's writing.

Following Caputo's argument, whether we heed Derrida or Heidegger makes a difference. Derrida provides a potent critique of logocentrism that can be applied to the modern account of technological disruption. Derrida provides ammunition against certain notions of language that permeate technological research and development programs, programs that present IT in a particular light, that assume that we are in control of technology, that promote technology as an outcome of the development of theory, that suggest that technology is an extension of ourselves—a supplement to the presence that is immediate bodily engagement. Derrida's arguments provide a clearing by dispensing with what has been written about technology in certain ways. But for the technologist who would rather design or make than be concerned with writing, there is less to grasp on to. The study of Derrida's writing inevitably leads to a focus on language. Derrida is logocentric in the ordinary use of the word—he focuses on words. In contrast, Heidegger draws us away from the peculiarities of words and wordplay and into the realm of practice—crafting (*techne*) and making (*poiesis*). We will return to this theme in the final section of this chapter.[118]

What does Derrida have to offer in our reflections on technology? In his later work, *Radical Hermeneutics*, Caputo embraces Derrida's project with greater enthusiasm. The intrigue of Derrida's writing is less in the details of his tortured arguments against Heidegger's logocentrism as in his advocacy of play, a theme also developed at length by Gadamer.[119] The "essential Derrida" is the Derrida who shows us how to keep the game in play. Lest we think that Heidegger has said the last word on Being or against logocentrism, Derrida reconvenes the game by indicating Heidegger's own logocentrism. As indicated by Caputo, this is a game that celebrates flux and change. Whereas Plato elevated the immutable, the unchanging, to the place of privilege in the realm of ideas, above the fluctuating uncertainty of the temporal world, deconstruction inverts this. According to Caputo, there are no underlying structures on which we build knowledge. The reverse is the case: "Structures are but inscribed on the flux";[120] "In the end, I want to say, science, action, art and religious belief make their way by a free play and creative movement whose dynamics baffle the various discourses on method."[121] This is not some statement of despair or futility. Caputo argues this is "the only really sensible, or reasonable, view of reason."[122] The elevation of play represents a profound reversal of the priorities of the ordering mind. The elevation of play is not vague, frivolous, or inconsequential. It results in a redefinition, or decentering, of subjectivity: "[T]he phenomenon of play destroys the traditional concept of self as substantial entity and reveals the self as an openness to various possibilities . . . a self process which never stops being a process in play."[123] According to Gadamer, the "players are not the subjects of play; instead play merely reaches presentation through the players."[124]

Meaning is disclosed in the ongoing play of signs. But it is the play of indeterminate meanings. "The stability of every meaning is undermined by the shifting play of signifiers."[125] Gallagher describes the play thus: "[E]very 'truth' that the interpreter closes in on becomes one of the plurality of fictions which constitute the play of differences within the system."[126] According to Caputo, the task of understanding is "to keep the trembling and endless mirror play, of signs and texts in play,"[127] lest meanings become fixed by the tradition.

Deconstruction is subversive but not irrational.[128] Derrida and Caputo talk of the "double gesture": combining professional rigor and competence with the subversion of the foundations of the professions:[129] "Institutions are the way things get done, and they are prone to violence. . . . Nothing is innocent."[130] These insights are applicable to design. The design, development, use, and integration of technologies and technological systems is less a matter of control than of artfully playing a role in a vast game—though in the case of IT, the nature of the game is more readily grasped through the metaphors of interpretation and praxis.

IT Praxis

So far in this discussion, we have outlined several responses to information technology and the critique afforded each of them by deconstruction. The first is the conservative or modern view that there are underlying truths that are being promoted or subverted by IT. The second is the critical view, as exemplified by Baudrillard: we are living in a world of delusion brought about in the technological age. The third is the position of McLuhan that IT is introducing radical changes for the better. We think differently thanks to the technologies we use and their involvement in senses of hearing and vision. The fourth is Heidegger's view that the essence of technology is the enframing to which we should respond by attending to the mysteries within things.

The response of deconstruction is to (1) present alternative language paradigms that deal with the concepts of origins, authorship, meaning reference, and truth content on which the modern rhetoric of technological disruption depends; (2) challenge the primacy accorded to writing over speech, presenting speech as a kind of protowriting; (3) reveal the metaphysical, logocentric element in philosophical and other writings; and (4) furnish us with techniques, largely through example, of how to generate "subversive" discourse that challenges the foundations even as they are being built.

What then of the concerns expressed in the modern account of technological disruption—about problems of significance, truth, and meaning brought about by IT? Is it of no consequence what words, images, and data signify? Do we not need to be concerned about truthful records and honest reporting? Are paintings, photographs, and computer images indistinguishable after all? Can we no longer speak of people as intending anything by their actions? Derrida says little about such matters, but deconstruction provides a valuable clearing for a reconsideration of the issues.

Derrida's talk of trace and difference leads in a particular direction of inquiry—meaning is in difference, a signified is but a trace, and so on. But there are other ways of talking about language, other metaphors that open different lines of inquiry. To say that the signifier does not map onto a referent, but means what it means by virtue of the play of difference, is to say that the signifier means what it means by virtue of its context.[131]

Opening the discussion to matters of context changes the emphasis from grammatology to community. It again places the emphasis on hermeneutics, the theme of Heidegger's that Gadamer promoted most vigorously.[132] As we have seen, hermeneutics focuses on the ubiquity of interpretation and on the contextual, historical, and social nature of any interpretive situation. As interpreter, one is both constrained and enabled by one's historical situation and one's prejudices. There are strands within Gadamer's thought that seek to disable the force of the Enlightenment's "prejudice against prejudice" and to locate method and logic as subservient to rhetoric and dialogue. Gadamer's understanding of the way interpretation proceeds also invokes the metaphors of dialogue and play.[133]

Where one stands in relation to interpretation brings out the various differences evident in contemporary philosophy. According to Gallagher, who applies hermeneutics to educational practice, the issue of interpretation comes down to the problem of "ambiguity and the finitude of understanding."[134] For Gallagher, the truth about interpretation lies in recognizing "the fundamental ambiguity of interpretation."[135] How do we address the problem of ambiguity? Gallagher's view is that conservative theory (the modern account of technological disruption) seeks to deny or partition ambiguity, critical theory (Baudrillard's simulacrum) seeks to control it by disarming the power that generates it, radical theory (deconstruction) celebrates and elevates it, and moderate theory (Gadamer's hermeneutics) acknowledges that we always have generated and promoted, and will continue to generate and promote, understandings according to the workings of the tacit conventions of the interpretive communities within which we are situated, in spite of, and possibly because of, the play of ambiguity.[136]

According to Gallagher's moderate position, the handling of ambiguity brings us back to the primacy of conversation and community, a theme developed by such writers as Kuhn, Foucault, Rorty, and Fish.[137] Rorty applies to philosophy the view developed by Kuhn (and, from a different tradition, Foucault) of the dependence of science and philosophy on the conversational, experimental, discursive, and other practices of communities. He develops the theme of the primacy of conversation in philosophy. For Rorty, the objective in philosophy is not to have the last word, rather it is to keep the conversation going. He posits this as a requirement of wisdom: "as consisting in the ability to sustain a conversation."[138]

How does the notion of interpretive communities address the modern account of technological disruption? It speaks to the issues of origins, verification, and intention. First, the modern account of technological disruption focuses on the distinctiveness of the originary moment—the original moment of creating an art work, composing a string of text, making a scientific observation, taking a photograph, or capturing some data. There is clearly a privileging of the originary moment in human praxis as a pivotal event. There are ample explanations of how this is so. For Derrida, the origin is present and all else follows as a supplement. Our concern with origins is conditioned by our logocentrism. From a different tradition, Lakoff accounts for the significance afforded to such moments as residing in the nature of metaphor and metonymy.[139] We favor metaphors of journey, progression, and linearity, and we take the simple moment of the journey's beginning as standing for the whole journey. Once we see the notion of an origin in this light, as contingent on historical, philosophical, and even metaphorical orientations, then we are in a position to study any particular identification of an originary moment.

For example, Sontag's description of photography provides a telling account of the praxis of taking photographs germane to computer imagery and information processing.[140] In photography, we favor the brief instant when the shutter opens and closes as the crucial originary moment. Without it there would be no picture.[141] But the identification of the originary moment depends simply on the context in which we wish to talk about origins. So, there may be different contexts and, therefore, different senses in which we speak of an origin. Or we may choose *not* to speak of an origin. This is the interesting contribution of deconstruction: where we choose to drop a conventional and limited metaphor (such as the metaphor of origins) and think anew about the phenomena of photography and computer imagery.

It may not be the origin that is of interest but the technological sophistication of some particular moment in a process. Or it may be that photography and computer imaging are not different because the former has an originary moment and the latter does not, but because photography is more often under the control of a single person, whereas computer imagery is often not. The "threat" of computer imagery is the challenge it poses to the professional and technical competence of practitioners of image making. Computer imagery challenges the modes of practice through which we understand our roles.

With respect to the originary moment, much of the modern account of technological disruption focuses on validity—the integrity of the originary moment. The Derridean recognition of the mimetic chain does not absolve us from questions of truth and falsity or deception. Far from it. In placing the moment of image capture in a context, we also place questions of verisimilitude in a context.[142] The picture is accurate or truthful for what purpose? It is a faithful record for whom and to what end? To decide on the accuracy of an image is to make a judgment—to enter into a long history of practices whereby we weigh evidence, appeal to precedent, follow the norms of our expert communities, indulge in debate, and involve ourselves in the situation, understood through the ancient intellectual virtue of *phronesis*. There are no "objective criteria" for deciding the matter, as though by algorithm; if we are able to generate criteria, they make sense only in an interpretive context. A photograph may be deemed more accurate than a painting in some situations but not in others. We need to know the credentials of the people involved, the nature of the technology, and what use will be made of the judgment; we need to be already inculcated into a set of practices, judgmental, technical, and otherwise. To assert that such judgments are always contingent is not to say that it does not matter or that we can think as we please, any more than a member of a scientific community can formulate theories independently of the theories and practices of that community.

We can say similar things about intention. Some ways of looking at actions obviate the need for intention, as in Heidegger's characterization of unreflective involvement in the world, notions of tacit knowledge, the pragmatic line on action as a form of thinking, Wittgenstein's identification of the elusive nature of intention in language, and Dreyfus's notion (borrowed from Heidegger) that we simply take over practices rather than act intentionally.[143] An intention is constructed in a context. We can speak about our intentions in making a painting, in composing a photograph, or in manipulating data in a computer. An intentional explanation may present itself differently in different contexts of explanation. When intention is removed as a criterion that distinguishes art from photography or from algorithmic manipulation on a computer, then we can focus on the different uses of technologies as tools. The difference between a painting and an ideal photograph or a computer image is not that one is a product of intention, the other a product of algorithm. It is people who make and store pictures and data in the context of their practices. Sometimes they do so in paint with very careful strokes of a brush, at other times by sending satellites into orbit to relay digital images back to earthbound computers. In the latter case, a vast technological system is devised and brought into play.

A further difference is that in the case of painting by hand, we are engaged in a human praxis, a tradition in which we are able to say we know what is going on. In the case of advanced technological systems, they sometimes appear to be "out of control"; in other words, we do not have a well-established praxis that incorporates them. According to Giddens, there is a breakdown in the systems of trust we have set up.[144] This brings us back to Heidegger's notion of technological enframing. We live in an age in which we think we are in control, but we clearly are not.

This emphasis on praxis and interpretation is what we are left with when Derrida's project against metaphysics is worked through. We cannot appeal to foundational principles and indisputable criteria, but we can appeal to a complex web or constellation that is human praxis,[145] an IT praxis that now incorporates as elements in the game the discourse of the analytical philosopher's quest for truth and validity through algorithm, critical theory's political skepticism, technological determinism's hope for the global village, Heidegger's *Gelassenheit*, and Derrida's deconstruction.

Deconstruction and Information Technology

Summary

I have investigated the contribution of deconstruction to an understanding of information technology. The chapter began by presenting two different accounts of a major disruption in thinking. The first, the modern account of disruption, asserts that such technologies as advanced electronic communications are challenging and breaking apart long-accepted values and preconceptions about reliability, truth, the intellect, place, and community. According to this account, technology and science are the source and driving force of this disruption. We are advised by those who promote the modern account to develop better understandings of technology and science (particularly pertaining to information technology) in order to develop appropriate modes of thinking.

The second account of disruption announces and develops the implications of the end of metaphysics and is the discourse of postmodernity. Metaphysics is that branch of philosophy concerned with establishing and investigating the ground and basis for all things—primary causes and origins. To give credence to the project of metaphysics is termed logocentrism. Postmodern rhetoric, which is against metaphysics and logocentrism, is well represented by the style of discourse promoted by Jacques Derrida, building on Nietzsche and Heidegger, known as deconstruction. I showed how deconstruction dampens the impetus of the modern rhetoric, which it identifies as logocentric. Deconstruction demonstrates the ubiquity of reproduction in language and art (mimesis), the complex and elusive relationship between the word (sign) and the thing it "represents" (signified), and the elusive nature of meaning. Deconstruction shows that these phenomena are not new or merely products of the electronic age but imbue the entire workings of thought and language. Language cannot operate without them. I examined some of the claims made about electronic communications in this light.

With this introduction to deconstruction, I was in a position to analyze its more powerful claims. I demonstrated how much of the rhetoric about information technology (including the concerns listed above) is permeated with metaphysics (logocentrism), that is, the quest for stability, some primal truth, an origin, or an immutable point of reference. Derrida interprets metaphysics as a concern with presence as opposed to the absent, the supplementary. I followed Derrida's demonstration of the contradictions inherent within logocentrism.

Derrida's challenge to metaphysics also extends to Heidegger's writing about Being. The notion of Being is vital in Heidegger's conception of technology. In spite of Heidegger's identification of the metaphysical element in Nietzsche and his sophisticated project against metaphysics and logocentrism, Derrida sees Heidegger as trapped within logocentrism, particularly in his writing about the primordiality of Being. I traced through Derrida's argument and touched on the implications for Heidegger's notions of technology. The apogee of Derrida's writing is therefore to challenge Heidegger from within and using the very deconstructive strategy that Heidegger championed. Deconstruction is therefore powerful, influential, and strongly influences our views of information technology at several levels: the critique it offers to conventional views of communication, in its challenge to metaphysics, and in its challenge to Heidegger's notions of Being.

On the way down from this summit (Derrida's clash with Heidegger), I encountered such Heidegger scholars as Caputo and Sheehan, who indicate Derrida's blindness to Heidegger's main point, which is to make a clearing for us to appreciate the mystery within things. In contrast, Derrida simply leaves us with a sense of being forever confounded by the vagaries of language. In the case of Heidegger, we are presented with a recognition of the enframing nature of technology and a working within it or past it to encounter things—in their essence and in their mystery. In the case of Derrida, we are presented with information technology's rendering obvious what has always been the case with language.

But Heidegger scholars like Caputo do not forsake Derrida. The essential Derrida is the Derrida who wants ideas to be in endless play, who shows the primacy of the flux, the complex interaction between convention and its subversion, and who also points to a "demythologized" Heidegger. This is radical hermeneutics.

Further in the descent from Derrida's wrestling with Heidegger, I showed that deconstruction presents another view of the hermeneutical enterprise. Hermeneutics is the study of interpretation. The study of hermeneutics provides a useful site for testing the differences among philosophical positions. I outlined how, at the level of our praxis, Derrida's special terminology of presence, trace, *différance*, and the like, are potent metaphorical supplements to the hermeneutical themes of context, dialogue, and community. The difference is that the hermeneutical metaphors open the discussion to interpretive praxis and community, features of language underplayed in Derrida's radical hermeneutics. The message about information technology, therefore, comes back to issues of interpretation and praxis, but with new insights.

Armed with these insights, we are in a position to examine further some of the claims made of information technology. With our pragmatic emphasis on community, it is tempting to see information technology as a means of sustaining and promoting community, as suggested by McLuhan, and of creating space. In total the claim is that information technology generates a world. The examination of information technology worlds brings us to an inevitable encounter with the phenomenological concept of world, as expounded by Heidegger.

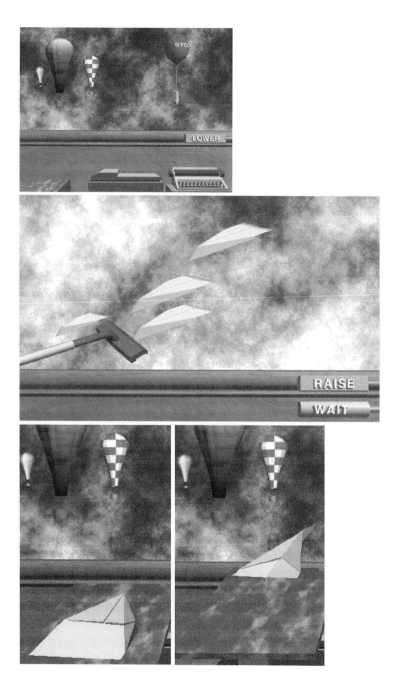

A fanciful animated multimedia interface to the cyberspace world of Internet e-mail by Zoltan Nemes Nemeth. The reader is suspended from a hot air balloon and intercepts messages from the maelstrom of flying paper airplanes with a vacuum cleaner. The balloon basket conveniently contains a typewriter and photocopier for dispatching messages into the maelstrom.

4

Where in the World Is Cyberspace?

The Phenomenology of Computer-Mediated Communications

The term "cyberspace" denotes the environment created by computerized communications networks.[1] Examples of such networks in the telephone system, local-area networks (LANs)—in which several computers are connected together in the same room or the same building for the passage of information, to share processing, or to facilitate communication—and wide-area networks (WANs), such as the Internet system (the international network of networks for academics and researchers), for the same activities across national and global networks. As with the telephone system, WANs tend to be organized so that there are many devices and routes through which connections can be made between computers (satellite links and land lines). This routing is under computer control, and it is generally not relevant to any user of the network how the connections are being made at any particular moment. The physical configuration of components is independent of the "functional configuration." Physical distance is also largely irrelevant in such networks. In the case of the Internet, Australia and New Zealand may each appear to be "closer" (response times are faster) to the West Coast of the United States than they are to each other, because most Pacific "traffic" is currently relayed through the West Coast. Communications proximity is largely a matter of where the control nodes happen to be located, which is in turn a product of the history of the development of the various parts of the network.

The Internet, or rather its precursor ARPANET, was originally developed with national defense in mind. The Internet does not have a vulnerable central control point, and there are many ways information can be routed between nodes. It is widely recognized that since the 1960s the network, its features, and its patterns of use have grown from the "bottom up." There has been no master plan, and it has been developed by the users of the system. The Internet is regarded largely as a grassroots phenomenon.

Until recently, for instantaneous communication between individuals, the Internet could only handle text-based communications. People communicated via instant "telegrams"—e-mail or "on-line chat," typed into a computer console. This use of text only is due to bandwidth limitations—limits on the volume of traffic the network can handle. With incremental improvements to the network and the development of sophisticated communications standards, it is now possible to engage in limited, but instant, communications via video, shared drawing and writing environments ("shared whiteboards") and sound, through the Internet system. The Internet now embraces such notions as computer conferencing, video conferencing, and computer-supported collaborative work (CSCW). The Internet (World Wide Web) is also becoming a "multimedia" environment. This designation "multimedia" is also a recognition of the increasingly amorphous nature of information technology.[2] A computer can assume a range of roles within a vast media matrix.

Computerized communications networks are now assuming many of the attributes we normally associate with the mass media—radio, television, and newspapers. We can characterize the mass media as what becomes of writing and the pictorial arts under the influence of mechanical and electronic reproduction—or mass production.[3] What are the characteristics of the mass media?[4] The mass media are concerned with reproduction—information is generated, copied, and reproduced many times over. They are concerned with dissemination—information is distributed widely, through media networks. The mass media involve editorial control—information received is not distributed indiscriminately but is moderated, sorted, and censored by editors, editorial boards, or referees. The mass media are ubiquitous—their artifacts are to be found in homes, workplaces, and as part of the landscape, as billboards, video displays, and radio and television broadcasts picked up on car radios, portable stereos, and portable televisions. The mass media are public—information is generally distributed indiscriminately or to "news groups" rather than used privately. Some aspects of the mass media display portability—products of the media (newspapers, magazines, portable radios, etc.) can be acquired and carried around by individuals. The mass media are ephemeral—the content of the mass media often has a short life, perhaps it is archived or repeated, but generally it is never to be revisited (newspapers have a life of one day, radio broadcasts a life of several minutes). Finally, the mass media are impressionistic—at their most characteristic, they generally trade in quick impressions rather than precisely crafted and accurate information.

The confluence of computerized communications and the mass media brings about an entity with certain emerging characteristics. The mass media have been interactive for a long time—with letters to the editor, talk-back radio, and the broadcasting of home videos on television programs—but now there is the possibility of sophisticated synchronous (real-time) interaction through computer networks, such as on-line bulletin boards and teletext.[5] The electronic mass media have the potential, therefore, to be highly interactive. The electronic mass media now rely substantially on computer networking. Computer networks, telecommunications, and media networks are merging.[6] The new mass media also increasingly rely on digital data manipulation: desktop publishing, digital image capture and manipulation, multimedia systems, talking books, and the use of CD-ROMs (digital compact disks).

According to some commentators, the mass media traditionally operated as "one-to-many" communication—one source, many recipients. The new emerging mass medium is "many-to-many"—any individual can instantly communicate with another individual or to a group. As such, the new mass media are thought to have the potential to revitalize the democratizing power once accorded to newspapers and broadcasting, which have more recently been usurped by commitments to partisan interests.[7] The new mass media herald a new democratizing force for reconstituting the Enlightenment ideal of the active and informed public.

Electronic communications and the mass media are also implicated in new conceptions of the computer as providing a total immersion environment.[8] Experiments in "virtual reality" are thought to herald a possible future in which our senses are plugged into a virtual world of information. This world has features of the physical world. It is said that we will enjoy the physical sensation of moving through simulated physical environments (buildings and landscapes), move through abstract information (such as medical records) as though it were transparent to all of the senses, and interact with other people as though we are with them, and assuming whatever role, status, and physical form suits us. We will be able to choose the role, status and physical form through which people "see" us.

Cyberspace is a vast media matrix of the actual and the potential that incorporates the activities of telephone conversations, data transfer, electronic mail, computerized financial transactions, ATM (automatic teller machine) transactions, on-line information services, video conferencing, the new mass media, virtual reality, and so on. The strangeness, power, ubiquity, and potential of this phenomenon has prompted commentators to see cyberspace as a kind of world in its own right. Cyberspace has been described thus:

Cyberspace: The juncture of digital information and human perception, the "matrix" of civilization where banks exchange money (credit) and information seekers navigate layers of data stored and represented in virtual space. Buildings in cyberspace may have more dimensions than physical buildings do, and cyberspace may reflect different laws of existence. It has been said that cyberspace is where you are when you are having a phone conversation or where your ATM [automatic teller machine] money exists. It is where electronic mail travels, and it resembles the Toontown in the movie *Roger Rabbit*.[9]

It is widely recognized among cyberspace commentators that there is a utopian strand to the development of electronic communications.[10] Cyberspace promises a bright and exciting technological future of unfettered communication and a reinvigoration of liberal and democratic community. The same commentators also indicate the possible dystopia of a cyberspace future in which not everyone enjoys equal access to cyberspace. This would produce a further disparity between the "haves" and the "have nots." Cyberspace users may also lose touch with reality. We may be producing a race of cyberspace "junkies" who eschew authentic, grounded, material pleasures in favor of the artificial, safe world of computer simulations and fleeting electronic encounters with other individuals. Whether the future is hopeful or grim, the basic assumption is that the cyberspace phenomenon is significant and powerful. Part of its power is in its ability to make space.

Cyberspace is thought to be space making in two senses: it shapes the physical infrastructure and physical form of our settlements, cities, and landscape; and it makes space within its own virtual environment. When you are using a computer, you are in cyberspace.

What is the ontological status of this strange and powerful entity? In the rest of this chapter, I compare the claims made about the cyberspace phenomenon with established commentary on space. In the process, I will answer the question "what and where is cyberspace?" What is the relationship between cyberspace and "real space," the space we inhabit in this universe?

According to most media and communications commentators, the most obvious relationship between cyberspace and "real space" is that electronic networks alter the effects of distance.[11] The ability for two people to engage in unmediated (face-to-face) communication is obviously sensitive to distance; a separation of a few miles, as opposed to a separation of a few yards, makes face-to-face communication impossible. Talking on the telephone is not exactly like having the other person in the same room, but whether or not the communicators are in the same country or speaking across the ocean makes little difference—except for the costs involved and that only a few more digits have to be entered on the telephone. This indifference to distance is even more pronounced with straight data transfer. A bank account in Sydney can be accessed immediately through an automatic teller machine in Boston. This reduction of distance is a phenomenon of the moment, when two people are in communication or as data is being exchanged. But the effects of communication networks on distance is said to extend beyond the communication event to a whole social milieu.

According to McLuhan, the mass media and electronic communications are ushering in a global village.[12] The world now seems smaller and assumes some of the characteristics of preindustrial village society. McLuhan maintains that people across the world are more involved with each other—"we wear all mankind as our skin." A concern for the world as a whole is comparable to the concern members of village society have for their own community.

Another aspect of the reduction of distance is that we are not bound to particular locations for particular tasks. Meyrowitz draws the analogy with nomadic rather than village society: "Many of the features of our 'information age' make us resemble the most primitive of social and political forms: the hunting and gathering society. As nomadic peoples, hunters and gatherers have no loyal relationship to territory. . . . [S]pecific activities and behaviors are not tightly fixed to specific physical settings."[13] Meyrowitz identifies some of the similarities between modern and nomadic society. Both tend to be egalitarian in terms of the roles of males and females, children and adults, leaders and followers: "The difficulty of maintaining many 'separate places,' or distinct social spheres, tends to involve everyone in everyone else's business."[14] So, electronic communications are said to substantially alter the effects of distance, which in turn has profound social ramifications.

Electronic networks do not only reduce distance. The claim is that they also define or invoke space—"cyberspace is where you are when you are having a phone conversation or where your ATM money exists."[15] Cyberspace is something that people or objects can be *in*. In what sense? Cyberspace as space invokes a range of notions—electronic communications as environment, context, domain, universe, background, medium, setting, situation, territory, area, region, province, sphere, system, realm, location, and site. Here I will concentrate on three key concepts: world, space, and place. These terms have wide currency, they have a substantial pedigree in philosophical discourse, and they cover most of the other concepts just listed. Cyberspace commonly refers to several senses in which we use the words "world," "space," and "place."

Cyberspace refers to the several senses in which we commonly speak of *world*.[16] I will consider the common uses of "world" before considering the deeper, more provocative, phenomenological use to be explored later. First, we commonly speak of *the* world as the total collection of physical entities. In the case of cyberspace, there is the world of objects, such as hardware, cabling, computer programs, and connections, the equipment of cyberspace. Cyberspace/world is here a subset of the common use of "world" as all physical entities.

Second, cyberspace is also a world in the sense in which we talk about the world of business, academia, music, or sports—in the sense of a community and its practices. In cyberspace, you have to do things in certain ways. In the case of automatic teller machines, the conventions for use are very strict. In the case of e-mail on the Internet, some very intricate conventions have developed for polite communication. There are also differentiations within cyberspace society: for example, "hackers" have full mastery of the technicalities of the system; "moderators" order, censor, and distribute material to user groups; and "lurkers" watch and listen to what is going on in the network without otherwise participating. As with any such world, there is also a specific terminology and language—all the trappings of a community. But cyberspace is a world as community in ways other than those enjoyed by business people and hobbyists (railway enthusiasts, stamp collectors, sports fans, and the like). The claim is that electronic communications facilitate creating community through the technology itself. Telephone users rarely constitute a community simply because of a common interest in telephones. The telephone is a tool of, or a means to, community. Writers like Rheingold make strong claims about this communal aspect of computer networks: "[W]henever CMC [computer-mediated communication] technology becomes available to people anywhere, they inevitably build virtual communities with it, just as microorganisms inevitably create colonies."[17] Furthermore, "the future of the Net [the Internet] is connected to the future of community, democracy, education, science, and intellectual life."[18] Cyberspace is a community that appears to "live" in the medium. In the case of the Internet, if you take away the medium, then the community disappears.

Third, cyberspace as world borrows from various concepts of alternative worlds. There is talk of worlds from the traditions of mathematics, logic, systems theory, and computer science. For example, in logic and artificial-intelligence research, there is the "blocks world," which is an imaginary, highly constrained environment of rectilinear blocks that can be moved around and placed on top of one another in various configurations, obeying certain laws.[19] This world is for exploring aspects of the logic of action sequences. A world is therefore a domain in which there are elements and laws. There are also worlds of topology, set theory, Euclidean geometry, and logical proof. In each case, the world entails elements, laws, practices, and all the possibilities that they allow. In a similar vein, the romantic and literary traditions furnish us with the idea of worlds as domains of possibilities. Certain kinds of events may occur in imaginary, distant, future, long-forgotten, parallel, or magical worlds, such as those revealed by Jonathan Swift in *Gulliver's Travels,* J. R. R. Tolkien in *Lord of the Rings,* and Lewis Carroll in *Alice's Adventures in Wonderland.* To qualify as a world it does not matter whether the world exists or not. It is necessary only that the possibility for certain kinds of events is opened up—interactions between giants and miniature people, battles between magical forces, or the inversion of Victorian sense and manners. We are adept at contemplating the existence of multiple, fanciful worlds. Cyberspace, as such a world, features prominently in science fiction writing, particularly in the popular novels of William Gibson.[20] This account of cyberspace reflects something of the cult and the populist aspect to the study of cyberspace. There are also on-line, sustained, and communal fantasy games in which people assume imaginary roles acted out through the computer network—for example, MUD (Multiple-User Dungeon Domain) and fantasy games popular on Minitel. Cyberspace is a world in the sense that it allows many possibilities for interaction, discovery, and exploring new combinations and configurations of information and new kinds of interaction between people.

Fourth, cyberspace is also a world in that it exists in the future, not the present. Cyberspace is a hope, an expectation, the future fulfillment of a current possibility, rather than a current reality. Its realization always seems to depend on future or newly emerging technologies and the development of legislation, standards, infrastructure, and social acceptance. Cyberspace is utopian. Cyberspace as world captures these ideas of cyberspace as an assemblage or infrastructure of enabling equipment, a community of devotees and users, and electronic communications as providing access to multiple and varied worlds.

How is cyberspace also a *space?* First, in mathematics, logic, and computer science, it is common to speak of a space as a subset of a world. Within a particular configuration of elements in the blocks world (say a red block stacked on top of a green block), there may be a space of possible maneuvers: the red block can be moved onto the ground, then the green block can be placed on top of it, or the red one can be put back again, and so on. For any initial configuration of elements and a set of rules, there is a space of possibilities defined. The system can assume many states, and the total of all states constitutes a space. Formal languages are similarly defined. A vocabulary, rules, an initial state, and a space of possible combinations of vocabulary elements constitute legal sentences. There is a sense in which cyberspace is such a space. To traverse through cyberspace in this sense is to explore its many possibilities, much as we might explore the space of a formal language by trying out its various word combinations.

Second, there is the sense of space as coordinate and measurable space. Things can be located in physical space and bear particular relationships to one another, such as adjacent, touching, near, and so on, and we can specify where a thing is in three-dimensional space with reference to some coordinate system. Similarly, objects can occupy cyberspace. They can be near to, or far from, each other, adjacent, and so on, and we can specify where we are in terms of an address, usually a "path name." In three-dimensional space, we can measure distances. In cyberspace we can measure path lengths in terms of the number of nodes traversed. Cyberspace is therefore a space in that it is a container, it is measurable, and it is specifiable, though these measurements and specifications are more fluid than in three-dimensional space. By analogy, we can readily plot the components of a particular area of cyberspace on a physical spatial diagram—a "logic diagram" of paths and nodes.

Third, cyberspace enables and constrains human interaction in ways similar to physical space. According to Meyrowitz, physical space provides walls, fences, passageways, and doors to direct the flow of people and determine to a large degree the way face-to-face interaction will proceed.[21] Physical spaces also take on particular significance in the way they include and exclude people. Meyrowitz says that advanced electronic communications and media override these boundaries and impose new ones. For example, conversing by telephone generally involves an intimacy that overrides any other social activity in the room at the time. As a further example, in considering whether we are somewhere private, we now need to pay heed not only to the kinds of walls surrounding us but to the presence of electronic surveillance devices. Furthermore, according to Meyrowitz, people seem to exhibit "on-stage" and "backstage" behavior in physical spaces. The waiter behaves differently in the kitchen (backstage) than with the patrons (on stage). Behavior patterns are intimately connected with space. People behave in a similar manner with electronic media, as when we adopt a formal telephone manner, though the mass media is very successful in exposing people's backstage behavior. As a further illustration of the relationship between cyberspace and physical space, watching television, or "lurking," is obviously similar to watching a stage from the dark anonymity of the auditorium or watching some activity through a one-way mirror.

Fourth, cyberspace is thought to reproduce or represent Cartesian space. If physical space can be represented with three-dimensional coordinates, then this information can be stored, manipulated, and transformed by computer and displayed, using monitors, plotters, digital manufacturing devices, flight simulators, and stereoscopic virtual-reality headsets. Furthermore, any information can be transformed into visual, audile, and now tactile form. In this sense, cyberspace reproduces and even transcends physical space.

Cyberspace is thought to be a space in these four senses. It defines spaces of possibilities, it is measurable and numerically specifiable, it enables and constrains social activity, and it reproduces physical space.

Cyberspace also involves space through the related notion of *place.* It is said that electronic communications destroy and create places. Within architecture and geography, it is common to distinguish between space and place.[22] Space is often regarded as measurable, coordinate space. It is homogeneous and without differentiation. On the other hand, place is a qualitative entity. According to Relph, places "are constructed in our memories and affections through repeated encounters and complex associations. Place experiences are necessarily time-deepened and memory-qualified."[23] A place is where one comes from, where one is known and knows others, where one is at home, and where one dwells. The elaboration of what constitutes place is a common theme within writing in geography, environmental studies, and architecture. Electronic communications and the mass media are commonly characterized as denying the sense of place. Because all places are accessible, we are nowhere in particular. Benedikt proffers the following definition (one of many) of cyberspace that illustrates the phenomenon:

Cyberspace: Accessible through any computer linked into the system; a place, one place, limitless; entered equally from a basement in Vancouver, a boat in Port-au-Prince, a cab in New York, a garage in Texas City, an apartment in Rome, an office in Hong Kong, a bar in Kyoto, a cafe in Kinshasa, a laboratory on the moon.[24]

If we can be anywhere, then we are in no place. But then cyberspace as place is said to have qualities of its own: "Billowing, glittering, humming, coursing, a Borgesian library, a city; intimate, immense, firm, liquid, recognizable and unrecognizable at once."[25] According to some commentators, however, cyberspace can be used to simulate spatial environments and thereby instill a rudimentary sense of place to the activities going on. Rheingold describes the experience of participating in an electronic conference, which is conducted using spatial metaphors from a normal academic or business conference. Particular topics are presented or are under discussion, in "rooms," topics for conversation are posted on a "blackboard" in the various rooms, and so on: "Computer conference conversations are dialogues that are situated in a specific place (the conferencing system, the conference, the topic) and time. The place is a cognitive and social one, not a geographic place."[26] Here space is stripped of the physical. It is a time-deepened and memory-qualified place *without* space. It is in the world of the imagination.

In keeping with the tenets of critical theory, electronic communications, rapid transportation, and many other features of this technological age are thought by some to have contributed to a sense of placelessness, or homelessness. Even if we were never to use a telephone, switch on a television set, or log on to a computer, we would still be caught up in this placelessness that, according to some commentators, is a condition of the electronic age.

So, cyberspace implicates concepts of world, space, and place. What are the relationships among these concepts? Further on in this chapter, I will juxtapose these common concepts of cyberspace with the phenomenological view, which attempts to schematize them and extend the concept of world. First I will review some of the major presuppositions of the cyberspace enthusiasm.

Presuppositions of Cyberspace

The enthusiasm for the phenomenon of cyberspace is sustained by at least two traditions of thinking. First is the liberal-pragmatic tradition that, as we have seen, imbues much research and development of computer systems. Second is the valorization of information. The enthusiasm for advanced telecommunications as "world making" can be traced largely to the influence of McLuhan. In chapter 1, I discussed the hallmarks of liberal pragmatism as they pertain to information technology in general. Cyberspace enthusiasts appear to be more interested in doing and making (practice) than in developing and following theories. They are interested in immediacy, the engagement of the senses. Some have a liberal and egalitarian orientation, manifested as an interest in empowering individuals and fostering community rather than creating systems that might be used to control processes or people. Others have a romantic orientation, expressed as an interest in other worlds and mythologies and giving scope to flights of fancy and the human imagination. Drawing on the history of communications media, Benedikt makes clear the Mc-Luhanesque and pragmatic orientation of cyberspace enthusiasm: "The broad historical movement from a universal, preliterate actuality of *physical doing,* to an education-stratified, literate reality of *symbolic doing* loops back, we find. With movies, television, multimedia computing, and now VR [virtual reality], it loops back to the beginning with the promise of a *post*literate era.''[27] Echoing McLuhan, cyberspace represents a return to a preliterate culture, in which physical doing had primacy over theorizing.

The enthusiasm for cyberspace is also sustained by the ideals of liberal democracy and notions of community and the public. Rheingold presents three ways in which electronic communications are changing society, which make this clear. First, computer-mediated communication (CMC) of the kind enjoyed by Internet users appeals to the intellectual, physical, and emotional needs of the television generation: "CMC spaces better fit their new ways of experiencing the world.''[28] Second, there is the new capacity for many-to-many communication, by which opportunities are provided to create community. According to Rheingold, cyberspace works as community forming because it offers an exchange of collective goods.[29] The collective goods are "social-network capital" (valuing communities in their own right, which are then available for other kinds of exchange), knowledge capital (exchanging expertise and developing the network as a "brain trust"), and communion (sharing personal and emotional support with people on the network). Third, a social change occurs at the political level. CMC further enhances the living web of citizen-to-citizen communication, the public sphere, continuing the Enlightenment tradition. It is taking this role over from the mass media, which are one-to-many and have become diluted with the flashy and phoney. CMC offers the potential to revitalize democracy, though it could also go the other way. According to Rheingold, the rival spatial metaphors are the citizen-centered electronic agora[30] and Jeremy Bentham's Panopticon. As Foucault described it, the Panopticon is the radial-plan prison in which the guard can see every prisoner but they each see only the guard: "Which scenario seems more conducive to democracy, which to totalitarian rule: a world in which a few people control communications technology that can be used to manipulate the beliefs of billions, or a world in which every citizen can broadcast to every other citizen?''[31]

The enthusiasm for cyberspace has little support from theory-oriented researchers, such as those engaged in formal systems and artificial intelligence. But the enthusiasm for cyberspace does rely substantially on a belief in the primacy of information. Information is the very stuff of life, according to Benedikt, "for the secret of life itself is wrapped up in the mystery of genetic encoding and the replication and motility of molecules that orchestrate each other's activity. Genes are information; molecules are media as well as motors, so to speak."[32] According to this view, cyberspace works as world and space because of its grounding in, and privileged access to, information. Cyberspace is an environment of pure information and hence has access to reality—to reproduce, to manipulate, and to transcend. From a more critical perspective, Meyrowitz makes similar claims. The essence of face-to-face encounters between people is information exchange: "To include mediated encounters in the study of situations, we need to abandon the notion that social situations are only encounters that occur face-to-face in set times and places. We need to look at the larger, more inclusive notion of 'patterns of access to information.'"[33] This insight allows Meyrowitz to discuss face-to-face encounters between people in the same light as communications through electronic media. The difference is one of a position on a spectrum.

Thus, while places create one type of information-system—the live encounter—there are many other types of situations created by other channels of communication. This wider view of situations as information-systems, rather than as places, is especially relevant to the study of *electronic* media because electronic media have tended to diminish the differences between live and mediated interaction. The speech and appearance of others are now accessible without being in the same physical location.[34]

If "being there" is a matter of information, then replicating the information is potentially indistinguishable from being there. Advances in electronic communication seem geared toward providing as many "information channels" (the senses) as we experience with physical proximity, and with as broad a bandwidth as possible (that is, conveying as much information per channel as possible).

Because cyberspace is made up of pure information, it is far more amenable to control, manipulation, and design than the real, physical world. The significance accorded to this phenomenon is summarized in Benedikt's identification of the major design issues posed by cyberspace.

The door to cyberspace is open, and I believe that poetically and scientifically minded architects can and will step through it in significant numbers. For cyberspace will require constant planning and organization. The structures proliferating within it will require *design*, and the people who design these structures will be called *cyberspace architects*. Schooled in computer science and programming (the equivalent of "construction"), in graphics, and in abstract design, schooled also along with their brethren "real-space" architects, cyberspace architects will design electronic edifices that are fully as complex, functional, unique, involving, and beautiful as their physical counterparts if not more so. Theirs will be the task of visualizing the intrinsically nonphysical and giving inhabitable visible form to society's most intricate abstractions, processes, and organisms of information. And all the while such designers will be rerealizing in a virtual world many vital aspects of the physical world, in particular those orderings and pleasures that have always belonged to architecture.[35]

This statement represents the apogee of the claims about cyberspace. It is a realm of total control. We will also have to take it into account as a legitimate space that contends with architectural space. New roles will emerge—these are filled by the professionals whose task it is to design and construct virtual worlds.

Notwithstanding these grandiose claims, serious challenges have been directed at the key assumptions of cyberspace, for example, challenges to the claims that electronic communications are capable of enhancing the power of the "public" and promoting the ideals of democracy. Some critical commentators are skeptical. For example, Roszak points to the failure in the 1960s and 1970s of citizen-band radio, which some regard as the precursor to community-based electronic communications networks, to provoke anything of political significance:[36] "For the most part, it became another consumer novelty. There are many signs that [networked] home computers will repeat that pattern, wasting their promise in frivolous, lightweight uses that have no great political relevance."[37]

Carey shows that this "mythology" of communications technology as ushering in social revolution is a fairly common claim of any new technology.[38] To make such claims is itself an Enlightenment legacy. Similar claims were made of newspapers in the eighteenth century. Then the steam engine, with its power to forge new commercial bonds through railroads and waterways, was similarly heralded as a benefactor of humankind. It would triumph over space and time and unite nations.[39] When people realized just how unpleasant and unhealthy was the industrialized world brought about by steam, they shifted their attention to the new technology of electricity. They saw electricity as clean and as bearing resemblances to "brainpower."[40] In fact, some employed electricity as a metaphor for social cohesion. After all, electricity united positive and negative forces. Computerization and citizen-based electronic communications are now similarly promoted in this light. Of course, the motivations for aligning technology with the ideals of an era are immense, be those ideals democracy, enlightenment, the banishment of poverty, efficiency, profitability, or the control of production.

The primacy accorded to information is also under question. Information is what appears on the printed page, as code, and courses through computer networks. According to Meyrowitz, it is also what is conveyed through personal communication. Carey explains this commitment to information as the transmission metaphor of communication,[41] in which communication is a process of transmitting messages at a distance for the purpose of control. Tying this metaphor to industrial development in the United States, Carey thinks it is related "strongly to the nineteenth-century desire to use communication and transportation to extend influence, control, and power over wider distances and greater populations."[42]

Needless to say, this metaphor of communication is under challenge from within language theory, particularly through pragmatism, critical theory, and poststructuralism.[43] The limitations and problems with the informational view of communication and information-processing models of cognition are discussed by Dreyfus and Winograd and Flores at length in the context of computers[44] and were alluded to in chapter 1. In summary, the focus on information amounts to a focus on representation, which in turn presupposes an "objective reality."[45] Knowledge can be stored in texts, rules, programs, and databases. We also think of communication as packaging ideas into code and transmitting them. We need large quantities of reliable information to make sound decisions. Group communication is conceived as a series of individual minds passing around representations so that we know what each other is thinking and intending. The essence of group collaboration is reliable information, so any tool that enhances the flow of information is seen as beneficial. However, we know from experience that information does not automatically produce group cohesion. Decisions are not made by manipulating texts, as attested by work on formal logic and experiments in artificial intelligence. What the information view seems to ignore is the central role of praxis in human affairs.

There are other metaphors of communication that bring praxis into play, particularly those offered by Gadamer's hermeneutics.[46] I presented these metaphors in chapter 2 in the context of information technology. Carey posits the ritual metaphor as a rival to the informational view as a means of explaining the mass media, and by implication aspects of electronic communications. I will briefly explore this metaphor, which accords in some respects with the hermeneutical view.

The ritual metaphor presents communication "as a process through which a shared culture is created, modified and transformed."[47] The ritual metaphor realizes that communication is not simply a matter of extending messages in space but maintaining society in a particular historical time. Communication is not simply imparting information or influence but creating, representing, and celebrating shared beliefs.[48]

Which of these two metaphors holds sway does have consequences. According to Carey, the basic questions posed through one metaphor do not necessarily connect with the basic questions of the other. For example, each leads to a different critique of the mass media (and electronic communication). According to the transmission metaphor, the problem is that the media do not always report accurately, or the message is often polluted with trivia. From the ritual perspective, on the other hand, the media may fail to reproduce or construct the reality of certain sectors of the community. Under the transmission metaphor of communication, the media of newspapers and television are instruments for disseminating news, knowledge, and entertaining diversions over great distances. According to Carey, the questions that arise pertain to the effects of such transmitted information on audiences. The news is either enlightening or it obscures reality. It changes attitudes or reinforces them; it presents material that is credible or doubtful. The metaphor also raises questions concerning the functions of the media. Do they integrate or fragment society? Do they make people stable or unstable? Carey claims, "some such mechanical analysis normally accompanies a 'transmission' argument."[49]

A ritual view of communication focuses on a different range of problems in relation to the media. Carey thinks that watching television or reading the newspaper (or, we may add, using the Internet) is less a process of sending or receiving information and more akin to attending a mass: "a situation in which nothing new is learned but in which a particular view of the world is portrayed and confirmed."[50] According to Carey, news reading and writing is a dramatic ritual act. The reader or television viewer is presented not with pure information but with a portrayal of conflicting world forces. This drama is not static, and the reader or viewer assumes different roles while reading as the dramatic focus shifts.[51] Communication is always historically situated. Contrary to the transmission metaphor, we do not address the effect or function of messages so much as "the role of presentation and involvement in the structuring of the reader's life and time."[52] On Carey's view, the news changes little and is intrinsically satisfying. It performs few functions and yet is habitually consumed. The news operates by presenting "what the world at root is."[53] Although Carey is describing the mass media, these accounts apply equally to the formation of community through any medium.

Under a ritual view, then, news is not information but drama. It does not describe the world but portrays an arena of dramatic forces and action; it exists solely in historical time; and it invites our participation on the basis of our assuming, often vicariously, social roles within it.[54] Of course, the ritual metaphor does not exclude the transmission metaphor. The latter is built on the former: "It merely contends that one cannot understand these processes aright except insofar as they are cast within an essentially ritualistic view of communication and social order."[55] If the mass media have this ritual quality, then it is never simply a one-to-many communication. If any medium is to survive with a viable constituency it is already many-to-many. A viewing audience or a readership participates in a community that uses the mass media or electronic communications to reinforce and sustain itself (for good or ill). Programmers, directors, journalists, news readers, and celebrities obviously have special roles, but, extending Carey's ritual metaphor, these are the priests, deacons, and choristers who have roles within the set service—so, too, the authors, moderators, and editors of Internet correspondence. The question of a message only makes sense within this background in praxis. A message is simply not understood unless it conforms in form and content to the ritual.

This ritual metaphor is compelling in providing a simple critique of cyberspace, but it does not vigorously address the issues of world and space as presented by the cyberspace phenomenon. Neither does it entirely capture the dynamism of the phenomenon of world and of electronic communications. For this we need to consider Heidegger's praxis-based phenomenology of world. We turn, therefore, to the phenomenological account of world and how it treats information, and thus cyberspace.

Phenomenology of World, Space, and Place

As we have seen, the link between computer-mediated communications and phenomenology,[56] particularly the phenomenology of Heidegger, is well established through such writers as Dreyfus, Winograd, Flores, and Heim.[57] There is also a strong pragmatic streak in Heidegger's writing, which strikes a chord with pragmatically oriented commentators and researchers in IT. At a superficial level, the language of Heidegger's phenomenology, particularly his notion of "being-in-the-world," has a seductive ring to people interested in total-immersion environments. The main difference between cyberspace enthusiasts and Heidegger's phenomenology is the former's enchantment with the notion of information, which, I will argue, has to be abandoned in order to appropriate Heidegger's rich concepts of world. I will show how the belief in the primacy of information is at odds with Heidegger.

As we have seen, the concept of world features prominently in cyberspace literature. It also features prominently in Husserl's and Heidegger's phenomenology.[58] The account of world given above seems to exhaust the subject, unless we can find another account. According to Heidegger, the traditional view of world leaves out important aspects of our experience. There is another concept of world that precedes those already considered. The clearest insight into Heidegger's notion of world comes from his introduction to the subject through the innocuous preposition "in"—what it is to be *in* a world. There are two meanings of "in." The first is inclusion, as though we, or objects, are located within a container. The second meaning is involvement, as in "being in a good mood," "being in business," or "being in love." We are engaged with something. Heidegger devotes several pages to articulating this concept of being in, or rather of "being-in." According to Heidegger, the etymology of the word shows that this latter meaning of "in" is more primordial than the former. The primordial sense is "to reside" or "to dwell," a meaning all but forgotten and consequently difficult to explain, but which we would do well to revive. The meaning of "in" as inclusion is possible only because of our prior understanding of "in" as involvement.

We need two further distinctions in order to progress to Heidegger's concept of world. Among the many new distinctions Heidegger makes in *Being and Time* is the distinction between the ontic and the ontological. The ontic is the representable, scientific, measurable, classifiable phenomenon. It is about beings or entities. The ontological, on the other hand, is about *ways* of being. The ontological is prior to the ontic, that is, it comes first chronologically (through the evidence of language and history), it is first in importance, and the ontic presumes the ontological. The ontological pertains to the whole. Our common uses of the word "in" provide a good example. Inclusion is possible in both an ontic and in an ontological sense, as is involvement. What do these different senses of "in" have to say about world? Through these distinctions, we are able to advance our understanding of world.

In the case of the ontic sense of "in" as inclusion, there is the world as a set of everything that is of a particular kind.[59] (This accords with the conventional views of world given above.) For example, there is the world as the universe, the set of all physical objects. There is also the world as a universe of discourse, as in mathematics.

There is the world of electronic components, microchips, cables, monitors, software, and so on, of electronic communications. A deeper, ontological meaning of "world" (still assuming "in" as inclusion) is the world as a set of entities and the essential characteristics that qualify them to be members of the set. So the physical world is not only the elements that make up the set but the abstract concepts and laws by which we explain the physical world. In this sense, the world of electronic communications includes the abstract concepts and theories (communications theory, protocol hierarchies, and so on) we use to explore and explain it. This is the "way of being," the ontology, of the entities of the ontic world under study.

The world of involvement, the world in which we dwell, can be considered at an ontic level as simply the world in which one lives or makes a living. There is the child's world, the world of fashion, the business world, the world of science, the disciplinary matrix. This is always a shared world, a field of tacit practices. In cyberspace jargon, this is the world of the computer hacker, the e-mail user, the cyberpunk, the systems designer, the virtual community.

These three understandings of world roughly correspond to those given earlier, though they are defined in terms of the distinctions between "in" as inclusion and "in" as involvement, and the distinction between the ontic and the ontological. But the major benefit of these distinctions is in enabling us to identify a fourth sense of world—understood through the ontological sense of "in" as involvement.

In a deep (ontological) sense, we are in *the* world. This sense is captured through Heidegger's important hyphenated term "being-in-the-world."[60] This is the "in" of involvement but with no presumption of differentiation between entity and environment. According to Heidegger, this conception of world has been passed over by the philosophical tradition (and it was passed over in the discussion given earlier of cyberspace as world). Being-in-the-world is not some strange ephemeral concept. It is just the reverse. Once it has been pointed out, it is obvious as a viable account of everyday experience. It implicates the most ordinary aspects of day-to-day living, involving everyday things. As if to emphasize the ordinariness of being-in-the-world, Heidegger explains it in terms of our involvement with equipment, such as hammers and the tools of the workshop. Dreyfus explains being-in-the-world thus: "This is the way of being common to our most general system of equipment and practices and to any of its subregions."[61] An important part of Heidegger's project is to lay out the structure of this world. This is the world of involvement and of being at home.[62] Being-in-the-world involves the transparent and unreflective use of equipment, as in the habitual use of a computer keyboard or a telephone. The keyboard and the phone do not enter into our awareness until they break down—a key gets stuck or the line is cut off—or when we employ signs, when we point something out. Using his own ontological term for the being who inhabits the world (*Dasein*), Heidegger describes this world: "The world is the wherein of Dasein's being."[63] According to this conception, the world is not a spatial container. We do not need to be placed in the world. We are already in it. We are *thrown* in it. This concept of world cannot be appreciated without the ontological concept of being-in.

Already we can see what this concept of world says about cyberspace. The cyberspace phenomenon is ordinarily described as somehow transcending the physical and material involvement of its users in equipment. Cyberspace is portrayed as some strange realm inside the network, in a theoretical realm, or in some utopia. The concept of being-in-the-world brings us back to the significance of everyday involvement in keyboards, desks, monitors, cables, workstations, and practices, not as a set of entities but as a context of total and undifferentiated involvement. This is the "ontological cyberworld."

From this understanding of world (as being-in-the-world), we then progress to a consideration of proximity. What is it to be near or close to something in this ontological sense of world? The world is what we care about, have concern for. In this world, Heidegger differentiates between the region that is our immediate sphere of involvement and concern and the world that is a totality of involvement.

What is ready-to-hand in our everyday dealings has the character of closeness. To be exact, this closeness of equipment has already been intimated in the term 'readiness-to-hand,' which expresses the Being of equipment.

Every entity that is 'to hand' has a different closeness, which is not to be ascertained by measuring distances. This closeness regulates itself in terms of circumspectively 'calculative' manipulating and using.[64]

For Heidegger, the term *readiness-to-hand* captures the sense of the ontological proximity of equipment. This closeness is not understood first as pertaining to measurable distance. Heidegger gives the example of walking down the street. The pavement is as near as anything could be (measurably), yet it is remote compared with the nearness of an acquaintance one encounters several paces away.[65] Extending the argument to electronic communications, the computer monitor or telephone is close, yet the person we are chatting with is closer still, even if the person is many miles away in terms of measured spatial distance. What brings proximity is not the mediation of electronic communications per se but the proximal region brought into being through our concern at the moment.

This region of concern is prior to measurable space. In fact, according to Heidegger, we can traverse through space only because we are already where we want to be ontologically.[66] It is only because we pervade space through our concern that we are able to go through spaces.

Rather, we always go through spaces in such a way that we already experience them by staying constantly with near and remote locations and things. When I go toward the door of the lecture hall, I am already there, and I could not go to it at all if I were not such that I am there. I am never here only, as this encapsulated body; rather, I am there, that is, I already pervade the room, and only thus can I go through it.[67]

At first reading, this passage may appear strange and mysterious, but, if we take on board Heidegger's "commonsense" notion of the primacy of concern, it could not be otherwise. Ontologically, we are with our concerns. We are already proximal to what constitute our concerns. Similarly, we are already with the person we are communicating with via the telephone, in our desire to make contact, in our involvement with that person over a period of time, or even just through the mutuality we may strike up with an otherwise complete stranger. Communications technology is no guarantee of ontological proximity in its own right.[68]

If ontological spatiality in the world is primary, what is the significance of scientific Cartesian or mathematical concepts of space—spatiality in the natural world? Heidegger articulates several different modes of being in terms of the ontic/ontological distinction and how they relate to one another. First, the most primordial and basic mode of being is that in which we are in-the-world, absorbed and involved in everyday practices, exercising our skills, unreflectively acting out our roles, involved with equipment. This is where we encounter things as ready and available, close by for action, proximal. It is where we are habitually typing at the keyboard, having a relaxed conversation on the telephone, reading our e-mail, dabbling with a computer paint system, filling in the details of a floor plan on a CAD system. It is only because we can be in the world in this way and the world can be so undifferentiated that we can encounter *things*. When there is a disturbance, a breakdown, in our deficient modes of concern (or a pointing out), then things emerge, for the moment and in the context of our practices. This is the second mode of being—a stuck computer key emerges as an object for concern when something goes wrong with my typing, the telephone emerges from the background when I am cut off, the paintbrush icon emerges as an object when I want to paint a line and I am unfamiliar with the paint program, the lines on a plan constituting a door swing emerge as objects when the ink smudges or when the library element in the CAD system is missing. The objects that present themselves pertain to our concern at the moment. If the telephone conversation is cut off, then it is unlikely that the television set in the corner of the room or the table under the telephone will come to the fore. It is also in this moment of breakdown that aspects of space are revealed, such as nearness and remoteness.

In the same way that objects present themselves in terms of our concern of the moment in the event of breakdown, so, too, with space. Space discloses attributes pertaining to our concerns at the moment: the journey through the forest is hard going, the building interior is oppressive, the mountain range is exhilarating. *This* space is always different from *that* space—space is heterogeneous. So, too, with distance: the supermarket is miles away when you have to walk to it, the waterfront is just down the road when it is reached through pleasant parkland, relatives live very near when they are just off the freeway, the United Kingdom and Australia are very close when we are on the phone, the United States and North Korea are a universe away when it comes to electronic mail. In this mode of being, we do not simply consider a subjective sense of distance, as opposed to an absolute or an objective one.

In this discussion, Heidegger is at pains to distance himself from relying on the notion of the subject, to distance himself from psychologizing.

When one is oriented beforehand towards 'Nature' and 'Objectively' measured distances of Things, one is inclined to pass off such estimates and interpretations of deseverance [distance] as 'subjective.' Yet this 'subjectivity' perhaps uncovers the 'Reality' of the world at its most Real; it has nothing to do with 'subjective' arbitrariness or subjectivistic 'ways of taking' an entity which 'in itself' is otherwise.[69]

Rather, these estimates of distance are pragmatic.[70] They constitute interpretations of distance in the midst of a practical situation, which is the only situation we can actually be in. We are always in a situation of acting and doing.

It is possible to abstract our encounter with space and distance into the practical, but privileged realm of measurement—Heidegger's third mode of being. Even here, measurement presumes the pragmatic concern with space. We know what to measure only because we already come to the measuring process with practical concerns. There are clearly many ways to measure something. The distance between two cities can be measured in terms of road distance, rail distance, a straight line assuming a particular cartographic projection, travel time, length of communications cables, numbers of communications nodes, cost of travel, cost of telephone charges, and so on. According to Heidegger, "Such thematization of the spatiality of the environment is still predominantly an act of circumspection by which space in itself already comes into view in a certain way."[71]

Finally, it is possible in some rare circumstances to strip space of any concern whatever—Heidegger's fourth mode of being: "The homogeneous space of Nature shows itself only when the entities we encounter are discovered in such a way that the worldly character of the ready-to-hand gets specifically deprived of its worldhood.''[72] In this rarefied consideration of space, any notion of being-in-the-world is lost. This is space as theory, devoid of practicalities.[73] It is as though we can just look at or contemplate space without being concerned about anything else. Space is neutralized into pure dimensions. This is Cartesian space, pure extension, in which objects can be placed anywhere. Space is a container without bounds, an infinity of possible positions for random things. This is also the homogeneous space of relativity and quantum theory, pure mathematical abstraction. (Though even here space is always "tainted" with a concern with explanation, prediction, and control.) This is also the space of the building model described as three-dimensional coordinates in a computer-aided design database; the space of the photorealistic, computer-generated perspective image; the space of the image on a flight-simulator screen; or the space projected through a virtual-reality headset.

For Heidegger, these latter spatial conceptions are abstract and derivative, not foundational and essential. Heidegger's view, therefore, presents a reversal of the conventional ontology. The space of nature/science is derived from our involvement in the world, and not the other way around. Heidegger's view is obviously holistic. It is nonreductive. It gives priority to experience (phenomena), and active engagement. It is also pragmatic. We are caught up in practices before we reflect and construct theories. Space is primarily what is experienced, though not understood subjectively, but as a being-in-the-world that is prior to any identification of subject and object. On the other hand, abstract space is decontextualized space.

From this ontology, we can see that we need to abandon the primacy of information if we are to get to the heart of being-in-the-world. The idea of information is a limited ontic construction. The concept of information has its place, but it cannot be understood without the ontological, and it certainly does not provide an account of space or of how communities are formed. Heidegger's ontology, therefore, defuses the power accorded to networked communications and their ability to create space and community.

Heidegger's ontology also throws into question the claim that electronic communications are breaking spatial barriers and creating new spaces. According to the above ontology, being-with is prior to measurable spatial proximity, and we are with each other or with a thing insofar as we have concerns that require or involve the other or the thing. We are already proximal to what constitute our concerns, so there is nothing special about electronic communications in this regard. Electronic communications are merely caught up in the practical world of involvement, the world of inconspicuous equipment use.

In his later writings, Heidegger pursues an interesting line of argument that indicates that world and space are created, or rather revealed, by everyday things.[74] We can say, in a sense, that equipment, artworks, or things in nature disclose.[75] But here again, this revelatory capacity of things has nothing to do with information. If the paraphernalia of cyberspace reveals anything, it is not through the information that it deals in.

In his later work, Heidegger makes a sharp distinction between things and objects. Things are artworks, equipment, or entities of nature (trees, rocks, rivers, and planets). The concept of a thing is prior to that of an object. Objects are what we understand ontically as the objects of science or the entities within some classification system. They are representable, decomposable, and can be located in Cartesian space. We can say of an object that it can be represented as information. Certainly an artwork can be an object—it can be bought, sold, hung in a gallery, digitally reproduced on a computer screen, treated as a *mere* object. So, too, an item of equipment, such as a cup or a hammer, can be objectified as something with properties, measured, accorded a utility value, located arbitrarily in space, described in a computer database. Entities of nature can also be turned into objects, to be exploited as fuel, as energy sources; scrutinized and measured as the objects of science; or depicted in geographic information systems (GIS). But for Heidegger, to objectify is to render everything the same, as made up of atoms, as measurable, as energy, as locatable in space on a coordinate grid, as representable, as information. This "artificial" way of looking at things is "correct," according to Heidegger, but it conceals the "thingly nature of the thing"—what it is that makes the thing under consideration unique or special. It prevents the thing from revealing something about itself and the world around it. It neglects the nature of a thing to gather.

Heidegger traces the etymology of the word "thing" to the old German word, which meant literally a gathering.[76] A thing gathers concerns—it is "anything that in any way bears upon men, concerns them, and that accordingly is a matter of discourse."[77] So a thing is situated, and it discloses world.[78]

How does this disclosure occur? The world is, of course, the ontological, historical, holistic world in which we are at home and in which we dwell. Things disclose the world (the world we are *in* in the sense of being-in-the-world) when we encounter them as things, which is simply to "let them be." We accomplish this by stepping back "from the thinking that merely represents—that is, explains—to the thinking that responds and recalls."[79] For the earlier Heidegger, this "thinking" was total, unreflective involvement, but for the later Heidegger, this thinking is meditative thinking that listens to the messages of Being presented through the ages and lets Being disclose itself. So it is not simply *things* that disclose world, but thinking of them *as* things, or allowing them to be. It is in letting them disclose their thingly character that world is revealed. When we allow them to do this, we are at home, we are in a place.

We considered Heidegger's concept of thinking in greater detail in chapter 2. Certainly this account of thinking strikes another blow against the primacy of information. Heidegger concedes that there is a kind of representational thinking, an information-processing view of thought, but it is an impoverished kind of thinking. Similarly, space is not essentially information, as coordinates in three dimensions. Space is primarily the heterogeneous space of lived experience. To store and manipulate coordinates in a computer system provides us with no special contact with reality. Neither is proximity primarily a matter of distance or the speed with which signals are passed through a network. In building community, it is our involvement in a shared world that constitutes our togetherness. Communicating with others, either "face to face" or across a network, is not to be understood primarily as passing information. Because we are in-the-world, we are already with each other, socialized, engaged, involved in shared practices. The construction that is "information" comes later as an ontic understanding of the phenomenon. To speak of passing information in a situation is to strip the experience of its context. This has its place but deprives us of a deeper understanding of human interaction. Contrary to Meyrowitz's view, the concept of information says very little about community and human social situations.

If it is not through information or representations, how do things reveal a world? Heidegger presents the example of a bridge. The bridge on the river brings the banks into presence and presents the towns on either side of the river as part of the same community. Things are not simply fitted into preexisting places but create place, or rather bring place into presence. It is not simply that a landscape, site, or environment has a set of features and attributes that are latent but that the bridge makes the river, or brings it into presence. Of course, no thing accomplishes this in isolation. There is an interconnection of things, or rather a whole that can be understood in terms of things. In this sense, things do not merely occupy space but disclose place. Neither do such things as artworks primarily *represent* place. Rather, they open up a place and show us what it is to dwell.[80] According to one commentator, "Art grows into a saving power by embodying places which preserve and hence save a place for dwelling."[81]

How do things reveal space? In Heideggerian terms, things understood in this way bring the thingly nature of things near. In gathering, they bring other things into proximity. This closeness is prior to the physical closeness of objects in Cartesian space.

What of technological things, equipment? What do they reveal? According to Heidegger, "Technology is a mode of revealing."[82] How does it reveal? Heidegger describes the "making" (*techne*) of technical equipment not as manufacturing but as revealing: "Whoever builds a house or a ship or forges a sacrificial chalice reveals what is to be brought forth. . . . This revealing gathers together in advance the aspect and the matter of ship or house, with a view to the finished thing envisioned as completed, and from this gathering determines the method of its construction.''[83] So the process of authentic *techne* is a process of revealing: the essence of the wood in fine joinery; the banks of the river in the case of an old, stone bridge; the early morning sun in the case of the gleaming, white temple. As things, hammers, jugs, windmills, peasant shoes, temples, and chalices gather. Hydroelectric dams, factories, coal mines, airplanes, typewriters, and television sets disclose nature as objects, as potential for exploitation. Heidegger speaks disparagingly but resignedly of the ''unlocking, transforming, storing, distributing, and switching about'' of power turbines, factories, coal mines, dams, and typewriters[84] as ways of revealing: ''Everywhere everything is ordered to stand by, to be immediately at hand, indeed to stand there just so that it may be on call for a further ordering.''[85]

Can electronic communications equipment constitute things? Can a telephone or a computer and its software be a thing that reveals? How do they gather? Heidegger offers few concessions to the virtues of electronic equipment.[86] We are trapped and alienated through them. They do not bring things closer but, according to one commentator, ''participate in the diminution of the very possibility of 'nearing' things.''[87] The technologies of the mass media and electronic communications seek to persuade us that we can be everywhere and anywhere. They are comparable to coal mines and power turbines. Through the primacy accorded to information, the mass media present everything for consumption; events are there as potential to be recorded, reported, and photographed. There is no differentiation brought about by actually being there and being involved or being concerned. In the case of electronic communications, we can turn our social engagements on and off by the touch of a key, we can ''lurk,'' we can be extroverted or introverted, we can deceive or tell the truth. Anything is possible, which means that very little is possible.

Heidegger's criticism differs from that of the reflections of some cyberspace commentators in that it is not the equipment or the systems themselves that are potentially dangerous. Thinking no doubt mainly of atomic weaponry, Heidegger remarks, ''The threat to man does not come in the first instance from the potentially lethal machines and apparatus of technology. The actual threat has already affected man in his essence."[88] As we have already seen, the threat was in place beginning around the time of Plato, when thinking became philosophy, when things became objects, and craft (*techne*) as revealing became manufacturing—in other words, when we became enframed. Heidegger is concerned with this enframing essence not the individual instances of technological apparatus. The danger of this enframing is that we become blind to other ways of looking at things, to letting things reveal their thingness. The instances of jugs, bridges, and typewriters are merely illustrative examples. We are already enframed, and Heidegger is *not* concerned about a new, enlightened form of design or engineering.

On the face of it, Heidegger offers little support, therefore, for thinking about computers as things that gather and disclose, nor for the concept that electronic communications disclose space as cyberspace.[89] Of course, they may disclose space in a negative sense. The impoverishment of cyberspace may reveal the reality of real space and place.

Where does this foray into Heideggerian phenomenology lead us in our considerations of cyberspace? Cyberspace can never lay claim to being a world in the ontological sense of the "in" of involvement, being-in-the-world. We can be in a region of concern, but that is never simply cyberspace. It is defined by our concerns: the people we are talking to, the community of which we are a part, the things that occupy our attention.

The effect is to defuse the cyberspace phenomenon of its sense of self-importance. Information does not make worlds or space. It does not usher in a new era of community. There are no new virtual cities on the horizon in which we may dwell. Cyberspace as a concept features in the rhetorical praxis of a community intent on promoting the importance of its technologies in whatever way it can.

But information technology clearly does reveal things to us. I will explore how by examining the claims and counterclaims about how computer systems *represent*, particularly in the area of virtual reality.

Photo-realistic rendering of a room using ray-processing techniques. The second image shows the configuration of the room model and scenery. The image was designed and implemented by Francis Kelly. The project was supervised by Sidney Newton.

5

Representation and Reality

The Phenomenology of Virtual Reality

Virtual reality is a computer technology that presents sensory information and feedback to give the convincing illusion that the technology user is immersed in an artificial world—a world that exists only inside the computer.[1] The technology is sometimes termed *immersion technology*. It uses specialized computer hardware and software to provide a highly sophisticated level of human/computer interaction. Virtual reality currently uses special helmets that place binocular images before the eyes of the technology user (stereopsis). The helmet also allows the position of the viewer's head to be tracked so that the images of a three-dimensional scene change according to the viewer's movements. Various devices, such as the control stick, three-dimensional mouse, and data glove, permit touching, moving, and feeling "virtual objects." Using this technology, one can "move through" and manipulate a three-dimensional environment, such as a building interior.

The proposed immediate practical applications of the technology are controlling robots located at remote and dangerous sites, controlling delicate surgery,[2] and enabling "walk-throughs" of uncompleted designs, such as those of buildings[3]—though virtual reality is also expected to apply to the fine arts, entertainment, education, and communication. Extensives summaries of various applications are provided by Helsel and Roth[4] and Hattinger et al.[5] Virtual-reality technology is also said to provide the opportunity for new modes of human-computer interaction, and is considered to provide a new medium for designing in three dimensions.

The study of virtual reality is fascinating because of the practical possibilities it seems to open up but also, as discussed in the previous chapter, because of the claims made about the "new worlds" it may open up to the senses—the electronic worlds of "cyberspace."[6] According to Heim, "The final point of a virtual world is to dissolve the constraints of the anchored world so we can lift anchor . . . so we can explore anchorages in ever new places."[7] Virtual reality technology is said by some to enable the depiction of "idea space" and the use of "visual metaphors for mental models of how the idea space is organised."[8]

It is also claimed that the technology is highly significant in that it will open up challenges to orthodox views of reality. According to Helsel and Roth, virtual reality is a topic "that will raise more (and perhaps more significant) questions concerning the nature of reality than the human race has faced to date."[9] Others add that it challenges our views of our bodies and ourselves. According to Walser, "[Y]our conditioned notion of a unique and immutable body will give way to a far more liberated notion of "body" as quite disposable and, generally, limiting."[10] According to some, we will find that with virtual reality it is possible to change from one body to another, according to what the situation demands. This will have profound effects: "The ability to radically and compellingly change one's body-image is bound to have a deep psychological effect, calling into question just what you consider yourself to be."[11] Virtual reality will also provide safe spaces. Spaces can be constructed in which there are no hazards. According to Heim, "Danger and caution pervade the real (existential) world, but virtual reality can offer total safety, like the law of sanctuary in religious cultures."[12]

Notwithstanding these claims, the current commercial manifestations of virtual reality are relatively mundane and include simulators, such as flight simulators[13] (though not usually exploiting stereopsis), arcade games, and theme park rides. At the time of this writing, virtual-reality researchers consider the technology to be at a rudimentary stage in relation to its potential. The binocular images are jerky, resolution is low, the scenes modeled have to be very simple, and there are problems in calibrating the equipment for individual users. The complete immersion environment is not yet with us, in which images are projected directly onto the retina and users wear bodysuits of "intelligent sensor effectors" or "data suits."

Studying the claims of virtual-reality technology is valuable, because it brings into sharp relief certain major assumptions that underlie the use of computer technology, particularly in human-computer interface (HCI) and computer-aided design (CAD) research. Virtual reality takes these assumptions to the extreme, and any testing of them will have implications for other aspects of CAD research. It also provides a good test case for the applicability of contemporary philosophical thinking to CAD. Does what we have outlined so far in this book have anything to say of which HCI, CAD, and virtual-reality researchers should take note? In this chapter, I further apply Heidegger's thinking on the nature of being-in-the-world, and his commentary on what happens when we take technologies to their extremes.

The idea of virtual reality relies on certain assumptions about perception and representation. Only a brief summary of these assumptions will be provided here. Broadly speaking, there appear to be two schools of thought on perception and representation that dominate research into HCI, CAD, and virtual reality. Virtual reality appears to favor one school over the other. Later we will see that both schools are under challenge from Heidegger's concepts of truth.

Data-Oriented and Constructivist Views of Perception

One view of perception is data oriented. Perception is seen largely as a matter of data input to the mind from the environment. This is considered to be the starting point for a consideration of perception. According to Fisher, "We obtain raw, directed information in the process of interacting with the situations we encounter."[14]

According to this view, we need more and more input to the senses to effect a sense of the real—"more" in the sense of a greater quantity of data and a greater degree of detail. This assumption is evident in the quest for visual realism in computer-graphics research generally. According to one textbook on computer graphics, in the real world, "[t]here are many surface textures, subtle color gradations, shadows, reflections, and slight irregularities (scuffs on the floor, chips in the paint, marks on the wall). These all combine in our mind to create a 'real' visual experience."[15] This view also seems to characterize the body as an elaborate input device. According to Rheingold, "our eyes are stereo input devices; our eyeballs and necks are sophisticated, multiple degree-of-freedom gimbals for moving our stereo sensors. We are elements in an information ecology that creates the useful illusion we call 'reality.'"[16]

It would be rare for this view to be held to the exclusion of other views. The data-oriented view is in tension with the counterview that our perceptions are primarily constructed—the constructivist orientation, according to which we rely on simple cues and clues from the environment. So we can be immersed in any environment, depending on our state of mind, our interests, what we have been taught to experience, our personal and corporate expectations, and our familiarity with the medium. The view suggests that simulators are effective because the users are immersed in their task and in the culture in which the simulation experience makes sense. The same applies to computer games and entertainment. The plausibility of the constructivist view of perception is widely acknowledged but is less privileged as a research drive in virtual reality. The constructivist view suggests that virtual-reality technology does *not* have to strive for realism through better and more complete sensory input.

The data-oriented and the constructivist views of perception are rarely seen as independent. The notions of environment (the object world) and organism (the subject) are closely coupled in J. J. Gibson's ecological view of perception.[17] According to Gibson, organisms are so enmeshed in their environment that one cannot be understood without the other. Hagen summarizes Gibson's position: "[T]o specify or describe the environment of the organism is to characterize, in general terms, the organism itself; to describe the organism is to outline the general character of its environment."[18]

VR seems to favor the opinion that the images generated by the technology and presented to the viewer are general, are invariant, capture the essence of the scene, and are independent of the viewer.

What is provided by a virtual-reality system is a universal field of sensory input. Viewers may apply their own constructions to this field and thereby engage in some kind of "filtering," though these constructions appear to receive less attention in virtual-reality research—which appears to be driven by the quest for more and better data input to the senses. Ignoring the constructed nature of perception suggests that a virtual-reality system for a frog would be little different from one for a human.

The Correspondence and Constructivist Views of Representation

Similar distinctions apply to understanding how representation and the presentation of visual images operate. The correspondence view of representation relies on the idea that a representation corresponds with what is out there in the object. So, according to Hagen, perspective images are realistic because "there is a one-to-one mapping of the visible surfaces of the world onto the picture plane, and from there to the eye."[19] The correspondence view also assumes the world contains structures, which we can discern and represent. The privileged view is that geometry and number provide the basic underpinnings of the world. (Some commentators think that whether or not these structures inhere within the world "out there" or in the mental constitution of the observer amounts to the same thing.[20]) The privileged view assumes that if we can capture the basic geometry of the world in a computer system then the representation of this information is an accurate reconstruction of reality. This appears to be implicit in the justification of research into the techniques of fractal geometry, as outlined by Barnsley.

Classical geometry provides a first approximation to the structure of physical objects; it is the language which we use to communicate the designs of technological products, and, very approximately, the forms of natural creations. Fractal geometry is an extension of classical geometry. It can be used to make precise models of physical structures from ferns to galaxies. . . . [Y]ou can describe the shape of a cloud as precisely as an architect can describe a house.[21]

A reliance on the geometrical underpinnings of the world is also evident in CAD research, as indicated by Mitchell.

Underlying any design medium is some method of geometrical description—some strategy for using geometrical entities to describe three-dimensional physical artefacts. . . .

In a CAD system they [the geometrical entities] are represented symbolically within the framework of a Cartesian co-ordinate system, and display hardware is used to translate them into visual equivalents.[22]

The primacy of geometry is also evident in models of how sense data reaches the eye, as in ray tracing, a technique for generating photo-realistic computer images. Some think ray tracing replicates the "real physics"[23] of light passing through lenses.

Recalling Scruton's and Mitchell's distinctions presented in chapter 3, the idea of truth in representation is implied when we talk about degrees of correspondence. Some representations seem to be closer to reality than others. This is implicit in the distinctions made among realistic, figurative, and abstract representations. Representations may also be accurate or ambiguous, denoted (actual) or connoted (implied), and they may fall along a continuum, as indicated in Foley and Van Dam's textbook on computer graphics.

At one end of the continuum are examples of what is often called photographic realism (or photorealism). These pictures attempt to synthesize the field of light intensities that would be focussed on the film plane of a camera aimed at the objects depicted. As we approach the other end of the continuum, we find images that provide successively fewer of the visual cues.[24]

According to some, the best kind of representation is one that does not need to package and unpackage the information inherent in a scene through the medium of a picture but confronts a duplicate of the real scene. According to Fisher, "A truly informative picture, in addition to merely being an information surrogate, would duplicate the physicality of confronting the real scene that it is meant to represent."[25] The correspondence view of representation generates certain research interests, such as developing models (computer algorithms) to produce greater photorealism and developing techniques for storing, processing, and presenting more-detailed data. This involves developing accurate data representations, complete and canonic data structures, and better simulation of perspective, color, texture, edge quality, illumination, light, haze, focus, motion blur, and movement.[26] Virtual reality adds research into other sensory data, such as sound, touch, and movement.[27] According to Foley and Van Dam, in the case of visual images, the objective is to "produce computer-generated images which are so realistic that the observer believes the image to be that of a real object rather than of a synthetic object existing only in the computer's memory."[28] This is a kind of Turing test for photorealism and virtual reality. The goal appears to be reached when we cannot distinguish between the computer image and the real thing, though this goal is elusive. As with artificial intelligence (AI), one may ask what will be the end point of the research process? What is the threshold of sophistication at which we will be able to say that a suitably convincing illusion of reality has been achieved? Some major unsolved technical problems include simulating the kinesthetic experience (e.g., walking), allowing the eye to change focus according to distance of object from the viewer, allowing for peripheral vision, and integrating the many theories and techniques that appear to constitute our perception of reality.

Virtual reality is also intriguing because it appears to take the idea of the underpinnings of number and geometry to a logical extreme. If virtual reality works, it vindicates one aspect of Cartesianism—the reduction of space to number. (This is similar to AI as a test of Cartesian cognitivism.[29] If AI works, then it would appear that logic and number underlie all human thought after all.)

The second common view of representation, as for perception, is constructivist, according to which the appreciation of "realism" has to be learned. Representation is a cultural phenomenon.[30] Hagen summarizes this position: "One learns to read the conventional symbols of a culture's pictures just as one learns to read the conventional words of a language."[31] According to this view, the language of representation is in a sense arbitrary. It involves a recognition that identifying structure is a human projection, and there may be many structures. This appears to be a less privileged view in virtual-reality research than the view of representation as correspondence. While supporting the basic tenor of virtual reality research, Helsel and Roth make passing reference to the challenge posed by the constructivist view to the research. It is readily acknowledged that history is always biased according to the historian's viewpoint—so, too, do drawings, models, and other artifacts bear the biases of their creators: "How will any individual or group carefully and sensitively, with a deep appreciation for cultural, racial, religious and gender bias, create virtual reality systems?"[32]

If the constructivist view is followed with conviction, it implies that *practice* has priority over any *theory* of correspondence (a view consistent with Turbayne's elaboration of a linguistic model of vision[33]). Any drawing or model makes sense by virtue of our immersion in a culture of particular practices, and in the context of our practices.[34] There is a way of considering drawings and models such that we need not appeal to the idea of their representing anything. They are a medium of exchange. Shop drawings, working drawings, diagrams, instructions, and schedules have the same "representational status." Each needs to be interpreted in a particular context of practice. This is a familiar idea to computer-graphics, HCI, CAD, and virtual-reality researchers but does not appear to feature prominently in their writing about images. (The discussion within media studies[35] appears to be more wide ranging however.)

The idea of practice is partly captured by the idea of language (as long as we do not see language use as following a system of rules). As we have investigated in chapter 1, there is no theory of practice—hence the priority within theory-oriented academic communities given to the idea of graphical images as corresponding to something and of realism as close and accurate correspondence.

The priority of the practice of reading drawings applies equally to working drawings, three-dimensional computer images, and figure drawing. We learn to "read" drawings. There are different styles of drawing. Our appreciation and understanding of a drawing changes over time, as we become part of the "appreciative community." We tend to privilege "accurate perspective," but perspective drawings are not superior, say, to medieval images, which adopt a different convention, or more realistic. Different conventions are in play, and conventions build on conventions.

Similar arguments can be applied to computer models of designs, such as building designs. The quality and appropriateness of the representation depends on how the computer model is used. There is no essential, closely corresponding, canonic description from which all others can be derived.

Applying the constructivist view to virtual-reality systems, we may assume that we learn to use these systems in a context of particular practices. As for the constructivist view of perception, the research quest need not be for realism. The computer can serve as a medium like any other, with its own idiosyncrasies. The idea that computer images may always look like computer images should not deter us, and the virtual-reality experience may be interesting and useful independently of what the experience might or might not correspond to—a view common among those who advocate computer graphics as a medium other than for realism.[36]

Needless to say, there is a tension between these two views—the appreciation of images through correspondence or through construction. It is not a simple matter to reconcile them, and the former appears to be highly privileged in the way HCI, CAD, and virtual-reality research is generally directed. It is in the interstice of such a dilemma that the application of Heidegger's thought proves valuable yet again.

Heidegger and Things

As we have already seen, Heidegger was very concerned about technology taken to an extreme—for example, what is happening in genetics research, space exploration, and computing.[37] We are in a technological age, and, according to Heidegger, technology is now so powerful that we define ourselves and our world in relation to it: "Our whole human existence everywhere sees itself challenged . . . to devote itself to the planning and calculating of everything. . . . and to carry this manipulation on past all bounds."[38] Heidegger was, of course, dismissive of computing. In the 1960s, he commented, "Today, the computer calculates thousands of relationships in one second. Despite their technical uses they [the relationships] are inessential."[39]

The constructivist argument given in the case of representation can be seen as a rough first approximation to a Heideggerian line of argument. Heidegger gave priority to the habitual and shared practices of making and doing over the specialized practice of theory construction. Theories are esoteric, belonging to the particular practices of scientific and related communities. But, as we have seen, there is a more radical reading of the Heideggerian position. Heidegger was concerned with constructing new understandings of what it is to be in the world, understandings that break down the conventions by which we must decide between (1) truth and reality as correspondence and (2) truth and reality as determined by social construct—also seen as a problem of objectivity versus subjectivity. He saw the posing of these and other distinctions as an unfortunate legacy of two thousand years of Western philosophical history, a history that culminated with Descartes's definition of the primacy of the divide between the thinking subject and the world of objects.

Heidegger was also strongly influenced by the later writings of the eighteenth-century German poet Hölderlin, from whom, to the frustration of the modern reader, he borrowed romantic metaphors, such as earth, sky, gods, and mortals, to elucidate his arguments.

It is worth briefly considering some Heideggerian arguments against the idea of virtual reality before considering his views on truth, through which it is possible to marshal some positive suggestions for the direction of virtual-reality research.

First, as explained in chapter 4 in relation to space, Heidegger posited a powerful counterargument to Descartes's priority of the subject-object distinction that underlies the oppositions referred to earlier (perception and representation seen as the input of sense data and correspondence, versus social construction). (Heidegger's ideas have been taken up in the context of perception, notably by Merleau-Ponty.[40]) Whereas Descartes began by asserting that the only thing beyond doubt was that he was there doubting (thereby positing the primacy of the subject), Heidegger pointed to our more primordial (basic) experience of being involved, unaware and thoroughly engaged in making and doing, in which there is no subject or object.[41] Such distinctions (subject and object) emerge in the event of some discontinuity in our working—a breakdown. They are fluid, contextual, and derivative, and they reflect our cultural preoccupations and prejudices. Similarly, the notion of pure sense data is illusive. No one has experienced it. It is a useful construct of certain kinds of scientific and philosophical investigation.

Heidegger was concerned to reverse the reductive Cartesian wisdom that an understanding of the world and our place in it can be accomplished by considering simple parts to make a complex whole—number as a basis of understanding space, logic as a basis for understanding thought, sense data as a basis for understanding being in the world. Heidegger would have had little time for a technology that claims to simulate reality by building up an experience from geometrical coordinates, or that barrages the viewer with sense data and then claims to have said something about reality.

Second, Heidegger argued strongly against the notion of "being" as "being made"—what he termed the "productionist metaphysic." That is to use technology as the driving metaphor for how we understand things in nature, as constructed, like technological equipment, though without purpose. Similarly, the productionist metaphysic presents *art* as something made, like equipment, but with "value added."[42] It is likely that Heidegger would have seen the idea of constructing reality (or its resemblance) through data and algorithms as untenable. The idea is the ultimate reduction—the ultimate manifestation of the productionist metaphysic. It is as if to say nature is constructed, so let us reconstruct it in a computer.

Third, according to Heidegger, our primordial understanding of being in the world is one of undifferentiated involvement. Things are disclosed through breakdown, in a situation. The idea of virtual reality is that everything in the field of view is presented to the senses. Heidegger observed that science operates with this "ontic" assumption. It treats things as ever "present-at-hand," laid out for our inspection, and knowable—a useful exercise, within limits.[43] Seen in this light, virtual reality is a literal enactment of the Cartesian ontology. It cocoons a person as an isolated subject within a field of sensations. In so doing it attempts to turn being into an ontic phenomenon. The claim is that everything is there, presented to the subject.

Because everything Heidegger suggests about our being indicates that we are not constituted like that (a subject in receipt of sense data), the fully realized virtual-reality environment would appear at best completely *un*real, at worse a world without differentiation, pulling us in every direction at once.

Fourth, the dark side of a technology is where it purports to make everything accessible as a potentiality to be exploited.[44] Heidegger sees some technologies as enabling, fitting into a new and emerging pattern of human practices, and revealing something about the environment in which they are situated. Recapping Heidegger's example of the bridge—the bridge reveals the banks and the character of the river, through the way it is reflected in the water and the way the pylons have to be built to withstand the river's flow. By way of contrast, a hydroelectric scheme appears to reveal "nothing of significance" about the river. The river becomes a potential to be exploited as an energy source. According to Heidegger, the hydroelectric technology brings all things to the same level. It tells us that the river is no different from coal dug up from the ground. Clearly there are also inappropriate bridges and appropriate dams (and the example is a romantic one, strongly influenced by Hölderlin's hymn to the Rhine), but Heidegger's point is clear. Certain technologies appear to exhibit a leveling characteristic through which whole slabs of the environment, or our experience, are reduced to some common denominator, such as energy, data, or measurement.

We could extract similar examples from the world of computing. A computerized drawing system is enabling in many ways, including in what it reveals about the geometrical and transformational aspects of line, color, and composition in the practice of drawing. The technology makes no claims of completeness. It does not purport to present the last word on drawing, present the complete drawing experience, or reduce drawing to an essential set of geometrical manipulations; neither are these goals necessarily built into the research that surrounds the technology. On the other hand, virtual-reality technology seems to be driven by the goal of presenting the last word on reality. Everything will be described and represented. Virtual reality places "reality itself" into the computer. Even other people can be objects in this world. Through this technology, it will be "obvious" that the appropriation of reality is simply a matter of data processing, and, as with the hydroelectric dam, everything becomes (according to this Heideggerian reading) a potential for exploitation.

Fifth, Heidegger also wrote about the nature of *things*—ordinary things, like jugs and shoes.[45] Needless to say, he did not see things merely as collections of properties. In the light of his sensitive consideration of the nature of materiality and culture (more specifically his complex argument about the collision between "earth" and "world"), it is implausible to imagine that we could model even a mundane thing, such as a jug, in a computer such that the model could manifest anything beyond what it was intended for: that we could warm it with our hands, feel the weight change as we filled it with water and flowers, hold it up to our ear and hear the sea, or watch our distorted reflection in the droplets forming on the outside as we remove it from the refrigerator. These irregularities are not inessential to what it is to manipulate a jug and make the experience.

These arguments suggest that we should be cautious in the development of virtual-reality technology, change the way it is talked about, and change the claims that are made of it. However, it is possible to embark on a more positive project from a reading of Heidegger. Bearing in mind these cautions, and an awareness of its limitations, what possible use could there be in virtual-reality technology?

Truth and Representation

In *Being and Time,* Heidegger directly addressed the issue of truth as correspondence.[46] His arguments have something to say about the idea of truthful representations, hence indirectly about virtual-reality technology's quest for realism. Heidegger did not object to the idea of truth as correspondence but pointed to a more primordial understanding of truth. He asked, how is it that the idea of correspondence is possible in the first place? Before we can make a statement that something corresponds to some state of affairs, there must be a particular comportment or disposition toward the thing or the state of affairs we are talking about. He argued that what enables us to identify a correspondence in the first place is our disposition to be open to the nature of things. In an "authentic" situation, we cultivate the freedom for things to disclose (i.e., reveal) themselves.[47] According to Heidegger, this idea of disclosure was evident in the original meaning of the Greek word for truth (*aletheia*). *Aletheia* meant nonconcealment, or disclosure, the idea of truth all but covered up by a subsequent philosophical concern with the notion of correctness, or correspondence. As with many of Heidegger's arguments (about sensation, knowledge, practice, theory, being, and truth), there is an appeal to something more basic or primordial than what is revealed through our modern orthodoxy.[48]

In the case of truth as disclosure, what is disclosed? Primarily it is a world that is disclosed, well understood in this context as a culture or some aspect of it—perhaps some aspect of human practice. Heidegger illustrates how the work of art discloses a world.[49] He describes a pair of peasant shoes depicted in a painting by van Gogh. We find out from the signs of wear and soiling about the life of toil working the land. It is less interesting to remark on whether the picture is a true likeness of something than what the picture discloses or, rather, how truth is at work in the picture. The notion of true likeness is only meaningful in a specialized realm, as in the *practice* of constructing or analyzing perspective compositions.

What is the immediate value of this notion of truth (as disclosure) outside of an appreciation of art? We can recall one of Heidegger's famous examples, that of the Greek temple. A modern analysis might be that first there is a context of people, plants, and topography; that these are stable and unchangeable; and that they may have constituted a fitting environment for building a temple.[50] The temple was added to this context at a particular moment in time. However, appreciating the disclosive nature of the temple (a consideration of "how truth is at work" in the temple) compels us to look at all this in reverse order. According to Heidegger, the temple "discloses a world." It brings the physical environment (earth) into presence (which is simply a stronger way of saying "it reveals something about it") and provides an identity for the people using it, an outlook on themselves (world). How did the temple bring the physical environment into presence? Its solidity reveals the ephemeral nature of the trees and the ocean. It brings them into presence in their many attributes (it reveals their many attributes). The columns catch the sun's rays at dawn and thereby reveal the nature of the sky. In the case of the temple as an authentic work, as part of the cultural practices of its day, it also brings the deity into presence. Nowadays the Greek temple is a museum piece, in which these aspects of how truth is at work are partially lost or changed. The world is now that of art connoisseurs, tourism, the culture of romantic painting, academic scholarship, history lessons, nostalgia, and so on. Similarly, a bridge discloses (brings into presence) the banks of the river and the movement of the water itself. It is not that these features are already there and the bridge simply draws attention to them. To assert as much is to make "ontic" claims— to assume that everything is basically there and present (part of the game of science).

What can be said about the disclosive capabilities of working drawings, such as the blueprints of a temple or a bridge? The orthodox account might be that blueprints convey information about objects, materials, sizes, and spatial configurations as instructions from the designer to the builder. What is in the drawings corresponds to how the structure is to be manifested. Heidegger does not discuss working drawings, but he writes about assertions (straightforward communicative utterances in language),[51] and we can extrapolate a Heideggerian line of argument in which the orthodox view takes second place.

There are construction practices—the activities of builders and tradespeople, who, left to their own devices, will skillfully build temples and bridges (as we see in the exercise of certain craft skills, such as erecting simple buildings and making simple furniture without working drawings, and some speculative building practice) in keeping with their practices. Drawings are interventions into those practices. Drawings make sense through familiarity with the skilled practices of producing and reading blueprints and of local construction. As such, the drawings contain cues or correctives to habitual practice: rather than continue the concrete of the column into the beam, place a steel support between them; rather than extend the rafters beyond the wall, stop the roof at a parapet. As interventions into construction practice, the drawings reveal aspects of the builder's own practice to the builder and, hopefully, to the designer. Successful architects seem to be those who have developed this rapport with local construction practice, and builders have been known to change their practice through working with architects. Seen in this light, the drawings can be said to reveal a changing world of practice. This revealing constitutes a predisposition within which it is possible to adopt the shorthand language of "this line corresponds to a wall" and "locate window *A* in wall *X.*" According to this Heideggerian understanding of working drawings, unless the drawings first disclose such a world, we cannot see them as corresponding to anything nor as providing sets of instructions.

Similarly, an integrated CAD system and database discloses the multifarious practices of consultants, contractors, and statutory authorities. Otherwise we might be deceived into thinking that the model in the database corresponded primarily to the essence of some built form. Similarly, a photo-realistic computer perspective seems to disclose a world of computer-graphics connoisseurs and marketing practices. What does a virtual-reality system disclose? How is truth at work in the virtual-reality system? In order to address these questions, it is helpful to look more carefully at an aspect of disclosure only hinted at so far. An important aspect of Heidegger's notion of disclosure is the role of difference.

Technology Opens up a World through Difference

Science and related fields seem to trade heavily in the importance of similarity: *this* situation is similar to *that* situation. Science searches for the underlying structures of things and phenomena. It is expected that once we get beneath the surface, we can find out what things have in common and thereby understand them better. Phenomena are abstracted so that they are describable in the same way. The medium of abstraction is commonly that of categories, entities, attributes, and quantification[52] or number, formula, logic, and rule. This interest in similarity is evident in the quest for the structures underlying language and social practices (as in structuralism). It is also evident in the concern in design fields, such as architecture, for identifying typologies, generic forms, and ordering principles.

In the field of computer graphics, computer images are often considered interesting because they are similar to photographs. It is also thought that images are fascinating because they are similar in some way to the real thing. Apparently virtual reality has the attraction of supposedly being so like the real world that we are deceived into thinking we are in the fabricated reality.

In our discussion of deconstruction in chapter 3, we examined Derrida's identification of the role of difference in language. It is not necessary to search far to discover evidence in human thought for the primordiality of difference as opposed to similarity. Saussure[53] demonstrated that it is difference that makes language possible—the difference between this word ("cat") and another word ("sat"). Clearly, categorization is not possible without difference. Foucault points to the triumph of difference over attempts to introduce conformity: "[T]he power of normalization . . . individualizes by making it possible to measure gaps, to determine levels, to fix specialities . . . all the shading of individual difference."[54] As we have seen, Derrida makes maximum play on the nature of difference, even to the extent of creating a new word (*différance*) that implies (in relation to language) "that meaning is always deferred, perhaps to the point of an endless supplementarity, by the play of signification."[55] To focus on difference is to embark on limitless discovery. By contrast, identifying sameness seems to close off discussion.[56] If we are intent on finding out what is the same about things, then our search ends when we achieve the goal. On the other hand, difference reveals further difference. Difference also opens up the possibility of dialectic, the revealing interplay between two entities discussed in chapter 2. (We tend to applaud the discovery of similarity as a basis for bringing people together. In the light of the importance of difference, an "authentic" community is not one in which everyone thinks the same way but one in which the differences are most revealing.)

The theme of difference runs through Heidegger's thinking. Heidegger talks about the disclosive nature of the friction between what he terms "earth" and "world." Traditional discourse on art focused on matter and form: how form was given to materials, how nature relates to culture, how chaos is tamed with order. Generally, it was a case of form being imposed on matter. This inevitably led to the orthodox dialectic about object and subject. Heidegger recast the issue through new metaphors, or rather old, primordial metaphors. For Heidegger, the distinction was between earth and world. Rather than chaotic or formless, the earth is that which is not knowable. What it "brings forth" (reveals) it also conceals. Earth offers the greatest resistance to the "openness" (truth) made possible by the work of art. World is well understood in terms of the culture of a people, in the sense of Hegel's idea of an epoch. So, the earth conceals, whereas the world reveals. However, rather than assert that the artwork exposes features hidden in the earth, that is, reveals or imitates nature, Heidegger says that in an artwork or an artifact, "the earth towers up within the work."[57] This towering up is in the direction of a world, with which it is in inevitable conflict. Kockelmans describes the phenomenon as follows. "The conflict and strife between world and earth is 'fixed' in the *Gestalt* [roughly, holistic structure] of the work and shows itself in and through it."[58]

How can we translate this lofty characterization of the importance of difference into a consideration of HCI, CAD, and virtual reality? According to Heidegger, a drawing (e.g., by Dürer) "draws out the fissure . . . between measure and that which is without measure."[59] In any drawing, there is a tension between an ordering scheme and that which defies order. The floor plan of a cathedral embodies a dialectic (the interplay between two entities enabled through difference) between a system of spatial and structural organization (world) and the materiality of the site, stone, mortar, timber, and glass (earth). There is a clash between order (a major preoccupation of the *world* of the designer) and the realized materiality of the building (earth). Seen in this light, identifying a grid system (what makes this building similar to that building) in the analysis of a building is relatively trivial. The excitement of a building lies in the difference between systems of order imposed on it (e.g., the imposition of a Christian order onto an Islamic one in the Cordoba mosque), the destruction of the grid, and the deviations from regularity. There appears to be no theory of difference, in the sense of a mathematical or symbolic formulation by which we can predict. What is interesting is what passes through the gaps, which is mostly everything.

As indicated above, working drawings open up a world through difference, for the contractor. First, there are differences in terms of signs.[60] The difference between two marks on the drawing enables us to identify one set of marks as a window and the other as a door. Second, there is the huge gulf between what the drawings are supposed to represent and what is actually realized. This difference is the building realized in materials on the site—the construction process as a kind of dialectic. Third, insofar as they describe anything, what the drawings do not describe are the skills base and experience of the contractor and those in the trades. In this way, the drawings reveal the world of construction practice through difference. Fourth, there are the skilled practices of building construction into which the drawings intervene. The builder would do one thing (perhaps build the wall entirely of brick), whereas the drawings are produced in such a way as to ensure that something different is accomplished (perhaps timber panels beneath the windows). The drawings bring the builder's own practices to light. Similar explanations related to the ubiquity of difference could be presented in the case of integrated CAD models.

How does difference operate in the case of a computer technology like virtual reality? The technology reveals, discloses, and opens up a world, but not primarily in the sense expected by virtual-reality writers. The world is disclosed through difference.

First, virtual reality brings the clash between "earth" and "world" into sharp relief. Taken as concrete materiality, the "earth" is the very thing virtual reality attempts to capture in its models. It does so with recourse to the "world" of number and geometry.

Second, the expectations of virtual reality differ from their realization as working computer systems. The dialectic this produces constitutes the basis of research programs—the world of research practice.

Third, virtual reality informs us about reality, primarily through the limits of the technology. A virtual-reality model can only ever be a "closed world." It is unlikely to offer security from real threats, such as starvation or electrocution. Virtual-reality real estate is unlikely to appreciate like actual real estate. Virtual reality is unlikely to enable the procreation and nurture of human beings. By most accounts, walking through a virtual building is nothing like the experience of being in a real building. Taking this point a little further, it may transpire that reflection on the difference between virtual reality and reality will engender new support for non-Cartesian notions of space and sensual experience—a non-Cartesian world of intellectual inquiry. In this sense, virtual reality will have informed us about reality.

Fourth, the enabling character of technology may lie precisely in the difference between the virtual-reality experience and the experience of reality. In fact, it is the difference between virtual reality and reality that seems to drive research. Virtual-reality researchers want people to be able to handle radioactive substances with alacrity and without contamination, perform delicate surgery on tiny organs that appear several yards wide, see straight through human flesh as though with X-ray vision, dissolve through walls, jump off buildings, shrink things so that one can look at them as models and then expand them so one can move around inside. Reality does not seem to afford these possibilities. Nor does it allow you to replay what you have just done, store the results on floppy disk, draw in space with a can of "foam," or swim in a pool of psychedelic colors. Some of this thinking about the unreality of virtual reality is expressed by Heim, though he considered this unreality to be optional rather than inevitable: "Something less than real evokes our power of imagination and visualisation."[61]

Recovering Virtual Reality

These reflections on Heidegger's thought about truth have led to a consideration of difference. The idea of truth as correspondence has given way to the more primordial (basic) understanding of truth as disclosure. Seen in this light, virtual reality fails to impress us with its claims to reveal something new about reality in the sense intended by certain virtual-reality writers. Heidegger's view, furthermore, does not support the data-oriented model of perception on which much virtual-reality research seems to be based. Thus, virtual reality fails, too, in its claims of presenting us with correspondences to reality, of which illusion will persuade us.

In the light of this commentary, any picture, and by extension a computer model presented to the senses through virtual-reality technology, discloses a world. These worlds are the vast, changing, and slippery realms of human practices (and culture). The edifice of correspondence built on the surface of this world (to mix Heidegger's metaphors) could appear almost anywhere. Dressed in headsets and armed with a data glove, I might be impressed with how well the experience corresponds to what I thought it would be like to observe a computer model with headset and dataglove; what it might be like having points, lines, and planes in the shape of a building in Cartesian space moving past my eyes; having a dream; moving through jelly. All of these constitute correspondences in a particular context. Virtual-reality research cannot ignore the substratum of a "disclosed world" revealed through the technology, as though the whole thing were simply a matter of direct mappings between objects, computer models, and something in the mind.

Would virtual-reality technology have been invented had perception and representation not been conceived of primarily in terms of data input and correspondence? Another way of looking at the phenomenon of the invention of the technology is by appreciating the power of metaphor to drive research projects, to be explored more fully in chapter 7. Seen in this light, virtual-reality technology did not need *theories* of perception or representation to drive it. In the world within which the technology has arisen, there are many privileged metaphors favoring a technological view of experience. Heidegger's characterization of the "productionist metaphysic" (natural entities as built up) is one example. But technologies like virtual reality trade heavily in other technologies, with which they can be seen to relate metaphorically. Aspects of virtual-reality technology are seen as wearing visual earphones ("eyephones"), wearing a space suit, taking drugs, being on a stage, operating puppets. These and other metaphors have extended the concepts of virtual reality and its research programs. Thus, virtual-reality research is enhanced by exploring interesting and enabling metaphors.

The other side of metaphor is difference. Virtual-reality research can be enhanced by considering how different it is from the metaphors through which it is conceived. In appreciating that virtual reality is not like operating puppets, we see that we are not constrained (as though by strings), that we can achieve something other than entertainment, that the puppets can change identity to become the people operating them, and so on. The virtual-reality experience is not like walking through a building, so we can fly through it, pass through walls, and shrink and expand the building around us. A geometrical model is not like the real thing, so we can distort the coordinate grid as we "move" through it and experiment with different geometrical transformations and projections (isometric or axonometric). Recognizing difference within the play of metaphors opens up the possibility of new metaphors. The issue of difference brings us back again to Heidegger's notion of disclosure.

Our discussion of virtual reality brings us to a consideration of metaphor and of difference, which clearly play a role in how we understand information technology. In the next two chapters, I develop the theme of metaphor more fully, initially by reconsidering the relationship between systems theory and information technology research and development.

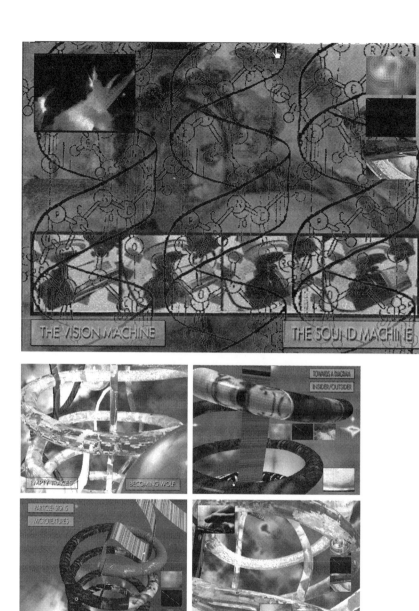

Scenes from an interactive multimedia CD-ROM titled *A Digital Rhizome* by media artist Brad Miller. The CD-ROM incorporates text and ideas from Gilles Deleuze and Felix Guattari on the rhizomic nature of becoming. The work appeared as part of an art installation at the Pompidou Centre in Paris.

6

Systematic Design

Methods, Theories, and Models in Design

Information technology comes under the purview of systems theory.[1] Computer programs and hardware configurations are undeniably systems, with identifiable interdependent components, inputs, outputs, feedback loops, control procedures, and nested subsystems. Computers and other information technologies can be understood as systems, but does the same apply to the design of computer systems? Can the place of computer systems in society, the processes by which computers come about, and the evaluation of computer systems be understood in systems terms? In this chapter, I investigate some of the many attempts to systematize the design process and how these sit in relation to postmodern theory.

At first glance there are several major discrepancies between postmodern discourse and systems theory. As we have seen, postmodernism wears several complexions, including critical theory, deconstruction, hermeneutics, and pragmatism. Whichever complexion it wears, postmodernism resists discourse, such as systems theory discourse, which confidently believes that having reduced a phenomenon to constituent parts and their interrelations, we thereby understand the phenomenon. Of course, systems theory also renounces reductionism. But while trading in the notion of wholes and asserting that the "whole is more than the sum of its parts," systems theory inevitably relies on identifying and manipulating parts and relations in its actual application. Postmodern discourse is also highly skeptical of metaphysics—of any discourse that

looks for fundamentals and foundations. Where it exhibits metaphysical tendencies in its own discourse, it seeks to undermine even
its own claims. Counter to this, general systems theory aims to discover principles common to all the sciences: "Developing unifying
principles running 'vertically' through the universe of the individual
sciences, this theory brings us near to the goal of the unity of
science."[2]

Postmodern discourse also renounces appeals to reason as residing in verbal propositions, formal logic or the syllogism. It avoids
discourse that trades in symbols and numbers other than for very
pragmatic uses. The rhetoric of systems theory by no means limits
itself to manipulating symbols, but systems theory of any operational
value results in mathematical and symbolic models. These models
manipulate signals, messages, and energy as quantifiable inputs and
outputs. Further, postmodernism rejects fields of endeavor that exhibit a bold confidence in appropriating the tenets of science outside its proven fields of operation—the formulation of testable
theories pertaining to natural systems and mathematics. Systems theory acknowledges such differences in domain, distinguishing between closed and open systems. Whereas the properties of closed
systems are considered to be well understood, open systems, such
as living organisms and human organizations, conduct complex
transactions with their environment and are poorly understood. According to systems theory, we should be cautious about generalizing
from the behavior of closed systems to open systems: "The very existence of an environment and interaction of the organization with
this environment is the most essential aspect of continuance of the
organization. Great caution is therefore needed in applying these
concepts of information and entropy to open systems."[3] This caution apparently does not prevent its advocates from applying systems
theory to open systems, notably in management and organization
theory, where "the organization is regarded as an integrated complex of interdependent parts capable of interacting sensitively and
correctly with one another and with their environment."[4] Nor does
this caution prevent its advocates from applying systems theory to
understanding the design process. Herbert Simon is one of the foremost advocates of applying systems thinking to design. According to

Simon, we need a "science of design": "The professional schools will reassume their professional responsibilities just to the degree that they can discover a science of design, a body of intellectually tough, analytic, partly formalizable, partly empirical, teachable doctrine about the design process."[5]

Postmodern thinking is not necessarily critical of systems theory as such but is skeptical of its claims to universality, of attempts to use systems theory as a measuring stick against which other fields of scholarship should be compared, of suggestions that education and understanding depend on it, and of attempts to extend its application beyond the natural sciences.

For postmodernism, the issue of systems theory is something of a dead letter. Its popularity and credibility in the 1950s and 1960s was due not only to its operational and technical promise in science and engineering but also its promise to provide a means of addressing major global and social issues. What are the global insights of systems theory? A report by the Club of Rome in the early 1970s invoked systems theory to propose that the world's problems have to be tackled as a whole rather than piecemeal, and we should take account of the mutual relationships among social class, population, food supply, and the environment.[6] This insight appears quaint in the postmodern age. From the point of view of postmodernism, systems theory has had its day. It now has little to say about major issues—about politics, freedom, equality, power, the impact of technology. The discussion has moved on, and, with the usurpation of systems theory in the discussion of global issues, it seems to have lost its appeal in the postmodern arena.[7]

Postmodern discourse does have a place for systems theory, however. Heidegger distinguishes between two levels of scholarly discourse: ontic study and thinking. Ontic study includes science, social science, psychology, philosophy, and theology. It is metaphysical but useful in its own domains of operation. It seeks causes. We may readily characterize disciplines that call on systems theory, whether "legitimately" or otherwise, as ontic. Heidegger suggests that he has no argument with these realms of scholarly reflection. Thinking is of course Heidegger's own particular brand of reflection by which he and the tradition in which he places himself lets things disclose themselves. This is ontological reflection and pertains to Being. According to Heidegger, science and other ontic modes of study have no part in this. Nor do they need to: "[S]cience itself does not think, and cannot think—which is its good fortune, here meaning the assurance of its own appointed course."[8] There is of course a criticism in Heidegger's distinctions. The claims of science and other ontic studies is that they are substantial and universal, and not only useful. They establish their credibility by claiming that they fit together, that they are part of a larger picture, that they present and seek to answer deep ontological questions. For Heidegger, this level of significant scholarship is reserved for thinking, which the philosophical and scientific tradition has been unable to appropriate. Let systems theory and other ontic studies be applied wherever they will. Heidegger is content to leave ontic scholarly reflection largely to its own devices. In Heidegger we find an implied criticism of ontic scholarship but no imperative for reform. Much postmodern writing follows this Heideggerian line. Studies in information technology or design that accord primacy to systems theory are categorized by postmoderns as ontic, useful in their own way if they are not extended beyond their own sphere of operation.

This "indifference" on the part of postmodernism to systems theory means that postmodernism focuses on its own agendas—power, how texts operate, ontological questions about the constitution of the subject, how we are constituted by our technologies, and the dismantling of metaphysics. Postmodern discourse therefore focuses largely on different issues than the theoretical and technical focus of systems theory. As I have shown, postmodern issues impinge profoundly on information technology design, but they are not necessarily the issues that systems theorists have identified. In keeping with Kuhn's characterization of rival paradigms in science, we have incommensurate domains of discourse largely ignorant of each other and at cross purposes. The theories and problems of one paradigm are largely ignored or misunderstood by the proponents of the rival paradigm.

A further postmodern response to systems theory is to discriminate between appropriate and inappropriate applications of systems theory and to identify those applications that perpetrate instrumental reason—dehumanizing agencies, causes of dislocation and ecological disaster, the promotion of hegemonic regimes, and the perpetration of disabling notions about human society and psychology. This is in part the legacy of critical theory (Horkheimer, Adorno, Marcuse), which promotes skepticism and suspicion of any system of understanding—any study, whether ontic or ontological. As we have seen, in the case of computer systems, this scrutiny is advanced by philosophers and computer scientists like Dreyfus, Winograd, Flores, and Weisenbaum[9] in the form of detailed critiques of the assumptions underlying artificial-intelligence and cognitive-science research. In part, this criticism targets the extension of systems theory into human cognition. In chapter 1, I highlighted how the extension of systems theory beyond science and engineering—revealing a rationalistic orientation—is in conflict with pragmatism. In this chapter, I outline in greater detail attempts to systematize design, and I show what uses, if any, can be made of the insights of systems theory from a postmodern perspective.

The view of design presented so far in this book has been pragmatic. Design is presented as a matter of doing, engaging the materials of specific design situations. The pragmatic tenets of postmodernism seem to militate against design as system and method. Postmodernism attempts to deliver design from such metaphysical pursuits. But the systems theory view of design holds sway in many quarters. Whatever the praxis of *doing* design is, the praxis of speaking about and teaching design is still largely dominated by the tenets of systems theory. We commonly use the language of systems theory if not its methods. This skepticism of systems theory is not to suggest that systems theory has provided no valuable insights into design. My thesis is that the best insights of these studies can be appropriated through metaphor, to be discussed in greater detail in chapter 7.

What is the appropriate and uncontroversial domain of systems theory? Systems theory provides an important function in structuring how we understand the technical aspects of computers. Computer science carries the hallmarks of a systematic and scientific discipline. Here computation is the subject of scientific study. A computer program can be usefully regarded as a system made up of interrelated parts, consisting of algorithms, as a series of steps defined by symbols, which takes data in the form of symbols and produces outcomes as symbols. Within computer science, this general algorithmic behavior constitutes the phenomenon under scientific study. The algorithmic phenomenon is comparable to what we find in other branches of science, such as chemistry and physics, which involve phenomena pertaining to chemicals, particles, mechanics, reactions, and so on. Computer science studies symbol manipulation. Algorithms also exhibit behaviors that can be generalized; there are categories of algorithmic behavior—algorithms can be determinate or indeterminate, decidable or nondecidable. There are also theories of computation (automata theory) by which we can categorize algorithms and by which we can predict their gross behavior. As one textbook on computer science puts it, "We are concerned with the Theory of Computers, which means that we form several abstract mathematical models that will describe with varying degrees of accuracy parts of computers and types of computers and similar machines."[10]

Computer systems engineering is not the only design discipline that has a scientific component. Science in other branches of engineering and architecture involves testing materials empirically and using formulas to predict the resistance of structural members to stress and weathering, or to scientifically study air flow, sound transmission, and heat transfer. This is not to say that architecture and engineering are sciences, only that they have a scientific component.

In this discussion, we have to be wary of the various uses of the term "science." We often distinguish between the natural and the social sciences. The classic examples of the natural sciences are physics, chemistry, biology, and mathematics. Outside of the natural sciences we have the human, or behavioral sciences. Some have described the human sciences as the hermeneutical sciences, because they involve interpretation and are not necessarily amenable to empirical study or systematization.[11] The appropriation of the term "science" to apply to any discipline is less problematic in languages like German—the term *Wissenschaft* has a much more liberal usage than the word "science" in English. In German the distinction is usually between *Naturwissenschaft* (natural science) and *Geisteswissenschaft* (human science).

In some quarters, what is rightly called a human science borrows terminology and methods from the natural sciences. A case in point is design, and Simon's ambition for it, mentioned above. What kind of a science, if any, is the study of design? Algorithms can be studied as objects in a natural science—computer science—but can the behavior of the designer or the organization that constructs those algorithms? The postmodern project presented in the preceding chapters points to a resounding "no," though the attempts to define it as a science have been influential.

What are the motivations for applying systems theory to design? From a Heideggerian and critical theory perspective, design is prone to instrumental reason and the desire to control people and outcomes. In its own terms, there appear to be three motivations within systems research for uncovering a systems-theoretic basis to design, that is, for rendering design amenable to systems theory. First, computer systems, hardware, and software are *designed*. If systems theory has something to say about design, then design can be researched, discussed, and enhanced, using the same methods and terminology by which one considers computer systems themselves. Second, computer systems are assembled that are meant to assist in some way, architectural, engineering, graphic, and other designers, including computer systems designers. So, the design of computer systems for drawing and communications has to take some account of the way designers do things. The systematic study of design is thought to assist this understanding. Third, the computer is thought to provide a testing ground for theories and models of what happens when designers design. If design can be systematized, then it can be coded into a computer. Programmers attempt to induce a computer to actually design, following some theory or other about what design is. The application of systems theory to design operates in three ways: it attempts to contribute to the better design of computer systems; it attempts to provide models that will help create useful computer systems for designers, and it seeks to develop and test models of designing on a computer.

Methods, Theories, and Models in Science

What is the systems view in science or in any other discipline? The technical definitions of systems have been presented at length in the vast literature on systems theory. The approach I will follow here is to focus on understandings of the key components of scientific discipline, which underpin systems theory and which have a much longer history. In appealing to science (and systems theory), we have access to three key phenomena that also appear in discussions about design: methods, theories, and models. My intention here is not to provide an account of science but to explain the major concepts appropriated from certain understandings of science into design studies.

Methods are procedures. According to Ong, method came to full flower in the validation of medical cures and the development of pedagogical procedures and curriculum organization in the Middle Ages.[12] Methods therefore began as explanations but later became procedures. Following Descartes, a method in philosophy is taken as a procedure for arriving at truth. In the natural sciences, a method is often a procedure or plan for verifying a hypothesis or inference.

It is common in science to refer to a specific method, such as an experimental procedure. But such methods are considered instances of the more general scientific method, so there is *the* scientific method, the procedure to which all scientific activity conforms and gains legitimacy. Identifying the scientific method has been, and still is, controversial. Contemporary philosophy of science, from Kuhn onward, frequently presents science as heterogeneous with many disparate methods and procedures. Nonetheless, some philosophers have persistently sought after *the* method of science. This pursuit is inevitably concerned with how propositional statements are derived through logic, a pursuit that many postmodern authors are at pains to avoid.

One of the simplest formulations of the scientific method is analysis and synthesis, though, as Turbayne indicates, the definitions of these terms have changed, and they have been used inconsistently.[13] According to Plato, the true scientist (the practitioner of *episteme*), as opposed to the mere technician, is engaged in deriving principles (analysis) followed by the application of those principles (synthesis) to establish new propositions. One argued the validity of the principles (analysis) prior to applying the principles (synthesis). According to this usage, to analyze is, therefore, to generalize, to derive rules that cover a large number of cases: parallel lines never meet, all fish breathe through gills, the sun rises in the East. To synthesize is to derive something specific or to effect a demonstration of the principles: this shape is an isosceles triangle, this fish is alive, tomorrow the sun will rise above that mountain. Identifying definitions and good examples of "analytical truths" and "synthetic truths" has been a major preoccupation of early philosophy of science.[14]

"Analysis" has two meanings. As suggested above, "to analyze" means "to generalize." This has been identified with the process of induction in logic. The scientist is confronted with many instances of birds with wings and induces the principle that all birds have wings. According to some, the idea of induction paved the way for experimentation as part of scientific method.[15] According to Newton, this analysis "consists in making experiments and observations, and in drawing general conclusions from them by induction, and admitting of no objections against the conclusions but such as are taken from experiments, or other certain truths."[16] According to this understanding analysis therefore entails experiment and observation.

The second meaning of "analysis" (not unrelated to the first) is to break a phenomenon down into constituent parts. This was Descartes's meaning of the analysis of a problem: "to divide each of the difficulties that I was examining into as many parts as might be possible and necessary in order to best solve it."[17]

"Synthesis" has also taken on two meanings. The first is to make logical deductions from premises and axioms, in the manner of a geometrical proof. Euclid's logical axioms regarding parallelism and congruence enable a geometrician to deduce (and to prove) that lines subtended from the endpoints of the diameter of a circle meet each other at the circumference at right angles. As another example, knowing that all birds have wings, and that an osprey is a bird, we can deduce that an osprey has wings.

The second meaning of "synthesize" is "to build up," as though from simple parts to something complex. Both definitions seemed to have informed Descartes's approach to scientific investigation.

Following on from analysis, he determined to conduct his thoughts "in an orderly way, beginning with the simplest objects and the easiest to know, in order to climb gradually, as by degrees, as far as the knowledge of the most complex, and even supposing some order among those objects which do not precede each other naturally."[18]

According to Descartes, every accomplishment of human knowledge is linked by long chains of causal argument of the kind evident in geometrical proof, such that "there is nothing so distant that one does not reach it eventually, or so hidden that one cannot discover it."[19] This synthetic process is not entirely deductive. It is not "foolproof," as in a proof. In assembly, components can go together in different ways, hence the necessity for enumeration. Descartes decided "to make such complete enumerations and such general reviews that [he] would be sure to have omitted nothing."[20] Implicit in this process is an evaluation—testing propositions against each other. So, one of the earliest characterizations of method is as analysis, synthesis, and evaluation. One of the earliest attempts to describe design in systems terms follows Descartes. In design, we break a problem down into parts (analysis), build up a solution (synthesis), then evaluate and enumerate solutions.

Systems theory applied to design also invokes the power of theories. In chapter 1 we considered the pragmatic view of theory that, in one form or another, most postmodern writers subscribe to, in which a theory (scientific or otherwise) is a tool, the application of which requires skilled and situation-specific practice. The understanding of theory as a means of generating and verifying logical and symbolic propositions takes second place. But it is the latter role of theory that is most prominent in the scientific tradition, and the one that design studies have most fervently appropriated. According to this tradition a theory is a generalization[21]—a statement that applies to many cases, such as "all birds have wings," or "force is mass times acceleration." According to Turbayne, "any set of postulates or basic laws is a theory. Indeed, any set of sentences adequate to the description of any subject-matter will count as a theory."[22] Theories are predictive. From the general principle that all birds have wings, we are able to predict that a particular bird we have heard about but not seen will have wings.

There are two other common definitions of "theory" that often confuse the discussion. As discussed in chapter 1, theory is commonly contrasted with practice. To theorize is to contemplate or speculate, in contrast to practical experimentation. According to Campbell, "it is perfectly correct to term 'theoretical' discussions which have no influence in active life."[23] "Theory," therefore, commonly carries the meaning of a hypothesis, or a hypothetical proposition, whether the proposition is general or not. To say "it is just a theory" is to state that a proposition is as yet unproven or, more precisely, that it is not yet empirically tested or believed by enough scientists (and may never be) to constitute a law or a certainty. Examples of current theories in this sense include the following: the earth is a self-regulating organism (the so-called Gaia hypothesis), carbon dioxide emissions produce global warming, and the quark is the smallest material particle. When theory is presented as something powerful and persuasive in science, it is rarely meant in this sense. The general theory of relativity is not called a theory because it is tentative, provisional, or speculative, but because of the formulaic relationships embodied in its generalizing formulas (and through which prediction is possible).

An even looser meaning of "theory" simply equates it with systematic thinking and debate within a domain, to be contrasted with the practice of a domain. Theory designates the speculative aspects of a discipline. Atomic theory, systems theory, hermeneutical theory, metaphor theory, art theory, and design theory are all theoretical in this sense. What is more commonly meant by "design theory" is "design studies."

From the point of view of pragmatism, the power of theories resides in their use as tools and in the skilled practices of the communities who apply the theories, design and conduct the experiments, make observations, and record, compare, and interpret results. But, according to the scientific tradition borrowed by the systems theoretical approach to design, the ability of theories to predict is discussed as if independent of notions of community. The importance of communities of scientists in the process of prediction and verification is a relatively recent consideration in the philosophy of science. According to the traditional view, the formula $f = ma$ is a theory in that it generalizes the relationships among phenomena in terms of the variables force (f), mass (m) and acceleration (a). The theory says that, ignoring friction, it is possible to predict the force with which a twenty-pound object will hit the ground. Automata theory enables computer scientists to predict what kind of algorithms are possible.

Theories are also said to have explanatory power, but, following Duhem,[24] it is clear that explanation is simply an extension of prediction. What constitutes a satisfactory explanation depends on context, and a theory is rarely sufficient on its own as an explanation. Asked to explain how it is that the osprey has wings, the theory that all birds have wings will be satisfactory only if one is convinced first of all that an osprey is a bird, and for that we probably will not appeal to theories so much as the authority of an expert or, more likely, our powers of observation picking out its general resemblance to a bird. We may also want to know how it is that some animals (birds) have wings and others do not. Similarly, the twenty-pound object's breaking when it hit the ground may be explicable in terms of $f = ma$, but we may be more interested in why it was dropped.

Some theories may be considered to explain with recourse to cause and therefore do not need to predict. The theories that solar flares cause radio disturbances and that salt causes corrosion in iron are also predictive. When a solar flare occurs, we can expect radio disturbance. Iron exposed to salt can be expected to corrode. There is presumably no such thing as a theory that explains but does not predict, and plausible explanations commonly require more than theories. Insofar as we assume that the power of theories resides in their ability to predict, to determine that a theory predicts well subsumes its explanatory status.

Whereas for some philosophers of science the power of science lies in its theories, for others, models are the means by which theories make sense. Models also secure the progress of science through to new discoveries. The view of science as driven by models, and the subsumption of theories within models, is more in keeping with a pragmatic orientation to science, though, as I will show, the pragmatic views of models is all but lost in the development of systems theory models in design. The purpose of models in science is explored at length by Black, Hesse, and Turbayne.[25] A model is an analogy—a set of assertions following the general form *A* is to *B* as *C* is to *D*. According to Hesse, we need models to make sense of, and to promote the development of, theories.[26] How do models work? Some observed phenomenon is expressed in an observation language.[27] In the case of sound, we may observe that sound is produced by the motion of gongs and strings, that there are such things as echoes, and that we can hear around corners. These are readily observable phenomena. Similarly, we may notice that a wave of water begins with an impact, that waves reflect, and that they diffract. These superficial observations may suggest that sound and the movement of waves in water are alike in more fundamental respects. Because water waves are more familiar and more is known about them, we may postulate that it is appropriate to investigate water waves in order to better understand sound. The model, as analogy, can be drawn up as a table showing the parallels between water waves and sound waves, based on such features as source, distance, amplitude, and frequency.

Some theories of water waves consist of equations, such as $y = a \sin 2\pi fx$, where y is the amplitude of a wave of frequency f and maximum amplitude a at distance x. Such theories will have been developed and tested and found to enable prediction when applied to water waves and before that to waves along a piece of chord. If the analogy between water waves and sound holds, we expect that sound is produced by the motion of air particles propagated in concentric spherical waves from a source of disturbance. The known theories of water waves and the analogies between them and sound enable us to construct a theory of sound. The formula $y = a \sin 2\pi fx$ can also be applied to sound. Loudness is identified with the amplitude of sound waves, and pitch is identified with frequency of sound waves. There is no guarantee that the analogy will work, but, having established these correspondences, we are then in a position to test the mathematical wave theories as theories of sound. The wave model enables us to predict (and explain) the behavior of sound.

A similar set of analogies helps explain light. Water waves provide a model for sound, which provides a model for light. The models reveal the causal relations amplitude and frequency (water) as similar to loudness and pitch (sound), which are similar to brightness and color (light).

Such model development is ubiquitous in any domain that calls itself a science. In the case of automata theory in computer science, two models are in common usage. The language model of computation involves the formal treatment of symbols, syntactic categories, and grammars. According to Cohen, "When we call our study the Theory of Formal Languages, the word 'formal' refers to the fact that all the rules for the language are explicitly stated in terms of what strings of symbols can occur. . . . In this basic model, language is not communication among intellects, but a game of symbols with formal rules."[28] A computer program contains strings of symbols resembling words. There are rules determining what constitutes a grammatical sentence. In computer languages, there are rules determining what constitutes a legal program, for example.

The second model is that of the Turing machine, a fictitious machine that allows a tape (paper or magnetic) to pass over a device (a tape head) that can read and write symbols onto the tape one at a time. The machine follows a given set of rules (a program). The movement of the tape and the writing of symbols onto the tape is determined by the rules in the program; the program, in turn, takes account of what is on the tape. The Turing machine is clearly a physical model that accomplishes for the study of algorithms what the wave model accomplishes for the study of light. The language model and the Turing machine model each structure different, though related, aspects of the behavior of algorithms; other models are based on networks and other kinds of machines.

That phenomena should be understood in science through models is not universally accepted. On the one hand, there is the view that what drives the natural sciences, such as physics, are theories alone. Theories are abstract and systematic. The ideal physical theories are mathematical structures with deductive structures, similar to Euclid's systems of geometrical proofs.[29] According to this view the theory of sound is well understood through such equations as $y = a \sin 2\pi fx$ without appeal to a model. Similarly, computers can be understood through automata theories without reference to natural language or Turing machines. Models may be psychological aids to discovery but are not essential. This view was expressed by the French physicist and philosopher Duhem, who, in reviewing a book on modern theories of electricity, complained that the book contained "nothing but strings which move around pulleys, which roll around drums, which go through pearl beads . . . toothed wheels which are geared to one another and engaged hooks. We thought we were entering the tranquil and neatly ordered abode of reason, but we find ourselves in a factory."[30]

In contrast to Duhem, an early advocate of the primacy of models was the English physicist N. R. Campbell,[31] who thought the arguments for the self-sufficiency of theory depended on notions of mathematical intelligibility and the formal characteristics of simplicity and economy. He argued that this is insufficient and that a theory also needs an intelligible interpretation in terms of an analogy or a model: "[A]nalogies are not 'aids' to the establishment of theories; they are an utterly essential part of theories, without which theories would be completely valueless and unworthy of the name."[32] He also draws attention to the dynamic nature of theory development. Theories are always being expanded and modified to account for new phenomena. Without a model, such extensions will be arbitrary. He shows how the billiard-ball model of gases promoted the development of the kinetic theory of gases. Models are essential for allowing predictions in new domains of phenomena: such as sound to light. According to this view, it is models rather than theories that drive science.

The power of models in science, therefore, lies in the similarities and differences they expose. In describing light in terms of sound, new properties of light are discovered. On testing, some properties are found to constitute disanalogies—for example, the property of requiring a medium for propagation. Identifying a major difference between the phenomena drives the quest for new models and theories. The language model of computation has similarly been a source of the development of ideas in computer science and is implicated in the development of "natural-language-understanding systems" and artificial-intelligence research.

Models are, therefore, analogies between phenomena articulated in terms of properties and relations, the latter expressed as generalizations, commonly as mathematical formulas (theories). The match between the properties and relations established for one domain will rarely be entirely adequate for the other. Such disanalogies prompt further investigation and the development of new models. In the case of computer science, there have been other models developed on and around formal language theory, notably the idea of "finite automata," trees, stacks, and transition networks, and around the Turing machine, notably the Mealy, Post, and Moore machines. Were it not that each of these models structure different aspects of the phenomenon of computation, one model would presumably suffice. There are also other models that rival those mentioned so far, such as "cellular automata" and "complex systems."

Systems theory commonly blurs the distinction between theories and models by referring to mathematical or symbolic models. Such models may include formulas for approximating some gross phenomenon, such as the behavior of populations, plant growth, and the behavior of markets. With such models, there may be no appeal to similarity from one domain to another other than to the domain of number and symbol. The title of "model" is considered fitting, because the models are often tentative, and researchers in the discipline may acknowledge that there are several such models. One may select from a range of incommensurate and contradicting predictive models in the course of one's investigations. Their designers and users commonly acknowledge them as simplifications:[33] for example, changes in population are treated as though they were continuous, or the movement of people through a building is described only in terms of nodes and connecting lines.

In the terms discussed above, such models are more accurately called "hypothetical theories," "noncausal theories," or, according to Black,[34] "mathematical treatments" that are, in turn, implicated in models. The actual models within which the theories fit may be assumed or no longer be of concern or be unrecognized. A "statistical model" of demography[35] is, therefore, a mathematical theory, with predictive capabilities, but the model may actually be human societies modeled on animal societies, which may, in turn, be understood with reference to several models: materiality (density and dispersion), explosions, waves, and mountain ranges. Systems theory generally ignores the analogical nature of models, or at least deprivileges it. This is hardly surprising. As a quest for a metascience, systems theory is considerably weakened if it shows itself to be dependent upon ordinary, everyday analogies rather than mathematics.

Independently of systems theory, models have also been characterized in other ways, such as iconic, which means literally embodying the features in the original object that are of interest,[36] such as in a scale model of a ship. This is one of Peirce's characterizations of a model.[37] There are also analog models,[38] in which an attempt is made to reproduce the structure of the original, if not the form, as in a symbolic model of the relationships among the working components of a ship. Some of these concepts are appropriated in design.

Methods, Theories, and Models of Design

Identifying and developing methods, theories, and models of design was a major concern of the design-methods movement in the period immediately after World War II and into the 1960s.[39] This movement sought to put design on a scientific footing—applying systems theory to design. Initially, these methods, theories, and models were thought to apply equally to architecture, engineering, and computer systems design. Because systems theory deals with theory that is common across disciplines, it was thought that design could be studied as a discipline in its own right, independently of domain. Systems theory applied to design was about principles that underlie all design activity, independently of the kind of artifact produced.

The triple of analysis, synthesis, and enumeration (or evaluation) was taken up by the design methods movement as both a model and a method of the design process. To be more precise, we could say that science was the model, and an understanding of one of its properties, namely, its method (as analysis and synthesis), was taken over by analogy into design. An early formulation of this method is succinctly articulated by Alexander, for whom analysis was a kind of breaking down, and synthesis was a building up. According to Alexander "[E]very design problem begins with an effort to achieve fitness between two entities: the form in question and its context."[40] A misfit constitutes a problem. Each instance of a misfit between form and context can be indicated with a variable. During design, as one misfit is eradicated another occurs, and the system of variables changes from one state to the next. Because of the complexity of interactions, it is necessary to consider the system of variables as forming subsystems. In traditional processes in which designs emerge and change over several generations of craft activity, in response to slow changes in context, the form is changed according to the dictates of relatively independent subsystems of misfit variables. According to Alexander, in modern-day "self-conscious" design, we divide problems into subproblems, in the manner of an inverted tree of related problems and subproblems. This process is analysis. At some stage, we reach a set of subproblems that map onto known solutions. The task is then to assemble these subsolutions into the total solution. On Alexander's view, this is the process of synthesis.

With this formulation of design we see the easy slippage into scientific terminology that accompanies the Cartesian method as adopted by the design methods movement. The concept of finding a fit between a form and its context is suggested with the same assurance as the suggestion that a scientist compares two items of data, or compares the prediction of a theory with the results of an experiment. Design variables, such as room sizes, beam lengths, wall color, and so on are presented as if they are variables in some scientific equation. Designed artifacts are broken down in the same way that the phenomenon of light is broken down into frequency, amplitude, and distance, and the design process is broken down into component procedures in the same way that a scientific procedure can be reduced to a series of steps to be repeated in different laboratory situations.

There is also a ready slippage into the notions of goals. In the same way that logic works toward proving a theorem, or a scientific experiment is set up to confirm (or refute) a hypothesis, design begins with a problem to be solved or a goal to be accomplished. As we have discussed already, Dewey's wrestling with the complexity of means and ends, Heidegger's denial of the primacy of propositions in\human action, and Derrida's presentation of the illusive and contingent nature of intentions render the tenets of the methods movement highly problematic. We will nonetheless pursue the models here and recover their best insights in chapter 7 by a further consideration of the nature of models, rather than through a detailed critique.

A common variation on Alexander's theme is the method of design as analysis, synthesis, and evaluation depicted spatially as a flow diagram. Analysis leads to synthesis, and evaluation is situated on a feedback loop to analysis again. In general terms, this is often interpreted as "define the problem," "seek a solution," and "evaluate the result." This evaluation may lead to a reappraisal of the problem definition and a number of iterations through the process. The body of computational techniques known as operations research fits within the analysis, synthesis, and evaluation method. For example, some operations research techniques optimize the performance of a structural system, by maximizing strength and minimizing cost.[41]

Within design studies, both rigorous and informal methods have been proposed based on analysis and synthesis. Christopher Jones provides an extensive catalog of design methods as codified procedures to be selected and rigidly applied to accomplish some design objective.[42] These mathematical procedures are often referred to as first-generation methods. In contrast to idealized methodologies, Broadbent[43] advocates the use of less-formal methods. These are empirical or "second-generation" methods and are intended to help designers collaborate and be creative: brainstorming, synectics, and the use of tables and checklists as aids rather than rigid procedures.

The advocates of these methods are generally working within the domain of computerization—computer-aided design (CAD) research and artificial intelligence. But the methods are also common currency within design studies generally. The model of analysis, synthesis, and evaluation provides the basic structure of the *Architectural Plan of Work;* in education, design studios are often structured according to these three phases, and debates about engineering education are often couched in terms of rival orientations toward analysis or synthesis (though here analysis is often taken to be evaluation, and synthesis is design). The advocacy of goal setting and planning in management and administration also relates to these methods.

Design studies that appropriate systems theory also appeal to the notion of generation—generative models. Within Descartes's method, we find a suggestion that synthesis involves combining and recombining the elements of an argument and testing the results. Here generation is one of the phases of a method. Generation is primarily a property of machines. It can also be a property of organisms, but organisms primarily understood as machines with interchangeable parts. Mitchell[44] traces the early discussion of generative systems back to Aristotle, who recognized that within the animal kingdom there are a small number of kinds of bodily components (such as legs, ears, eyes, and tails) but many different forms these components can take (such as ears that are short or long, round or pointed). Animals seem to exhibit these forms in different combinations.[45] Aristotle argues that cities could be so arranged, by combining alternative components.

The relationship between mechanical generation and thought certainly dates to the thirteenth century. Ramón Lull produced a machine consisting of wheels annotated with symbols in order to generate new combinations of words, hence, hopefully, new knowledge. Generative systems can similarly be identified with artists and architects, such as Leonardo da Vinci and J. N. L. Durand.[46]

The machine model and the generative properties of machines have obviously influenced mathematics and computer science, which in turn have influenced cognitive science and design studies. In the same way that sound as a model for light yields vibrations, frequency, and amplitude, the machine model yields for design the components of states, state transition operators, and controls. In the same way that there are theories linking the components of light, there are theories linking the components of design. The language and Turing machine models and the automata theory (for proving the properties of algorithms and classifying different generative systems) also furnish models of the design process.

The product of a generative system can be a string of symbols or words. Chomsky's language theory links syntactic categories, words, and grammar rules through the process of sentence parsing. The related algorithmic theories of Post and Markov have influenced the development of various generative models of design, notably that of shape grammars,[47] in which design is treated as a formal language—the use of formal rewrite rules to define and generate patterns of shapes consisting of lines and markers.

According to the generative model, the design process can be understood as a transition through a space of states. There is an initial state, in the case of a building design, possibly an empty site; and there is an end state, the completed design. In the states in between, the design is only partially realized. There is also a set of requirements or goals (though goals are not essential in formal language theory and shape grammars). The end state is identifiable as that in which a set of requirements is met. Operators, which are rules or actions (or rewrite rules in formal language theory and shape grammars), facilitate the transition from one state to the next. In the case of the design of a house, we may start with the empty site and conclude with a state in which certain requirements are met: such as suitable for a family of four, low-cost, and single-storied. The operators are actions, such as drawing a square, converting a line into a wall, adding a bedroom next to the hallway, deleting the bay window. In the case of designing a computer program, the initial state may be a skeleton of a program or some core procedure that already exists. The ''rewrite'' process involves filling out the skeleton with more-detailed procedures or expanding on the core procedure.

Of course, applying all candidate actions at each state produces a vast space of possible designs, partial designs, and impossible designs (designs not complying with the requirements). The model is, therefore, extended by some theorists (particularly in artificial intelligence) to the consideration of strategies to make the process tractable. There are heuristics (rules of thumb) for deciding between actions (if cost is to be low, then only employ actions that keep the floor area small), rules about what to do if you reach a dead end (go back to the last state in which most requirements were met), rules for avoiding unproductive searches (apply only actions that keep options open), and rules for planning action sequences (apply actions in the order of greatest consequence to least consequence). The process can be seen as having multiple levels of control. There may be actions, tasks, strategies, and metastrategies.[48]

Some models of design also rely on typologies. Many models are amenable to hierarchical ordering and classification, but the model through which such systems of hierarchy derive their descriptive power is commonly biological—with such terminology as "family," "species," and "inheritance." Steadman draws attention to the interest in classification of nineteenth-century natural historians, whose aim was to define new species. J. N. L. Durand had a similar concern with generating new building forms.[49] Durand's writings were accompanied by large numbers of plates with drawings of buildings laid out as if they were specimens in some work of natural history.

If analysis, or induction, is the process of deriving generalizations from many instances, then design is thought by some to be the production of an instance from generalizations. There are general types (or classes or species) of designs, such as temples, bridges, and wagons; various subtypes (or subclasses or subspecies), such as Doric, Ionic, or Corinthian; and various instances, such as the Temple of Athena in Syracuse and the Temple of Poseidon in Paestum. According to this model, to design is to instantiate from a class. The simplest manifestation of the process is selecting a particular design from a catalog of designs according to some criteria, a rudimentary design method. Typology seems to play a large part in computer systems design, from the categorization of variables and data structures into types to the use of generic procedures. Object-oriented programming uses the typing of program elements known as "objects," which are related to one another in hierarchies that entail properties and inheritance links. This structuring, in turn, seems to play into the design of programs, which are assemblages of objects and instantiations of classes of programs.

Disanalogies of Design

According to Hesse, models work not only by way of analogy between two domains but also by identifying differences among components within domains, that is, by disanalogy. In positing sound as a model of light, it is apparent that the two phenomena differ in certain ways, notably, sound requires a medium whereas light does not. The failure of experiments to yield a detectable medium for light led to further investigations and model building. The model and theories were eventually modified (to Maxwell's electromagnetic model) and their limits defined. This is typical of any model and theory development.

It would appear that the disanalogies in design models are more severe than in science. There are widely recognized disanalogies between the methods, theories, and models proposed above and design as it is experienced. There is little evidence that designers analyze, synthesize, and then evaluate in either their small-scale or their large-scale design activity. (There is also little evidence for it in science.) Furthermore, where the three phases are advocated as a method, and where there is an attempt to follow the method, it does not appear to yield a faster or better outcome.

In light of these disanalogies, some early advocates of systems theory applied to design have reappraised their approach to design and adopted wholly different models, or moved into a discourse or mode of practice in which systems theory no longer holds sway. Such changes are akin to participating in a paradigm shift—such as adopting a more pragmatic or postmodern orientation to design. But the power of models and analogies is such that some advocates of systems theory see fit to retain the models and marshal them to show that design is a phenomenon that is, after all, difficult to understand. The models provide an explanation of the difficulty and intransigence of design. The fact that design does not comply with the tenets of systems theory is taken as a statement about design rather than a pointer to the inadequacies of systems theory or its application. In this case the disanalogies in the models serve to define further research programs based in systems theory. In the process new models and variations of models emerge.

The difficulty of design and its resistance to the use of methods has been explained in terms of analysis and synthesis. The argument to account for the difficulty of design appeals to the operations of propositional logic. It is thought that evaluation or refutation can readily proceed by means of deduction, but the synthesis or generation of a design seems to bear little relation to logical deduction. Nor does it proceed in a manner akin to induction, that tentative process by which we generalize rules from a number of specific instances.

Design has been described as operating by way of a third process, that of abduction,[50] an even more circumspect operation, by which we produce premises from conclusions and rules—"reasoning backward." For example, we may be informed that creature X has wings and decide that X is, therefore, likely to be a bird. That this kind of reasoning is only provisional is obvious when we reflect that some creatures with wings are not birds, bats for example. It is supposed that such inferences are made on the basis of evidence, taking account of information not explicit within the propositions, including context and situation. It may also involve generating hypotheses and testing them against evidence: supposing X to be a bird and then looking for supporting evidence, such as feathers. The evaluation of a design can proceed by logical deduction, but to produce a new design from a given evaluation or set of requirements requires a range of reasoning strategies. In this way, the analysis, synthesis, and evaluation model has yielded definitions and explanations of what is problematic about the study of design. It has also yielded new models more akin to hypothesis testing in science.

Similarly, there are disanalogies with the generative model, which is the formal structure of design as a transition through a space of states, each state changed by means of operators, and the whole system heading toward a certain set of goals. Simon and Newell have developed a variation on the state-space search model as a general model of human problem solving.[51] Clearly, one of the difficulties with the model is in accounting for how the expert human problem solver is often able to home in on a solution without being overwhelmed by the vast range of possible solution paths—the so-called combinatorial problem. Simon and Newell describe in their model the process by which evaluations are made for selecting the appropriate operator at each step. It involves a kind of means-ends analysis. One considers the goal and the best means for accomplishing it given the current state. But the rules and formulas for such analysis in the case of design (and most problem solving) appear to be elusive. For example, it is not possible to predict that placing the kitchen east of the dining room (as a possible operation to get from the current state to the next) will reliably result in a floor plan that fits the site, has minimum area, or provides morning light to the bedrooms. To assume as much is to assume that design is like climbing a hill—as long as every step one takes is higher than any other possible step, one will eventually reach the summit.

Systems theorists consider generation to be a reasonable description of a puzzle or a game. There are legal moves, a clear objective to win, and a clear starting state. By way of contrast, design has been characterized as a "wicked" or "ill-defined" problem domain, in that the rules keep changing, the goals are formulated as the design proceeds, and the starting state may be different each time.[52] The generative model has yielded the "wicked problem-solving model" of design through disanalogy.

Similar disanalogies are evident in design as instantiation through typologies. The classification of designs rarely conforms with strict hierarchies, as in animal genera, not only because of ambiguity in interpreting evolutionary lineage, as may occur in biology, but also because of the overlapping nature of the many typologies that can be constructed. For example, there are temples that are also meeting places and markets, houses that are also offices, and kitchens that are also living rooms. Furthermore, classification systems based on structure, form, function, ownership, size, siting, and cost differ. Component hierarchies seem similarly nonconforming. Whatever classification scheme we devise will always be to some purpose and can readily be violated when we move to another purpose. Such observations have led to other models of design, such as Alexander's network model (of cities, but also of designs) and pattern language.[53] They have also led to the identification of the phenomenon of emergence, as in the case of new shapes emerging from overlapping shapes, and design as the emergence of descriptions that cross classification boundaries.[54]

Whether these disanalogies actually yield workable insights into design is open to question. The design models discussed so far seem to function mostly in explaining what design is *not* rather than what it is. The disanalogies between the phenomenon of light and the sound model eventually led to Maxwell's electromagnetic model of light and the production of new theories and an enhanced ability to make predictions. The same cannot be said of design models, on two counts. First, the initial design models (analysis/synthesis model, the generative model, and the typology model), though lacking, are operational. They provide clearly understood methods to produce unambiguous outcomes. On the other hand, their rivals or enhancements—the abductive model, the wicked problem model, and the emergence model—are not operational. They define research fields, but they do not in themselves produce operational outcomes. There is no known method for abduction; for producing results from a system in which rules, states, and goals are continuously changing; or for allowing shapes to emerge. The new models are as poorly understood as design itself. There are, of course, models for understanding these phenomena, and no doubt models for explaining *their* inadequacies, too, and so on to infinite regress. Second, design models clearly do not lead to theories for making predictions. What would a predictive theory in design be? In computer science, the automata theories allow us to predict whether we will find any new kinds of algorithms and whether an algorithm will run out of control. It is extremely difficult to find comparable predictions arising through design models. If they are models at all, design models appear to be of a totally different kind from scientific models. This leads us to the unremarkable and commonplace observation that design is not a science. More controversially, it suggests that design is not amenable to a systems-theoretic treatment. It also casts a shadow over the plausibility of research programs that attempt to so model design.

Cognitive Models

Before dispensing with models altogether it is necessary to inspect the broader class of models that deal with human cognition or thought processes. The models outlined above do not lay any claim to cognitive reality. They are models of what design is "in the abstract" (which is itself a questionable enterprise). On the other hand, cognitive models are models of human reasoning and perception (cognition). They are developments on the models outlined above and their disanalogies. Their sources are similar to the design models, and they have also influenced design studies. A proliferation of models of human cognition have been posited to explain such phenomena as language, memory, and problem solving.[55]

As for the design models already discussed, these models are entirely dependent on notions of reason as propositional and informational. As discussed in previous chapters, these are notions strongly refuted by postmodern thinkers. Cognitive science as a discipline is prone to all the criticisms advanced in previous chapters against instrumental reason, rationalism, and so on, though many advocates of cognitive science attempt to justify their studies through their adherence to *models* of cognition as somehow separate from the realization of the models in living human beings. I recount these models here to show cognitive science as much as possible in its own terms, and as a prelude to a discussion of its best insights appropriated through the notion of metaphor.

Aristotelian logic clearly bears little relation to human thinking, though some cognitive models use it as a starting point. There are various enhancements to the logical model of cognition. One is to describe logical reason in terms of beliefs, evidence, certainties, and probabilities—one of the ways of describing abduction. According to this model—the plausible-inference model[56]—the rule by which we might decide that all winged creatures are birds carries a probability value. We may believe that the thing we see is a creature with wings, with a certain probability. Our conviction that it is therefore a bird will follow with a value determined by some combination of the probability value of the rule and that of the observation statement. This conviction value must therefore be compared with the value determined by other rules, for example, about bats and penguins, and with other conflicting observations, for example, that the thing we see is not a creature but a buoy or a beacon. The rules may, of course, chain together to form long lines of "plausible" argument. The final, reasoned conclusion is therefore determined by comparing calculated probabilities. The most plausible conclusion wins. This model has been used to explain, predict, and simulate medical diagnosis and various other kinds of expert problem solving, within very narrow domains.

Fuzzy logic is a variation on this idea and applies particularly to our use of classes and properties.[57] It recognizes that the categories we use rarely have fixed boundaries. If we say that a building is tall, we have in mind a range of height values: anything above twenty stories is certainly tall, heights under twenty becoming progressively less tall. Hence we get the notion of variable set membership. Fuzzy set theory attempts to explain how we can reason from such statements as "this building is moderately tall" and "very tall buildings require a lot of wind bracing" to "this building may need a small amount of wind bracing."

Nonmonotonic inference is another "enhanced logic" which attempts to explain how we hold on to contradictory beliefs right up to the point when we need to make a decision.[58] According to this model, we keep multiple traces of lines of inferential reasoning. These traces are called dependencies. So I may feel that it is appropriate to specify brick walls in my design because brick is readily available, durable, and fits in with the rest of the street. The brick-wall proposition depends on three beliefs. I may also think that timber is desirable because it is ecologically sustainable and reflects the owner's individuality. The choice of timber cladding may depend on only two propositions. During the process of designing, I may decide that the building will be raised on stilts and that the roof will be lightweight. These decisions make sense only if the walls are timber. So two propositions depend on the timber-wall propositions. Eventually a commitment is called for—a suggestion has to be presented to the client, the specifications for the building have to be written, bids have to be taken. In the decision-making process, we regard building the wall of timber and building it of brick to be a contradiction. A resolution is called for. We have kept a record of how tentative decisions depend on each other. Various heuristics are brought into play to help us decide. The brick option is supported by three beliefs, whereas the timber option is supported by two. One of the beliefs supporting timber is only a tentative opinion about the owner's preferences. It may therefore carry less weight. However, at least one decision (to build on stilts) depends on building the walls of timber. By weighing up these dependencies, we may decide on the timber wall after all. Through this complicated procedure, we keep mental note of parallel lines of argument and defer a final choice until as late as possible. (This is the so-called least commitment principle.) We also use metarules about reasoning to resolve conflicts between different lines of argument.

As cognitive models, such models depend for their plausibility entirely on the propositional nature of thought. Of course, there are those advocates of the models who argue that the models do not say that thought is propositional, only that it can be regarded as such for certain ends, as when they wish to code knowledge into a computer system.

Cognitive models have also been developed around classification.[59] The models are based on the idea of mental schemas or generic descriptions of objects and situations. We know how to act in situations by identifying the generic description that a particular situation most closely matches, then instantiating from the range of possibilities presented by that generic description. The common example used is that of entering a restaurant. Certain cues from the situation invoke in us the recollection of the appropriate generic description, called a "schema" or a "script." When the waiter asks are you ready to order? we know what this means in the restaurant context. In other contexts and other schemas, it may mean something very different. There are certain expectations and certain appropriate responses. Similarly, in designing an artifact, such as a kitchen, we will have a generic description of a kitchen, a kitchen schema, through which we will have certain expectations of appropriate factors to consider. There are benches, which will usually be eighteen to twenty-seven inches deep and twenty-nine to thirty-five inches high. There are also different bench configurations, such as U-shaped, L-shaped, and galley-shaped. We also know we will have to consider the location of the stove and the sink. What the schema will exclude from consideration is the location of a bed or a bath. These belong to different schemas.

Schemas can be considered as existing hierarchically. The overall room schema leads us to expect walls, a ceiling, and a floor, and the kitchen schema belongs to it. Other schemas, such as the bathroom and the bedroom, are also related to the same room schema. These kitchen, bathroom, and bedroom schemas inherit the properties of the overall room schema. In this way, schemas are structured and related to one another in terms of inheritance (the "kind of" relation).

They are also related in terms of the component relation (the "part of" relation). Kitchens, bedrooms, and bathrooms are components of houses. The final major component of the model is the set of methods, rules, or procedures attached to the various components of schemas through which we can select from among competing instantiations. In the case of the kitchen schema, the method for selecting a bench configuration may be to consider such rules as "if the kitchen is also connecting two other spaces, then consider a galley configuration" or "if unsure, then ask which the client prefers."

According to this model, designing involves building up complex networks of such generic descriptions through experience, matching new situations to schemas, navigating through these schemas by considering inheritance and component linkages, and implementing rules and problem-solving strategies associated with instantiations within schemas.

A model somewhat counter to the classification model asserts that we reason from specific cases.[60] These cases are stored in memory and accessed when the appropriate situation presents itself. But we never simply recall a case. We modify and adapt the recollection so that it is applicable to the current situation. According to this view, human reasoning involves a very efficient and sophisticated indexing system. Language understanding is therefore explicable largely in terms of lexicons of phonemes (fragments of words) and of words themselves. When we understand a sentence, we have successfully looked in our "internal dictionary," taking account of words in their context in the sentence. Similarly, in design, we store cases of previously encountered designs and design situations. To design is to make an appropriate recollection and to apply the appropriate modification so that the old design fits the new situation.

There is a well-known division in cognitive science between those who advocate models of cognition based on symbols or propositions, sometimes called "classical cognitivism," and those who advocate connectionism.[61] The cognitive models described above fall within the classical camp. Rather than seek to model thought as symbol manipulation, connectionism seeks to study the operations of the human nervous system and brain (the "cognitive hardware") and simulate their operations on computer systems. The ends in view range from attempts to understand human nervous dysfunction and the processes of learning, to producing useful computer systems that respond to visual patterns and control simple machines. Some postmodern writers who are dismissive of classical cognitivism are less scathing about, and even supportive of, connectionism. There are several reasons why this is the case. First, in keeping with pragmatic and phenomenological understandings of psychology, connectionism denies the centrality of propositions, representations, and goals in human cognition. Second, connectionism seeks to simulate the microprocesses of the biological and chemical processes within cells, a study that has long been held to be the safe preserve of scientific investigation. Third, there is a scaling factor that distances connectionist research from any pretense at replicating human intelligence. The differences in scale and complexity between any computer model and the human brain and nervous system are immense, and are undisguisably so. Fourth, connectionism supports the phenomenological proposition that the entire nervous system, the human body, and its environment are implicated in thought. It suggests that for a computerized connectionist system to function as an "intelligence" it would require "inputs" comparable to the entire sensory field of the human body, a comparable environment, and even a comparable community within which to operate. Fifth, in keeping with phenomenological views of perception, connectionism emphasizes the importance of memory in any cognitive activity. In fact, it maintains that any response to a new situation depends upon past experience. Sixth, connectionism gives priority to the habitual in human action rather than the reflective. Connectionism as a model of cognition is very weak at accounting for notions of reflection and linear argumentation.

As realized, most connectionist systems are actually computer systems that manipulate numeric symbols. They are sometimes called "neural networks." A system can be understood as networks of nodes connected in complex ways. Values are attached to the connections and nodes, and threshold values are attached to the nodes. Learning about something, as when we learn to associate white linen with silverware (as in restaurants) or kitchen sinks with refrigerators (because they occur together so frequently in kitchens), involves strengthening linkages between nodes within neural networks in such a way that when one item is present, the other will also occur to us. Such models do not suggest that nodes (or neurones) within physical neural networks correspond to such items as sinks and refrigerators, but, by making this assumption, the idea can be demonstrated and simulated with a computer.

Rumelhart and McClelland conducted an interesting experiment,[62] and Coyne, Newton, and Sudweeks replicated it to demonstrate the applicability of the model to design.[63] A connectionist network is "trained" about a large set of rooms in the following way. In this model, each of the possible features of a room is represented as a node on the network. The features are descriptors, such as the fact that there is a sofa in the room or that the room has a large window, a carpet, or a refrigerator. If there are fifty possible features, then there are fifty nodes in the network. Each room is considered in turn, that is, when the first room is presented to the system, its features are activated on the network. An algorithm is applied to make adjustments to the parameters of the network (actually, weights on the connections between the units and threshold values on the units). These adjustments ensure that if at a later time the network is presented with a partial description of this room, a general purpose algorithm will bring the pattern of activation to life. The system exhibits a rudimentary kind of "memory."

When other rooms are presented to the system, it "learns" these patterns of mutual activation as well. Some patterns of feature combinations may be in conflict. For example, a table and chair may appear in combination when in the presence of a sideboard (typical of a dining room configuration), but a chair will perhaps not appear with a table when in the presence of a washing machine (typical of a laundry room). The parameters of the network take account of all these complex associations and inhibitions between features.

The system can be used to recall feature combinations from a single feature. So we may ask what is the most typical combination of features that includes a washing machine. The system will recall such features as cupboard, sink, ironing board, and table, because these features were strongly linked together through the examples by which the weights were set up in the network. It has recalled a typical laundry. If we ask what is normally associated with a washing machine and a refrigerator in combination, then the system may list such features as stove, sink, table, chair, cupboard, and window, which are typical of the less-common examples of kitchens that contain washing machines. By "clamping" features in this way, it is possible to recall combinations of features that are typical and those that are less typical. In all this there is no description of what constitutes a kitchen or a laundry as in the schema model outlined above. In connectionist models, these schemas emerge from a network trained on specific examples. This is considered to be a useful model of cognition, because it does not rely on the idea of mental representations or the storage of schemas, which, although they feature in explanations, are notoriously difficult to identify.

The connectionist model is also used to account for certain aspects of creativity, such as those in design. The network is able to "recall" combinations of features that did not exist in the original training set. These are not random combinations but take account of the complex web of associations and inhibitions between features. We can ask the system to recall the set of features consistent with the two features bed and stove (assuming they were not present together in any of the examples). The outcome may be a list of features that includes refrigerator, sofa, and sink. This constitutes a new room type ("unknown" to the system) of a combined bedroom and kitchen. With no more effort than is required for recollection, the system is able to generate an example of a new type. The new type is not merely the union or the intersection of known types, but takes account of the complex affinities and inhibitions between features.

There are many neural network models. The one described above involves an entropy or landscape model. It is as though a trained network were a multidimensional landscape, with as many dimensions as there are features, and with complex patterns of valleys conforming to known types (kitchens, bedrooms, bathrooms). Less well established types (such as kitchen-laundry combinations) appear as shallow dips within valleys and between valleys. Clamping a particular feature distorts the landscape in a particular way—as though it were made of rubber—and it becomes deformed or stretched at a particular point.

The simulation process involves traversing the landscape to find its lowest point, and the traversal of the landscape can be imagined as the movement of a table-tennis ball across the landscape. To assist the table-tennis ball to find the lowest point its movement may have to be made slightly erratic. It needs to rattle around a little so as not to get caught in any shallow dips. The model is therefore stochastic, it involves randomness. When the table-tennis ball has settled, its coordinates are read off to describe the feature combination. Of course, it is a very strange landscape, because the coordinate axes have only two values—the feature is either present or absent.

The model is more accurately described as an entropy model, in which the system has to be prompted to find its lowest energy state. The analogy often used is the cooling of molten metal. As a metal cools, its constituent molecules form a crystal configuration that has either a high or a low level of latent energy depending on how the cooling took place. In cooling, the movement of the molecules goes from random (high entropy) to more constrained (low entropy). One of the neural network models actually bears the name "simulated annealing," where annealing is the repeated heating and cooling of metal to maximize its strength. Connectionism therefore trades in many models. Although it involves intensive computation, the advocates of connectionism claim it as a rival to symbolic models of cognition. One of the difficulties of connectionism is that although it is operational, the behavior of computerized connectionist systems is not well understood. The model also relies for its plausibility substantially on analogies between simple algorithmic processes and the functions of neurones, for which the biological evidence at the moment is scant. In the case of design applications there is no effective means of evaluating the results of connectionist experiments. As well as producing plausible new room types, the system was able to produce many less-plausible combinations of features. As with any computer experiment the quality of the output depends substantially on the initial data, in this case the initial room examples. There is no connectionist model or theory that assists in selecting the best examples, nor in deciding on what features to use.

There are further models that feature in cognitive science discourse. One such model trades on the idea that reasoning is best understood in terms of cooperation and negotiation—what Minsky terms "society of mind."[64] There are many agents, each arguing the case for a particular problem-solving strategy or solution. The emphasis in this model is on communication among the agents, and conflict-resolution strategies. The behavior of the whole system exceeds the sum of the parts. Design therefore involves negotiation among internal agents, each with different priorities and strategies. In the case of the design of a house, there may be different agents concerned with such issues as optimizing the spatial layout, optimizing energy use, maximizing good views, deciding where to put the plumbing, and resolving how to provide a sense of home. This would appear to accord with design experience in which there are many conflicting motivations and strategies, though it puts a great deal of stress on the process of negotiation, for which the theories and models are very scant.

A further model reduces agents to extremely simple entities obeying very simple rules.[65] The gross behavior of a very large number of very simple entities is considered to lead to complex overall behavior. An obvious example from nature is a hive of bees or a colony of ants. A single insect does not appear to be doing anything of great significance, yet the whole hive or colony is producing a very complex structure or negotiating a route across a very complex terrain. The model assumes that individual ants do not plan or have complex goals, yet the overall system seems to exhibit these characteristics. Human problem solving is considered to be describable in a similar way, in terms of insignificant units, the gross behavior of which is more profound and purposeful.

The cognitive models outlined here seem to represent a commerce in a large number of models—rolling dice, overlapping circles with soft edges, objects strung together, actors' scripts, networks, filing cabinets and catalogs, landscapes, molten metals, societies, and insects. On investigation, we find that each of these models is as prone to disanalogy as the design models described in the previous section. The disanalogies lead to the development of further models of even greater sophistication. Some of the models lead to predictive theories of human behavior under controlled experimental conditions. But they fail the cause of design. It is extremely difficult to break design activity down into activities amenable to experimentation, where variables can be readily identified, isolated and controlled. If design is broken down, the isolated phenomena bear very little relationship to design in total, and there appears to be no theory for how the larger picture can be reconstructed from the study of the isolated phenomenon. Many of the models are based on the primacy of propositions, whereas design appears not to be a process of manipulating propositions or logical statements. Many of the models assume that design is goal-directed, whereas goals, where they do feature, often seem to emerge in the act of designing, or of explaining a completed design. Many of the models assume that design, like thinking, is an individual process, that there is a private introspective activity that precedes and is independent of the process of communication. As discussed in chapter 1, the models seem to deny that thinking involves engagement in a material world or a world of the senses and, in the case of design, of drawing and other media. In short, we are left with a plurality of inadequate and speculative models for which there is no unifying theory or overarching model. This goes against the grain of systems theory that it should be so. This plurality also highlights that models for understanding design are used differently from the way they are used in science.

Design Models and Information Technology

There appears to be one dominant model of design, that of the mind as a machine, understood computationally and symbolically. The stakes for the plausibility of the models proposed above are high. If design is to be understood through these and other models, then information technology clearly extends our ability to design. Information technology has been put forward as a means of implementing design methods. This was particularly the case with first-generation methods, in which methods were seen as logical steps to some solution. The trilogy of analysis, synthesis, and evaluation has been adopted within numerical techniques (operations research) for solving certain classes of design problems. Computerized optimization programs were once posited as tools for synthesizing designs, as in the case of finding optimal window sizes and glass thicknesses, taking account of the conflicting considerations of heat transfer, lighting levels, glare, cost, and building-code constraints.[66] Alexander implemented the statistical technique of cluster analysis for building up appropriate combinations of components as a main ingredient in the synthesis of a design.[67] To be feasible, the technique required a computer. Computers are also used in certain kinds of design evaluation, as in calculating stresses, bending moments, and deflections of structural systems.

If the synthesis of a design follows some variation of logic, then computers can help construct logical deductions. This would include set-theoretic operations on constraints, as in computerized map-overlay techniques for selecting suitable building sites.[68] But the projected applications of information technology extend further. If design is an exercise in logical deduction, then that logic can be automated on a computer. Logic programming (as exemplified by the computer language Prolog[69]) makes it possible to formulate logical axioms, prove that certain theorems are consistent with the axioms, and deduce new theorems. Expert systems are computer programs that attempt to make this idea operational.[70] Axioms are described in terms of expert rules and facts. The truth or falsity of propositions is established by a question-and-answer dialogue with the user of the system, access to a database, or by logical deduction. The style of inference may be modified by appealing to the cognitive models of plausible inference, fuzzy sets, or nonmonotonic reasoning.

If state-space search is accepted as a reasonable description of what design is, then information technology can extend design activity in various ways. First, computers provide a medium in which states can be represented, as in the database of a CAD system. The computer serves in much the same way as a sheet of paper in providing a medium for recording what the mind is incapable of storing— large and complex descriptions of designs as they progress. Second, the computer is a means of storing the vocabulary elements of such descriptions. These are the element libraries of CAD systems, consisting of lines, circles, rectangles, windows, doors, and columns. Third, the computer provides a medium for storing and manipulating sets of requirements—the goals of the state-space search system.

Fourth, the computer provides a means of operationalizing certain actions (operators), such as drawing or deleting a line; filling; cutting; performing geometrical transformations, such as rotation, scaling, and translation; performing set operations on shapes; and drawing in stairs and column grids. Fifth, the computer provides a means of keeping a trace of states, so that it is possible to return to earlier states in the development of the drawing or design.

What I have just described is fairly characteristic of any CAD or drawing system, but if we adopt the state-space search model of design it enables us to extend the idea further. So far we have assumed that the designer controls the system. But, according to the model, the computer should be able to take over certain aspects of the control of the actions. Algorithms can be applied that automatically select and implement operators, as in the case of rule-based generative systems. Such systems may be created so that they operate in tandem with a designer, doing what computers do best, which is generating patterns and allowing the designer to monitor and manage the process and intervene with actions and strategies that are beyond the computer's capabilities. Beyond that, it is possible to conceive of more-sophisticated control mechanisms that actively seek out design solutions consistent with a set of requirements, marshaling the various theories of cognitive models.

Similarly, the typological model of design suggests that the computer can extend our ability to store and recall schematic descriptions. Some CAD systems use such descriptions as a means of storing generic parameterized descriptions of designs or design elements. It provides a basis for organizing the CAD system's element library. Such descriptions include parameters that can be varied to generate a unique instance. An example is the generic description of a window in a building, where the width and height of the window are unspecified. The frame profile may already be specified, but the user of the system decides its width and height when the window is put in place. Parameterization is a powerful concept in computer applications to design.[71]

This idea has been extended to the conjecture of automated design systems and design "assistants" that contain large numbers of hierarchically organized schemas of the kind suggested by certain cognitive models. So a system for designing kitchens would contain hierarchical descriptions of different kinds of kitchens and their components. There are also automated procedures for navigating through the inheritance "kind of" and component "part of" relationships among schemas and through algorithmic and rule-based methods for instantiating unknown values. Such systems are posited as forming part of computerized expert systems for designers.

As long as design is modeled as involving social interaction among agents, then the computer can be seen as a device that provides a communicative medium for design agents. These agents are commonly understood as different computer programs that need to be integrated through a common database and some kind of overseer. Artificial-intelligence programs called "blackboard systems" attempt to exploit this approach.[72]

An understanding of design as driven by connectionist principles suggests that complex symbolic descriptions and formalized schemas do not adequately model cognition and design. Connectionism is commonly regarded as offering a counterparadigm to cognition as symbol processing (classical cognitivism). Three outcomes are possible if this view is taken. One is to accept that any technological extension based on classical cognitivism is bound to fail, because it is founded on inadequate models. The second is to accept that computers operate with symbols. This is what they do best. So in the symbiotic relationship between human and computer, computers are best constructed around symbol-processing models. The third possible outcome is to construct computer systems around the connectionist models. The problem here is that the models themselves and their computer implementations are generally considered to be mere shadows of actual brain functioning. No computer can currently simulate the vast number and complexity of neural connections apparently necessary for even rudimentary cognition, such as recognizing an object. (There are of course demonstrations of this faculty, but these work only in heavily constrained contexts.) In this case, technology is scarcely able to extend or amplify design.

A second role of information technology is in simulating, and thereby testing and refining, these models, though it is unclear quite what it means to test a model of cognition in this way. It is common in science to process observational data using a computer program in which the theories of a model are embodied. The predictions that emerge may then be compared with further observational data. If the data match, then the model and its theories may be vindicated.

It is also common to compare one model with another. Rather than observational data, the data is generated by a computer program built on tried and trusted theories and models. The results of the less-certain model are compared with those of the established model. This is done when new theories are tested in some kind of simulation, as when some large-scale geographical intervention (such as deforestation) is tested in an elaborate climate simulation.

Cognitive science has a tradition of testing a model, through its computer implementation, against empirical observations of subjects. Experiments with connectionism have been conducted along these lines. For example, some model is posited as providing a good theory of language-acquisition skills. The theory is implemented as a computer program and the results compared with observations about the language skills of human subjects. The correlation between the results and the observations are presented to vindicate the model. To merely implement the model on a computer as a program is commonly referred to as providing "proof of concept." This is hardly a vindication, however. For the research program to function as science, a reasonable test is not simply that the model can be constructed but that its theories exhibit reasonable predictive power.

A great deal rests on the credibility of design models. If they are credible, then they indeed provide impetus for developing computer systems. But how plausible are design models? Their credibility appears to rest on the credibility of models in science. As already indicated, however, there are major differences between the use of models in science and in design.

I have established that in science a model is an analogy with a particular domain, systematized in terms of properties or features linked by generalizations, which are often formulaic. The theories within models are subjected to empirical testing. Models commonly bring disanalogies to light, and it is through these that we change models and their theories.

Methods are prescriptions—procedures, that if followed will produce a particular result. In the case of science, these are experimental procedures. A method is reliable if it produces the same results over a range of experiments that exhibit the same set of experimental conditions.

The problems with method in design are well known. There is no reliability criterion. Methods are commonly used in an educational context as a means of organizing the curriculum or structuring the discourse. In practice they may be used to identify the stages of a project. But they are not followed to produce a design in the same way that experimental methods produce scientific results. Nor is a method a reliable way of producing a design with a guaranteed result.

Furthermore, there appear to be no formulaic *theories* of design. We make many generalizations about design: every design has a starting point, good rules produce good designs, good designers are masters of a design language, form follows function, design is metaphor play, methods are rarely successful. But these generalizations do not necessarily fit within models. They are not necessarily formulas linking together the elements of a model, and where they are predictive or testable they are often tautologous or trivial.

Hesse outlines four different kinds of analogy and shows what happens when models are extended beyond the realm of science.[73] Recognizing these helps us understand models of design. A model in science depends on two kinds of relationship. There is the similarity between the components of one domain and those of another. In the case of sound and light, these relationships are between loudness and brightness, pitch and color. Within each domain, the relationships are considered causal, or dependent. A change in one component may change others, and we can calculate these relationships by formula (theories).

In another kind of model, the horizontal relationships of the model are recognized as shared properties. For example, the planet Venus is understood in terms of our understanding of the Earth. The horizontal relationships include the fact that both planets are roughly spherical and both have an atmosphere. What is known about one, but not about the other, is that Earth supports human life. What was unknown (until recently) was what kind of life Venus supports. Until recently, this question, prompted by the analogy, was an interesting area of speculation. The model opened up the inquiry.

Another kind of analogy is that of a classification system. The horizontal relationship is similarity of structure or function. The vertical relation is that of whole to parts. As an example, a bird has wings, lungs, and feathers, which correspond to fins, gills, and scales in a fish. Wings and fins provide propulsion, lungs and gills are for breathing, feathers and scales are a covering.

A final model type is persuasion in political rhetoric. For example, the family is promoted as a model for society. Parents are to their children as the state is to its citizens. Such models attempt to persuade rather than predict. There is no arguing from known terms to the unknown. The model is concerned rather with pointing out moral or normative consequences. The vertical relation (between parents and children or state and citizens) is not specifically causal. Rather there are several relationships, including that parents provide for their children and that children are respectful to parents. The implication is that as parents are to be obeyed, so is the state. There is no horizontal relation independent of the vertical relation. The use and detailed structure of the model is unspecific. There is no problem in the use of such models, and the strengths and limitations of the family as a model of the state are generally understood. The only danger is when the model is not recognized as such and is paraded with more conviction than is warranted. The very idea of a model carries enormous weight in some quarters, thanks to its associations with science. Design models commonly bear characteristics of all these model types, but more commonly the latter.

In the next chapter, we will see that the phenomenon of models is subsumed within the idea of metaphor. Models are systematized metaphors.[74] Apart from providing an extremely informative account of aspects of human cognition, metaphors carry far fewer pretensions than models. To assert that the machine or logic or connectionism provide *metaphors* for design or the mind, rather than *models*, leads to a different line of inquiry, opens them up to scrutiny in different ways, and presents different research programs. I will show that these inquiries are more in keeping with postmodern inquiries. The idea of metaphor also circumvents many of the problems with design models outlined above. A metaphor need not be predictive. It is primarily a discursive tool to keep a conversation alive, and its efficacy resides in its adoption and use in discourse, which appears to be a better description of the functions of design models than those posited through systems theory.

The Antisystematic Tradition in Design

Before closing this discussion of design models, we should note another strand of design studies that does not trade in systematized design models but draws on the romantic tradition.[75] The romantic philosophers were those who built their ideas on the primacy of the subject as opposed to the object (the rationalists). Fichte, Schelling, and particularly Hegel were the great "systematizers" of thought on the self, spirit, and nature.[76] With its roots in philosophical idealism, romanticism found full flowering in music, art, and literature, where it operated as a force against the cold rationalist spirit. As a strand of thought within design studies, romanticism is less coherent than rationalism. It does not exercise the same access to arguments that appeal to "pure logic" and "objective truth." It is more an influence, characterized by elevated notions of imagination, intuition, emotion, feeling, and the primacy of the individual.[77] In this tradition, design is commonly promoted as an art, a product of the individual, who must be given free reign to exercise creativity. Designers are visionaries and need to ward off the influences of mediocrity, a theme developed in Rand's popular novel *The Fountainhead.*[78] This theme is prevalent in design discourse, particularly in architectural design and criticism. Its influence is apparent in many contemporary histories of architecture that characterize the story of design as the story of "hero architects." Of course, the relationship between romanticism and rationalism is often ambiguous. Rand's hero places himself among the great scientists and seems to elevate reason above mere emotion and fellow feeling. The self-image of science also seems to take up on romantic themes: "scientific discovery as the work of genius, the pursuit of knowledge as a disinterested and heroic quest, the scientist as actor in a dramatic history, the autonomy of a scientific elite.''[79] Contrary to these sentiments, romanticism is also commonly characterized by a suspicion of "progress" and represents a return to craft values and the vernacular.[80]

The rationalism of the systems theory school and romanticism represent two regimes that feed on one another. Both are commonly defined in terms of their opposition to one another. Of course, they each have their own dominant metaphors. In the case of rationalism, they are metaphors of systems, mechanisms, order, and the object. Romanticism is fueled by metaphors of individuality, flow, spirit, and the subject.

A third strand to design studies attempts to stand aloof from both of these. The metaphors of pluralism attempt to lay out rival philosophical positions on a spectrum or continuum, so they can be scrutinized and compared. Such attempts are evident in the divide between rationality and intuition, even within design methods. According to one design methodologist, "[N]one of the design methods that have appeared so far is as complete as it looks and . . . some mixture of both rationality and intuition is needed in the solving of any design problem.''[81] Broadbent seeks to reconcile different views of designing, by means of a typology. There are four types of design: pragmatic, iconic (typologic), analogic, and canonical (syntactic).[82] Pragmatic design is associated with pure function, iconic with designing to an accepted type, analogic with appropriating from other problems or areas design ideas for the current problem, and canonical with designing to rules or a system. Broadbent also gives recognition to the role of intuition and states that among the common polarities of creativity versus intelligence, rational versus intuitive, divergent versus convergent, "both are needed in a fully creative act.''[83]

Rationalism as a pure doctrine of commitment to logic is very difficult to find in design theory. We generally find concessions to a more romantic disposition, a recognition of the importance of intuition and imagination, and machinations about the irreconcilability of the art and the science of design. An advanced form of pluralism adopts a dualistic approach to design, as advocated by dual-knowledge theorists.[84]

Of course, postmodern discourse attempts to dispense with such polarities. Questions about the art versus the science of design and about subjectivity versus objectivity are overruled by new modes of discourse.

Even though design models do not appear to meet the criteria applied to models in science, they do provide some insights into design.

The phenomenon of models itself provides an interesting metaphor of design. Models in science develop and change through the identification of analogies and disanalogies. Design can be characterized as a progression through different "models." As I will describe it in chapter 7, this is the process of seeing the design *as* different things during its development, described as metaphor "play." One way to characterize design is as a dialectic between a formal view (the model) and the phenomenon. There is a tension between the model and the situation to which it is applied. This tension brings to light various insights. Design can be so characterized as a projection into a situation. The idea of design as hypothesis testing also implies some notional design or partial design projected into the design situation. The hypothesis is tested against the situation and accepted, rejected, or modified. Clearly, designs emerge from experience in some way. From schema theory, we gather that designers project recollected past designs, in modified form, into the current design situation. From connectionism, we gather that schema boundaries are fluid and that the "cognitive effort" of recollection and creation may be equivalent.

What of language models? Design competence appears to have similarities to language competence. Skills are acquired through practice and experience and through "acculturation" into a language community. What of generative models? Design has the appearance of the exploration of worlds. It is productive and generative. What of nonmonotonic reasoning? Design reasoning appears to be provisional; designers hold off from making commitments until the appropriate moment. But these and other insights cannot be attributed to a systems theory view of design. They emerge from the interstices of the models proposed rather than from their substance.

Mixed metaphor of the information superhighway as ocean in which a fishing net dredges up information. Interactive multimedia interface to an information network by Zoltan Nemes Nemeth.

7

Metaphors and Machines

Metaphor, Being, and Computer Systems Design

The effective use of metaphor seems to be an important consideration in computer interface design. Many computer systems incorporate pictures, ideograms, and icons that depict objects, tools, files, and other operational and organizational devices displayed on the computer screen, and the use of the hand-held "mouse" or touch screen as a means of pointing at, and clicking on, objects. The computer screen is arrayed with metaphorical objects that exhibit certain properties and with which one can interact. According to one systems developer, Erickson,[1] "Just about everyone at Apple knows the phrase 'desktop metaphor' and fervently believes that a good metaphor is essential to an easy-to-use human interface."[2] Of course, the use of metaphor in computer systems design goes deeper than the simple deployment of pictures and familiar key words. The structures of the operating system[3] and other computer programs and subroutines are commonly designed as a network of (invisible) objects. These objects have properties, generate and receive "events," and send "messages" to one another.[4] They take on meanings of the software designer's own choosing, ranging from the abstract (such as the algebraic variable x) to the more concrete, though bizarre, "demons" or "autonomous agents" that monitor what is going on in the computer system and act in response to some problem. Computer hardware can also be considered in metaphorical terms. Many electronic components are named after familiar entities: memory, gate, chip, processor, and so on. In these senses, the entire computer system is imbued with metaphor, from the structure and configuration of hardware to icons and the designation of objectlike names attached to program subroutines.

Adopting metaphor as a design concern seems to appeal to pragmatically oriented systems designers. It suggests an engagement with the world of the computer user and programmer through familiar and recognizable objects, as opposed to esoteric commands and formal logic. An emphasis on metaphor also represents a liberal attitude to design. Through such emphasis, design is cast largely in terms of devising appropriate metaphors rather than solving a problem through theoretical analysis. Design becomes a process of comparing the efficacy of metaphors rather than matching solutions to problems through objective criteria. A metaphorical approach to design can be cast in much looser and more pragmatic terms than the idea of method suggests. Metaphor also elevates the role of the imagination in design. The screen is an imaginary sheet of blank paper; a screen window is an imaginary opening into a world of information. Metaphor also implicates the human body. In pointing and clicking on the computer screen, we imagine we are touching and grasping real objects, a precursor to "virtual-reality" systems and "tactile computers."

There are further ways in which metaphor appeals to computer systems designers. (Traditionally, the study of metaphor belongs within the study of rhetoric, language, literature, psychology, and philosophy.) The appeal may reside in the implication that a computer system is a blank slate or a lump of clay for designers to manipulate in any way they choose.[5] We can fashion whatever we want out of the computer—a desktop, a filing cabinet, a stage play—much as we can make almost anything out of words. In other design areas, such as architecture or mechanical engineering, the designer feels more constrained by tools, techniques, materials, and a physical setting. It seems that principle and method assume greater importance. By way of contrast, the medium of the computer-software designer is pure, malleable strings of electrical impulses, subject to laws, but waiting to be fashioned through whatever metaphors we desire.[6]

Not everyone agrees that talk of metaphor is useful. Some systems developers operate within the pragmatic mode of design but are skeptical of metaphor. Nelson,[7] for example, maintains that the "metaphor business has gone too far."[8] He argues that the link between the objects on the computer screen (the picture of a trash can) and real objects (a real trash can) is very tenuous, and it hinders rather than helps human-computer interaction. Such pictures are mnemonic gimmicks. They assist memory but do little more, and, according to Nelson, the metaphors are usually ill chosen. They become a dead weight—the whole computer program has to be structured around them. The metaphors become "forced." They also introduce inconsistencies into the operation of the program—for example, the trash can is used to dispose of files but also to eject disks (ready for safe-keeping).

What is the alternative? Nelson proposes a consideration of the whole of a system rather than a collation of assorted metaphors: "The alternative to metaphorics is *the construction of well-thought-out unifying ideas,* embodied in richer graphic expressions that are not chained to silly comparisons. These will be found by overall virtuality design . . ., and not by metaphors, which I consider to be using old half-ideas as crutches."[9] Nelson's criticism appears to be directed mainly against a particular kind of metaphor use, the fairly "trivial" one of having a pictograph on the screen that looks like a folder or a trash can and expecting it to behave like one. Nelson advocates that systems developers follow the pattern set by film production. A film is planned and directed to form an artistic whole. But of course, we can regard what Nelson is proposing here simply as a different metaphor, a grand, holistic metaphor of computer software as a movie.

Nelson points out that some computer systems have had this holistic "nonmetaphorical" character. Apparently the Visicalc spreadsheet had no reference to anything that had gone before: "To replicate a column and its formulas corresponds to nothing that was on earth previously; and when metaphoric thinking was dismissed, it could be designed cleanly with no reference to anything that had come before."[10] Nelson describes this as discovering a new principle. But then it could equally be described as discovering a new metaphor, and this by the melding of existing metaphors: work sheets, bookkeeping, timetables, truth tables, formulas, and so on. The sound advice Nelson is offering can be translated simply into metaphorical terms: do not get fixated on trivial and obvious metaphors, allow metaphors to play against one another and new metaphors to emerge, situate yourself in the problem domain rather than immediately fixating on a particular metaphor, look for the grand metaphor, do not take metaphors too literally by fixating on one-to-one correspondences between the metaphor and the object, and carefully evaluate your metaphors.

Kay also criticizes metaphor:[11] "My main complaint is that metaphor is a poor metaphor for what needs to be done."[12] He posits another term, "user illusion," contending that it may be helpful for part of the computer screen to resemble a sheet of paper onto which one can type words or draw, but it is the "magical" qualities of that paper, those that escape the analogy, that are the most valuable. What can you accomplish with magic paper? You can layer things on it, animate drawings, and erase much more easily than on real paper. If computer systems designers simply followed the metaphor, the screen paper would be no more enabling than real paper. To further illustrate, Kay draws out some of the shortcomings of Hyper-Card, a high-level computerized database system that exploits the metaphors of stacks, cards, buttons, and fields. According to Kay, the difficulty is that you can write only on cards, not on buttons; you can place cards in stacks but not stacks in cards, and so on. Kay argues that the distinctions between stacks, cards, buttons, and fields are unnecessary; a much better idea is simply to have random containers. Kay's advice is that rather than have arbitrary and limiting metaphorical distinctions, the systems designer should adopt a more unitary concept. But here again the appeal is to more efficacious metaphors, random containers rather than differentiated objects, holistic metaphors rather than reductive and disparate ones. As we will see, it is precisely the "magical" qualities of metaphors that enable them to work. Every metaphor brings to light differences, and a substantial part of the power of metaphor resides in difference.

But the application of metaphor to computer systems extends even further than is suggested by the discussion so far. As most systems developers and commentators acknowledge, the appeal to metaphors extends beyond what appears on the computer screen or in the computer program. Our whole conception of the computer is driven by a varied range of "metaphorical orientations." These orientations are apparent when we think of the common terms "interface," "memory," "artificial intelligence," "problem solving," "state space," as well as many specialized terms, such as "motherboard," "bandwidth," "register," "packet switching" and "system crash." Each of these terms can be regarded as a metaphor that associates a computer component with some other domain or human practice. Such metaphors are often anthropomorphic: "memory," "intelligence," and so on. So the metaphorical orientation is of the computer as a human entity. In arguing for a new view of the computer and how it might fit into the workplace, commentators frequently appeal to some new metaphor or metaphorical orientation: Laurel promotes the idea of the computer as theater; Turkle as Rorschach inkblot; Kay as medium; Nelson as movie machine; Weiser as ubiquitous facility—pens, paper, and the electricity grid. The computer itself also serves as a metaphor for other things. The computer is implicated in various conceptions of the workplace, education, society and the workings of language, and the mind and communication. A prime example is the famous information-processing metaphor of cognition. So metaphor practically permeates our entire conception of the computer.

Several major questions underlie the issue of metaphor in computer systems design. Is it possible to get back to some reality beyond metaphor? Are all metaphors feasible in all situations? Are there any constraints posed by the computer medium that restrict the possibility of certain metaphors? Is computer systems design metaphorical all the way through? Is metaphor so ubiquitous and universal as to be a meaningless concept? What of the grand metaphors through which we see ourselves in the computer? In what follows, I consider the different views on metaphor and how different traditions of thinking impinge on the issue. In the process, I develop some valuable insights on the efficacy of metaphor in computer systems design. We will also be in a position to evaluate the role of the design models outlined in chapter 6.

Theories of Metaphor

What is metaphor?[13] According to Aristotle, "metaphor consists in giving the thing a name that belongs to something else."[14] Metaphor is an example of imitation (mimesis), which, according to Aristotle, is the integrating principle of poetry, tragedy, comedy, and music. Aristotle also shows how metaphor is an integral part of "style" in rhetoric.[15] According to Aristotle, metaphor is also the use of figurative, exotic, or ornamental language. The appeal of figurative language is that "the discourse must be made to sound exotic; for men are admirers of what is distant, and what is admired is pleasant."[16]

Terms related to metaphor include *trope,* which is a general term for the figurative use of a word (for example, to describe someone as radiant, normally a property of a hot or luminous object); *synecdoche,* in which we substitute a part of something for the whole (as in one hundred head of cattle); *metonymy,* in which we substitute an attribute for the thing that is meant (as in the use of "the crown" to refer to "the monarch"); *catachresis,* in which we misuse, deliberately or otherwise, a word that sounds similar; and *ellipsis,* in which we deliberately omit words in a sentence. As we will see, the most important terms related to metaphor are *analogy* and *simile.* Derrida explores these and other terms in an illuminating article on metaphor, "White mythology."[17] Derrida is one of the most celebrated practitioners of the use, and even deliberate abuse, of such devices in philosophical argument.

For Aristotle and much of the philosophical tradition up until the twentieth century, metaphor was an element of language to be used cautiously. Metaphor was regarded as an embroidering of truth. It was Nietzsche who vividly drew attention to the impossibility of formulating truths independently of metaphor.

What therefore is truth? A mobile army of metaphors, metonymies, anthropomorphisms; in short a sum of human relations which became poetically and rhetorically intensified, metamorphosed, adorned, and after long usage seem fixed, canonic and binding; truths are illusions of which one has forgotten that they are illusions; worn out metaphors which have become powerless to affect the sense, coins which have their obverse effaced and now are no longer of account as coins but merely as metal.[18]

Coupled with metaphor's rise in importance in the twentieth century is an appreciation, within the contemporary German and French philosophical tradition at least, of the importance of rhetoric and all its devices. As indicated by Aristotle's treatise on the subject, metaphor comes within the study of rhetoric. The primacy of rhetoric over logic is an important theme in postmodern writing. According to Gadamer,[19] the ubiquity of rhetoric is "unlimited." Even the pursuit of scientific understanding comes within its ambit: "There can be no doubt . . . about the fundamental function of rhetoric within social life. But one may go further, in view of the ubiquity of rhetoric, to defend the primordial claims of rhetoric over against modern science, remembering that all science that would wish to be of practical usefulness at all is dependent on it."[20] In the study of rhetoric, we consider the means by which we persuade, including conventions, systems of legitimation, the authority of the speaker (or writer), the authority of sources, the nature of the community in which the discourse is taking place, the situation of the writer and the reader, and the metaphors used. According to Ricoeur,[21] the study of rhetoric has been maligned through sophistry, but also through the rise in prominence of logic, grammar and classification: "[R]hetoric is given over to playing with distinctions and classifications. The genius of taxonomy occupies the space deserted by the philosophy of rhetoric."[22] So the study of metaphor falls within this tradition of the study of rhetoric, and in appealing to metaphor we appeal to a tradition of thought dating back to antiquity. The tradition has undergone a transformation. Now rhetoric and metaphor are regarded by many contemporary thinkers not merely as embroidery but as essential to truth and understanding.

How does metaphor work? To speak metaphorically is simply to relate two entities (or terms) through the verb "to be" (or the copula "is")—a house is a machine, that person is a beast, design is following a procedure—or the preposition "as"—I regard the house as a machine, men as animals, design as following a procedure. The juxtaposition of the terms in the metaphor commonly (but not always) involve assigning an instance to a class, or a species to a genus, though obvious metaphors (such as a house is a machine) usually have the appearance of assigning an instance to the "wrong" class, or a species to the "wrong" genus.

Metaphor is not regarded only as a linguistic phenomenon. For such writers as Goodman,[23] metaphor is implicated in perception: I see the drawing as a square and a circle overlapping, the floor plan as a flow diagram, the arrangement of pixels on the screen as a sheet of paper. "Seeing as" is a basic phenomenon of perception—so too with sound. According to phenomenologists, we do not hear abstract noises, which we then interpret, but we hear sounds immediately *as* car engines, *as* bird calls, *as* people speaking. According to this view, we are constantly engaged in metaphorical projections. We project one term, concept, or situation onto another.

As a further means to understanding metaphor, it is helpful to look at the view of metaphor generally attributed to Aristotle. This is the substitution, or comparison, view of metaphor. The substitution view asserts simply that it is always possible to rephrase a metaphor in literal language. To speak metaphorically is to embroider plain language. So to say that a house is a machine is to imply that a house has certain properties: it has simple functionality, it has inputs and outputs, it can be mass produced, and so on. According to this view, a metaphor is an abbreviated form of simile. A simile has the form *A* is like *B*. The statement could be expanded to "a house is like a machine," and then we may append a list of properties: "in that it has certain properties." According to the comparison view, when we extract meaning from the statement "a house is a machine," we invoke a list of properties pertaining to a machine and compare them with those of a house. The substitution view also treats metaphors as implied analogies. An analogy has the general form *A* is to *B* as *B* is to *C*—the supply of services is to a house as energy is to a machine.

Seen in this light, some view metaphor as not belonging to serious discourse. Metaphor obviously features in poetry but not in scientific or philosophical study, or in other cases when we wish to make our meaning absolutely clear. The rationalist, empiricist, and Enlightenment projects were bent on cutting through the obscuring effects of figurative language. But this concern was also revived by logical positivists in the 1930s who maintained that figurative language has meaning only insofar as it can be translated into literal language. Furthermore, logical positivists thought that confusion within figurative language was responsible for many philosophical and logical errors.[24]

This concern to get back to the realities of a situation unencumbered by metaphor echoes the argument outlined by Hesse about the role of models in science.[25] (As we will see, a model is arguably the formal treatment of a metaphor.) There are those who say that science does not need models—such as the wave and particle models of light—but simply sound theories, rules, and formulas that unite observable and measurable variables and predict outcomes. A model is merely a pedagogical tool we can dispense with once we have grasped the principles. Certainly there is more than a hint of this suspicion of metaphor in the criticisms leveled at computer interface design. In analyzing the metaphor of the computer screen as a sheet of paper, we think of the properties of paper and those of the computer screen. A sheet of paper is flat, can be written on, can be overlaid with other sheets, and so on. The screen display is also flat, can be written on and overlaid, but it is usually vertical rather than horizontal. You cannot fold it down the middle or make it into a paper airplane, and you can do lots of things with it that are impossible with real paper. Seen in this light, the paper metaphor appears unnecessary, except perhaps as a temporary learning device for novices. The substitution view of metaphor suggests that the paper metaphor can be substituted by a literal collection of concepts. We could strip away the interface metaphors and get down to the realities of the system, which should be founded on sound principles.

But some metaphors clearly cannot be reduced to lists of features. Poetry provides many obvious examples of this. Some poetical expressions appear to lose most of their meaning if they are paraphrased in literal terms. To analyze "Juliet is the sun" in the terms outlined above (as a list of features) would involve an endless regress of metaphors. As a simile, Juliet is like the sun in that they both radiate warmth, are spectacular, give life, rule over the day, and so on, but Juliet and the sun do not exhibit these features in the same literal sense. Each feature is also a metaphor that needs to be elaborated further. Furthermore, the expression is a poetical one, whose value is considerably diminished by such analysis. The metaphor is irreducible. The metaphor is explicable rather in terms of understanding Juliet in a new way by associating her with the sun. The two terms of the metaphor interact to produce a new and extended meaning to "Juliet." This new meaning is clearly open to wide interpretation and will vary depending on context and what we understand by the two terms.

Counter to the substitution view of metaphor, the interactionist view asserts that metaphors are always of this kind, whether poetical or not.[26] According to Black, a metaphor has a primary and a secondary subject. In the metaphor "a house is a machine," the primary subject is "house" and the secondary subject is "machine." The secondary subject is to be regarded as a system rather than an individual thing. So "machine" is a set of concepts rather than an instance of a machine. It is clearly not *that* machine over there—the old electrical fan in the corner, or any other particular machine. On the other hand, "house" can be a particular house or, in this case, *any* house. A metaphor commonly ascribes an instance to a class or a species to a genus. According to the interactionist theory, the metaphor works by projecting a set of "associated implications" onto the primary subject—machineness and its entailments are projected onto the concept of a house. The two subjects interact in several ways. The primary subject incites the hearer to select some of the secondary subject's properties: being functional, having inputs and outputs, and so on. The metaphor constructs a parallel "implication complex" that can fit the primary subject: a house is functional, has inputs and outputs, and so on. There are also parallel changes in the secondary subject—we regard in a new light what it is to be a machine. By virtue of this usage a machine takes on houselike qualities. New metaphoric uses for "machine" are opened up as well as new ways of conceiving of machines.

Although Black highlights the notion of properties, this is not to reduce metaphors to lists, as in the substitution view. The interactionist view holds that any analysis of a metaphor in terms of feature or property lists is a contextual activity, an expedient for particular kinds of analysis. The workings of any particular metaphor can never be fully captured in an "objective" sense. For example, to regard part of the computer screen as a sheet of paper (the paper metaphor) cannot be reduced to lists of features. The juxtaposed terms enhance understanding in some way, and that understanding is contingent on the situation. To understand a metaphor is always to interpret it, and there are different interpretations according to context. The computer systems designer exploring the metaphor may focus on writing conventions, the background/foreground property, rectangular format, orthogonality, and erasure. There is no exhausting such lists, and in certain contexts, analysis might also focus on other, less-obvious properties, such as reflectance, color, stiffness, topology, and so on. But a metaphor need not be broken down in order to be useful or meaningful, and our everyday, unreflective engagement with a metaphor does not require such analysis.

Much contemporary debate about metaphor elaborates these two basic understandings: the substitution view (that every metaphor has a literal equivalent) and the interactionist view (that metaphors are irreducible and rely on the context-dependent interaction between two terms). Clearly artificial-intelligence research and studies into cognitive modeling find greatest potential in some variation of the substitution view, because it implies that metaphors can be represented and controlled.[27]

There are two other poles in the debate about metaphor. One position holds that the designation "metaphor" is simply a category of utterance (like a question or a command), and metaphor is not a fundamental constituent of language. According to this view, all language is literal, including such statements as "a house is a machine" and "Juliet is the sun." The second view maintains that all language is metaphorical, including such matter-of-fact utterances as "that is a table" and "the earth revolves around the sun."

The Literal and the Metaphorical

The foremost proponent of the literal language view is Davidson.[28] He maintains, "Metaphors mean what the words, in their most literal interpretation, mean, and nothing more."[29] But Davidson does not thereby hold to the substitution view. Metaphors are not *reducible* to literal language; they *are* literal language. Davidson contends that there are problems with the interactionist view. The interaction view of metaphor regards metaphors as containers and suggests that they have a special cognitive status. According to Davidson, metaphors do not convey ideas; a metaphor does not have a special meaning. As a language theorist influenced by pragmatism (along with Austin, Searle, Wittgenstein, and most of the proponents of the interactionist view), Davidson argues that "metaphor belongs exclusively to the domain of use":[30] "If we are to think of words in metaphors as directly going about their business of applying to what they properly do apply to, there is no difference between metaphor and the introduction of a new term into our vocabulary."[31] Davidson furnishes a colorful illustration. He gives the example of teaching an alien from another planet the concept of "floor." We may teach the concept by pointing to the floor and presenting contrived pedagogical situations in which the floor features in some use context, much as Robinson Crusoe might have taught English to his servant Friday. Then we accompany the alien into outer space to visit its planet. En route, we point through one of the portholes to the spectacle of the receding earth and exclaim "floor!" We would probably assume that to refer to the earth in this context as the "floor" is a metaphor. But according to Davidson, whether the declaration is meant metaphorically or not makes no difference to the alien. Nor does it matter. As far as the alien is concerned, the term "floor" is simply given a new context of use. Who is to say where the literal meaning of "floor" ends and its "metaphorical" use takes over? Davidson is careful to point out that the new use of "floor" is not simply an extension of a common use. Words are constantly being used and reused in different contexts. The quest for original uses will not lead us very far.

In view of this, we could say that to designate a part of a computer screen as a sheet of paper works by virtue of a particular speech community's acceptance and use of the term in that context, rather than some special cognitive operations associated with the special notion of metaphor. In fact, some terms appear to have greater currency in the new context. How often do we use the term "desktop" other than as a descriptor for a computer screen?

To emphasize how words work in a context, Davidson also casts the issue of metaphor in terms of the nature of a lie—some commentators prefer the terms "myth" or "fiction." According to Davidson, the major difference between simile and metaphor is that "all similes are true and most metaphors are false."[32] (We will forego considering poststructuralist revisions of notions of truth.) Only when we take a sentence to be false do we entertain its possibility as a metaphor. Then we "start to hunt out the hidden implications."[33] How are all similes true? Because everything can be deemed to be similar to everything else in some sense, all similes are trivially true. A computer is *like* anything we care to imagine, in some sense—a tool, a medium, a person, a book, even an umbrella or a steam train. On the other hand, most metaphors are statements that are patently false, or fictional. "A house is a machine" is false; so too "the computer screen is a sheet of paper" and "a computer is an intelligent assistant." Of course sometimes metaphors are statements that are true but in a very trivial sense. Such expressions as "business is business" and "no man is an island" are so trivially true that we are prompted to take the expressions metaphorically. We can therefore say that except for the trivial case metaphors are untrue statements that, by virtue of their context, are not to be dismissed but are worthy of consideration and have particular uses. According to Davidson, metaphors are untrue statements that are not lies.

How do we decide that a statement is a lie? Whether or not a statement is a lie or a metaphor depends on context. Davidson gives an example. The statement "my neighbor is a witch" could be one of three things. If we believe in witches, it could be either a lie or a truth. Or it could have a metaphorical meaning. (Or it could be a mistake.) The final arbitrator as to which meaning applies is simply the context of the utterance.

What makes the difference between a lie and a metaphor is not a difference in the words used or what they mean (in any strict sense of meaning) but in how the words are used. . . . What distinguishes metaphor is not meaning but use—in this it is like assertion, hinting, lying, promising, or criticizing. And the special use to which we put language in metaphor is not—cannot be—to 'say something' special, no matter how indirectly. For a metaphor says only what shows on its face—usually patent falsehood or an absurd truth. And this plain truth or falsehood needs no paraphrase—it is given in the literal meaning of the words.[34]

According to Davidson, there is no content to be captured by a metaphor; rather the metaphor makes us notice certain things.[35] (Davidson's critics deny his charge that they see metaphor as having "content" in the simple way he suggests.) Davidson's view of metaphor is considerably closer to the interactionist view than it is to the substitution view. Davidson effectively conflates the phenomenon of language into a single pragmatic system of words in context. This word usage does not require that words be broken down into definitions, schemas, or lists of similarities, and we do not need a special theory to account for metaphor.[36] The counterview to Davidson (that all language is literal) is that all language is metaphorical. I will return to this proposition in the next section.

Two additional polarities feature in discourse on metaphor. These cast further light on the implications of Davidson's view. Nearly all commentators on metaphor offer some account of the distinction between living and dead metaphors. For some commentators, the term *dead metaphor* is synonymous with "the literal." A living metaphor is a juxtaposition of terms that still has some power to strike us as incongruous, shocking, novel, strange, interesting, or in other ways informative—a house as a machine, Juliet as the sun, a computer as an intelligent being, the computer as theater, and so on. In Davidson's terms, these expressions are metaphors because we cannot account for them as lies. On the other hand, a dead metaphor is an expression that no longer invokes investigation, reflection, or new insights. Examples of dead metaphors include "this object is a table," "a computer is a calculating machine," "a pixel is a colored dot on a computer screen." There are many less-obvious examples. Ascribing memory to a computer chip could be regarded as a dead metaphor; so too are computer file, command, menu, and so on. These terms are so much a part of computer parlance and practice that they are generally taken "literally." We have mostly forgotten that the terms are "borrowed" from other fields—memory is a human faculty, a file is a folder or a box to store documents, a command is an order, a menu is a list of food dishes.

But who is to say that memory is not simply the storage of information, a faculty shared by both people and computers; that a file is not simply a means of storing documents, whether in cardboard or magnetic media; that documents are not simply information, whether in paper or electronic form; that a command is not simply an order, whether to a person or a machine; or that a menu is not simply a short list of items for selection, whether presented in a restaurant or on a computer screen? What Davidson's arguments bring to light is that all terms are borrowed in some way or other. The distinction between living and dead metaphors follows the distinction between the metaphorical and the literal. The distinction is determined by use.

A full account of the debate surrounding Davidson's ideas is beyond the scope of this book. As I will show, Heideggerian concepts of truth as disclosure rather than correspondence provide a fruitful account of language and metaphor use contrary to Davidson's view.

Furthermore, Davidson's theories do not adequately account for the privilege that certain words carry from one context of use to another. It is not that Davidson is wrong but that the literal language view seems to close off a whole domain of fruitful inquiry into the privileging of terms. The domain of computerization provides a good illustration of privileging. Ascribing human terms to the computer and computational terms to people are not matters of indifference or coincidence. They indicate, among other things, a privileging of certain conceptions of ourselves and the world that has a history. If we follow the arguments of Heidegger and critical theorists, then linking the computer to human intelligence provides one of many examples of our technological "enframing." Pre-Socratic concepts of thought have given way to the technological. The discourse on metaphor provides a useful forum for analyzing these aspects of such terms as "computer" and "intelligence." Rather than focus on individual terms, we can inspect the "baggage," or "entailments," that certain metaphors carry, their "structures" and relationships, and how they have risen to prominence.

The counterview to Davidson is that all language is metaphorical. Lakoff and Johnson are among the foremost proponents of this view. They also offer an account of how we privilege certain metaphors.

Metaphor and the Body

Lakoff and Johnson argue that the key to this privileging lies in grounding language in the human body.[37] How does this work? Metaphors are related to one another in ways that we can analyze as structures—metaphor structures. According to Lakoff and Johnson, our direct, early, and shared experiences dictate and shape basic metaphor structures, which we call on when going about our day-to-day business. Lakoff cites evidence from linguistics, particularly cross-cultural studies, that abstract ideas, such as those pertaining to how we describe thought, are couched in terms that belong to the world as we interact with it physically. This is particularly evident in the use of categories. The category names to which we have immediate affinity, such as "table," "chair," "tree," and "dog" (basic categories), are more important to us than the more specific categories of "writing table," "Breuer chair," "elm" and "cocker spaniel."[38] The argument is that it is more important to distinguish between a table and a chair than between different types of tables, say a dining table and a writing table, because of the way we use the objects. The basic categories are also more useful in day-to-day living than the more generic terms "furniture," "vegetation," and "animal." Lakoff also notes that because of their widely different behaviors, it is vitally important to make certain distinctions among the animal class. We are not generally content merely to group dogs, cats, and spiders together in the category "animal." Beause of our involvement in various pleasant and unpleasant experiences, we are more likely to declare "there is a spider in the bath" than "there is an animal in the bath." So our whole understanding of what constitutes an object and how we designate it relates to our communicated experience.

A similar analysis can be presented for our understanding of "abstract" objects. A similar hierarchization of categories applies to action words, such as "seeing," "touching," "running," and "making." These verbs denote basic category terms that are experientially based. Of course, all category terms vary as our experience changes and as our interests and vocations develop. They also vary across cultures. Language, however, has a conserving effect on these basic categories.

Even language pertaining to more complex aspects of our experience retains the vestige of these basic experiential terms—seeing, hearing, touching, and making. According to Lakoff and Johnson, abstract and complex activities, such as thinking and designing, are understood and described in these basic category terms. So we *see* the answer to a problem, are deeply *touched* by a situation, and *make up* our minds.

The next step in Lakoff and Johnson's argument is to see that categories of objects and actions do not exist merely in isolation but are formed into experiential gestalts—basic metaphor structures. Lakoff identifies several of these. There is a metaphor structure pertaining to containment: "a schema consisting of a boundary distinguishing an interior from an exterior. The *container* schema defines the most basic distinction between *in* and *out*. We understand our own bodies as containers—perhaps the most basic things we do are ingest and excrete, take air into our lungs and breathe it out."[39] Other metaphor structures pertain to paths, links, forces, balance, the up-down orientation, the part-whole relationship, and the center-periphery relationship.[40] Similarly, a journey schema is derived from basic experiences. Tied in with the journey metaphor are notions of intention and means. In order to satisfy a particular desire, a small child may need to embark on a journey across the room. According to Lakoff, this experientially based metaphor structure incorporates and sustains our basic ideas about intention and causality. Lakoff and Johnson use these basic and simple metaphor structures in analyzing more-complex linguistic and social phenomena. So exchanges within relationships between people can be seen as driven by certain dominant metaphors (for example, dialogue as war). These can be further broken down to particular schemas or basic metaphor structures.

According to Lakoff and Johnson, metaphor structures have their own internal relationships. How is it that certain aspects of a metaphor structure gain primacy over other aspects? Lakoff points to the importance of the phenomenon of metonymy: "It is extremely common for people to take one well-understood or easy-to-perceive aspect of something and use it to stand either for the thing as a whole or for some other aspect or part of it."[41] In the case of a journey, we may take the origin to stand for the whole thing. In response to the question "How did you get here?" the answer "I got on a bus" is often sufficient. The answer does not require a long explanation, because the rest follows from our knowledge of the bus-ride experiential gestalt. Of course, using another part of the journey metaphor, as in the answer "I got off a bus," is less usual and may lead to confusion. We may add that some computer screen icons appear to work metonymically (as do logos, symbols, crests, and so on). They depict a part of something in order to draw our attention to the whole—a pencil tip to depict a pencil, the letter A to indicate text, a compass to depict a drawing system, and so on. Metaphors have these and other internal structures.

According to Lakoff and Johnson, our understanding of logic is also driven by metaphor. They identify three main metaphors. The first is that of the experience of containment and its transitivity. The statement "all As are Bs" followed by "C is in A" informs us that therefore C is in B. This is a characterization of the syllogism. The metaphor of containment comes through our experience of inside and outside, supported by basic bodily experience. The containment schema is evident in everyday expressions, such as "let out your anger," and in comments about supposedly abstract reason, such as "let's start out from the following assumption" and "that assumption will lead you astray." A second metaphor is that of force. The conclusion from a set of logical propositions is considered to be inevitable. We are led to the conclusion through the force of inference. So we get another characterization of the same syllogism: A implies B, and A is true; therefore B is true. Force as the bodily activity of pushing against something leads to ideas about inevitability and causality. A third metaphor is that of balance. We weigh evidence; in making logical judgments, we balance conflicting requirements; and, in mathematical reasoning and formal logic, we balance both sides of an equation or a logical clausal statement. Schön also elaborates on this metaphorical theme of balance.[42] The use of this metaphor is evident where the consequences of certain actions have to be weighed against each other. We talk of the weight of evidence being in favor of a particular decision. Ethical problems are frequently discussed in these terms—"on *balance* it seemed appropriate to favor the needs of those dependent on public transport."

Schön adds that we make liberal use of such metaphors as working with tools ("sharpening our wits") and social interaction ("my will and reason are at odds") in understanding thought. There are also metaphors of social processes. Here there are different parts to the self: "I told myself . . ." "my conscience told me . . ." "my will and reason are at odds." Under this metaphor structure, decision making (or designing) becomes a conversation between "internal advocates" of different kinds of rationality (or advocates making use of different metaphor structures)—"It seemed logical to keep the structure simple, but I wanted the design to be a bold statement." There are also metaphors of mechanism and dynamism in which the mind is a machine. According to some process models, decisions appear as switches or taps. Schön suggests that arguments about freedom and determinism are also essentially appealing to the mechanistic metaphor structure.[43]

How does the bodily basis of language and metaphor impinge on computer systems? There are two major ways. First, Lakoff and Johnson's arguments linking reason to bodily experience, in keeping with the tenets of pragmatism, defuse the claim that reason is a pure and transcendent phenomenon. In so doing, they challenge the claim that the computer may someday be a repository of reason, an intelligent device.[44] They also challenge many of the models of chapter 6. Human cognitive ability does not reside in propositional logic but in such phenomena as metaphor use, which are irreducible to propositions. As long as cognitive science and artificial-intelligence research focuses on propositional logic, it will never meet its more ambitious goals. Second, Lakoff and Johnson's arguments indicate that the computer is not an abstract "reasoning" device, whose internal logical structure renders it independent of human concerns. In the same way that Johnson demonstrates the presence of the body in the mind, we can readily point to the presence of the body in the computer, or in any other human artifact. As confirmed by many critical commentators, the computer is not an impartial, value-neutral tool to be used for good or ill. But, at a more pragmatic level, Lakoff and Johnson also indicate that the computer is an embodiment of practical, bodily based concerns.

Following Lakoff and Johnson what is the bodily basis of the computer? We need look no further than the prevalence of the containment, force, and balance schemas in the conception and design of computer systems, or indeed of any machine, for evidence of the presence of the body. As far as containment is concerned, the registers in the microprocessor contain values, files contain data, and directories are organized hierarchically as nested containers. As far as the metaphor of force is concerned, the computer clock ticks away indefatigably at thirty thousand or more pulses per second, passing binary strings into and out of registers and logic circuits to ensure that the logical instructions produce their effects on the data. On the subject of balance, logic circuitry ensures that a statement like "A" balances with a statement like "not not A." The basis of the modern-day computer in binary logic also fits Lakoff and Johnson's account of the primacy in human cognition accorded to the metaphor structure of containment: in/out, near/far, on/off, right/left, up/down. According to Lakoff and Johnson, these oppositions are derived from experiential, bodily based gestalts.

But if they are right about the bodily basis of metaphor, the main contribution of Lakoff and Johnson's insights is to note that we need not accept as inevitable the current form and structure assumed by the computer. Computer systems are thought to work so well because of the generality of their basic grounding in binary logic. Computer programs, such as drawing systems or CAD systems can be constructed because Cartesian notions of geometry map so well to this basic logic structure. In a computerized drawing system, lines are commonly defined as connections between points located anywhere in space, planes are bounded by lines, and volumes are spaces bounded by planes. The metaphors of containment, force, and balance outlined by Lakoff and Johnson are clearly very basic and map readily onto reductive Cartesian notions of space and geometry. But what if we reverse the priority of constructing drawing systems on binary logic and instead begin with the concept of drawing? What sort of machine or computer system would support a non-Cartesian view of drawing? Other interpretations of the grounding of metaphor in bodily experience do not reduce geometry to containment, force, and balance but focus on the line as a boundary arc between near and far drawn by the sweep of the arm, on geometry as a generative device that has a life of its own, and on the production of drawings as a journey by which we project an image into a situation and then return to find ourselves and the image changed.[45] Such an account of drawing is more amenable to exploring the experience of manual drawing than reductive geometry is. We may then contemplate how a machine could be invented to facilitate drawing understood as such. By beginning with the bodily activity of drawing rather than the general mechanism of binary logic, a different kind of computer may be produced.

Such a line of inquiry is not so far-fetched. Some of the earliest computational devices controlled the deflection of an electron beam aimed at the center of a cathode-ray tube—early radar devices and oscilloscopes. Much research and development effort has been directed to suppressing the arc in favor of the straight line, and suppressing the natural propensity for mechanical and electronic components to exhibit states that are continuously variable and non-linear in favor of discrete and linear states. The point is that once we accept the grounding of the computer in bodily metaphors, we are in a position to explore new aspects of those metaphors, or new interpretations of the metaphors. Where this may lead in terms of computer systems design is unknown at this stage. Needless to say, there are many experiments exploring different paradigms of computation.[46]

No one would deny that the development of the computer has followed the best path technically, but what constitutes the best path is substantially a product of what fits within a complex matrix of other systems and inventions and what accords with our experience and expectations. According to the Lakoff and Johnson model, the cards are stacked heavily in favor of binary logic, and this is not because of some Platonic primacy of two-valued logic but because of our bodily engagement in a world of living, surviving, consuming, and moving: "the massive complex of our culture, language, history, and bodily mechanisms that blend to make our world what it is."[47]

Metaphor and Metaphysics

According to the Heideggerian view and that of Derrida, critical theorists, and poststructuralists, the impetus for developing modern technologies, such as the computer, and the reason they occupy such a place of privilege is metaphysical thinking. Can metaphysical thinking be explained by Lakoff and Johnson's account of bodily based metaphors? From a Heideggerian viewpoint, the computer is caught up in a series of developments dating back to Plato and Aristotle. Technology's "essence" is our will to control, manipulate, manufacture, dissect, reduce, and "enframe." The development of the computer is abetted by this ethos. According to Hegel, Heidegger, and others, this takeover by Aristotelian logic—the reduction of reason to a manipulation, a technology—is to be contrasted with pre-Socratic thought, or dialectic, which celebrates opposition and contradiction. The idea of oppositions seems to feature prominently in both pre-Socratic and Aristotelian discourse on reason. Both pre-Socratic thought and Aristotelian logic are clearly "based in the body" in this sense (in relying on right-left and up-down oppositions). The major difference is that Aristotelian logic (at least according to the dominant tradition) denies its grounding in the world.[48] According to the pre-Socratic view, reason is contingent and is based in contradiction—a dialectic between "is" and "is not." According to the Aristotelian view, reason is logic that can be divorced from the day-to-day and manipulated as symbols on paper, and eventually on a computer. For pre-Socratic thought, the ground of reason is shifting and indeterminate. For Aristotelian thought, certainties underlie reason; there is structure that can be uncovered and decided. Metaphysics is that branch of philosophy that seeks out the grounds for reason, the overarching principles, the framework that binds together all human knowledge. Needless to say, metaphysics is regarded with profound suspicion by most philosophical traditions since Nietzsche, though metaphysical thinking runs deep in our institutions and in the forces that drive the development of technology.

There are four ways in which Lakoff and Johnson's view of metaphor impinges on the issue of metaphysics: first, the view that metaphor imbues all language presents a challenge to metaphysics; second, metaphysics can be described metaphorically; third, a challenge to the grounding of any understanding of cognition in the body must itself answer to the charge that it is metaphysical; and fourth, Heidegger charges that the entire metaphorical enterprise is metaphysical. I will consider the first three now, deferring the fourth until a later section.

First, Lakoff and Johnson address the issue of metaphysics indirectly. They devote considerable attention to challenging "objectivist" views of reason, which appear to deny the contingency of reason and insist on the existence of a literal, objective language independent of metaphor use. Having argued against objectivism, can Lakoff and Johnson be cast as relativists (subjectivists)? The answer is "no." Lakoff and Johnson also point to the contingent and metaphorical nature of notions of subjectivity. Both objectivity and subjectivity are metaphors within the Cartesian master metaphor of subject versus object. In adopting the primacy of contingent metaphor use, Lakoff and Johnson's view attempts a direct challenge to metaphysics.

Second, their view provides a valuable explanation of the metaphysical orientation—the quest for foundations. The strange ally in this argument is Derrida,[49] who says the key to understanding metaphysics rests in our propensity to see things in terms of presence and supplement. Metaphysics is not an appeal to deeply embedded structure or pure transcendent reason so much as the simple recognition of things that are near and things that are far. For example, to say that there is both literal language and metaphorical language is metaphysical. It implies that the literal is the true, essential, and immediate meaning; the metaphorical is the supplemental, additional, unnecessary, and distant. The distinction between speech and writing is also metaphysical—Derrida's primary example. Speech is near and essential; writing is a copy of speech. It is incidental and distant. (Indirectly, Derrida is deflating the claims of metaphysics to transcendence by showing its grounding in the everyday issue of proximity.)

Applying Lakoff and Johnson's (bodily) point of view to Derrida's argument, metaphysics is grounded in the most basic metaphorical image schema we can imagine, that of inside versus outside—the containment schema. Derrida's identification of presence versus supplement is little more than an identification of the basic schema by which we identify what is contained and what is outside, what is within our reach and what is outside it. As already discussed, Johnson describes this schema at great length and shows both its grounding in bodily experience (ingesting food, discovering limits to the reach of our arms, and so on), and its prominence in language. We can extend the containment schema to a consideration of the pre-Socratic, Pythagorean identification of binary oppositions. The oppositions between straight and curved, up and down, and right and left are not symmetrical. As Derrida has shown us, there is always a privileging. In other words, as Pythagoras said of these oppositions, they pertain to the limited and the unlimited. There is only one way for a line to be straight. A straight line is present. A curved line is a deviation from straight, and there are unlimited ways for a line to be curved. A curved line is supplemental to the "ideal" of a straight line. So the containment schema is based in bodily experience, it is ubiquitous, and it is implicated in pre-Socratic binary dialectic, in ordinary and abstract language (according to Lakoff and Johnson), and in metaphysics (according to Derrida). In view of this, our propensity for metaphysical thinking should come as no surprise. We think metaphysically because we are grounded, bodily beings, and our bodily experiences lead us to see things in terms of containment.

Of course, Derrida's project is to show the tenuous nature of metaphysical thinking, how the privileged term in a binary opposition can be shown to be the lesser term, how speech depends on writing (protowriting), and how literal language depends on metaphor. Derrida suggests a return to the pre-Socratic view of thought (*logos*) as being in constant flux. He does this by showing us how committed we are to metaphysical notions, while at the same time he removes their certainty.

We have shown how one aspect of Derrida's account of presence and supplement can be explained in bodily terms. This brings us to the third meeting point between the metaphorical and the metaphysical. What does Derrida have to say about the bodily basis of thought?

Derrida already posits a sophisticated deconstruction of the containment schema by showing that what is present depends on what is supplemental, not as a universal rule, but through many specific cases pertaining to language use—meaning, naming, metaphor, writing—and philosophy, specifically Heidegger's notions of Being. Given this, a Derridean critique of Lakoff and Johnson's view of metaphor would not be to refute it, but to play with it, to show it as contingent and self-referential.

To date Derrida has not specifically addressed the writings of Lakoff and Johnson, but a critique comes in the form of Derrida's identification of the present and the supplemental in Heidegger's writing about the hand, which is a bodily metaphor of some potency in Heidegger's writing.[50] In *Being and Time* and elsewhere, Heidegger makes great use of the hand as a means of distinguishing between the immediacy of our involvement in the world and our abstract theorizing. There is the readiness-to-hand of immediate involvement and the presence-at-hand of the world of measurable objects. Derrida thinks Heidegger is unwittingly succumbing to metaphysical thinking in uncritically according to the hand this immediacy and power. If the charge of metaphysical thinking can be leveled at Heidegger over the issue of the body, then the same charge certainly applies to Lakoff and Johnson. They privilege the body without apparently acknowledging the contradictions and reversals this entails. To trace language and metaphor use back to the immediate realm of bodily experience is a metaphysical exercise. It assumes a base, a solid foundation for understanding reason. As Derrida points out, we can only ever present our arguments in such a way, but postmetaphysical writing presents such ideas as ''under erasure.'' We indicate the contradictions they entail and show their provisional status. Of course, Lakoff and Johnson are writing in a scientific and analytical context rather than a philosophical or literary one. Although their theorizing is far from objectivist, it is pragmatic. The rules of the game are different from those enjoyed by literary deconstruction. Their thesis about the bodily basis of metaphor opens up avenues for exploration, and the ultimate arbitrator of the validity of these ideas is their usefulness.[51]

Other Derridean arguments can, however, be advanced against Lakoff and Johnson's view. Johnson identifies containment, force, and balance as bodily based image schemata. He shows how they are each implicated in both everyday argumentation and in Aristotelian logic. In keeping with Derrida's deconstruction of concepts of speech and writing, we can show that the notions of containment, force, and balance are not simply borrowed from the physical world of human action and applied to formal logic but depend on notions in formal logic. How is this so? Containment, force, and balance were obviously not invented by logicians to be applied only to the world of physical action later on. Rather the terms we normally take to apply to putting something inside a container (containment), pushing against a physical object (force), and ensuring that we do not fall over (balance) are but manifestations of more-basic notions of containment, force, and balance. These are preembodied notions. As preembodied, these notions may be partially lost to everyday language but are partially uncovered in the consideration of the abstract world of Aristotelian logic.[52] That these image schemata are present in logic, which makes no overt claims to being embodied, provides evidence at least that there are other nonembodied uses of the terms "containment," "force," and "balance."

The best proponent of this kind of deconstruction is Heidegger, particularly in his notion of the primordial "in."[53] For Heidegger, the spatial "in" of containment is subservient to a primordial notion of "in" as involvement. There is the nonspatial "in" of being-*in*-the-world, being *in* a good mood, being *in* love. Seen in this light, Lakoff and Johnson's notion of containment is subservient to the more primordial notion of involvement. Prior to our bodily experience of containment is our being-in-the-world, an altogether more primary and important concept. Similarly, Heidegger offers a revision of notions of causality, which for Lakoff and Johnson is related to the bodily experience of force. For Heidegger, causality is subservient to care. From our being-in-the-world, we direct our attention within a region of concern. Notions that we may cause something to happen and that we may exercise control over a situation are derivative of this more-basic understanding of our place as exhibiting care. As a further illustration of the subservience of notions of force, Heidegger points to our ability to already be where we want to go. Before I move across the room, I am already there ontologically by virtue of my involvement in a sphere of concern that includes my "destination." It is only because I am already there that I am able physically to go there.

These arguments are obviously counter to those proffered by Lakoff and Johnson. Heidegger argues that there is a more basic experience than embodiment. Even orientation has a grounding prior to our bodily experience of orientation. So Heidegger conspires with his later opponent Derrida in identifying a preembodied mode of being. Whereas Heidegger's identification of preembodied experience could be construed as yet another instance of discovering a foundation (not in the body, as for Lakoff and Johnson, but experience *prior* to the body), the preembodied has the appearance at every turn of being undecided. It is a fluxional involvement that defies pinning down. Heidegger's primordial concepts are not foundations but excursions into pre-Socratic concepts of contradiction, flux, and play. How else could we characterize being-in-the-world?

In a strange way, this Heideggerian-Derridean critique of embodiment also finds some support from Davidson. The use of a term such as "in" is never limited to the metaphor of containment. A floor can be part of a building or apply to the earth or any solid grounding, a file is not just a cardboard folder but storage for information, and a desktop is not just a place to rest books when I am reading them but a computer display. In the same way "in" is not simply the spatial relationship between an object and a container but applies to whatever uses our language community is able to find for the word. In this sense, all words have a "prior" meaning that goes beyond any notion of an "original" meaning. The small word "in" is a placeholder in a complex of varying contexts and practices, best captured by the notion of use. This is consistent with pragmatic theories of meaning. As a variation on this pragmatic theme, a Derridean reading of the word "in" places it, along with all other words, in a complex play that is difference and deferral. In either event (whether we adopt the Davidsonian or the Derridean understanding), the meaning of "in" does not reside in the association we establish between an image schema of containment and some new domain of abstract reason. At every turn, Lakoff and Johnson's claim for the primacy of bodily based metaphors is under challenge. Derrida, Heidegger, Lakoff, and Johnson each challenge metaphysics, though Lakoff and Johnson's insistence on the primacy of the body appears to undermine their own intentions here.

But then again, Lakoff and Johnson's notions of the embodiment of metaphor have uses—provided we see embodiment itself as a metaphor and not as having some absolute foundational status. The uses of Lakoff and Johnson's notions of embodiment include restoring dignity to the body in philosophical discourse, refuting certain Cartesian dualisms, rehabilitating reason as grounded in worldly concerns (as opposed to transcendence), and showing how we can see ourselves in our technologies.

Metaphor and Science

Metaphor challenges metaphysics, but what about the scientific basis of computer systems? It is commonly thought that designers of computer systems may use metaphors as heuristics, as ways of talking about systems, interfaces, and so on, but the computer is best understood scientifically.[54] If we strip away the devices designers use for talking about design, such as metaphor, we will arrive at the scientific underpinnings of computer systems. But even if we hold to this view, we find that these "scientific underpinnings" are also metaphoric. This strikes another blow to the idea of metaphysical underpinnings beyond metaphor.

One of the foremost proponents of the view that science is driven by metaphor is Hesse.[55] If she is right, then whichever way we look at it the computer is pervaded through and through by metaphor. As I discussed in chapter 6, the link between science and metaphor is forged through the idea of a model. We will now develop the idea of models further. According to Ricoeur, "The function of a model is to describe an unknown thing or a lesser-known thing in terms of a better-known thing thanks to a similarity of structure."[56] In describing scientific activity, it is common to distinguish between the thing observed and the means at our disposal for explaining it. The thing observed is described in an observation language—a language that scientists develop for describing what they observe—for example, "light and dark bands appeared when light is passed through two parallel slits onto a white card." Then there is the model or theory for explaining the phenomenon—the wave model of light. Hesse actually describes these in terms of a primary and a secondary system. The primary system is the observed phenomenon and the general terms used to describe it—the behavior of light; the secondary system is the system of explanation—the wave model. According to Hesse, "in scientific contexts the primary and secondary systems may both be highly organized by networks of natural laws."[57]

In the case of computer systems, computation provides many models for other phenomena. There are computer models of natural processes, chemical reactions, weather, the behavior of populations, and so on. But there are also models of computation, and these provide its scientific base. As we have seen, the Turing machine is one such model.[58] A simple machine consisting of paper tape, a mechanism that can move the tape backward and forward, and a device for reading and writing to the tape make up a universal machine for simulating all algorithmic processes, including those of any computer. The Turing machine model incorporates theories about properties of algorithms, such as decidability, consistency, regularity, and determinism. The theory is generally known as automata theory.[59] In this case, the primary system is the behavior of an algorithmic process, the behavior of a computer; the secondary system is the system of explanation, the Turing machine as a model.

How are the primary and secondary systems linked? Hesse contrasts the deductive with the metaphoric view of science. According to the deductive view, the thing explained (say, the interference pattern of light shone through two slits of paper or the observation that an algorithm is running in a loop without generating an outcome) is deducible from the scientific explanation (the wave model of light or the theories of the Turing machine). That is, science posits explanatory models, and given the model we should be able to derive the phenomenon observed. The explanatory model must be capable of prediction. In order to do so, the explanation must contain at least one general law that must not be empirically falsified to date. In the case of the wave model (and other models), one such law is that light intensity diminishes inversely to the square of the distance from the source.

As Hesse indicates, there are problems with this deductive view. Since Popper, it is widely accepted that observation is theory-laden. The observation language already betrays a commitment to some theory or other. The observation that an interference pattern was observed presumes a theory of interference—patterns reinforcing and canceling each other out in some way. The observation about a runaway algorithmic process presumes some notion of looping. Further, the law or theory for predicting an observation from a model is problematic. The fit between the model and the observation is always approximate. How approximate is a matter of interpretation, and there appear to be no laws for determining what constitutes a close fit between the two systems. The deductive view of models offers no explanation of the link between the primary system and the secondary system. This is the case for computation as much as for models of light. The difficulty of making connections between Turing machines (and automata theory) and the behavior of computer programs is legendary. Very few programmers are willing or able to make use of it in any practical sense to predict the behavior of their programs.

By way of contrast, what is the metaphorical view of scientific models? According to Hesse, a scientific model is a metaphor. The primary system, the observation language, is the first term of a metaphor. The model is the second term. The wave model of light can be cast in metaphoric terms: light as waves. The Turing machine model presents the metaphor of the computer as a machine for reading and writing to tape. Scientific models can therefore be accounted for according to the interaction theory of Black and others. But there are important differences between metaphors in science and metaphors in literature. At first blush, metaphors in science appear to support the similarity view of metaphor. Scientific metaphors appear as similes, and they can be reduced to literal statements. There are two ways that this appears to be the case.

First, according to Black's interaction theory of metaphor, the metaphor *creates* the similarity rather than bringing to light some preexisting similarity. In contrast, in science it is generally assumed that the model reveals some preexisting similarity. Light simply *does* behave as waves, independently of any models or metaphors we care to fabricate. Computer programs simply do behave as Turing machines. Second, whereas in literature any metaphor offers something illuminating—Juliet as the sun, a rainbow, an autumn mist, a thunderstorm—in science not every metaphor is applicable in every situation: "[N]o model even gets off the ground unless some antecedent similarity or analogy is discerned between it and the explanandum [the thing explained]."[60]

But Hesse indicates that in spite of these differences the substitution theory does not hold even for metaphors in science. In projecting a model/metaphor onto an observational situation, the scientist never knows how far the comparison extends. There is never a definitive list of similarities that exhausts the comparison, and it is the unexpected extensions of the comparisons that promote the development or rejection of a model: "[A]s long as the model is under active consideration as an ingredient in an explanation, we do not know how far the comparison extends—it is precisely in its extension that the fruitfulness of the model may lie."[61] According to Hesse, there are two further differences between metaphors in science and those in literature and poetry. First, metaphors in literature and poetry are initially striking and unexpected. They are not meant to be analyzed in pedantic detail, and such analyses destroy the metaphor. In science, models/metaphors may be only initially unexpected. They are not meant to be peculiar but are meant to be consistent and tightly knit internally. For a model/metaphor in science, contradiction is not desirable. Science seeks to find the "perfect metaphor."

Second, in literary language, a metaphor is not put forward as explaining something: "[I]n literary metaphor in general there is no hint that what is metaphorically described is also thereby explained."[62] But in science, models are counted as explanatory. What is explanation? The deductive view of science assumes that the explanatory power of a model resides in correspondence rules joining the two languages: observation and explanation. As has been pointed out by many commentators, this is a problem for the deductive view. On the other hand, according to the metaphorical view, there are no correspondence rules. Furthermore, there are not two languages, the observation language and the explanation language (the language of the model). There is only one language, the observation language, which is continually being extended by metaphoric uses. For example, it is extended into the terminology of the explanation—light is described not only in terms of light and dark bands but in terms of waves, frequency, amplitude, and interference (from the wave model/metaphor). As a further example, under the influence of the Turing machine model, computer programs are described in terms of symbols, start conditions, and rewrite rules (the action of the read/write device in the Turing machine). So the use of models/metaphors in science is no different from the use of metaphors in literature or in day-to-day language. According to Hesse, this process of extending language through metaphor use is not necessarily well understood, but it is a process of language generally and is not peculiar to science.

According to the metaphoric view, predictions become possible by the shifts in meaning and extensions of vocabulary brought about by metaphor. These predictions may or may not turn out to be empirically verifiable: "They will however be rational, because rationality consists just in the continuous adaptation of our language to our continuously expanding world, and metaphor is one of the chief means by which this is accomplished."[63] So, following Hesse, even if we regard the computer as a product of scientific reasoning this does not exempt it from its grounding in metaphorical thinking.

Metaphor and Technology

We have appealed to the usefulness of metaphor. What is the efficacy of metaphor use in understanding information technology? We can summarize the implications so far. There are several means by which the link between metaphors and technology can be forged. Technology provides metaphors through which we understand phenomena, metaphor is implicated in the setting of problems, dependencies between technologies can be understood as metaphorical, and metaphors provide a basis for evaluating technologies.

Technology provides metaphors through which we understand phenomena—the mind as computer and the house as a machine—and technologies in turn are understood through other phenomena. Basalla provides an example of the metaphorical relationship between technology and biology.[64] He notes that early philosophers, such as Aristotle, wrote extensively on biology but did not make much use of mechanical metaphors. With the Renaissance development of machines, Renaissance writers drew parallels between the mechanical and the biological: "Structures and processes in living organisms were described and explained in mechanical terms."[65] In the nineteenth century, the relationship was reversed. With developments in geology and Darwinian evolution, technology was described organically. Basalla cites the example of various tables and charts drawn up during this time that placed artifacts (such as axe heads and weapons of tribal cultures) into evolutionary trees, with genera, species, and varieties. This is still common practice today. Technologies are described biologically, and biology is sometimes understood in terms of technology. We see similar reciprocity between technology and organism in the case of computers and mind. As pointed out by Ryle, Schön, and Sternberg, the technology of mechanization has also furnished us with the metaphor of the mind as a machine, but certain machines (computers) are also understood in terms of mind.[66]

Technology as a source of metaphor can also operate in more subtle ways. Metaphor provides a way of accounting for the power accorded to technology by such writers as McLuhan and Ong, who, as we saw in chapter 1, assert that the technologies of literacy and print have contributed substantially to the primacy of method, individualism, and notions of objectivity, leading the way for Descartes, the Enlightenment, and modern science.[67] According to Ong, people from literate cultures (like ours) have so "interiorized" the technology of writing "that they organize, to varying degrees, even their oral expression in thought patterns and verbal patterns that they would not know of unless they could write."[68] Our deference to the syllogism illustrates this. Ong makes an even stronger point. The technology of print has persuaded us to think of mind in spatial and "objective" terms.

By removing words from the world of sound where they had first had their origin in active human interchange and relegating them definitively to visual surface, and by otherwise exploiting visual space for the management of knowledge, print encouraged human beings to think of their own interior conscious and unconscious resources as more and more thing-like, impersonal and religiously neutral. Print encouraged the mind to sense that its possessions were held in some kind of inert mental space.[69]

By this metaphorical construction, McLuhan and Ong are positing grand master metaphors that influence the way we see the world. McLuhan also ascribes such movements to the engagement of the different senses, particularly hearing and vision. So print also gains its metaphorical power due to its involvement in the sense of sight.

The second link between metaphors and technology is that metaphors appear to generate problems that technologies are presented to solve. Problems emerge as the entailments of metaphors. The view that technology and metaphors interact puts to one side any idea that technologies arise as a response to some abstract need or problem. It suggests that technologies, metaphors, and problems are interrelated. This relationship is made clear by Schön,[70] who says that different metaphors promote different problems. Technologies are commonly advanced as the solutions to particular problems, yet it is apparent that the technologies have brought about the metaphor shifts that define and even create the problems in the first place. Thought is shaped by the technologies in such a way that the technologies are readily accommodated. Information processing provides a good example of this complex play between technology, metaphor, and problem.[71]

When we operate with the information-processing metaphor, certain problems present themselves. For example, problem solving and design, seen as information processing, lead to a concern with accuracy of information transfer—minimal disruption to the flow of information from the "coder" to the "decoder." In architectural and engineering design practice, this may be seen as the problem of accurately communicating information from the designer to the manufacturer or tradesperson. The technological solution might be better CAD (computer-aided design) database techniques or more-complete specifications. However, in an age in which the metaphor of information processing had less force, we would expect other problems to have presented themselves. So problems (such as accuracy) emerge from the metaphors provided by the technologies (information processing).[72]

We can also see that changing the dominant metaphors redefines the problem. There are other metaphors of human communication, cognition, and design. For example, design can be seen as a process of enabling within a community of expertise. The problem of accurate information transfer then becomes a problem of facilitation. How can clients, consultants, authorities, contractors, and tradespeople be enabled to do their job or carry out their roles better? This new way of looking at the domain may result in a spectrum of actions, ranging from the adoption of new media or new ways of using computers to different modes of education within the professions and trades. The solution may not involve technology at all but rather new practices.

The third linkage between metaphors and technologies is that dependencies between technologies can be understood as metaphoric. Metaphor features in an understanding of important dependencies among technologies. In the history and "evolution" of a family of artifacts, such as pottery jugs or certain building types, certain features persist that seem to serve no functional purpose. "Skeuomorphism" is a term coined by archaeologists to designate a "nonfunctional" feature of a design that derives from some precursor to the current design.[73] For example, the projecting ends of wooden beams appearing originally in timber buildings reappeared as ornamental dentils beneath the eaves of Greek temples built of stone. Early plastic laundry baskets were fashioned in imitation of the reed and wood construction of the earlier artifacts. The phenomenon relates mainly to changes in materials, but skeuomorphism can be evident in any aspect of an artifact or a technology. We understand and develop new technologies and new designs in the light of our experience of existing technologies and designs. This is a metaphoric phenomenon. The early technology sheds light on the new technology. New technologies, inventions, and designs are seen in terms of existing technologies, inventions, and designs: stone construction is seen as carpentry; plastic is seen as reeds and wood. The phenomenon is certainly evident in the design of computer systems. As I stated at the beginning of this chapter, the success of the personal-computer interface is largely attributable to the deliberate use of particular organizational metaphors (desktop, folders, windows, and trash can). Certain computer-aided drafting systems make extensive use of metaphors wrought through a consideration of manual drafting tools: the screen cursor looks like a pencil or a paintbrush.[74]

When we consider the interactive nature of the terms of a metaphor, we see that the relationships among technologies are not static. In the same way that "house is a machine" can inform us about both terms ("house" and "machine"), new technologies shed light on old methods of working. Construction in stone tells us something new about construction and structure. Understanding stone's resistance to compression and its susceptibility to shear informs us about the unique behaviors of timber. We look at timber construction in a new light. The plastic laundry basket informs us about the unique properties of reeds and wood. We understand a computerized drawing system through our knowledge of manual drawing, but a computerized drawing system also informs us about drawing in general. There are new operations that we formerly did not consider part of drawing (stretching, inverting, smoothing). We look afresh at conventional drawing tools, and we learn new things about creating images. We may value the uniqueness of manual drawing in a new way—seeing drawings not merely as points and lines but as extensions of bodily movements, something CAD drawings clearly are not. We may presume that this dynamic relationship between technologies informs the development of new technologies, inventions, and designs.

The fourth link between metaphor and technology is that metaphor provides a basis for evaluating technologies. Evaluation proceeds on the basis of the efficacy of the metaphors that the technology brings to light. How does this occur? According to this model, evaluating a technology involves identifying the dominant metaphors that influence the user at the work task and that are attributable to the presence of the technology. This involves understanding the experiences of the computer user. The next step is to identify the sets of problems these metaphors define. We can then evaluate the efficacy of these problems in terms of the extent to which they facilitate the work task, the extent to which they represent the imposition of "false" problems that disappear once new metaphors are adopted, the extent to which problems are a product of the metaphors imposed by the technology, and the extent to which problems change their definition once new metaphors are introduced.

The actions that follow from this analysis may include introducing technologies, practices, and interactions that provide more-enabling metaphors; arguing for the adoption of new metaphors for understanding tasks (new ways of looking at tasks); recommending new metaphors through which the technology can be understood; and redesigning, changing, or abandoning the technology in particular situations.

The critique of information processing given above follows this kind of analysis. On a smaller scale, one could apply this method of critique to some aspect of a computer system, such as the screen cursor in a computerized drawing system. A system design in which the cursor looks like a pencil presents problems of control. Screen pencils are notoriously difficult to use. We may expect the cursor to work like a pencil only to find that we are unable to use broad strokes or change the thickness of the line as we draw. The problem may disappear once we see the tool as something else, perhaps as a fine paintbrush or an etching tool. We may also circumvent the problem of controlling the cursor in a pencil-like way by analyzing the metaphor of control itself. The idea of control is heavily promoted through the technology of computation. What appears on a computer screen is so heavily mediated by electronics that we do not have immediate access to the work surface (the screen) other than through the control of keyboard, mouse, and numbers. When we use a physical pencil, we do not so much control the pencil as make use of a tacit understanding, or familiarity, with the tool within a context of skilled practices. The problem of the pencil-like screen cursor can be recast as a problem of an inappropriate expectation due to an inevitable distancing by the technology.

The metaphor of distancing may suggest that the computer medium is useful for performing abstract operations, such as geometrical transformations. What becomes important is not getting the marks onto the screen but how one manipulates them once they are there. This may involve abandoning the pencil cursor or changing the screen display in some way that makes the mediated nature of the pencil cursor apparent. This is just a simple example of how an understanding of the ability of technologies to furnish us with metaphors can be brought to service in evaluating aspects of technologies in use.

In summary, metaphor and technology converge in several ways. Technology functions as a source of metaphors, and technologies are understood metaphorically through other phenomena. Metaphors, problems, and technologies are interrelated. Metaphors set problems that technologies are commonly put forward to address. These technologies in turn promote metaphors that set the problems. Technologies also provide metaphors of each other. This particular technology or artifact is seen as that previous technology or artifact, and the reverse also applies. We revisit previous technologies in the light of what is now available. Finally, metaphor provides a means of evaluating technologies.

Metaphor proves its efficacy in these areas, but what is its role in design? Before we can address this question, we need to deal with Heidegger's criticism of metaphor, which brings to light further issues that impinge on design.

Metaphor and Being

We have explored at length Heidegger's view that technology brings about a covering over of Being in favor of a focusing on beings. In other words, thanks to technological thinking dating back to Plato, we have lost sight of what it means to be. We now focus on simple entities, objects as causally related, and human thought as a matter of manipulating propositions according to causal laws. In the pre-

Socratic mode of thinking, to which Heidegger wishes us to return, we let things be in their essence.[75] That is to say, we allow things to be different in unique ways, to fit their context, to be their own causes. This is not to exclude causal thinking as a valid mode of investigation, as long as we recall the derivative and provisional nature of such thinking. In his later work, Heidegger indicates how the technological enframing to which we are now committed is inescapable and not "caused" by humankind so much as "sent" by Being. Being covers over and reveals itself at different times and in different ways throughout history. As we have seen, Heidegger's later thinking is controversial and complex and borrows substantially from the German theological and mystical traditions. Heidegger's life's work therefore focuses on the matter of Being. How do Heidegger's investigations into Being relate to metaphor?

Heidegger begins his first major work, *Being and Time,* with an argument for the resurrection of interest in the verb "to be"—the "sum" ("I am") of Descartes's foundational proposition "Cogito, ergo sum" ("I think, therefore I am"). As discussed earlier, metaphor in language is the linking of two terms through the copula "is"—the computer *is* an intelligent assistant, and a house *is* a machine. It would seem that metaphor, then, is central to Heidegger's project to develop an understanding of Being. Unfortunately for the cause of metaphor theory, Heidegger attacks any claim to the primacy of metaphor.

Although Heidegger does not mention metaphor in *Being and Time,* his later attack on metaphor is consistent with his explanation of the "as" structure in *Being and Time.* The preposition "as" is the other connecting term used in metaphor—the computer *as* an intelligent assistant and a house *as* a machine. In *Being and Time,* Heidegger distinguishes between the hermeneutical and the apophantic "as." The hermeneutical "as" is the immediate recognition or projection that derives from being-in-the-world, encountering the ready-to-hand as part of our circumspective awareness, our dealings in which we exhibit concern.[76] We have this understanding in advance. This is the primordial, premetaphorical use of "as." On the other hand, the apophantic "as" is the ontic, representational way in which we assert something *as* something.[77]

Heidegger's later assertion of the primacy of a prelinguistic mode of understanding that eschews metaphor is consistent with this. Dreyfus summarizes Heidegger point: "[A]t an early stage of language the distinction metaphorical/literal has not yet emerged."[78] This is not to deny that there is metaphor. Heidegger is simply asserting that there is a more-basic understanding that precedes metaphor use. There is a more-basic use of "as" that is not metaphoric.

Heidegger's argument can be taken two ways. If we take metaphor to be a mere phenomenon of language, then we have to agree that there is prelinguistic, premetaphorical understanding. However, if we take Lakoff and Johnson's view about metaphor as understood in terms of experiential gestalts, then metaphor runs deep in human experience—"as our mode of being-in-the-world or our way of having-a-world," according to Johnson.[79] According to this view, Heidegger's commentary on the "as" structure points to a redefinition of metaphor to include ontological as well as ontic use. There is hermeneutical as well as apophantic metaphor. By this interpretation, metaphor runs deep in our involvement in the world, and it is a prelinguistic phenomenon, as Lakoff and Johnson suggest.

Elsewhere in *Being and Time*, Heidegger describes this hermeneutical, prelinguistic "metaphor use" in his description of projection. This description covers both the way we deal with everyday situations and with analytical study. According to Heidegger, all interpretation begins with a background that we take for granted (a fore-having). There is also always a point of view (a fore-sight), and there are expectations (a fore-conception). This is Heidegger's "three-fold structure" of interpretation—fore-having, fore-sight, and fore-conception.[80] This structure can be taken as a description of metaphorical projection of the kind Lakoff and Johnson describe. To interpret a situation is to engage in metaphorical projection. It is to see the current situation *as* another situation. Every experienced moment is a candidate "second term" of a metaphor for the present moment. It is to project a point of view and an expectation into a situation. There is therefore ample support within *Being and Time* for the primacy Lakoff and Johnson and other metaphor theorists accord to metaphor—as long as we see metaphor as more than a phenomenon of language.

What of Heidegger's specific criticism of metaphor? In his later writing, he asserts that to interpret certain statements as metaphoric is to show a commitment to metaphysics: "The metaphorical exists only within metaphysics."[81] Wood makes Heidegger's argument clear.[82] According to Heidegger, to explain his own work as comprised of metaphors is to maintain the possibility of the literal. To assert as much is to maintain the presence of some absolute. It is to get back to old metaphysical notions of language as reference—a stable world to which words refer. Heidegger's attack comes in the context of his discussion of seeing and hearing as ways of thinking, presented in *Der Satz vom Grund* (*The Principle of Reason*).[83] Lest the reader think Heidegger is merely being illustrative in characterizing seeing and hearing as ways of thinking, Heidegger asserts that he is not speaking metaphorically. Nor is he speaking literally. To assert as much is to maintain that there are sensory levels of experience (seeing and hearing) as distinct from intelligible (thinking) ones. According to Heidegger, such a dichotomy rests on Cartesian and metaphysical distinctions between body and mind. According to Wood, to assert that Heidegger's reference to thinking as seeing and hearing is metaphoric "would rest on the assignment of seeing and hearing to the *sensory* level and thinking to the intelligible or *non-sensory*."[84] The observation about perception given earlier—that we do not hear noises that we then translate into meaningful sounds, but that we directly hear cars, birds, and bells—takes a more radical turn. To hear and see is to interpret, which is to say, to think. In breaking down the mind-body dualism, this argument, also developed by Wittgenstein in *Philosophical Investigations*,[85] is an attack against metaphysics itself, and by implication against metaphor. But, according to Wood, it need not imply a serious challenge to metaphor.[86] The argument relies on drawing a general conclusion from particular examples. To assign Heidegger's discussion of seeing and hearing as thinking to the realm of metaphor may be an "error" in this particular case, because he is making a point about breaking down the sense-thinking dichotomy, but not every categorization of an utterance as metaphoric is in "error." The criticism against metaphor need not always hold. To Wood's argument in defence of metaphor, we can add that Heidegger is again assuming metaphor to be a phenomenon only of language, and a superficial phenomenon at that—ideas strongly refuted by the contemporary metaphor theorists referred to so far.

The second occasion on which Heidegger eschews metaphor is in his essay *Letter on Humanism*. Metaphysics is that tendency within philosophy and reflection to mask Being in favor of beings, in other words, to miss the basic questions of Being that the pre-Socratics pursued and to see the existence of beings as important—the dominant aspect of the philosophical tradition since Plato. How is metaphor metaphysical in this sense? As an example, Heidegger at one point describes language as "the house of Being." On first reading, this comes across as a metaphor—a rich, evocative, enigmatic metaphor. However, in his *Letter on Humanism*,[87] Heidegger explicitly says that the expression is not to be taken metaphorically: "The talk about the house of Being is no transfer of the image of 'house' to Being. But one day, we will, by thinking the essence of Being in an appropriat(ing) way . . . more readily be able to think what 'house' and 'to dwell' are."[88] One point of the essay is that we do not understand what it is to dwell. Our need and ability to dwell has been covered over by the philosophical tradition. For Heidegger to dwell is to "be-in-the-world." In recovering the primordial meaning of "dwelling" and "house," we are returning to an immediate ontological use of the word "house." Language as the house of being should not, therefore, conjure up an image of a house with something called "Being" in it, and the whole thing bearing the label "language." Nor, obviously, should the phrase conjure up some lists of features attributable to the three entities language, house, and Being so that we can compare them. If we have attended to Heidegger's careful arguments in his essay, then we are already familiar with his newly rehabilitated notion of dwelling and house. The statement is indeed not to be taken metaphorically. The statement relies on a more-primordial notion of house that transcends the literal/metaphoric.[89]

Derrida takes Heidegger's suspicion of metaphor as a key theme in his argument about metaphor. Derrida's argument follows four stages. First, every attempt within philosophy to explain metaphor is itself imbued with metaphor, and every description of metaphor depends on philosophical ideas.[90] A mutual dependence is therefore in play—philosophy depends on metaphor, and metaphor depends on philosophy. Second, Derrida rejects meaning as depending on reference (that is, *this* word refers to *that* object) in favor of meaning as dependent on difference. According to Derrida, to distinguish between words and meanings is to affirm the tenets of metaphysics and the possibility of the literal. With the disappearance of the idea of the literal, metaphor also withdraws from the scene. But, according to Derrida, we use metaphysics against itself. We borrow from metaphysics. Deconstruction is that strategy by which we construct arguments, inevitably depending on metaphysical assumptions, but we write "under erasure," showing the provisional nature of our terms. It is never possible to get outside of metaphysics. One can only hope to work within it, but in a way that is subversive of the arguments of others and of one's own arguments. So too with metaphor. We use it, refer to it, and subvert it.

Third, metaphor itself is located within the play of differences. It is not based simply on the opposition of sensible/nonsensible (the senses and the intellect), as suggested by Heidegger, but on a whole range of distinctions. In the literature on metaphor, notably from Nietzsche, there is talk of wear and tear (worn-out metaphors), life and death (dead metaphors), and use and profit (coins that are no longer of account).[91] Derrida is keen to show that metaphor does not depend on one opposition but on many. The very idea of metaphor is slippery. Whereas Heidegger looks for dwelling and a sense of stability, of being at home, Derrida indicates permanent dislocation.

Fourth, Heidegger talks of the withdrawal of Being. This is Being's doing. Yet Being has accomplished this in such a way (a series of guises, turns, modes) that we are tempted to describe Being through all the ruses of metaphor. There is no nonmetaphorical sense in which we can talk of the withdrawal of Being. As in all Derrida's arguments, this brings us back to the primacy of difference and deferral.

In summary, Heidegger addresses the issue of being. At first reading, this seems to implicate metaphor, which, with its heavy investment in the copula ("is"), appears somehow central to our being-in-the-world, as Lakoff and Johnson suggest. But Heidegger eschews talk of metaphor as belittling his insights into primordiality and prelinguistic understanding. He seems though to have a very linguistic-centered view of metaphor. The view of metaphor of Lakoff and Johnson and others accords more with Heidegger's notion of the hermeneutical "as"—the prelinguistic recognition of this *as* that. For Heidegger, the question of Being is resolved by our attending to our home, or dwelling in the world, with all the implications of stability. Again, for Heidegger, the reference to home is not a metaphor but strikes at the essence of Being. Derrida, on the other hand, thinks Heidegger is caught up in all the ruses and turns of metaphor in his accounts of Being. Most significantly, whereas Heidegger seeks stability, Derrida seeks permanent dislocation—the constant reminder of uncertainty. This latter insight points again to the workings of metaphor and the role of difference and deferral.

Metaphor and Design

Before returning to the matter of difference, I will review what metaphor tells us about design. It is clear that metaphor provides insights into the workings of the design process. Design can be characterized as generating action within a "play" of metaphors.[92] We see the design as particular things during its development. This is evident in the case of geometrical manipulation. We see the configuration of marks on the drawing board or computer screen as triangles, squares, circles, diamonds. The things we see suggest "problems" (or opportunities). We know about a square and the manipulations we can perform with it. These are the entailments of the metaphor. So perhaps we draw in a diagonal. New shapes and figures emerge. We cannot help ourselves. Our experience is constantly bringing metaphoric projections to bear on the current situation. It is constantly undergoing transformation in the light of the current, changing situation. Of course, even when playing with geometry, the process is never entirely geometrical. Shapes are never just shapes but also sunbursts, leaves, rays, clouds, tokens, wings, crystals, window panes, and symbols. And each metaphor suggests new action.

Presumably design communities have access to certain metaphors that are considered enabling within particular domains of action. So there are different ways of understanding a design in progress as the designer shifts from one metaphor to another. Different metaphors have currency within different design communities. For example, an architect may see spaces as having the properties of a fluid ("space as fluid" metaphor). This metaphor suggests and opens up possibilities (or problems) of "shaping" spaces, improving their "flow," and identifying their "source." If a designer is operating within a "form as mass" metaphor, it may lead the designer to consider "emphasis," "giving weight" to an element, and providing "balance." Some of the metaphors used by architects enable them to see their designs in terms of focal points, concepts, points of departure, themes, ordering principles, and types. There are also various analogs—shells, pine cones, praying hands—and precedents that arise as metaphors. Certain metaphors are unique to certain design disciplines, such as architecture—providing a sense of address, defining the street, interface, accentuating, articulating, providing a transition, providing an interplay of spaces. But metaphor play is also evident in the supposedly "practical aspects" of design—a building as a system, machine, energy sink, circuit, ledger item, resource, or liability.

So too in the design of software and computer systems. We find overarching metaphors through which problems are set, such as the computer as intelligent assistant, theater, environment, ubiquitous resource, and so on. As long as we see the computer as an intelligent assistant, we set ourselves the agenda of codifying knowledge, replicating human thought, modeling cognition. To see the computer as theater is to think in terms of scripts, actors, spectacle, engagement, and so on. These metaphors may not present themselves as exclusive. We may shift from one metaphoric orientation to another. At one time we see the computer as intelligent assistant, at another time we are overwhelmed by the dramatic possibilities of the computer.

Such orientations do not pertain only to the early conceptualization of a particular computer system design. Working with computers carries the added interest that a single program is usually a

collaboration by systems developers influencing one another indirectly through the environments they create. For example, the developers of programming languages provide environments and sets of
metaphoric orientations for those who write high-level programming tools, such as HyperCard, Macromedia Director, and so on.
Other developers then use these tools to create environments in
which computer users can customize their own tools. Of course this
is never a simple top-down process. The way programmers formulate
their environments is strongly influenced by the metaphors prevalent in the user's domain. A field of metaphors pervades the various
intersecting communities of developers and users.

There may also be major shifts in metaphorical emphasis, analogous to Kuhnian paradigm shifts in science. Some major shifts that
have filtered through the various levels of systems development at
one stage or another include the computer program and the problem domains they serve conceived as a flow of control through an
intricate network of decisions. The original Fortran programming
language required the programmer to make these control flows explicit, through "go to" statements and subroutine calls. Then there
were structured programming languages, such as Pascal, which al-
lowed for constructing the computer program and conceptualizing
the problem domain in terms of autonomous subtasks or procedures
understood hierarchically. These procedures exist as modules that
can be assembled and linked together to accomplish higher-level
tasks. There are also object-oriented programming languages, which
encourage the systems designer to think in terms of autonomous
objects with behaviors and properties. The kit of parts becomes very
flexible. The idea of object-oriented programs now pervades the design of most programs, from word processors to CAD systems. And
no doubt there are other potentially pervasive metaphorical orientations in the pipeline or about to be resurrected.

So in software design, we are being encouraged to participate in
the metaphors we set for each other. Some high-level programming
tools ("authorware") encourage particular orientations to the computer through the metaphors they present to systems designers. For
example, some programming environments for creating expert sys-

tems are designed around notions of autonomous agents, group decision making around a "blackboard," "inference engines," knowledge bases, and so on. Some multimedia systems are designed around scripts, frames, and cast members—metaphors derived from animation and film production.

Metaphor play also applies at the level of software programming, writing the code or "hacking." The programmer frequently copies segments of programs from elsewhere. Segments of programs are taken from one situation and applied to a new situation. This involves "seeing as"—seeing a previous problem as this problem and this problem as a previous problem. Program components, such as variables, operators, and data structures, take on different characteristics. For example, variables are sometimes seen as containers, at other times as algebraic terms, generalizations, placeholders, pointers, or handles. The program is treated as a conduit into which the programmer pours effort, code, data, or it is seen as a defective structure that needs repairing, or an experiment that involves testing.

The power of metaphors to define problem regimes and prompt action suggests a particular approach to design practice. The architectural design practitioner does not come to a situation with fixed, predefined problem statements but undertakes an investigation and engages in dialogue through which appropriate metaphors emerge. These metaphors are arrived at by both the practitioner and the client in the specific situation. Problems are presented and addressed through such exchanges and collaborations. The metaphoric view of design points to design as a richly collaborative activity. So too does software design. Clear and unambiguous problem statements are rare. Any problem statement needs to be interpreted in a situation. Most software design proceeds by rapid prototyping. A computer system is proposed and developed for a particular understanding of a problem situation and tested either informally or formally. The requirements of the program emerge as the program undergoes development. The program results from an interplay between what is wanted and what is possible. There is always a collaboration among designers, sharing and developing metaphors as suggested above, and with clients and users, who bring their own developing understandings and metaphors to the situation.

There are, therefore, at least two extreme modes of software-design practice. On the one hand, the methods orientation relies on the distinction between problem and solution and on hierarchical design procedures progressing from problem statements to performance specifications to flowcharts to informal pseudocode to operational programming to testing and evaluation. On the other hand, there is the mode of software-design practice that recognizes what every programmer knows—that you are a skilled programmer by virtue of skills and experience acquired by many years of practice, that each new project involves a new "method," and that you frequently do not know what a program should deliver until you have investigated what is possible, which is often not known until the end of the project. Of course there are contractual requirements from the client that the project will be completed on time and to a particular specification. The management of the project and the professional practice of the company (with their metaphors of timelines, milestones, and the assurance of total control) are often at odds with the metaphors of the design and development team.

So metaphor is implicated in the design of computer systems. Metaphor provides a metaphor for understanding design. It is not the only metaphor, nor is it the most perspicacious in all situations. But then to appeal to logic, flow diagrams, rewrite rules, Turing machines, and other paraphernalia of programming theory is not to abandon metaphor but to shift to a different set of metaphors. The appropriateness of any metaphor depends on the context. The pragmatic view of metaphor asks is this metaphor enabling in this situation?

Metaphor theorists have said little about design explicitly, though Johnson and Ricoeur in particular have related metaphor to the workings of the imagination. Design, whether of buildings or of software, is an intensely imaginative activity. But then is this any different from other supposedly rational/logical activity? Johnson emphasizes that the workings of the imagination are not to be distinguished from *rational* thinking. There is a strong presupposition promoted throughout the philosophical tradition, notably by the empiricists, that the imagination is different and subservient to rational thinking. Hume, for example, described the image as the residue of an impression, which is to imply that imagination is a secondary, derivative faculty.[93] To reinstate the importance of the imagination is also one of the missions of romanticism. Though it elevates imagination, romanticism trades heavily on upholding a distinction between the imagination and reason. Pragmatism (and phenomenology) seeks to unite the two, showing that the distinction is one of word usage but not of substance. According to Dewey, thinking that is of any consequence at all pertains as much to the aesthetic and the imaginative as to what we may choose to call pure reason, whether practiced by the artist or the scientist. In keeping with the pragmatic tradition, Johnson seeks to reinstate the imagination as essential to all aspects of human cognition.

Imagination is a pervasive structuring activity by means of which we achieve coherent, patterned, unified representations. It is indispensable for our ability to make sense of our experience, to find it meaningful. The conclusion ought to be, therefore, that imagination is absolutely central to human rationality, that is, to our rational capacity to find significant connections, to draw inferences, and to solve problems.[94]

This imaginative structuring implicates metaphor. To see this thing *as* that thing is creative and imaginative through and through. According to Johnson, "Metaphorical projection is one fundamental means by which we project structure, make new connections, and remould our experience."[95]

Ricoeur adds support to Johnson's view. Following Kant, he says, "we have to look at imagination as the place of nascent meanings and categories rather than as the place of fading impressions."[96] For Ricoeur, theories of imagination return us to the pre-Socratic tradition. Metaphor works through opposition, dialectic, and difference.

According to Ricoeur, to "see sameness in difference is the genius of metaphor."[97] On his view, the tension is not just between the two terms of the metaphor (e.g., "house" and "machine" in "a house is a machine") but in the relation itself, in the copula ("is"). The tension is between sameness and difference. In metaphor, we detect sameness in spite of the overwhelming presence of difference.[98]

Ricoeur does not advance a full theory of imagination but asserts that imagination is "the emergence of conceptual meaning through the interplay between sameness and difference."[99] Metaphor makes obvious the process that is covert in all attempts to derive meaning, namely, the conflict between sameness and difference. Metaphor brings this conflict between sameness and difference to light. It does this by defying categories. Metaphor bypasses accepted categories to reveal "unnoticed similarities in the field of our experience."[100] A metaphor is a classic case of what Ryle and Turbayne characterize as a "category mistake."[101] We "misclassify" a house as a machine.

To highlight the tensional structure of metaphor echoes our earlier discussion about metaphoric versus literal language. There is a tension inherent in asserting a metaphor: is the assertion a truth, a fiction, or a metaphor? This tension is always present in language but is rendered obvious through the issue of metaphor. The identification of this tension echoes the tensional relationship between the "is" and the "is not," being and nonbeing, outlined in the philosophical tradition of Hegel and Heidegger. It could be said that metaphor resides at the interstice between "is" and "is not." Translating this insight into the world of information technology, every assertion about the computer is in tension with a denial of the assertion. The computer is/is not an intelligent entity. The configuration of pixels on the computer screen is/is not a sheet of paper.

This tensional, dialectical account of metaphor accords with Heidegger's notions of truth. The conventional view of truth, dating from Plato and made explicit by the empiricists and logical positivists, pertains to how assertions correspond to some state of affairs. For example, the truth status of the proposition "the computer is intelligent" is thought to reside in the degree of correspondence between the proposition and the evidence of our senses to support the claim. According to logical positivism, for a statement to be meaningful it must at least be testable. The truthfulness of "the computer is intelligent" resides in our ability to elaborate and define the terms of the expression and to establish some means of testing or refuting it. (The Turing test is such a test.) According to the correspondence theory of truth, the statement is meaningful but false. Similar statements subject to truth testing include the "computer is a theater," "a movie," "an inkblot," and so on. In terms of correspondence, these assertions are patently false. From Davidson's view, we may infer that although these statements are false, their meaning, which is simply their use, resides in their status as metaphors. By this account, the idea of metaphor is subservient to the idea of correspondence. Metaphor accounts for the uses we are able to make of untruthful statements.

Heidegger's notions of truth as disclosure take us in a different direction of inquiry, however, and in a different direction regarding the workings of metaphor. Whereas truth as disclosure has its place and is "correct" according to Heidegger, that is not the "essence" of truth. We use the term *truth* in many different contexts. We say of a painting that it is truthful. According to the correspondence theory of truth, this means that the painting corresponds to something else—a scene or a particular person. But this is clearly an impoverished view of truth in art. For Heidegger, the truth of a painting is what it discloses or reveals. Any work of art both reveals and conceals, and appreciating that truth is clearly a matter of interpretation in a context of understanding. If this is so of art, then it is equally the case in other contexts—including observations in science, the evaluation of mathematical models, and the interpretation of assertions in language. Language has a revelatory property for Heidegger, and this is where truth resides—not in what words correspond to but in what they reveal. Heidegger thinks this view of truth is far removed from a murky relativism. Its roots are in the flux and play of strife, conflict, and tension—human rationality as understood by the pre-Socratics and appropriated by Eckhart and Hegel.

The dialectical tensions in a situation of interpretation are described in different ways by Heidegger and others—as the strife between earth and world, revealing and concealing, and so on. Ricoeur is more straightforward. He uses the idea of poetical language to illustrate this tension. Poetic, or metaphoric, language changes our way of looking at things: "What is changed by poetic language is our way of dwelling in the world. From poetry we receive a new way of being in the world, of orientating ourselves in this world."[102] How does this occur? According to Ricoeur the purpose of metaphorical language is not to improve communication nor to ensure clarity of argument, "but to shatter and to increase our sense of reality by shattering and increasing our language. The strategy of metaphor is heuristic fiction for the sake of redescribing reality. With metaphor we experience the metamorphosis of both language and reality."[103]

Elsewhere Ricoeur shows how poetry brings to light the tensions within language. The conventional distinctions between the literal and the metaphoric point to the "paradox" of the copula. This paradox preserves our sense of being-in-the-world.

Here are summed up all the forms of 'tensions' brought to light by semantics: tension between subject and predicate, between literal interpretation and metaphorical interpretation, between identity and difference. . . . They come to completion finally in the paradox of the copula, where being-as signifies being and not being. By this *turn* of expression, poetry, in combination with other modes of discourse, articulates and preserves the experience of belonging that places man in discourse and discourse in being.[104]

Poetry and metaphor are therefore primordial, and, in opening up the possibility of alienation, they allow us to reflect on being and dwelling: "What is given to thought in this way by the 'tensional' truth of poetry is the most primordial, most hidden dialectic—the dialectic that reigns between the experience of belonging as a whole and the power of distanciation that opens up the space of speculative thought."[105] What can be said of poetry and metaphor can be said of technology. Technology is a means of establishing difference and thereby establishing a sense of dwelling, if we let it. In this regard technology functions as metaphor. The progress and upheaval of technology is like the changes in metaphor that excite our sense of belonging.

The notion of difference has implications for the design of computer systems. We can appropriate the differences that a metaphor reveals as a stimulus to design activity. The notion of difference also suggests that designers, developers, and users of computer technology are not as helpless as it seems. We need not succumb to technological enframing but, by attending to it in a particular way, can exploit technology as a source of upheaval that intensifies our sense of dwelling. Here technology is not a means of amplifying or extending our powers but, through its ability to alienate, paradoxically provides a means of jarring us into realizing where our home really lies.

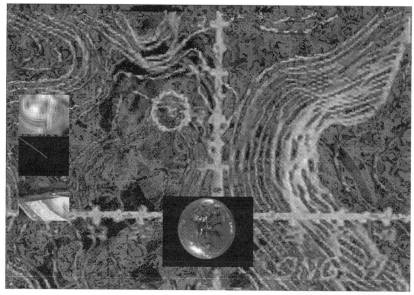

Scenes from *A Digital Rhizome* by Brad Miller—fresco and satellite map.

8

Conclusion

In my examination of information technology and postmodern thinking, I have favored the priority of praxis, understood through the writings of pragmatic and hermeneutical philosophers. The pragmatic approach to information technology emphasizes the importance of everyday practices. Pragmatism recognizes that we are always socially situated. The way that praxis operates is summed up in Theodor Adorno's understanding of cultural and social phenomena through the concepts of "force field" and "constellation."[1] By "force field" he means "a relational interplay of attractions and aversions that constitute the dynamic, transmutational structure of a complex phenomenon."[2] By "constellation" he means "a juxtaposed rather than integrated cluster of changing elements that resist reduction to a common denominator, essential core, or generative first principle."[3] In the context of work and leisure, the constellation of activities are our practices as professionals, administrators, managers, technologists, and users—our irreducible, interacting work and leisure practices.

The nature of praxis is evident when we consider the relationships among members of a firm, particularly those relationships that cross over organizational structures and the formal roles of the participants: the tacit understandings of the boundaries to each other's knowledge; knowing who to turn to for help; knowing who is reliable and trustworthy; and the teams of alliances that are set up. Such dynamic phenomena generally defy attempts at systematization and the imposition of structure and can easily be destroyed when such impositions are attempted.

According to the pragmatic theme, technologies are similarly connected to each other. Items of technological equipment form parts of complex technological systems that involve different kinds of dependencies. Some dependencies are physical, such as the dependence of computer systems on the electricity grid and the telephone system. Some dependencies are metaphoric—computer-aided design (CAD) systems are related to manual drawing tools, multimedia is related to film and video, aspects of electronic mail are metaphorically related to telex and CB radio, and so on. Also there are institutional dependencies through industries, systems of distribution, regulations, training, and education systems. Other dependencies are local—the computer requires the printer, the modem connects the computer to the telephone line, and so on.

These technological constellations are enmeshed with the complex constellation that is praxis. The role of the professional designer is engaged with the technology of the drawing board or CAD system and related technologies. The role of the manager is caught up with spreadsheets, the cellular telephone, and the company car. Secretaries and administrative assistants are involved with typewriters, word processors, and telephones. This interconnection of praxis with constellations of technology is particularly evident if any of the components change. A simple example is the introduction of word processing, which is gradually changing, in some cases reducing, the role of the administrative assistant. But the effects are not just in one direction. Word processing has been designed and developed through understandings of typing practice, and the technology is responding to changes in that practice as word processing incorporates more features of interest to management, such as dynamic charts and tables.

Introducing a new technology has the potential to perturb the constellation of conventions currently in place in our praxis. As the technology is taken up, we discover new ways of acting and thinking. New technology is always taken up in a context. According to this model, any account of the "impact" of a new technology should take into account the conventions currently in place and how they are changing.

The pragmatic theme also recognizes that new technologies *reveal* aspects of our practices. Computer-aided design reveals architectural and engineering practices as custodians of databases on buildings and systems. Computerized desktop publishing reveals the firm as a kind of publishing business. Multimedia reveals the firm as a dealer in advertising, presentation, and even fantasy. So technologies do not merely meet needs but are implicated in the defining and redefining of practice.

What I have outlined so far is consistent with Heidegger's view of technology as equipment, in *Being and Time*. There is an equipmental whole which we reduce to specific items in a particular context of breakdown or of pointing out. It is also consistent with my Heideggerian exploration, in chapter 5, of how *things* reveal our practices.

By way of contrast, the conservative approach to information technology trades in the notion that there is something to be conserved, to which we should return, or a deep structure to be uncovered. This is also a metaphysical orientation. In the case of information technology, this theme is revealed most potently in the tenets of systems theory applied to design, particularly in presenting methodologies for research and development. According to one such theoretical method, we make observations about the practices of a group of people (such as designers). Then we attempt to identify variables, to find correlations between variables, and to form generalizations. In so doing, we attempt to uncover the underlying structure of the practices under study. We then move into a new experimental context in which the generalizations serve as tools for prediction. So we apply our findings to new situations, such as architects or engineers working with computers. We would know from our generalizations about architects and engineers that they require large drawing surfaces, they need somewhere to display their work, they work with three-dimensional models, and they sketch. If the method were successful, it would help us plan for emerging technologies, such as computer-mediated collaborative work. We would know that architects and engineers need common drawing surfaces, a means of exchanging information, audit trails, and face-to-face contact with groups of people. Such generalizations would thereby guide our research programs, curriculum development, systems development, and decision making about computer resources.

However, experience with the invention, design, and integration of computer technologies shows a different pattern to design activity. The process is more usually one of prototyping and informal testing in use. Technologies are not designed simply to address needs, but the formulation of the design task is influenced by technologies already at hand. It is well known that design relies heavily on precedent. In spite of attempts at automated case-based reasoning, principles underlying our use of precedent prove elusive.

Under the conservative theme, one also posits models that carry the weight of science. But on inspection, we see that these models are rarely productive in the same way that models are in science. I have indicated that models can be more accurately described as metaphors. But to describe models as metaphors is problematic for conservatism, which also maintains a sharp line between the literal and the metaphoric. Literal meaning is what is conserved, irrespective of the metaphors we use. To hand our scholarly deliberations over to metaphor is hardly scientific. It is not uncovering principles, nor is it uncovering structure.

For the pragmatic position, the use of metaphor is far less problematic. By recognizing the role of metaphor, it is possible to abandon the idea that there must be underlying principles governing practices. Where there are principles, they are themselves artifacts, tools of practice. Recognizing the role of metaphor involves recognizing how research and decision making actually occur. Pragmatism in its many guises affirms the priority of engagement in the world over theoretical constructs. Its understanding of science resides with the materiality of instrument use, laboratory practices, the nature of communities, and theories as tools. But then pragmatism does not depend on science as the sole means of legitimation in a field. Aware of the nature of communities, it is also wary of adopting scientific terminology as a means of legitimating discourse and research programs. For pragmatism, metaphors of design are not second best to scientific accounts. Pragmatism seeks to break the divide that asserts a difference in objective truth and subjective construction, or between literal truth and metaphoric gloss. It renders such distinctions unimportant by presenting new terminology and new modes of discourse, or it shows such distinctions to be contingent.

Seen in this light, an appeal to metaphor is not an appeal to second best. On examination, metaphor can be shown to preserve the tensional and indeterminate nature of understanding. If we are our technologies, then we are also our metaphors. Metaphors are implicated in how we see ourselves, and they define the problems that we set. The workings of metaphor are implicated in modes of being.

Metaphor also provides the critical theme with a focus for its critique. Instrumental reason, technical rationality, presents its metaphors as fixed. It closes off interpretation. One way of looking at Heidegger's misgivings about the enframing essence of technology is that technological thinking promotes totalizing and fixed ways of looking at things rather than allowing things to reveal themselves as different and situational. In other words, technological thinking attempts to call a halt to the disclosive, dialectical play of metaphor. In a sense, the critical-theorist seeks to expose the metaphors within what is taken to be the literal, investigate their entailments, and posit rival metaphors.

Under the radical theme, metaphor finds full flower as a commerce between the "is" and the "is not," the play between metaphoric truth and literal falsehood. Metaphor's assertion of patent "falsehood" sets up a distance that is also a space for imaginative thought.

Changing Metaphors of Computer Systems

The utility of the pragmatic view of metaphor is further illustrated in the way metaphor structures discourse and action. There are metaphors of the design process, design practice, the clientele, the design organization, the task domain, thinking, and the computer. Metaphors reveal and conceal. Seeing one thing as another reveals something about the thing: a problem to be solved, an action to be undertaken, a scenario to be acted out. Metaphors assist us in setting the problems we try to solve. Certain prevalent metaphors appear to guide the organization of work practices and decision making in organizations. These metaphors relate to how we see the organization and its constituents, including personnel, clients, customers, users, managers, and equipment. Metaphors emerge through the practices of the organization; its relationships to the wider world; the ideologies of related professions, trades, and institutions; and pervasive technologies. The metaphors set the problems of the organization and define its successes and failures. Reflecting on the prevalent metaphors within organizations can bring about change and provide pointers to future practice. In the course of this book, I have identified several prominent metaphors of computer systems. It is worth recounting some of these to reinforce how the metaphors we adopt are implicated in our practice.

The currency of the metaphor of the computer *as* a calculating device is beyond dispute—the computer as an adding machine, slide rule, ledger, codebook. Coincident with this conception is the computer as a drawing tool—the computer as a drawing surface and pen, a dynamic chart, as demonstrated in the earliest radars and oscilloscopes. Coincident again is the conception of the computer as an intelligence. For Turing and his contemporaries, the intrigue of the new calculating machines and the theories surrounding them also lay in the implications about human intelligence.[4] Calculation, drawing, and intelligence were each implicated in the development of the computer at the outset.[5]

What are the entailments of these three metaphors? The computer as calculating device has clearly fostered sophisticated computer systems for bookkeeping and accounting, structural analysis, and so on. In terms of educational programs, it has fostered courses in computer programming that focus on arithmetic operations, numerical data manipulation, and so on. For architectural and engineering education, it has promoted the use of the computer for structural and statistical analysis. The computer as calculating device has also promoted understandings of design, cognition, and society in terms of calculation. The power of the calculation tool also increases the force of the metaphor of all things as calculable.

The computer as drawing tool presents a different set of entailments, culminating in the development of sophisticated CAD systems. In architectural and engineering design, the computer as drawing tool has focused on precision, comprehensive information, intricate detail, completeness, and the integration of disparate graphical information. The variation on the drawing metaphor is to see the computer as a modeling tool. Drawing and calculation conspire to construct the powerful metaphor of the design model. A drawing is a two-dimensional model. Cartesian geometry is used to specify values for points, lines, and planes, which are in turn models, or perhaps metaphors, of designed artifacts.

The computer as intelligence has spawned prolific research projects on modeling human cognition on computer systems, developing expert systems that purportedly solve real-world problems, and so on. More subtly, under this metaphor, the computer also provides a point of comparison. The computer and its organizational structure become a benchmark against which we can compare our own flawed reasoning powers. When we see the mind as a machine, it appears as a very flawed machine.

Beyond the computer as calculator, drawing device, and intelligence, other metaphors are emerging, promoted by both changes in the technology and in the rhetoric of those who wish to encourage some kind of change. In its earliest years, the computer appeared as a large, expensive mainframe facility, now replaced largely by networked desktop computers. The latter suggest the metaphor of the computer as a distributed facility. More recently, and as a development on the idea of distributed computing, some have promoted the computer as a ubiquitous resource.[6] This metaphor trades in metaphors promoted through recent developments in computerization that apparently devolve control to the computer user: personal computers, local-area networks, international networks, electronic communications, file sharing, miniaturization, portable computers, high-level software tools, and iconic interfaces. But it also trades on metaphors of the everyday—those things we take for granted. Weiser appeals to the metaphor of books, magazines, candy wrappers, and street signs: the "constant background of these products of 'literacy technology' does not require active attention."[7]

The ubiquitous computing metaphor fits comfortably within the ethos of pragmatically oriented computer systems development, and arguably with Heideggerian notions of the equipmental whole. We recognize that computers will not necessarily supplant books, manual drawing, or hand writing. The computer will be one of several resources at hand to assist in a task. This militates against the possibility of the complete, fully integrated, totalizing electronic work environment. It also suggests that computers will appear wherever we happen to be. The computer can be taken onto the construction site and into meetings with clients at their homes. Students can use word processing and CAD in the library, in the student lounge, at home, or in the coffee shop. There are at least two interesting scenarios provided by the ubiquity of computing in office practice. One emerges through the metaphor of the office as club outlined by Francis Duffy.[8] Professionals join general-purpose business establishments that provide infrastructure, a pleasant working environment, and the opportunity for strategic face-to-face contact. The environment is nonspecific. The specific work-related support is provided through the computer. Obvious examples of organisations suited to this kind of arrangement are those related to finance—specific needs are met by communication and access to databases. In a second (and not unrelated) scenario, the professional is either itinerant, works from home, or works in a very task-specific environment, such as a studio. In this case, the computer provides support for the more-general business activities, such as communications.

The ubiquitous computing metaphor obviously trades heavily in the computer as a communications device. It also conspires with the notion of the computer as a total-immersion environment and the computer as a mass-media device. I outlined these metaphors critically in detail in chapters 4 and 5. There is clearly a difference between the emphasis on the computer as a precision three-dimensional modeling device, as in CAD, and the computer as a communications and mass-media device. Already we see a trend within some organizations, notably universities, toward acquiring computers as a means of communication rather than as a calculating, word processing, or drawing tool. With widespread access to the mass media through computer links, perhaps the primary reason for acquiring a computer will be to connect to the information superhighway of communications, information, and mass media. It is an open question as to what kinds of metaphors this usage promotes and how it will change work practices. Already in architectural firms there is evidence of a new, emerging orientation to practice that implicates the computer as a mass-media device. In a recent survey on computers in practice, we detected something of this media orientation.[9] One survey respondent indicated how the conception of the firm had been influenced through this metaphor: "So we've been a mixed media communications company as much as an architectural firm. We go from the dream making end of it all the way."

We have noticed a similar difference in orientation promoted through introducing architecture students to computers as a means of processing video images as opposed to generating precision three-dimensional models. The former arguably presents a media orientation to design—taking quick video images of a building site or context; capturing related imagery, either through a camera or by "lifting" it from television or commercial videos; displaying the images on a computer screen and projection facility; and capturing and enhancing the images digitally. The techniques also involve mixing media: producing hand sketches, which are then scanned, digitally enhanced, and collaged together to form a multimedia presentation. The images can then be transmitted to another party for comment and critique or some kind of remote collaborative design session. The tools are now quick and easy to use. Working with digital video is more like sketching than model making. The technology promotes different ways of working and different metaphors of the design process than the highly constrained techniques of precise three-dimensional model manipulation on a computer, which has been one of the usual means of introducing computers to architecture students. Presumably the mass-media metaphor influences computer use in schools in which multimedia is often a preferred medium for presenting project work. How the computer as mass-media device will affect engineering and other disciplines with a less-graphical orientation to design is unknown at this stage.

What kind of work practices will this use of the computer instill, where designers are working within a vast media matrix, cutting and pasting ideas from everywhere, and in turn contributing to such a pool? Following the arguments of chapter 3, we may discount the possibility that the design enterprise will degrade through an endless spiral into simulations of simulations, and on into "hyperreality," but there will most certainly be new modes of practice, new conceptions of the design process, and new forms of designed artifact brought about by new technologies and metaphors.

Being and Resistance

We cannot conclude without returning to the grand, master metaphor that, thanks to Heidegger, inevitably intrudes into any discussion of technology—the metaphor of Being. Hubert Dreyfus provides a telling summary of contemporary thinking by contrasting the writing of Heidegger and Foucault.[10] The contrast provides us with two options for pursuing the matter of technology. We will use Dreyfus's summary here to emphasize Heidegger's position and its consequences. The consistent theme in Heidegger's writing from *Being and Time* on is the theme of being. For Foucault, the dominant theme is power, understood not only as a tool of domination but of positive enablement.[11] Each writer employs his major theme to similar ends; however, one of the major differences between them is that Heidegger focuses on things and how they become objects, whereas Foucault focuses on human beings and how they become subjects. So Heidegger challenges the objectivity of modern, metaphysical thinking, and Foucault challenges its subjectivity.

Even though Heidegger is concerned with the essence of technology and not its multifarious manifestations, the kinds of technologies Heidegger invokes are the physical machinery, electronic systems, bridges, dams, and airplanes that populate our technological world. On the other hand, the technologies Foucault names are welfare systems, schooling, military establishments, prisons, and bureaucracies—the institutions through which power is transferred and deviations are rendered manageable. For both, technology is implicated in a kind of pervasive distress; this includes treating things and people as resources. More profoundly, Heidegger sees a distortion of our ability to appreciate things in their essence, as different and revealing. This distortion comes about through the essence of technology—that is, its enframing. For Heidegger, the essence of technology objectivizes. For Foucault, technologies also subjectivize. The technologies (institutions) of the Christian confessional and those of Freudian psychiatry have brought about the construction of intro-spective subjects, driven by a logic of desire. For Foucault, the distress is through disciplinary bio-power, which affects the social order and the relationships among people. For both writers, enframing and disciplinary bio-power are totalizing and normalizing; it is a de-pendence on technology (Heidegger) or on social technologies like welfare (Foucault) that presents the danger.

But both Heidegger and Foucault identify elements of resistance to enframing and disciplinary bio-power. For Heidegger, the resis-tance is within things. The metaphor is of the earth in things. The earth is inviolable and shatters every attempt to penetrate it. Dreyfus demystifies Heidegger's concept of the earth within things by re-lating it to Kuhn's characterization of anomalies in normal science. Heidegger's impenetrable earth is analogous to an anomaly that forces a revolution in science. As long as there are such anomalies and we are aware of them as such, there is the possibility of a break-down in the current paradigm and the development of a new one. In the new paradigm, the anomaly becomes the focus of a new truth. For Heidegger, there is the possibility of resistance and hence of a saving from the all-pervasive technological enframing: ''[F]or Hei-degger the resistance intrinsic to things holds open the possibility of a saving breakdown of the total ground plan of modern culture.''[12] Foucault, on the other hand, focuses on people and their positive resistance to disciplinary bio-power. There is something within groups of people and within individuals that responds inversely to attempts to render them docile. People seek to disengage themselves from incursions of power. According to Dreyfus, these notions of earth, resistance, anomaly, and disengagement ''are meant to en-courage us to pay attention to what remains of the different, the local, and the recalcitrant in our current practices.''[13] We do not need to resist particular technologies but rather ''our totalizing, nor-malizing understanding of being.''[14] The task then is to strengthen those practices that have so far escaped or successfully resisted the spread of technology or disciplinary bio-power ''and so might be-come the elements of some different understanding of being.''[15]

Heidegger thinks this is accomplished through developing an understanding of our historical condition, which is the task of "thinkers." The thoughtful understanding of history weakens the grip of the totalizing, enframing worldview and makes it possible to disengage ourselves from our current direction. Of course, for Heidegger, this is not accomplished simply through the study of schoolbook history but by reflection on how Being reveals itself, or how Being "happens," or on the epochs of Being.

By way of contrast, Foucault thinks there is no essence or special way of thinking. There is no historical essence to be recovered. His nonessentialist rhetoric denies him an account of why we should resist disciplinary bio-power or why it should be a source of distress. Foucault's strategy of resistance is to seek to reform specific instances of disciplinary bio-power. "This view of his role, Foucault calls his hyperactive pessimism."[16]

Dreyfus contrasts Foucault's "hyperactive pessimism" with Heidegger's "superpassive optimism." For Heidegger, what is lost in the enframing is receptivity, so he does not advocate intervention but a letting be—*Gelassenheit*. As do the thinkers who know their history of Being, Heidegger appeals to the poetic work, the work of art, the Greek temple, and nearness to God. According to Dreyfus, letting be also represents the fostering of a new sense of community, a new cultural paradigm. Under Dreyfus's pragmatic interpretation of Heidegger, *Gelassenheit* is a community enterprise: "A cultural paradigm focuses and collects the scattered practices of a culture, unifies them into coherent possibilities for action, and holds them up to the people who can then act and relate to each other in terms of the exemplar."[17] According to Dreyfus, a new paradigm would focus upon practices that are now at the margins of our culture and make them central. Conversely, it would marginalize practices now central to our cultural self-understanding: "[W]e must preserve the endangered species of practices that remain in our culture in the hope that one day they will be pulled together in a new paradigm rich enough and resistant enough to give new meaningful direction to our lives."[18] For Dreyfus, this "superpassive optimism" of Heidegger's contrasts radically with Foucault's "hyperactive pessimism." On Heidegger's view, we become receptive to the marginal, the resistant, and we wait for the change. On Foucault's view, we react and reform. Dreyfus presents the two possibilities as an unresolved choice.

The path of superpassive pessimism is interesting from the point of view of information technology. Whereas Heidegger would have us focus on what is distinctly untechnological (history and poetry), it is intriguing to speculate on the value of probing within the world of information technology for the marginal, the resistant, and the anomalous—anomalies that are inevitably bringing about transformations of information technology and of ourselves and that may one day herald the "turning" Heidegger seeks. Such anomalies may include the world of computer programmers who are so steeped in machine logic that they instinctively know its failings and its limits; e-mail users who, while appearing trapped in an electronic world, are desperately establishing and promoting the value of human contact; virtual-reality users who develop a heightened sense of the essence of things as opposed to objects described in a database; travelers armed with portable computer, telephone link, micro-video camera, and instant access to one hundred media channels who, knowing what this connectivity can and cannot provide, have a heightened sense of the value of place. It is an interesting prospect that perhaps the deeper one probes and the greater one's commitment to, and dependence on, information technology, the more resistant one may become to its essence.

Notes

Introduction

1. S. Gallagher, *Hermeneutics and Education.*

2. In describing structuralism as conservative, I am not denying the radical impact of Saussure's innovative theories of meaning (not mentioned here), and the great advances that his theories brought about in linguistics, nor the debt of radical theorists such as Derrida to those theories.

3. J. Caputo, *Demythologizing Heidegger.*

4. M. Heidegger, *Being and Time,* 39.

5. M. Heidegger, *The Question concerning Technology and Other Essays,* 12.

6. T. Fry, *Remakings: Ecology, Design, Philosophy,* 14.

Chapter 1

1. According to Ihde, pragmatism is one of the three dominant "styles" of philosophy evident this century. The other two are phenomenology and logical positivism. All three incorporate critiques of Cartesian rationalism, but, from the point of view of pragmatism, logical positivism (which has evolved into the analytic school) exhibits the strongest allegiance to the tenets of rationalism. See D. Ihde, *Philosophy of Technology: An Introduction.*

2. The theory/practice distinction has a long history. For Aristotle, theory (*theoria*) was both contemplation and strenuous disciplined activity, to be contrasted with practice (*praxis*), which involved doing, living well, and exercising practical wisdom. See R. J. Bernstein, *Praxis and Action.*

3. Rorty presents the similarities and differences between Heidegger's thought and

philosophical pragmatism. See R. Rorty, *Philosophy and the Mirror of Nature;* R. Rorty, *Contingency, Irony and Solidarity;* R. Rorty, "Heidegger, contingency and pragmatism," *Heidegger: A Critical Reader,* 209–30; and R. Rorty, "Overcoming the tradition: Heidegger and Dewey," *Consequences of Pragmatism (Essays: 1972–1980),* 37–59. For a summary of the practical implications of Heidegger's philosophy on computer-aided design, see S. McLaughlin, "Practices and primordial understanding: Major implications of Heidegger's philosophy for computer-aided architectural design research"; and I. Hybs, "Beyond the interface."

4. See, for example, H. Marcuse, *One-Dimensional Man: Studies in the Ideology of Advanced Industrial Society;* and D. Ingram and J. Simon-Ingram, eds., *Critical Theory: The Essential Readings.*

5. See J. Derrida, *Of Grammatology;* and J. D. Caputo, *Radical Hermeneutics: Repetition, Deconstruction, and the Hermeneutical Project.*

6. See R. Descartes, *Discourse on Method and the Meditations;* and F. Copleston, *A History of Philosophy,* vol. 4, *Descartes to Leibniz.*

7. See Rorty, *Philosophy and the Mirror of Nature;* and R. J. Bernstein, *Beyond Objectivism and Relativism.*

8. See R. Schank, "What is AI anyway?" *The Foundations of Artificial Intelligence: A Source Book,* 3–13.

9. Ibid., 4.

10. Ibid., 5.

11. Ibid., 5.

12. See, for example, Mas'ud Zavarzadeh and D. Morton, "Theory pedagogy politics: The crisis of the subject in the humanities," *Boundary* 2 (15): 1–22.

13. See A. Barr and E. A. Feigenbaum, eds., *The Handbook of Artificial Intelligence,* vol. 1.

14. For a discussion of the uses of the term *model* in artificial intelligence and cognitive science, see Y. Wilks, "One small head: Models and theories," *The Foundations of Artificial Intelligence: A Source Book,* 121–34; and A. B. Snodgrass and R. D. Coyne, "Models, metaphors and the hermeneutics of designing," *Design Issues,* (1): 56–74. For a discussion of models in science, see M. Hesse, *Models and Analogies in Science;* and C. M. Turbayne, *The Myth of Metaphor.*

15. See H. Simon, *The Sciences of the Artificial.*

16. See M. M. Gardiner and B. Christie, *Applying Cognitive Psychology to User-Interface Design;* D. A. Norman, *The Psychology of Everday Things;* R. E. Eberts and C. G. Eberts, "Four approaches to human computer interaction," *Intelligent Interfaces: Theory, Research and Design,* 69–127; B. Laurel, ed., *The Art of Human-Computer Interface Design;* and P. Falzon, ed., *Cognitive Ergonomics: Understanding, Learning and Designing Human-Computer Interaction.*

17. See R. C. Schank, *Dynamic Memory: A Theory of Reminding and Learning in Computers and People;* and R. C. Schank and R. Abelson, *Scripts, Plans, Goals and Understanding.*

18. Strictly speaking, analytic philosophers like Ayer would maintain that the question "can machines think?" is undecidable and therefore meaningless. But such philosophers demonstrate their allegiance to the calculative (and Cartesian) view of reason with such comments as the following:

> [T]he questions with which philosophy is concerned are purely logical questions; and although people do in fact dispute about logical questions, such disputes are always unwarranted. . . . [W]e may be sure that one party in the dispute has been guilty of a miscalculation which a sufficiently close scrutiny of reason will enable us to detect. (A. J. Ayer, *Language, Truth and Logic,* 144)

See also A. J. Ayer, *The Central Questions of Philosophy.* For a brief summary of the history of artificial intelligence, see E. Dietrich, "Programs in the search for intelligent machines: The mistaken foundations of AI," *The Foundations of Artificial Intelligence: A Source Book,* 223–33.

19. See L. March,"The logic of design and the question of value," *The Architecture of Form,* 1–40; G. Stiny, *Pictorial and Formal Aspects of Shape Grammars;* and W. J. Mitchell, *The Logic of Architecture: Design, Computation, and Cognition.*

20. See W. J. Mitchell, "Computer-aided design media: A comparative analysis," *Computers in Architecture: Tools for Design,* 53–62.

21. See C. Alexander, *Notes on the Synthesis of Form;* and J. C. Jones, *Design Methods: Seeds of Human Futures.*

22. See D. Cooper and M. Clancy, *Oh! Pascal;* and A. Macro and J. Buxton, *The Craft of Software Engineering.*

23. Eberts and Eberts, "Four approaches to human computer interaction."

24. See T. Winograd and F. Flores, *Understanding Computers and Cognition: A New Foundation for Design;* and T. Winograd, "Thinking machines: Can there be? are we?" *The Foundations of Artificial Intelligence: A Source Book,* 167–89.

25. See F. Nietzsche, *Beyond Good and Evil: Prelude to a Philosophy of the Future;* and M. Heidegger, *Being and Time.* For a summary of Heidegger's complex thought, see H. Dreyfus, *Being-in-the-World: A Commentary on Heidegger's "Being and Time,"* Division I.

26. See H. L. Dreyfus, *What Computers Can't Do: The Limits of Artificial Intelligence;* H. L. Dreyfus and S. E. Dreyfus, *Mind over Machine;* and Winograd and Flores, *Understanding Computers and Cognition.*

27. See Marcuse, *One-Dimensional Man.*

28. See J. Weizenbaum, *Computer Power and Human Reason: From Judgement to Calculation.*

29. See M. J. Stefik, "Book reviews: Understanding computers and cognition—a new foundation for design, *Artificial Intelligence*, 31:213–61, for both the book reviews and the response by Winograd and Flores.

30. Bernstein, *Beyond Objectivism and Relativism*.

31. This impatience with philosophy is directly attributable to the analytic school, which distinguishes between "speculative philosophy," in which "undecidable" (and therefore meaningless) propositions are debated, and analytic philosophy, which serves science by showing the nature of formal propositions and how we can test their validity. See Ayer, *Language, Truth and Logic*.

32. Stefik, "Book reviews," 226.

33. Ibid., 229.

34. Ihde points out that technology has only recently appeared as a cause for philosophical study. It did not appear in the philosophy of science, because it was thought that modern technology "derives simply from theoretically and formally constructed science as a theory activity." (Ihde, *Philosophy of Technology*, 22)

35. See the report by the Tavistock Institute, *Interdependence and Uncertainty: A Study of the Building Industry*.

36. See Dreyfus, *Being-in-the-World*.

37. Analytical philosophers like Ayer indicate their bias toward the primacy of the self (the subject) over community when they argue the case for our certainty about the existence of other minds. They argue for the existence of community from the starting point of the individual subject. See Ayer, *Language, Truth and Logic*.

38. This theme is developed further by R. D. Coyne and A. B. Snodgrass, in "Cooperation and individualism in design," *Environment and Planning B: Planning and Design* 20:163–74.

39. Analytic philosophy supports this position indirectly in its assertion of the calculability of reason and in its silence on the role of technology. See Ayer, *Language, Truth and Logic*.

40. In keeping with its origins in empiricism, analytic philosophy places great emphasis on sense experience. But priority is given to the theoretical. For example, in Ayer's *Language, Truth and Logic*, the senses first make their appearance in their role in the processes of observation by which we confirm or refute logical propositions (p. 16).

41. See H. Rheingold, *Virtual Reality*.

42. In analytic philosophy, the priority of the end or problem statement is expressed in terms of the hypothesis. In reasoning, we are actively engaged in confirming or refuting hypotheses. See Ayer, *Language, Truth and Logic*, 92.

43. See B. Latour and S. Woolgar, *Laboratory Life: The Social Construction of Scientific Facts;* B. Latour, *Science in Action;* and D. Ihde, *Instrumental Realism: The Interface between Philosophy of Science and Philosophy of Technology*.

44. It is common to use the term *pragmatic* rather than *practical* in this context. Both pertain to practice (praxis), but the latter implies "able to produce useful and menial outcomes," whereas the former implies "advocating behavior that is dictated more by practical consequences than theory."

45. M. Weiser, "The computer for the twenty-first century," Scientific American 265 (3): 66.

46. A. Kay, "Computer software," Scientific American 251 (3): 42.

47. See also A. Kay, "Doing with images makes symbols: Communicating with computers," *Industry Leaders in Computer Science;* A. Kay, "User interface: A personal view," in *The Art of Human-Computer Interface Design,* 191–207; and A. Kay, "Computers, networks and education," Scientific American (September): 100–107.

48. B. Laurel, *Computers as Theatre,* 45.

49. See G. Bell and C. Mead, "How things really work: Two inventors on innovation," *Industry Leaders in Computer Science.*

50. Weiser, "The computer for the twenty-first century," 75.

51. R. Stults, "Experimental uses of video to support design activities," *Report SSL-89–19 [P89–00019],* 3.

52. Ibid.

53. Ibid., 4.

54. Ibid.

55. See J. Dewey, *Democracy and Education: An Introduction to the Philosophy of Education;* P. Freire, *Pedagogy of the Oppressed;* and I. Illich, *Deschooling Society.*

56. Kay, "Computers, networks and education," 105.

57. C. Davidson, "The man who made computers personal," New Scientist (June): 34.

58. Ibid., 35.

59. Kay, "Computer software," 42.

60. See K. Carter, "Computer-aided design: Back to the drawing board"; and S. L. Minneman, "The social construction of a technical reality: Empirical studies of group engineering design practice," *Report SSL-91-22 [P91-00160].* Xerox.

61. Davidson, "The man who made computers personal," 35.

62. Laurel, *Computers as Theatre,* 32.

63. See S. Turkle, "Computer as Rorschach," *Society* (January/February): 15–24; and S. Turkle, *The Second Self: Computers and the Human Spirit,* 84.

64. Kay, "User interface: A personal view."

65. Davidson, "The man who made computers personal," 34.

66. Weiser, "The computer for the twenty-first century."

67. Laurel, *Computers as Theatre.*

68. Turkle, *The Second Self,* 13.

69. Ibid.

70. S. K. Helsel and J. P. Roth, eds. *Virtual Reality: Theory, Practice and Promise,* vii.

71. See C. S. Peirce, "Some consequences of four incapacities," *Writings of C. S. Peirce: A Chronological Edition,* 211–42; C. S. Peirce, "How to make our ideas clear," *Charles S. Peirce: Essays in the Philosophy of Science,* 31–56; and W. James, *Pragmatism, a New Name for Some Old Ways of Thinking.*

72. See J. Dewey, *Essays in Experimental Logic;* J. Dewey, *Experience and Nature;* J. Dewey, *Philosophy and Civilization;* J. Dewey, *Art as Experience;* and J. Dewey, "The public and its problems," in *John Dewey: The Later Works, 1925–1953,* vol. 2, *1925–1927,* 235–372.

73. See Peirce, "Some consequences of four incapacities," 212. Peirce also argued, "the essence of belief is the establishment of a habit; and different beliefs are distinguished by the different modes of action to which they give rise" (Peirce, "How to make our ideas clear," 39) and "what a thing means is simply what habits it involves" (ibid., 41).

74. Pragmatism is also characterized as taking a nonrepresentationist view of knowledge. Dewey also used the term "instrumental logic." For Dewey, pragmatism means "only the rule of referring all thinking, all reflective considerations, to consequences for final meaning and test" (Dewey, *Essays in Experimental Logic,* 330). Peirce chose the term *pragmatism* to avoid confusion with Kant's use of the term *practical* (to Kant this was a priori moral laws). Kant's "pragmatic" meant "rules of art and technique derived from experience." For an explanation of pragmatism, see Dewey, *Philosophy and Civilization,* 13–14. See also J. P. Murphy, *Pragmatism from Peirce to Davidson,* for an account of the history of pragmatism; and L. A. Hickman, *John Dewey's Pragmatic Technology,* for a recent account of Dewey's thought.

75. Dewey, *Philosophy and Civilization,* 178.

76. Dewey, *Experience and Nature,* 124.

77. Ibid., 122–23.

78. Hickman, *John Dewey's Pragmatic Technology,* 83.

79. Ibid., 99.

80. Dewey, *Essays in Experimental Logic,* 12.

81. Dewey, *Experience and Nature*, 67.

82. Ibid., 67–68.

83. Dewey, *Experience and Nature*, 435.

84. Ibid.

85. More recently Dewey's work has featured, with little approval, in debates about education. See A. Bloom, *The Closing of the American Mind*; E. D. Hirsch, *Cultural Literacy: What Every American Needs to Know*; and S. Aronowitz and H. Giroux, *Education under Siege: The Conservative, Liberal, and Radical Debate over Schooling.*

86. Dewey, *Democracy and Education*, 275.

87. Ibid., 160.

88. Dewey, *Art as Experience*, 7.

89. Ibid., 5–6.

90. Ibid., 200.

91. Ibid., 319–320. The pragmatic interest in the power of art to inform us about other human endeavors, such as science, is in marked contrast to the chasm between art and science set up by analytic philosophy. For example, see Ayer's exclusive attribution of the possibility of truth to scientific propositions. (*Language, Truth and Logic*, 28)

92. As also maintained by Heidegger and the phenomenologists. See M. Merleau-Ponty, *Phenomenology of Perception.*

93. As maintained by empiricists and analytic philosophy. See Ayer, *The Central Questions of Philosophy*, 71.

94. Dewey, "The public and its problems," 371.

95. Dewey, *Art as Experience*, 115.

96. Dewey, "The public and its problems," 323.

97. See E. Carpenter and M. McLuhan, eds., *Explorations in Communication*; M. McLuhan, *The Gutenberg Galaxy: The Making of Typographic Man*; M. McLuhan, *Understanding Media: The Extensions of Man*; and M. McLuhan and Q. Fiore, *The Medium is the Massage.* For critical reviews of McLuhan's work, see L. Grossberg, "Interpreting the 'crisis' of culture in communication theory," *Journal of Communication* 29 (1): 56–68; A. Kroker, "Processed world: Technology and culture in the thought of Marshall McLuhan," *Philosophy of the Social Sciences* 14:433–59; R. Wasson, "Marshall McLuhan and the politics of modernism," *Massachusetts Review* 13 (4): 567–80; R. Gambino, "McLuhanism: A massage that muddles," *The Midwest Quarterly* 14 (1): 53–62; D. W. Shriver, "Man and his machines: Four angles of vision," *Technology and Culture* 13 (1): 531–55; W. P. Dommermuth, "How does the medium affect the message?" *Journalism Quarterly*, 51 (3): 441–47; and M. Ferguson, "Marshall

McLuhan revisited: The 1960s zeitgeist victim or pioneer postmodernist," *Media, Culture and Society* 13:71–90.

98. See Kay, "User interface: A personal view"; and Rheingold, *Virtual Reality*, 85. There do not appear to be any direct formative links from Dewey and pragmatism to McLuhan. We can surmise, though, that McLuhan was a party to Dewey's liberalism through the education system—in his case that of Canada. Within McLuhan's extensive references to luminaries in the history of ideas, he makes only passing reference to Dewey. Hickman indicates that Dewey anticipated many of McLuhan's insights but does not indicate that McLuhan was in fact influenced by Dewey. One unusual commonality between the two men was an interest in religious issues. Dewey was raised in the Calvinist tradition but wrote extensively from a liberal Christian perspective (S. C. Rockefeller, *John Dewey: Religious Faith and Democratic Humanism*). McLuhan was a Catholic convert. Kroker traces the development of McLuhan's ideas through the legacy of the Canadian Catholic humanism he inherited as a convert, and his indebtedness to the methods of inquiry of Thomas Aquinas (Kroker, "Processed world"). According to Wasson,

> [A]s some medieval scholars read the book of nature as symbols revealing God's grace and law, so McLuhan reads the new technological environment as a book of symbols which reveals the Incarnation. Because everything in the world is a symbol, McLuhan can offer endless symbolic interpretations. (Wasson, "Marshall McLuhan and the politics of modernism," 577)

Dewey was a philosopher and McLuhan was a professor of English literature (though originally trained as an engineer). As such McLuhan belonged to the New Critical movement, which asserted that a poem or other artwork is to be understood in relation to its own inner structure and should not be studied as though its content could be removed from its form, as in a paraphrase. This idea of the inextricability of form and content became translated into McLuhan's famous aphorism "the medium is the message." Irrespective of the links between the two thinkers, the strong influence of both on contemporary thought is undeniable. Furthermore, they represent philosophical positions that are highly supportive of each other.

99. See W. J. Ong, *Rhetoric, Romance, and Technology: Studies in the Interaction of Expression and Culture;* E. A. Havelock, *The Muse Learns to Write: Reflections on Orality and Literacy from Antiquity to the Present;* M. Heim, *Electric Language: A Philosophical Study of Word Processing;* and I. Illich and B. Sanders, *ABC: The Alphabetization of the Popular Mind*. According to these writers, print technology has introduced notions of continuity, uniformity, and repeatability, important features of the scientific and intellectual enterprise. Ong, a former student of McLuhan's, writes about the "spatialization of thought" completed in the writing of the sixteenth-century educationist Peter Ramus. Ramus developed an extreme schematic treatment of knowledge and introduced a bookkeeper's stress on method and analysis. He contributed to an intellectual climate receptive to Descartes's promotion of the importance of method. For Ong, Ramism also represented a final phase in the steady decline of the preliterate, oral tradition of (critical) dialogue. According to this argument, print was indirectly responsible for the rise in individualism, ideas about linear organization, centralist control, uniformity, and visual abstraction. This account is a long way from the rationalist claim of the primacy of theory.

100. McLuhan, *Understanding Media*, 47. Counter to the view that electronic media instill a sense of social responsibility, critics of McLuhan are quick to point out the

irresponsibility engendered by believing that "the medium is the message." As long as we focus on the medium, we do not listen to what people are saying. McLuhan was no social activist and is accused by critical theorists of selling out to capitalism. See Ferguson, "Marshall McLuhan revisited."

101. McLuhan, *Understanding Media*, 323.

102. McLuhan, *Understanding Media*, 5.

103. Ibid.

104. McLuhan, *Gutenberg Galaxy*, 39.

105. McLuhan, *Understanding Media*, 18.

106. McLuhan, *Gutenberg Galaxy*, 40.

107. McLuhan, *Understanding Media*, 84.

108. Ibid., 154.

109. Ibid., 11.

110. Ibid., 4.

111. Ibid., 12.

112. Ibid., 171–72.

113. Ibid., 15.

114. McLuhan sees E. M. Forster's novel *A Passage to India* as an allegory of a transition from the visual, typographic culture to an aural and seemingly irrational one. In succumbing to the reverberations and the cacophony of sounds in the Marabar caves the heroine lapses into what appears to the typographic culture of the nineteenth-century British Empire as a kind of madness. According to McLuhan, the "moment of truth and dislocation from the typographic trance of the West comes in the Marabar cave." (Ibid.)

115. Ibid., 24.

116. Ibid., 22.

117. Ibid., 39. For an introduction to further explorations into the nature of television, see T. Fry, ed., *RUA TV? Heidegger and the Televisual.*

118. Ibid., 329.

119. Ibid., 12.

120. See H.-G. Gadamer, *Truth and Method;* S. Fish, *Doing What Comes Naturally: Change, Rhetoric and the Practice of Theory in Literary and Legal Studies;* and Dreyfus, *Being-in-the-World.*

121. See M. Polanyi, *The Tacit Dimension.*

122. "Theory talk" is the term Fish uses to indicate that theory is after all a kind of practice. See Fish, *Doing What Comes Naturally.*

123. A notable exception is the pragmatic design philosophy of Schön, a scholar of Dewey. See D. Schön, *Displacement of Concepts;* and D. Schön, *The Reflective Practitioner.*

124. G. Broadbent, *Design in Architecture: Architecture and the Human Sciences,* xiii.

125. See C. Alexander, *Oregon Experiment.*

126. See M. Minsky, "Logical versus analogical or symbolic versus connectionist or neat versus scruffy," *AI Magazine* 12 (2): 34–51.

127. Stefik, "Book reviews," 256.

128. Dreyfus, *Being-in-the-World,* 119.

129. McLuhan, *Understanding Media,* 357.

130. Ibid., 358.

131. McLuhan, *Gutenberg Galaxy,* 248.

132. Ibid., 248.

133. M. Heim, "The computer as component: Heidegger and McLuhan," *Philosophy and Literature* 16 (2): 317.

Chapter 2

1. See C. Shannon and W. Weaver, *The Mathematical Theory of Communication.*

2. By this meaning dialectics is a method of argument attributed to Zeno (c.490 B.C.) that involves taking a thesis and showing its impossibility by demonstrating that the consequences of the thesis entail contradictions. See J. Marías, *History of Philosophy.* See Cornford, *The Republic of Plato,* 223 for a discussion of Plato's use of dialectic.

3. See J.-F. Lyotard, *The Postmodern Condition: A Report on Knowledge.*

4. G. E. R. Lloyd, *Polarity and Analogy: Two Types of Argumentation in Early Greek Thought.*

5. Ibid., 2.

6. Heidegger's work is a major source for critical theory. However, as we will see, they part company in important ways.

7. See J. D. Caputo, *The Mystical Element in Heidegger's Thought.*

8. In a negative way, Hegel provided a target for Russell (1872–1970), who spent much of his career refuting Hegel. See S. Houlgate, *Freedom, Truth and History: An Introduction to Hegel's Philosophy*, 2.

9. See J. D. Caputo, *The Mystical Element in Heidegger's Thought;* and A. Snodgrass, "Hermeneutics, the university, and the letting-be of technology," *Proc. Universities as Interpretive Communities*, 75–94.

10. Such a study is also appropriate because some think that logic and the binary system underpin the invention and understanding of information technology. It is important to note that the distinctions being made here do not focus around two ways of thinking, but two ways of thinking about thinking. According to critical theory one of the errors of technological thinking is that it does not acknowledge that it is grounded in the pretechnological. In critical theory, the diagnosis, prognosis, and remedy of "the problem of technology" are couched in terms of this characterization of pretechnological versus technological rationality.

11. Aristotle, *Metaphysics*, in R. E. Allen, *Greek Philosophy: Thales to Aristotle*, 316; and Lloyd, *Polarity and Analogy*, 16.

12. Language studies have also placed great significance on the existence of oppositions. To point to something is to single it out from its background, to mark off or limit part of our experience from the unlimited, which is everything else. (The identification of figure and ground indicates a similar focus in gestalt psychology.) One of the tenets of structuralist linguistics is that words and signs entail antonyms or opposites and that there is a privileging of one over the other: raw and cooked, clean and unclean, male and female. In the case of structuralist anthropological studies, these oppositions are considered revealing of the deep structures of human societies. See T. Hawkes, *Structuralism and Semiotics*.

13. See P. Redding, "Hegel's logic of being and the polarities of Presocratic thought," *The Monist* 74 (3): 438–56; and Lloyd, *Polarity and Analogy*, 91. See also Allen, *Greek Philosophy*.

14. Lloyd, *Polarity and Analogy*, 99.

15. Aristotle, *Metaphysics*, in Allen, *Greek Philosophy*, 332.

16. Lloyd, *Polarity and Analogy*, 100.

17. Ibid., 102. From this logical point of view, there are clearly different "modes of opposition." (Lloyd, *Polarity and Analogy*, 86–88) These modes are articulated in terms of logic by Aristotle. A pair of logical propositions can be *contradictory* or merely *contrary*. A contradiction arises if we assert that all swans are white and some swans are not white. It is a contradiction because if the first proposition is true the second must be false. They cannot both be true. Contrary propositions are such that if one proposition is false, it does not follow that the other is true—for example, all swans are white and no swan is white; if the first is false, it does not follow that the second is true. Aristotle also identified *subcontraries*—some swans are white and some swans are not white; if the first is true, it does not follow that the second is false; but if the first is false, then the second must be true. Similar distinctions apply to *terms* (qualities or properties) themselves, such as white and black, independently of truth propositions. Examples of contrary oppositional terms include pairs that admit inter-

mediates: for example, black and white have the intermediate gray in between. So if a thing is not black, it is not necessarily white. It can be gray or another color. If we consider the set of rational numbers (that admits fractions,) odd and even are also contraries. Whereas it is true of all whole numbers that if a number is not odd it must be even, this is not the case with rational numbers. Similarly, certain oppositions, such as short and tall, are applicable in different contexts taking account of different relations. If a thing is short, it does not follow that it is not tall, as it is possible to be at once tall and short, in relation to different things (tall in relation to an ant and short in relation to a giraffe). There are also asymmetrical oppositions, such as straight and crooked, and stationary and moving. In these oppositions, each term is defined in relation to the other. To be straight is to be not crooked, and to be stationary is to be not moving. But they also embody a one-to-many relationship. There are many crooked lines between two points but only one straight one. There is only one way to be stationary but many ways in which a thing can move. It can be shown that these oppositions are also contraries.

Some opposite terms, however, are not contraries. In such cases, there is a contrast or antithesis explicable in terms of sets of opposite properties. Sun and moon, for instance, are not contraries (neither, of course, are they contradictions). Their oppositional nature is identified in terms of their properties. One is the main source of light during the day, and the other is the main source of light at night. Earth and sky are also opposites when we note that one is down and the other up, one looks flat and the other curved, one is solid and the other ephemeral, one is within reach and the other out of reach, and so on. According to Lloyd, such sophisticated logical distinctions were not necessarily recognized by the pre-Socratics.

18. Houlgate, *Freedom, Truth and History*, 61. See also T. Pinkard, "The successor to metaphysics: Absolute idea and absolute spirit," *The Monist*, 74 (3): 295–328; and Redding, "Hegel's logic of being." Hegel's logic is described in his voluminous *Science of Logic* first published in German in 1812. See G. W. F. Hegel, *Hegel's Science of Logic*.

19. Hegel, *Hegel's Science of Logic*, 70.

20. Houlgate, *Freedom, Truth and History*, 47.

21. Ibid., 64. According to Hegel, "Now starting from this determination of pure knowledge, all that is needed to ensure that the beginning remains immanent in its scientific development is to consider, or rather, ridding oneself of all other reflections and opinions whatever, simply to take up, *what is there before us*." (Hegel, *Hegel's Science of Logic*, 69)

22. See Marías, *History of Philosophy*, 12. See also A. B. Snodgrass, *Architecture Time and Eternity*.

23. Houlgate, *Freedom, Truth and History*, 50.

24. Houlgate quotes the criticism by Schopenhauer, Hegel's contemporary and colleague, who accuses Hegel of "the greatest affrontery in serving up sheer nonsense, in scrabbling together senseless and maddening webs of words, such as had previously been heard only in madhouses. . . . [Hegelianism] became the instrument of the most ponderous and general mystification that has ever existed, with a result that will seem incredible to posterity, and be a lasting monument to German stupidity." (Ibid., 1)

25. Ibid., 51. According to Hegel, "we call dialectic the higher movement of reason in which such seemingly utterly separate terms pass over into each other spontaneously, through that which they are, a movement in which the presupposition sublates itself. It is the dialectical immanent nature of being and nothing themselves to manifest their unity, that is, becoming, as their truth." (Hegel, *Hegel's Science of Logic*, 105)

26. Houlgate, *Freedom, Truth and History*, 52.

27. Ibid., 53.

28. Ibid., 56. According to Hegel, "Becoming, as this transition into the unity of being and nothing, a unity which is in the form of being or has the form of the one-sided *immediate* unity of these moments, is *determinate being*." (Hegel, *Hegel's Science of Logic*, 106) He says further, "This unity now remains their base from which they do not again emerge in the abstract significance of being and nothing." (Ibid., 108)

29. Houlgate, *Freedom, Truth and History*, 59.

30. Ibid. As I will conclude in this article, modern hermeneutical scholarship challenges this imperative to relate reason to formal logic.

31. Houlgate, *Freedom, Truth and History*, 64.

32. For Hegel's complex analysis of the different forms of the syllogism and how they each presume the universal and the individual, see Hegel, *Hegel's Science of Logic*, 664–704.

33. Houlgate, *Freedom, Truth and History*, 65.

34. Houlgate sees Hegel's epochs as foreshadowing Kuhn's paradigms. (Ibid., 17)

35. Ibid., 18.

36. Ibid., 19.

37. Ibid., 27.

38. See M. Heidegger, *What Is Called Thinking?* M. Heidegger, "The origin of the work of art," *Poetry, Language, Thought*, 15–87; M. Heidegger, "The thing," *Poetry, Language, Thought*, 163–182; M. Heidegger, *The Principle of Reason;* M. Heidegger, "The principle of ground," *Man and World*, vol. 7, 207–22; M. Heidegger, *The Question concerning Technology and Other Essays;* M. Heidegger, *Early Greek Thinking: The Dawn of Western Philosophy*.

39. The term *autonomy* here reflects the way that thought is spoken about. As I will show, it is consistent with Heidegger to see thought as totally connected with day-to-day life, involved and situated.

40. M. Heidegger, *Being and Time*, 25.

41. Ibid., 27.

42. Caputo, *The Mystical Element in Heidegger's Thought.*

43. Ibid., 79.

44. Heidegger uses the term *ontic* to designate scientific understanding, as opposed to *ontological,* which denotes that which pertains to Being.

45. Caputo, *The Mystical Element in Heidegger's Thought,* 69.

46. Heraclitus, frag. 50. See Allen, *Greek Philosophy,* 40.

47. Caputo, *The Mystical Element in Heidegger's Thought,* 79.

48. Ibid., 80.

49. Ibid., 72.

50. Ibid.

51. According to Heidegger, this acceptance of things in themselves and as they present themselves was the early Greek understanding of *physis* prior to the scientific, causal understanding. *Physis* originally meant "presentation" rather than its common modern translation as "nature."

52. For the identification of these and other issues, see Caputo, *The Mystical Element in Heidegger's Thought;* and A. Borgman, "The question of Heidegger and technology: A critical review of the literature," *Philosophy Today* 31 (2/4): 97–194; M. E. Zimmerman, *Heidegger's Confrontation with Modernity: Technology, Politics, Art;* R. Bernstein, *The New Constellation: The Ethical-Political Horizon of Modernity/Postmodernity.*

53. Heidegger, *The Question concerning Technology,* 6.

54. Ibid., 13.

55. Ibid., 16.

56. Caputo, *The Mystical Element in Heidegger's Thought,* 185.

57. Ibid., 188.

58. See T. Adorno and M. Horkheimer, *Dialectic of Enlightenment,* 3.

59. See W. Benjamin, "The work of art in the age of mechanical reproduction," *Illumination,* 217–51; Adorno and Horkheimer, *Dialectic of Enlightenment;* J. Habermas, *The Philosophical Discourse of Modernity: Twelve Lectures;* H. Marcuse, *One-Dimensional Man: Studies in the Ideology of Advanced Industrial Society;* D. Ingram, and J. Simon-Ingram. eds., *Critical Theory: The Essential Readings.*

60. Marcuse, *One-Dimensional Man,* 124.

61. Ibid., 131.

62. Ibid.

63. Ibid., 125.

64. Ibid., 126.

65. This contrasts with Heidegger's understanding of the essence of a *thing*. For Heidegger the essence of a thing is to disclose by virtue of its capacity to gather. The thing is a thing by being situated. See Heidegger, "The thing," 174.

66. Marcuse, *One-Dimensional Man,* 131.

67. Ibid., 127.

68. Ibid.

69. Ibid., 128.

70. Ibid.

71. Ibid., 129.

72. Ibid., 131.

73. Ibid., 124–25.

74. Ibid., 132.

75. Ibid., 133.

76. Ibid., 135.

77. Ibid., 146.

78. A position of contempt for Marcuse, who argued against all forms of idealism.

79. Marcuse, *One-Dimensional Man,* 147. Marcuse sees the objective world becoming more and more dependent on the subject (as exemplified in Heisenberg and Popper) as indicative of the triumph of idealism.

80. Ibid., 136.

81. Quoted by Marcuse, ibid., 137. See Horkheimer and Adorno, *Dialectic of Enlightenment,* 22.

82. Marcuse, *One-Dimensional Man,* 138.

83. Ibid., 144.

84. Ibid.

85. Ibid., 145.

86. Ibid., 154.

87. Ibid., 158. According to Adorno and Horkheimer, the "basis on which technology acquires power over society is the power of those whose economic hold over society is greatest. A technological rationale is the rationale of domination itself." (Adorno and Horkheimer, *Dialectic of Enlightenment*, 121)

88. Ibid., 123.

89. Ibid., 154.

90. T. W. Adorno, "How to look at television," *Critical Theory: The Essential Readings*, 74.

91. As well as such writers as Huxley, Chomsky, Ellul and Baudrillard.

92. See A. Feenberg, *Critical Theory of Technology;* Bruce Berman, "The computer metaphor: Bureaucratizing the mind," *Science as Culture* 7:7–42; T. Forester, *Computers in the Human Context: Information Technology, Productivity and People.*

93. Benjamin identifies this great divorce in the case of art as due to mechanical reproduction. Art is no longer in a context. It is available for all to see, including the untrained masses. It has lost its place in ritual and in history. See Benjamin, "The work of art in the age of mechanical reproduction."

94. These arguments can be extended further. Mass production also involves the exercise of power and influence over a large arena. The complexity and detachment of the consequences from consumption become the subject of ethical investigation. There is a separation between the gathering of raw resources, manufacture, distribution, and use. There is a concealment of who is affected.

95. This distance clearly masks our responsibility toward resources and sustainability.

96. See H. L. Dreyfus, *What Computers Can't Do: The Limits of Artificial Intelligence;* J. Weizenbaum, *Computer Power and Human Reason: From Judgement to Calculation;* T. Winograd and F. Flores, *Understanding Computers and Cognition: A New Foundation for Design.*

97. It is common for the popular imagination to see the human genome project in this light.

98. G. T. Marx and S. Sherizen, "Monitoring on the job," *Computers in the Human Context: Information Technology, Productivity and People.*

99. See for example R. Stults, "Experimental uses of video to support design activities," *Report SSL-89-19 [P89-00019];* and M. Weiser, "The computer for the twenty-first century," *Scientific American*, 265 (3): 66–75.

100. The use of electronic mail on the Internet provides such records.

101. As reported in relation to the Reagan election campaign.

102. Berman, "The computer metaphor."

103. Marcuse, *One-Dimensional Man,* 227.

104. Ibid., 231.

105. Ibid., 227.

106. Ibid., 228.

107. Ibid., 234.

108. Ibid., 254.

109. Ibid., 256.

110. Ibid., 256–57.

111. For example, see A. Giddens, *The Consequences of Modernity.*

112. S. Gallagher, *Hermeneutics and Education.*

113. Ibid., 262.

114. H.-G. Gadamer, *Truth and Method,* 315.

115. Quoted by Caputo, *The Mystical Element in Heidegger's Thought,* 174. From M. Heidegger, *Die Technik und die Kehre.*

116. Ibid.

117. M. Heidegger, *Discourse on Thinking.*

118. See A. Borgman, *Technology and the Character of Contemporary Life: A Philosophical Inquiry.*

119. Leder points out Borgman's favoritism toward handmade artifacts, such as violins, as focal things, ignoring highly technological devices, such as a sound-mixing board in a music studio, as a focus for enriching, engaging, corporeal, and communal activity. The same could be said for networked computers. See D. Leder, "The rule of the device: Borgman's philosophy of technology," *Philosophy Today* 32 (spring): 17–29.

120. Habermas indicates the right and left directions taken by Hegelianism in his *Philosophical Discourse of Modernity,* 56.

121. Houlgate, *Freedom, Truth and History,* 61.

122. Ibid., 88.

123. Ibid., 89.

124. Ibid., 106.

125. Ibid., 111.

126. Ibid., 123.

127. See for example M. Heidegger, "Letter on humanism," *Philosophy in the Twentieth Century*, vol. 3, *Contemporary European Thought*, 192–224. This is discussed in Bernstein, *The New Constellation*, 123.

128. He was accused by the de-Nazification committee of 1945 of holding office in the Nazi regime; introducing the "Führer principle" into the University of Freiburg, where he was rector, engaging in Nazi propaganda, and inciting students against anti-Nazi professors. See Bernstein, *The New Constellation*, 129.

129. Ibid., 122.

130. Ibid., 133.

131. Heidegger, *The Question concerning Technology*, 34. See also Bernstein, *The New Constellation*, 115.

132. Ibid., 122.

133. There are power struggles, funding for humanities is being cut in some institutions, and computer networking is denied to some, but the desirability of access to computing and advanced communications is rarely at issue.

134. See H. L. Dreyfus and P. Rabinow, eds., *Michel Foucault: Beyond Structuralism and Hermeneutics;* M. Foucault, *Discipline and Punish: The Birth of the Prison;* M. Foucault, "Afterword: The subject and power," *Michel Foucault: Beyond Structuralism and Hermeneutics,* 208–26; and M. Foucault, *The Foucault Reader: An Introduction to Foucault's Thought.*

135. According to Foucault, a "society without power relations can only be an abstraction." (Foucault, "Afterword," 222–223).

136. Ibid., 221.

137. Ibid., 220.

138. Foucault, *The Foucault Reader,* 61.

139. Foucault, *Discipline and Punish,* 226.

140. Foucault, *The Foucault Reader,* 61.

141. See Gadamer, *Truth and Method;* P. Ricoeur, *Hermeneutics and the Human Sciences;* and A. B. Snodgrass, (1991) "Asian studies and the fusion of horizons," *Proc. Gadamer, Action and Reason,* 35–42.

142. See J. C. Weinsheimer, *Gadamer's Hermeneutics: A Reading of "Truth and Method."*

143. See for example the application of hermeneutics in education by S. Gallagher, *Hermeneutics and Education;* and in law by S. Fish, *Doing What Comes Naturally: Change, Rhetoric and the Practice of Theory in Literary and Legal Studies.*

144. See H.-G. Gadamer, *Philosophical Hermeneutics.*

145. Similarly, Heidegger does not have exclusive access to thought. His exposition of thought makes sense thanks to the tradition of Hegel and the mystics, and it establishes distance thanks to the tradition of rationalism against which it is posited.

146. See S. Fish, *Is There a Text in This Class?: The Authority of Interpretive Communities.*

147. But such mechanical metaphors to describe complex phenomena invariably prove inadequate. The metaphor of community itself provides the most revealing metaphor.

148. See Heidegger, *Being and Time*, 87–98.

149. As already discussed, though, for the later Heidegger the realization of this interconnectedness is not a moment of analysis and reflection but a standing back and letting be: "When and in what way do things appear as things? They do not appear *by means of* human making. But neither do they appear without the vigilance of mortals. The first step toward such vigilance is the step back from the thinking that merely represents—that is, explains—to the thinking that responds and recalls." (Heidegger, "The thing," 181)

150. See R. D. Coyne and A. B. Snodgrass, "Cooperation and individualism in design," *Environment and Planning B: Planning and Design* 20:163–74.

151. This trust is realized in the formation of consumer groups, the green movement, community architecture, and design for sustainability. However, some dispute the "good will" assumed by hermeneutics. The debate is recorded in G. L. Ormiston and A. D. Schrift, eds., *The Hermeneutic Tradition: From Ast to Ricoeur.*

152. See M. Heim, "Humanistic discussion and the online conference," *Philosophy Today* 30:278–88.

153. Seen from the point of view of an equipmental whole, these developments can be seen in terms of their dependence on, and development from, such technologies and practices as telegraph, citizen-band radio, and newspapers.

154. None of these criticisms dispense with Heidegger. We will return to his best insights in subsequent chapters.

Chapter 3

1. See F. Nietzsche, *Beyond Good and Evil: Prelude to a Philosophy of the Future;* F. Nietzsche, *A Nietzsche Reader;* M. Heidegger, *Being and Time;* M. Heidegger, *Basic Writings;* M. Heidegger, *The Question concerning Technology and Other Essays;* and J. Derrida, *Of Grammatology.* The postmodern project is described in J.-F. Lyotard, *The Postmodern Condition: A Report on Knowledge,* R. J. Bernstein, *Beyond Objectivism and Relativism;* and R. Rorty, *Philosophy and the Mirror of Nature.* Giddens presents a contrary view to the one presented here. He characterizes the current age as one of *radical modernity* rather than *postmodernity.* See A. Giddens, *The Consequences of Modernity.*

2. For a sample of metaphysical discourse that purports to present new and challenging ways of thinking, informed by advances in science and mathematics, see

S. W. Hawking, *A Brief History of Time: From the Big Bang to Black Holes;* P. Davies, *Superforce: The Search for the Grand Unified Theory of Nature;* D. Bohm and D. Peat, *Science, Order and Creativity;* J. Gleick, *Chaos: Making a New Science.* For an account of how computer systems in the form of virtual-reality systems are changing notions of space, see M. Benedikt, Introduction to *Cyberspace: First Steps,* 2–25.

3. Modernist discourse can also masquerade as postmodernism. See the debate between Wexler and Kurtzman for a telling commentary on the appropriation of postmodern thinking within psychology. See P. Wexler, "And now for a little deconstruction: A response to Kurtzman," *New Ideas in Psychology* 5, (1): 73–76; H. Kurtzman, "Deconstruction and psychology: An introduction," *New Ideas in Psychology* 5, (1): 33–71; and H. Kurtzman, "Deconstructionist psychology and human liberation: A reply to Philip W.," *New Ideas in Psychology* 5 (1): 77–94. See also G. G. Globus, "Deconstructing the Chinese room," *The Journal of Mind and Behaviour* 12 (3): 377–92.

4. See S. Houlgate, *Freedom, Truth and History: An Introduction to Hegel's Philosophy.*

5. See J. D. Caputo, *Radical Hermeneutics: Repetition, Deconstruction, and the Hermeneutical Project;* and S. Gallagher, *Hermeneutics and Education.*

6. See W. J. Mitchell, *The Reconfigured Eye: Visual Truth in the Post-Photographic Era.*

7. Ibid., 52.

8. Ibid.

9. Ibid., 31.

10. Ibid., 17.

11. See R. Scruton, "Photography and representation," *The Aesthetic Understanding,* 102–26.

12. According to Scruton,

> With an ideal photograph it is neither necessary nor even possible that the photographer's intention should enter as a serious factor in determining how the picture is seen. It is recognized at once for what it is—not as an interpretation of reality but as a presentation of how something looked. . . . (Ibid., 111)

> It follows, first, that the subject of the ideal photograph must exist; secondly, that it must appear roughly as it appears in the photograph; and thirdly, that its appearance in the photograph is its appearance at a particular moment of its existence. (Ibid., 112)

13. Mitchell, *The Reconfigured Eye,* 30.

14. Ibid.

15. Mitchell provides several interesting examples of published photographic images whose veracity has been called into question at some time. The book focuses on techniques for digitally altering images.

16. Ibid., 52.

17. See W. Benjamin, "The work of art in the age of mechanical reproduction," *Illumination*, 217–51.

18. Ibid.

19. For a sample of the critical theory discourse, see: D. Ingram and J. Simon-Ingram, eds., *Critical Theory: The Essential Readings;* T. Adorno and M. Horkheimer, *Dialectic of Enlightenment;* H. Marcuse, *One-Dimensional Man: Studies in the Ideology of Advanced Industrial Society;* J. Habermas, *The Philosophical Discourse of Modernity: Twelve Lectures;* J. Baudrillard, *Revenge of the Crystal: Selected Writings on the Modern Object and Its Destiny, 1968–1983;* and J. Baudrillard, "Simulacra and simulations," *Jean Baudrillard: Selected Writings,* 166–84.

20. Baudrillard, "Simulacra and simulations," 170.

21. Ibid.

22. Ibid., 172.

23. For a summary of the issues, see chapter 1. See also M. McLuhan, *The Gutenberg Galaxy: The Making of Typographic Man;* and M. McLuhan, *Understanding Media: The Extensions of Man.* A similar line of argument is developed in W. J. Ong, *Rhetoric, Romance, and Technology: Studies in the Interaction of Expression and Culture.*

24. Derrida makes specific reference to global communications in his essay on apartheid, J. Derrida, "Racism's last word," *Critical Inquiry* 12:290–99; and in his book *Of Grammatology.* See also A. Argyros, "Narratives of the future: Heidegger and Derrida on technology," *New Orleans Review* 17 (2): 53–58; and S. Crowell, "Text and technology," *Man and World,* 23:419–40.

25. F. de Saussure, *Course in General Linguistics.*

26. C. Lévi-Strauss, *Structural Anthropology,* 31–32. For an explanation of the structuralist project, see also H. Gardner, *The Quest for Mind: Piaget, Lévi-Strauss and the Structuralist Movement;* and T. Hawkes, *Structuralism and Semiotics.*

27. Note that these arguments are not exclusively Derrida's (they also find support in New Criticism, with its challenge to "authorial intent," and in aspects of the pragmatic language theories of Austin, Searle and Wittgenstein), nor do they represent his most potent contribution to philosophy. Derrida's main target is metaphysics. The purpose here is to build up a picture of Derrida's thought and its relevance to information technology.

28. See J. Culler, *On Deconstruction: Theory and Criticism after Structuralism.* Valuable summaries of Derrida's thought are also provided in C. Norris, *Deconstruction: Theory and Practice,* and G. C. Spivak, translator's preface to *Of Grammatology,* ix–lxxxvii. For commentaries on Derrida's life and times, see R. Bernstein, "Serious play: The ethical-political horizon of Derrida," *The New Constellation: The Ethical-Political Horizon of Modernity/Postmodernity,* 172–98; and Peter Dews, *Logics of Disintegration: Poststructuralist Thought and the Claims of Critical Theory.*

29. Culler, *On Deconstruction*, 186–87.

30. The rehabilitation of mimesis, the art or craft of imitation, so much discredited by Plato, is also a popular project among such writers such as Riceour. See P. Ricoeur, *Hermeneutics and the Human Sciences.*

31. Culler, *On Deconstruction*, 187.

32. The matter of practice is not one that deconstruction readily illuminates.

33. Culler, *On Deconstruction*, 188.

34. Ibid.

35. Ibid., 189.

36. Ibid.

37. Derrida places enormous weight on the importance of the signifier: "From the moment that there is meaning there are nothing but signs. We think only in signs." (Derrida, *Of Grammatology*, 50) Derrida's arguments for the sign are also presented in his article "Fors," *The Georgia Review* 31:64–116; and in his book *Glas.* The argument is explained by Culler. In asserting the arbitrary nature of the sign, Saussure excludes onomatopoeic words. They need not be taken into account in a theory of signs. They do not merely mimic but commonly accord with convention. Neither are their origins always in resemblance. Their evolution is fortuitous, unintentional, unmotivated. Derrida points out the inconsistency in argument here. If a sign is arbitrary, then how can a particular phenomenon of language, namely, the use of onomatopoeic words, be discounted on the basis that it is arbitrary? The arbitrary and the motivated are obviously intertwined in some way. Some phenomena of language are arbitrary and yet essential to the nature of language (such as the arbitrariness of the connection between the sign and the signified), and some phenomena of language are arbitrary and inessential (such as the arbitrary fact that some words sound like the things they signify). The structure of a language is not affected by the fact that some words sound like the things they signify. The issue of arbitrariness is being decided on the issue of motivation. Culler comments, "But Derrida asks whether this contamination of arbitrary signs by suggestions of motivation, by possibilities of remotivation, might be not accidental and excludable but inseparable from the working of language." (Culler, *On Deconstruction*, 190) In poetry, words gain force and potency through the "accidental" nature of their phonic resonances.

> Though the motivating of signs is in a sense extraneous to the internal system of a language and thus available as a specific poetic technique for making symbols more persuasive or increasing the solidity of important thematic connections, it functions powerfully and covertly within the system of language and now appears to be central to other textual constructs and discursive practices. (Culler, *On Deconstruction*, 191)

The proper name provides an obvious example. It ought to be pure reference, but it assumes meaning, because of its coincidental sound, etymology, familial connections, or in other ways.

38. Culler, *On Deconstruction*, 95.

39. Saussure, *Course in General Linguistics.*

40. Culler, *On Deconstruction,* 96.

41. See J. Derrida, *Positions,* 26. (Culler, *On Deconstruction,* 99)

42. Derrida, *Positions,* 26. As will be discussed subsequently, there is another construction that can be placed on this notion of trace, which is simply to say that every meaning depends on context.

43. Gallagher, *Hermeneutics and Education,* 284.

44. Mas'ud Zavarzadeh and D. Morton, "Theory pedagogy politics: The crisis of the subject in the humanities," *Boundary* 2 (15): 1–22.

45. Ibid., 2.

46. Ibid., 4.

47. See chapter 5 for a discussion of Heidegger's concepts of truth.

48. Saussure, *Course in General Linguistics,* 24.

49. See McLuhan, *Gutenberg Galaxy;* and Ong, *Rhetoric, Romance and Technology.*

50. See J. Dewey, *The Public and Its Problems.*

51. Derrida, *Of Grammatology,* 57.

52. Ibid., 56.

53. As I will discuss subsequently, there is a difference brought about by electronic communications, but it is not necessarily the difference indicated by these writers.

54. Dewey, *The Public and Its Problems,* 218–19.

55. See D. Ihde, *Philosophy of Technology: An Introduction.*

56. See A. J. Ayer, *Language, Truth and Logic.*

57. Ibid., 3.

58. Ibid., 24.

59. Ludwig Wittgenstein's *Philosophical Investigations* provides the authoritative refutation of this whole approach to language (and its reliance on the "verification principle").

60. See J. Derrida, *Spurs: Nietzsche's Styles;* and Heidegger, *Being and Time.*

61. See Culler, *On Deconstruction;* Norris, *Deconstruction: Theory and Practice;* and Spivak, translator's preface to *Of Grammatology.*

62. Derrida, *Positions.*

63. Ibid., 41.

64. Ibid.

65. Ibid.

66. Ibid., 42.

67. Ibid., 43.

68. Spivak, translator's preface, to *Of Grammatology*, xxviii–xxix.

69. Derrida, *Of Grammatology*, 11.

70. J. Derrida, "Différance," *Margins of Philosophy*, 9.

71. J. Derrida, *Limited Inc*, 93.

72. Ibid.

73. Culler, *On Deconstruction*, 93–94.

74. Ibid., 94.

75. Derrida, *Of Grammatology*, 166.

76. Culler, *On Deconstruction*, 95.

77. Ibid., 95; Derrida, "Différance," 13.

78. See J. Caputo, *The Mystical Element in Heidegger's Thought.*

79. Spivak, translator's preface to *Of Grammatology*, xxxiii.

80. Nietzsche's identification of the "will to power" is in part a response to Schopenhauer's "will to live." See J. Marías, *History of Philosophy*, 338–40.

81. Spivak, translator's preface to *Of Grammatology*, xxxiv.

82. Ibid., xxxvii.

83. See Derrida, *Spurs.* The strategy of this work is summarized by Norris:

> The unsettling power of Nietzsche's text is such as to place it beyond reach of a philosophy aimed, like Heidegger's, towards truth and the ultimate presence of meaning. Hence the style [in *Spurs*] of outlandish virtuosity—the ruses of metaphor and image—which Derrida by contrast brings to his reading of Nietzsche. Interpretation is no longer turned back in a deluded quest for origins and truth. Rather, it assumes the vertiginous freedom of writing itself: a writing launched by the encounter with a text which itself acknowledges no limit to the free play of meaning. (Norris, *Deconstruction*, 70)

84. Norris, *Deconstruction*, 70.

85. Ibid., 69–70.

86. Ibid., 70.

87. Ibid.

88. See Derrida, *Spurs;* Derrida, "Différance," 1–27; Jacques Derrida, "*Ousia* and *Gramme:* Note on a note from *Being and Time*," *Margins of Philosophy,* 29–67; and J. Derrida, "The supplement of copula: Philosophy before linguistics," *Margins of Philosophy,* 175–205.

89. Heidegger writes of the forgetting of being. Derrida observes that forgetting seems to be part of being's nature: "Forgetting, then, not only *attacks* the essence of Being . . . inasmuch as it is apparently distinct from it. It belongs to the nature of Being . . . and reigns as the Destiny of its essence." (Derrida, *Spurs,* 143) If presence is under question then "one questions the limit which has always constrained us, which still constrains us—as inhabitants of a language and a system of thought—to formulate the meaning of Being in general as presence or absence, in the categories of being or beingness (*ousia*)." (Derrida, "Différance," 10)

90. Derrida, "Différance," 21.

91. Ibid., 22.

92. Ibid.

93. Ibid., 22.

94. Ibid., 23.

95. Ibid.

96. Ibid., 24.

97. Ibid.

98. Ibid., 26.

99. See J. Derrida, "*Geschlecht* II: Heidegger's hand," *Deconstruction and Philosophy: The Texts of Jacques Derrida,* 161–96.

100. See M. Heidegger, *What Is Called Thinking?*

101. Derrida, "*Geschlecht* II," 169.

102. M. Heidegger, *Parmenides,* 118.

103. Derrida, "*Geschlecht* II," 178.

104. Ibid., 171. Derrida also brings out the political motivations here: Heidegger is speaking out against the professionalization of the university; aligning thinking with the rustic artisan class.

105. Heidegger also characterizes the hand as *not* about the animal act of grasping. The hand is best understood through the act of giving.

106. Derrida, "*Geschlecht* II," 176.

107. Ibid., 180.

108. Ibid., 181.

109. See J. Caputo, "From the primordiality of absence to the absence of primordiality: Heidegger's critique of Derrida," *Hermeneutics and Deconstruction*, 191–200; and T. Sheehan, "Derrida and Heidegger," *Hermeneutics and Deconstruction*, 201–18.

110. Caputo, "From the primordiality of absence," 196.

111. Ibid., 197.

112. Ibid., 196–97.

113. Ibid., 197.

114. Ibid.

115. Ibid.

116. Ibid., 197–98. Caputo adds,

> Far from delivering us over to signs and supplements and substitutes, the movement of absence is an initiation into a sphere of primordiality and aboriginality. And if it is true that such an origin is likewise a non-origin, this is not because we have always and already to do with derivatives, but because, in a genuine alethiology, the origin is always already concealed and withdrawn. Instead of the substitute, Derrida should speak of the aboriginal abyss; instead of the supplement, the hidden depths; instead of masturbation, the primal birth of things in *lethe* [abyss]. (Ibid., 199)

117. Ibid., 199–200.

118. Sheehan reminds us of Derrida's debt to Heidegger. Sheehan also maintains that "there is a strong suspicion, for this reader at least, that when Derrida does get matters right and proposes some truly interesting issues for philosophical reflection, he does so in large measure by reinventing what is already to be found in Heidegger's thought." (Sheehan, "Derrida and Heidegger," 202)

119. See H.-G. Gadamer, *Truth and Method*.

120. Caputo, *Radical Hermeneutics*, 211.

121. Ibid., 211.

122. Ibid.

123. Gallagher, *Hermeneutics and Education*, 51.

124. Gadamer, *Truth and Method,* 92.

125. Gallagher, *Hermeneutics and Education,* 284.

126. Ibid.

127. Caputo, *Radical Hermeneutics,* 278.

128. Ibid., 234.

129. See J. Derrida, "The principle of reason: The university in the eyes of its pupils," *Diacritics,* 13:3–20.

130. Caputo, *Radical Hermeneutics,* 235.

131. Derrida is well aware of the issue of context and discusses it critically in *Limited Inc.*

132. See Gadamer, *Truth and Method;* S. Fish, *Is There a Text in This Class?: The Authority of Interpretive Communities;* and S. Fish, *Doing What Comes Naturally: Change, Rhetoric and the Practice of Theory in Literary and Legal Studies.* For a critical view of Gadamer's hermeneutics, see J. Habermas, "A review of Gadamer's *Truth and Method,*" *The Hermeneutic Tradition: From Ast to Ricoeur,* 213–244; and J. Habermas, "The hermeneutic claim to universality," *The Hermeneutic Tradition: From Ast to Ricoeur,* 245–72.

133. Derrida has engaged the issue of hermeneutics in a series of debates with Gadamer. For Gadamer, the act of conversation requires the "good will" of each party to understand the other. Derrida objects that the idea of "good will" has its roots in Kant's metaphysics. To assert the primacy of conversation and the ability of the participants to be trusting and fair-minded in the interpretive process is to imply a degree of control by the participants—to presume a kind of subjectivity. According to Derrida, everyone is aware, however, of the phenomenon of distorted communication. In characteristic fashion, Derrida opposes Gadamer's hermeneutics of trust with a hermeneutics of suspicion. Trust implies a preservation of tradition. Suspicion, the center of deconstruction, implies transformation. See J. Derrida, "Three questions to Hans-Georg Gadamer," in *Dialogue and Deconstruction: The Gadamer-Derrida Encounter,* 52–54; H.-G. Gadamer, "Reply to Jacques Derrida," in *Dialogue and Deconstruction: The Gadamer-Derrida Encounter,* 52–54; and H.-G. Gadamer, "Reply to my critics," *The Hermeneutic Tradition: From Ast to Ricoeur,* 273–97.

134. Gallagher, *Hermeneutics and Education,* 343.

135. Ibid., 344.

136. Ibid., 343.

137. See Rorty, *Philosophy and the Mirror of Nature;* M. Foucault, *The Foucault Reader: An Introduction to Foucault's Thought;* T. Kuhn, *The Structure of Scientific Revolutions;* S. Fish, *Is There a Text in This Class?* and *Doing What Comes Naturally: Change, Rhetoric and the Practice of Theory in Literary and Legal Studies.*

138. Rorty, *Philosophy and the Mirror of Nature,* 378.

139. See G. Lakoff, *Women, Fire, and Dangerous Things: What Categories Reveal about the Mind.*

140. S. Sontag, *On Photography.*

141. But there would also be no picture without loading the film or processing it. But then perhaps it is what happens in front of the camera at that particular moment that distinguishes this picture from that one. Perhaps it is not the click of the shutter that is the originary moment but composing the picture and arranging the camera and the subject matter. Composing images through the viewfinder of a camera is, in turn, conditioned by a vast legacy of photographic practice instilled through the traditions of painting, particularly the picturesque tradition, and through photography itself, with picture postcards, the use of designated scenic vantage points for tourists, notions of genre, and conformity to "standard shots," such as "the standard wedding photograph," "the standard mountain shot," and so on. Taking a photograph is mimetic in two senses. It purports to be a copy of what is before the camera, and it imitates the conventions of photography. In this case, the originary moment of the photograph seems to have escaped us.

But the originary moment may be a crucial step in a technological process. In the case of photography, there is a substantial technological investment in the moment at which the shutter opens and closes. The quality of the image depends substantially on what happens to the light as it passes onto the film at that moment. The moment is a consummation of several processes, many of which are often automatic, such as adjusting duration, aperture size, and focus. In this case, the originary moment is actually the end of a series of measurements and adjustments, all of which find their consummation in the opening and closing of a shutter.

For computer imagery, the originary moment is equally variable. But here the intervention through technology is longer and more complex. Some computerized image capture involves scanning devices that take analog images (such as photographs) and scan them over several seconds, one pixel and one line at a time. As pointed out by Mitchell and others, images can be modified and stored in ways that make identifying an original extremely problematic.

142. See Fish, *Doing What Comes Naturally,* for a full discussion of the matter of judgment in a legal context.

143. See H. Dreyfus, *Being-in-the-World: A Commentary on Heidegger's "Being and Time,"* Division I.

144. See A. Giddens, *The Consequences of Modernity.*

145. See R. Bernstein, *The New Constellation: The Ethical-Political Horizon of Modernity/ Postmodernity.*

Chapter 4

1. The term *cyberspace* was reputedly first used by William Gibson in the popular science fiction novel, *Neuromancer.* An introduction to computer networking and communications can be found in S. R. Hiltz and M. Turoff, *The Network Nation: Human Communication via Computer;* H. Rheingold, *The Virtual Community: Homesteading on the Electronic Frontier;* and J. Galegher, R. E. Kraut, and C. Egido, *Intellectual Teamwork: Social and Technological Foundations of Cooperative Work.*

2. See J. Barker and R. N. Tucker, *The Interactive Learning Revolution: Multimedia in Education and Training.*.

3. See W. Benjamin, "The work of art in the age of mechanical reproduction," *Illumination*, 217–51. The media metaphor has been brought to prominence in the context of computer systems design by U.S. research and development centers such as the MIT Media Lab and Xerox PARC. See S. Brand, *Media Lab: Inventing the Future at MIT*, and R. Stults, "Experimental uses of video to support design activities," *Report SSL-89-19 [P89-00019]*.

4. The following summary fits in with some of the observations in Marshall McLuhan and B. R. Powers, *The Global Village: Transformations in World Life and Media in the Twenty-first Century;* J. Meyrowitz, *No Sense of Place: The Impact of Electronic Media on Social Behaviour.* Clearly we are already influenced by the computer in how we think about the mass media. Defining the mass media in terms of information transferral is itself partly a product of information systems theory developed in the context of electronic systems and computers. Computing has informed contemporary notions of the mass media, often to the exclusion of other interesting characterizations.

5. See S. Rafaeli and R. J. LaRose, "Electronic bulletin boards and 'public goods' explanations of collaborative mass media," *Communications Research* 20 (2): 277–97.

6. See M. Weiser, "The computer for the twenty-first century," *Scientific American* 265 (3): 66–75.

7. See Rheingold, *Virtual Community.*

8. See H. Rheingold, *Virtual Reality;* Benedikt, introduction to *Cyberspace: First Steps*, 2–25; S. K. Helsel and J. P. Roth, eds., *Virtual Reality: Theory, Practice and Promise;* and Michael Heim, *The Metaphysics of Virtual Reality.*

9. Heim, *Metaphysics of Virtual Reality*, 150.

10. See Rheingold, *Virtual Community.*

11. For a comprehensive discussion of the social ramifications of this phenomenon, which involves the "restructuring of capitalism," see Manuel Castells, *The Informational City: Information Technology, Economic Restructuring and the Urban-Regional Process.*

12. McLuhan, *Global Village.*

13. Meyrowitz, *No Sense of Place*, 315.

14. Ibid.

15. Heim, *Metaphysics of Virtual Reality*, 150.

16. Some of these senses are outlined by Lefebvre in his book *The Production of Space:* physical space (nature and the cosmos); logical spaces (including logical and formal abstractions) and the social (spaces of knowledge, spaces of social practice, space occupied by sensory phenomena, "including products of the imagination such as projects and projections, symbols and utopias"). (Ibid., 12) In *Objective Knowledge: An Evolutionary Approach,* Karl Popper outlines three worlds. World 1 is the physical world, world 2 is the world of conscious experience, and world 3 is "the world of

the logical *contents* of books, libraries, computer memories." (Ibid., 74) So concepts of multiple spaces and worlds belong substantially to various traditions of Western thinking, including logical positivism and analytic philosophy. For mythic conceptions of space not discussed here, see A. B. Snodgrass, *Architecture, Time and Eternity*.

17. Rheingold, *Virtual Community*, 6.

18. Ibid.

19. For an application of the blocks world in language theory, see T. Winograd, "Understanding natural language," *Cognitive Psychology*, no. 3, 8–11.

20. See for example Gibson, *Neuromancer*.

21. Meyrowitz, *No Sense of Place*.

22. See E. Relph, "Geographical experiences and being-in-the-world: The phenomenological origins of geography," *Dwelling, Place and Environment: Towards a Phenomenology of Person and World*, 15–31. See also G. Bachelard, *The Poetics of Space*.

23. Ibid., 26.

24. Benedikt, introduction to *Cyberspace*, 1.

25. Ibid., 2.

26. Rheingold, *Virtual Community*, 61.

27. Benedikt, introduction to *Cyberspace*, 12.

28. Rheingold, *Virtual Community*, 12.

29. Ibid., 13.

30. Ibid., 23.

31. Ibid., 14.

32. Benedikt, introduction to *Cyberspace*, 7.

33. Meyrowitz, *No Sense of Place*, 37.

34. Ibid., 38.

35. Benedikt, introduction to *Cyberspace*, 18.

36. T. Roszak, *The Cult of Information: The Folklore of Computers and the True Art of Thinking*.

37. Ibid., 171.

38. J. W. Carey, *Communication as Culture: Essays on Media and Society*.

39. Ibid., 120

40. Ibid., 122.

41. Carey, *Communication as Culture*. For an example of the extensive application of the transmission metaphor applied to the media, see J. Fiske, *Introduction to Communication Studies*.

42. Carey, *Communication as Culture*, 43.

43. See for example, L. Wittgenstein, *Philosophical Investigations;* and M. Reddy, "The conduit metaphor—a case of frame conflict in our language about language," *Metaphor and Thought*, 284–324.

44. See H. L. Dreyfus, *What Computers Still Can't Do: A Critique of Artificial Reason;* and T. Winograd and F. Flores, *Understanding Computers and Cognition: A New Foundation for Design*.

45. Information-based theories of communication cannot account for our ability to understand what is said as it is said and before a sentence is completed. They cannot explain how it is that certain ideas cannot be expressed in certain languages; how we often say things we did not expect to say or "did not mean"; or how in animated conversation we "borrow" each other's ideas so that they cannot be said to belong to any individual. Again, they ignore forms of language that seem not so much to convey a message as simply to repeat social conventions, as when we exchange greetings or comment on the weather.

Reddy ("The conduit metaphor") highlights some of the problems of the systems theory of communication. In the view of Shannon and Weaver, the success of a communication is independent of any role played by the receiver of the message. Failure to pick up a message is attributable to poor transmission or interference. Reddy points out, however, that words and sentences are not isolated "packages" of meanings that are conveyed in a conduit to a receiver who "unpacks" and then "reads" them, but occur within a speech community that has certain preconceptions concerning likely or unlikely meanings in a particular context. The understanding of the "message" involves interpreting a code, and interpretation is a function of the recipient. According to Reddy, it is the "decoder" as well as the message that is transmitted, though, of course, the understanding of the "decoder" depends on the wider context of the history involving other communicative acts.

The information model of language also presupposes that meanings exist independently of, and prior to, the act of communication, so that language expresses preformed meanings. Wittgenstein questions this presupposition: "When I think in language, there aren't 'meanings' going through my mind in addition to the verbal expressions: the language is itself the vehicle of thought." (Wittgenstein, *Philosophical Investigations*, 139).

46. See H.-G. Gadamer, *Truth and Method;* and Stanley Fish, *Doing What Comes Naturally: Change, Rhetoric and the Practice of Theory in Literary and Legal Studies*.

47. Carey, *Communication as Culture*, 43.

48. Ibid.

49. Ibid., 20.

Notes to Pages 164–168

50. Ibid.

51. Ibid.

52. Ibid., 21.

53. Ibid. Furthermore, according to Carey, the idea of the news is itself an invention we can locate in history:

> It is a form of culture invented by a particular class at a particular point of history—in this case by the middle class largely in the eighteenth century. Like any invented cultural form, news both forms and reflects a particular "hunger for experience," a desire to do away with the epic, heroic, and traditional in favour of the unique, original, novel, new—news. (Ibid.)

54. Ibid.

55. Ibid., 21–22.

56. Radical phenomenology seeks to explicate the nature of things *in themselves*, as the thing shows itself, rather than through theories or concepts. Phenomenology shares this approach with empiricism, but empiricism appeals to a theory of objectivity. According to empiricism, there is pure sense experience, and we make inferences from this. The domain in which the distinction between phenomenology and empiricism is commonly made is perception. In hearing a sound of a car engine passing by the window, we do not first hear the noise as pure sense data, which we then distinguish as the sound of a Volkswagen or a Mercedes Benz (Heidegger's example), but we hear it first as that. It requires an especially contrived frame of mind to be able to hear it as nothing at all, as pure noise.

Heidegger radicalizes the phenomenological project by attending to the issue of the being who conducts such investigations. Whereas Husserl took the subject, the thinking entity, for granted, the thinking being who projects intentions into the world, Heidegger focuses on the being engaged in phenomenological inquiry, *Dasein*. And the issue of the inquiry is Being. Heidegger is also interested in what remains unthought in the appeal to the things themselves. See J. Sallis, "The origins of Heidegger's thought," in *A Companion to Martin Heidegger's "Being and Time,"* 89–103.

57. See Dreyfus, *What Computers Still Can't Do;* Winograd and Flores, *Understanding Computers and Cognition;* and M. Heim, "The computer as component: Heidegger and McLuhan," *Philosophy and Literature,* 16 (2): 304–19.

58. Heidegger modified Husserl's concept of "life world." Here we will focus on Heidegger's "radical phenomenology." Heidegger's early concepts of space and world are explained in *Being and Time*. See also Martin Heidegger, *History of the Concept of Time*. For commentaries on space and world in these difficult works, see H. L. Dreyfus, *Being-in-the-World: A Commentary on Heidegger's "Being and Time," Division I;* E. F. Kaelin, *Heidegger's "Being and Time": A Reading for Readers;* J. J. Kockelmans, ed., *A Companion to Martin Heidegger's "Being and Time";* Sallis, "The Origins of Heidegger's thought"; G. F. Sefler, "Heidegger's philosophy of space," *Philosophy Today* 17:246–59; and M. E. Zimmerman, *Heidegger's Confrontation with Modernity: Technology, Politics, Art.*

59. See Heidegger, *Being and Time,* 93; and Dreyfus, *Being-in-the-World,* 89.

60. *In-der-Welt-sein* in German.

61. Dreyfus, *Being-in-the-World,* 91.

62. Kaelin, *Heidegger's "Being and Time,"* 66.

63. Heidegger, *History of the Concept of Time,* 168.

64. Heidegger, *Being and Time,* 135.

65. Ibid., 141–42.

66. M. Heidegger, "Building, dwelling, thinking," *Poetry, Language, Thought,* 143–61.

67. Ibid., 157.

68. In fact, Heidegger and other commentators express profound suspicion of the claims of communications technologies to bring people together, to reduce distances. According to Heidegger, everything is brought close. But this closeness does not make them any more present to us. We are still alienated from things. It is possible to be alienated from things even though they are measurably close.

69. Heidegger, *Being and Time,* 141.

70. Dreyfus, *Being-in-the-World,* 138.

71. Heidegger, *Being and Time,* 146.

72. Ibid., 147.

73. We may surmise that according to Heidegger this is the starting place for space as considered by analytic philosophers, who seem interested in the resolution of spatial paradoxes, the validity of truth statements about space and time, and the gounding of truth about space in empirical data and logic. See B. C. van Fraassen, *An Introduction to the Philosophy of Time and Space;* C. Ray, *Time, Space and Philosophy;* and Richard Swinburne, *Space and Time.*

74. Heidegger's thinking underwent some changes after *Being and Time.* In his later essays, he places less emphasis on his systematic ontological categories and develops a more poetical account of being. Heidegger moves on to other metaphors.

75. See M. Heidegger, "The origin of the work of art," *Poetry, Language, Thought,* 17–87; Martin Heidegger, "The thing," *Poetry, Language, Thought,* 165–86; Martin Heidegger, *The Question concerning Technology and Other Essays;* and M. Heidegger, "Art and space," *Man and World* 6 (1): 3–8.

76. Heidegger, "The thing," 174.

77. Ibid.

78. Heidegger gives the example of a jug and shows how, as a thing, it gathers what he poetically calls the "fourfold"—earth and sky, divinities and mortals—or, as a unity, the "onefold." For our purposes here, we can translate these terms roughly

as the materials from which the jug is made, which bear a dialectical relationship with light and day, and the seasons into which its use is set; and the jug as a sacred vessel, as a part of abiding ritual in a dialectical relationship with our finitude and mortality. This interplay of gathered concerns (however poetically we may wish to describe it) constitutes the world: "This appropriating mirror-play of the simple onefold of earth and sky, divinities and mortals, we call the world." (Ibid., 179) Elsewhere Heidegger describes the revelatory nature of artworks as a clash between "earth" and "world." For an explanation of the disclosive power of art according to Heidegger, see S. L. Bartky, "Heidegger's philosophy of art," *British Journal of Aesthetics* 9:353–71. These concepts are discussed further in chapter 5.

79. Heidegger, "The thing," 181.

80. See K. Wright, "The place of the work of art in the age of technology," *Southern Journal of Philosophy* 22:565–83. See also R. L. Hall, "Heidegger and the space of art," *Journal of Existentialism* 8 (29): 91–108; and J. J. Kockelmans, *Heidegger on Art and Art Works*.

81. Ibid., 579.

82. Heidegger, *Question Concerning Technology*, 13.

83. Ibid.

84. Ibid., 16.

85. Ibid., 17.

86. For similar critiques of mass media, see also T. W. Adorno, "How to look at television," *Critical Theory: The Essential Readings*, 69–83; and Paul Adams, "In TV: On 'nearness,' on Heidegger and on television," *RUA/TV?: Heidegger and the Televisual*, 45–66.

87. Ibid., 49.

88. Ibid., 28.

89. As discussed in chapter 2, Borgman develops the distinction between devices and "focal things" as a way of showing how we can "let be" in the technological age. See A. Borgman, *Technology and the Character of Contemporary Life: A Philosophical Inquiry*.

Chapter 5

1. See H. Rheingold, *Virtual Reality;* and S. Brand, *The Media Lab: Inventing the Future at MIT*.

2. M. Bajura, H. Fuchs, and R. Ohbuchi, "Merging virtual objects with the real world: Seeing ultrasound imagery within the patient," *Proc. Computer Graphics (Siggraph '92)* 26 (2): 203–10.

3. M. Deering, "High resolution virtual reality," *Proc. Computer Graphics (Siggraph '92)*, 26 (2): 195–202.

4. S. K. Helsel and J. P. Roth, eds., *Virtual Reality: Theory, Practice and Promise.*

5. G. Hattinger, M. Russel, C. Schöpf, and P. Weibel, eds., *Ars Electronica 1990,* vol. 2, *Virtuelle Welten.*

6. W. Gibson, *Neuromancer.*

7. M. Heim, "The metaphysics of virtual reality," *Virtual Reality: Theory, Practice and Promise,* 33.

8. M. B. Spring, "Informating with virtual reality," *Virtual Reality: Theory, Practice and Promise,* 13.

9. See Helsel and Roth, *Virtual Reality: Theory, Practice and Promise,* vii.

10. Walser, quoted by Rheingold, *Virtual Reality,* 191.

11. Walser, quoted by Rheingold, ibid., 191.

12. See Heim, "The metaphysics of virtual reality," 33.

13. R. Reisman, "A brief introduction to the art of flight simulation," *Ars Electronica 1990,* vol. 2, *Virtuelle Welten,* 159–69.

14. S. S. Fisher, "Virtual environments: Personal simulations and telepresence," *Virtual Reality: Theory, Practice and Promise,* 102.

15. J. D. Foley and A. Van Dam, *Fundamentals of Interactive Computer Graphics,* 560.

16. H. Rheingold, *Virtual Reality,* 63.

17. See J. J. Gibson, *The Perception of the Visual World;* and J. J. Gibson, *The Ecological Approach to Visual Perception.*

18. M. A. Hagen, *Varieties of Realism: Geometries of Representational Art,* 6.

19. See Hagen, *Varieties of Realism,* 87.

20. See C. Norris, *Deconstruction: Theory and Practice.*

21. M. Barnsley, *Fractals Everywhere,* 1.

22. W. J. Mitchell, "Computer-aided design media: A comparative analysis," *Computers in Architecture: Tools for Design,* 53.

23. A. S. Glassner, ed., *An Introduction to Ray Tracing,* x.

24. J. D. Foley, A. Van Dam, S. K. Feiner, and J. F. Hughes, *Fundamentals of Interactive Computer Graphics,* 605. This discussion recalls our investigation of photographic realism in chapter 3.

25. S. S. Fisher, "Virtual environments," 101.

26. See S. Upstill, *The Renderman™ Companion: A Programmer's Guide to Realistic Computer Graphics;* T. Saito and T. Takahashi, "Comprehensible rendering of three-dimensional shapes," *Proc. Computer Graphics (Siggraph '90)* 24 (4): 197–206; and D. R. Baum, S. Mann, K. P. Smith, and J. M. Winget, "Making radiosity usable: Automatic preprocessing and meshing techniques for the generation of accurate radiosity solutions," *Proc. Computer Graphics (Siggraph '91),* 25 (4): 51–60.

27. See S. J. Teller and C. H. Séquin, "Visibility preprocessing for interactive walkthroughs," *Proc. Computer Graphics (Siggraph '91)* 25 (4): 61–69; and M. Deering, "High resolution virtual reality," *Proc. Computer Graphics (Siggraph '92)* 26 (2): 195–202.

28. See Foley and Van Dam, *Fundamentals of Interactive Computer Graphics,* 539.

29. See H. L. Dreyfus, *Being-in-the-World: A Commentary on Heidegger's "Being and Time," Divison I,* 119.

30. N. Goodman, *Languages of Art.*

31. See Hagen, *Varieties of Realism,* 86.

32. See Helsel and Roth, *Virtual Reality,* ix.

33. C. M. Turbayne, *The Myth of Metaphor.*

34. This view was elaborated on in chapter 3 in relation to photographic images.

35. B. Jones, "Computer imagery: Imitation and representation of realities," *Leonardo,* 31–38.

36. See M. Weiser, "The computer for the twenty-first century," *Scientific American* 265 (3): 66–75; K. Carter, "Computer-aided design: Back to the drawing board"; P. Haeberli, "Paint by numbers: Abstract image representations," *Proc. Computer Graphics (Siggraph '90)* 24 (4): 207–14; and S. Schofield, "A general approach to interpretive (non-photorealistic) rendering."

37. See J. J. Kockelmans, *Heidegger on Art and Art Works;* M. E. Zimmerman, *Heidegger's Confrontation with Modernity: Technology, Politics, Art;* and H. L. Dreyfus and H. Hall, *Heidegger: A Critical Reader.*

38. M. Heidegger, *Identity and Difference,* 34–35.

39. Ibid., 41.

40. M. Merleau-Ponty, *Phenomenology of Perception.*

41. See Dreyfus, *Being-in-the-World,* 124.

42. See Kockelmans, *Heidegger on Art and Art Works,* 136.

43. R. Brandom, "Heidegger's categories in *Being and Time*," *Heidegger: A Critical Reader,* 61.

44. See M. Heidegger, *The Question concerning Technology and Other Essays;* D. Vesely, "The nature of creativity in the age of production," *Scroope Cambridge Architecture Journal* (4): 25–30; and D. Vesely, "The question of technology."

45. M. Heidegger, "The thing," *Poetry, Language, Thought,* 165–86.

46. M. Heidegger, *Being and Time.*

47. See Kockelmans, *Heidegger on Art and Art Works,* 157–58; and J. Haugeland, "Dasein's disclosedness," *Heidegger: A Critical Reader,* 27.

48. J. P. Fell, "The familiar and the strange: On the limits of praxis in the earlier Heidegger," *Heidegger: A Critical Reader,* 65.

49. M. Heidegger, "The origin of the work of art," *Poetry, Language, Thought,* 17–87.

50. See Kockelmans, *Heidegger on Art and Art Works,* 143.

51. Brandom, "Heidegger's categories," 57.

52. G. Lakoff, *Women, Fire and Dangerous Things: What Categories Reveal about the Mind.*

53. F. de Saussure, *Course in General Linguistics.*

54. M. Foucault, *The Foucault Reader: An Introduction to Foucault's Thought,* 196–97.

55. See Norris, *Deconstruction: Theory and Practice,* 32.

56. A. B. Snodgrass, "Asian studies and the fusion of horizons," *Proc. Gadamer, Action and Reason,* 35–42.

57. See Kockelmans, *Heidegger on Art and Art Works,* 184.

58. Ibid., 184.

59. Ibid., 185.

60. See Saussure, *Course in General Linguistics.*

61. See Heim, "The metaphysics of virtual reality," 30.

Chapter 6

1. See for example C. Shannon, and W. Weaver, *The Mathematical Theory of Communication.* For introductions to systems theory, see C. West Churchman, *The Systems Approach;* and Nic J. T. A. Kramer and Jacob de Smit, *Systems Thinking.*

2. L. von Bertalanffy, "General system theory," *General Systems, Yearbook of the Society for the Advancement of General System Theory,* vol. 1, 2.

3. Kramer and Smit, *Systems Thinking,* 66.

4. Ibid., 7.

5. H. A. Simon, *Sciences of the Artificial*, 58.

6. See D. H. Meadows, N. L. Meadows, J. Randers, and W. W. Behrens, *The Limits of Growth, a Report for the Club of Rome's Project on the Predicament of Mankind*. The authors state their purpose as follows:

> First, every assumption we make is written in a precise form so that it is open to inspection and criticism by all. Second, after the assumptions have been scrutinized, discussed, and revised to agree with our best current knowledge, their implications for the future behaviour of the world system can be traced without error by a computer, no matter how complicated they become. (Ibid., 22).

7. Note that systems theory is also undergoing revision and has resurfaced at one time or another as a significant contributor to the discussion of major issues in the development of complex systems, self-organizing systems, and chaos and catastrophy theory. See E. Jantsche, *The Self-Organizing Universe;* and C. G. Langton, "Artificial life," *Santa Fe Institute Studies in the Sciences of Complexity*, vol. 6 *Artificial Life*.

8. M. Heidegger, "What calls for thinking?" *Basic Writings*, 373.

9. See H. L. Dreyfus, *What Computers Can't Do: The Limits of Artificial Intelligence;* T. Winograd and F. Flores, *Understanding Computers and Cognition: A New Foundation for Design;* and J. Weizenbaum, *Computer Power and Human Reason: From Judgement to Calculation*.

10. D. I. A. Cohen, *Introduction to Computer Theory*, 3.

11. Some commentators say that all sciences involve interpretation, so the distinction is not a useful one. For a summary of the issues, see C. Taylor, "Understanding in human science," *Review of Metaphysics* 34:3–23; and R. J. Bernstein, *Beyond Objectivism and Relativism*.

12. W. J. Ong, *Ramus: Method, and the Decay of Dialogue from the Art of Discourse to the Art of Reason*, 227.

13. C. M. Turbayne, *The Myth of Metaphor*, 30.

14. See J. Hospers, *An Introduction to Philosophical Analysis*. In chapter 5 we saw Heidegger's attempt to get behind such propositional notions of truth with his exploration of *aletheia*.

15. Commentators like Dewey, however, ascribe the development of science to an engagement with experimental tools rather than to theoretical principle. See J. Dewey, *Experience and Nature*.

16. I. Newton, *Opticks: or a Treatise of the Reflections, Refractions, Inflections and Colours of Light*, book 3, part 1, 404.

17. R. Descartes, *Discourse on Method and the Meditations*, 41.

18. Ibid.

19. Ibid.

20. Ibid.

21. For an early account of theory in science, see P. Duhem, *The Aim and Structure of Physical Theory*. According to Duhem, "A physical theory is not an explanation. It is a system of mathematical propositions, deduced from a small number of principles, which aim to represent as simply, as completely, and as exactly as possible a set of experimental laws." (Ibid., 19)

22. Turbayne, *Myth of Metaphor*, 220.

23. N. R. Campbell, *Foundations of Science: The Philosophy of Theory and Experiment*, 120.

24. Duhem, *The Aim and Structure of Physical Theory*.

25. See M. Black, *Models and Metaphors*; M. Hesse, *Models and Analogies in Science*; and Turbayne, *Myth of Metaphor*.

26. Hesse, *Models and Analogies in Science*, 11.

27. As we will see in the following chapter, in treating models as metaphors, we can dispense with the distinction between the observation language and the language of the model.

28. Cohen, *Introduction to Computer Theory*, 10.

29. Hesse, *Models and Analogies in Science*, 3

30. Duhem, *The Aim and Structure of Physical Theory*, 70–71. Duhem contrasts the French theoretical approach to science with the English approach that depends on models.

> Understanding a physical phenomenon is, therefore, for the physicists of the English school, the same thing as designing a model imitating the phenomenon, whence the nature of material things is to be understood by imagining a mechanism whose performance will represent and simulate the properties of bodies. The English school is completely committed to the purely mechanical explanations of physical phenomena. (Ibid., 72)

31. Campbell, *The Foundations of Science*. The conflicting views of Duhem and Campbell are brought out in a mock debate in Hesse, *Models and Analogies in Science*.

32. Ibid., 129.

33. Black, *Models and Metaphors*, 224.

34. Ibid., 223.

35. See E. A. Wrigley, "Demographic models in geography," *Models in Geography*, 189–215.

36. Black, *Models and Metaphors*, 221.

37. See C. S. Peirce, *Collected Papers of Charles Sanders Peirce.*

38. Black, *Models and Metaphors,* 222.

39. See T. Heath, *Method in Architecture.*

40. C. Alexander, *Notes on the Synthesis of Form,* 15.

41. See for example J. L. Cohon, *Multiobjective Programming and Planning;* and A. D. Radford and J. S. Gero, *Design by Optimization in Architecture, Building and Construction.*

42. See J. C. Jones, *Design Methods: Seeds of Human Futures;* and Tavistock Institute, *Interdependence and Uncertainty: A Study of the Building Industry.*

43. G. Broadbent, *Design in Architecture: Architecture and the Human Sciences.*

44. See W. J. Mitchell, *Computer-Aided Architectural Design.*

45. Ibid., 29.

46. P. Steadman, *The Evolution of Designs: Biological Analogy in Architecture and the Applied Arts.*

47. G. Stiny, *Pictorial and Formal Aspects of Shape Grammars,* and W. J. Mitchell, *The Logic of Architecture.*

48. In artificial-intelligence research there are so-called blackboard systems, which attempt to codify the "knowledge" by which a group of people might reason through these hierarchies of control. See B. Hayes-Roth and F. Hayes-Roth, "A cognitive model of planning," *Cognitive Science* 3 (4): 275–309.

49. Steadman, *The Evolution of Design,* 29.

50. See J. Feibleman, *An Introduction to the Philosophy of Charles S. Peirce;* L. March, "The logic of design and the question of value," *The Architecture of Form,* 1–40; U. Eco, *Semiotics and the Philosophy of Language;* and R. D. Coyne, *Logic Models of Design.*

51. Simon, *Sciences of the Artificial;* A. Newell and H. A. Simon, *Human Problem Solving.*

52. See C. W. Churchman, "Wicked problems," *Management Science,* 4 (14): B-141 and B-142; and H. W. J. Rittel and M. M. Webber, "Wicked problems," *Man-Made Futures,* 272–80.

53. See C. Alexander, "A city is not a tree," *Design after Modernism,* 67–84; and C. Alexander, *A Pattern Language.*

54. See G. Stiny, "A new line on drafting systems," *Design Computing,* 1:5–19.

55. See P. N. Johnson-Laird, *The Computer and the Mind: An Introduction to Cognitive Science;* M. Boden, *Artificial Intelligence and Natural Man;* and M. Boden, *The Philosophy of Artificial Intelligence.*

56. See for example E. H. Shortliffe and B. G. Buchanan, "A model of inexact reasoning in medicine," *Mathematical Biosciences,* 23:351–79.

57. L. A. Zadeh, "The role of fuzzy logic in the management of uncertainty in expert systems," *Fuzzy Sets and Systems* 11 (3): 199–228.

58. See J. de Kleer, "An assumption-based truth maintenance system," *Artificial Intelligence* 28 (2): 127–62.

59. See R. C. Schank and R. Abelson, *Scripts, Plans, Goals and Understanding*.

60. See C. Stanfill and D. Waltz, "Toward memory-based reasoning," *Communications of the ACM* 29 (12): 1213–28.

61. See A. Clark, *Microcognition: Philosophy, Cognitive Science, and Parallel Distributed Processing*. See H. Dreyfus, *What Computers Still Can't Do* for a phenomenological treatment of the subject.

62. See D. E. Rumelhart, P. Smolensky, J. L. McClelland, and G. E. Hinton, "Schemata and sequential thought processes in PDP models," *Parallel Distributed Processing: Explorations in the Microstructure of Cognition*, vol. 1, *Foundations*, 7–57.

63. See R. D. Coyne, S. Newton, and F. Sudweeks, "A connectionist view of creative design reasoning," *Modelling Creativity and Knowledge-Based Creative Design*, 177–209.

64. See M. Minsky, *The Society of Mind*.

65. L. A. Suchman, *Plans and Situated Actions: The Problem of Human-Machine Communication*.

66. See Radford and Gero, *Design by Optimization*.

67. Alexander, *Notes on the Synthesis of Form*.

68. See I. L. McHarg, *Design with Nature*.

69. See W. F. Closksin and C. S. Mellish, *Programming in Prolog*.

70. See F. Hayes-Roth, D. A. Waterman, and D. B. Lenat, eds., *Building Expert Systems*; and R. D. Coyne, M. A. Rosenman, A. D. Radford, M. Balachandran, and J. S. Gero, *Knowledge-Based Design Systems*.

71. For example see G. Stiny, "Introduction to shape and shape grammars," *Environment and Planning B*, 7:342–51.

72. See Hayes-Roth and Hayes-Roth, "A cognitive model of planning."

73. Hesse, *Models and Analogies in Science*.

74. Black, *Metaphors and Models*, 236.

75. See A. Cunningham and N. Jardine, eds., *Romanticism and the Sciences*.

76. See J. Marías, *History of Philosophy*.

77. See L. R. Furst, *Romanticism in Perspective: A Comparative Study of Aspects of the Romantic Movements in England, France and Germany*.

78. See A. Rand, *The Fountainhead.*

79. See Cunningham and Jardine, *Romanticism and the Sciences.*

80. The return to craft values in architecture could be regarded as romantic. See for example Charles, Prince of Wales, *A Vision of Britain: A Personal View of Architecture.*

81. Jones, *Design Methods,* 62–63.

82. Broadbent, *Design in Architecture,* 456–57.

83. Ibid., 322.

84. See B. Edwards, *Drawing on the Right Side of the Brain;* and D. Kolb, *Experiential Learning: Experience as the Source of Learning and Development.*

Chapter 7

1. T. D. Erickson, "Working with interface metaphors," *The Art of Human-Computer Interface Design,* 65–73.

2. Ibid., 65.

3. The computer operating system is the suite of programs that controls the interface and the operations common to all programs, such as reading from, and writing to, files.

4. For a description of object-oriented programming, see A. Goldberg and D. Robson, *SMALLTALK-80 The Language and Its Implementation.*

5. See S. Turkle, "Computer as Rorschach," *Society* (January/February): 15–24.

6. As I will show, principle and method can be made subject to the idea of metaphor.

7. See T. H. Nelson, "The right way to think about software design," *The Art of Human-Computer Interface Design,* 235–43.

8. Ibid., 236.

9. Ibid., 237.

10. Ibid., 241.

11. A. Kay, "User interface: A personal view," *The Art of Human-Computer Interface Design,* 191–207.

12. Ibid., 199.

13. For an introduction to metaphor, see D. E. Cooper, *Metaphor;* G. Lakoff and M. Johnson, *Metaphors We Live By;* A. Ortony, ed., *Metaphor and Thought;* I. A. Richards, *Philosophy of Rhetoric,* and M. Salner, "Introduction: Metaphor and human understanding," *Saybrook Review* 7: 1–19. For a discussion of metaphor and models in the

context of design, see A. B. Snodgrass and R. D. Coyne, "Models, metaphors and the hermeneutics of designing," *Design Issues* 9 (1): 56–74.

14. Aristotle, *Poetics,* 1457b. See W. D. Ross, ed., *The Works of Aristotle,* vol. 11.

15. Aristotle, *Rhetoric,* 1404b.

16. According to Aristotle, there are four kinds of metaphor in poetry and rhetoric. There is metaphor as a transferral from genus to species, from species to genus, and from species to species, and metaphor by analogy. See Aristotle, *Poetics,* 1457b.

17. J. Derrida, "White mythology: Metaphor in the text of philosophy," *Margins of Philosophy,* 207–71.

18. F. Nietzsche, *The Complete Works of Friedrich Nietzsche,* vol. 2, *Early Greek Philosophy and Other Essays,* 180.

19. H.-G. Gadamer, *Philosophical Hermeneutics.*

20. Ibid., 24.

21. P. Ricoeur, *The Rule of Metaphor.*

22. Ibid., 12.

23. N. Goodman, *Ways of Worldmaking.*

24. As explained in David Wood, *Philosophy at the Limit,* 29.

25. See M. Hesse, "The explanatory function of metaphor," *Revolutions and Reconstructions in the Philosophy of Science,* 111–124.

26. M. Black, "More about metaphor," *Metaphor and Thought,* 19–43.

27. See for example D. Gentner, B. Falkenhainer, and J. Skorstad, "Viewing metaphor as analogy," *Analogical Reasoning: Perspectives of Artificial Intelligence, Cognitive Science, and Philosophy,* 171–77.

28. D. Davidson, "What metaphors mean," *On Metaphor,* 29–45.

29. Ibid., 30.

30. Ibid., 31.

31. Ibid., 32.

32. Ibid., 39.

33. Ibid., 40.

34. Ibid., 41.

35. Ibid., 44.

36. See also R. Rorty, "Unfamiliar noises: Hesse and Davidson on Metaphor," *Journal of the Aristotelian Society* (July): 283–96; and Mary Hesse, "Unfamiliar noises—tropical talk: The myth of the literal," *Journal of the Aristotelian Society* (July): 297–311.

37. See G. Lakoff, *Women, Fire, and Dangerous Things: What Categories Reveal about the Mind;* M. Johnson, *The Body in the Mind: The Bodily Basis of Meaning, Imagination, and Reason;* and Lakoff and Johnson, *Metaphors We Live By.*

38. See M. Turner, "Categories and analogies," *Analogical Reasoning: Perspectives of Artificial Intelligence, Cognitive Science, and Philosophy,* 3–24; and E. Rosch, "Categorization of natural objects," *Annual Review of Psychology,* 32:89–115.

39. Lakoff, *Women, Fire and Dangerous Things,* 271.

40. Ibid., 267.

41. Ibid., 77.

42. See D. Schön, *Displacement of Concepts;* and D. Schön, "Generative metaphor: A perspective on problem-setting in social policy," *Metaphor and Thought,* 254–83.

43. As discussed later in this chapter, arguments about the origins of metaphor turn in on themselves. The quest for an origin indicates a particular metaphorical orientation. Grounding metaphor in bodily experience (a view criticized by Dreyfus) suggests that there are foundations for our metaphors, a particularly Cartesian metaphorical orientation. Metaphor theorists generally recognize (and celebrate the fact) that we are never able to free ourselves from metaphorical orientations. There is no nonmetaphorical language at our disposal for explaining what metaphor is and how it works. All statements about metaphor are metaphorical. That a metaphor is the juxtaposition of two ideas is a metaphor. According to Ricoeur, there is no mastery and control of metaphor by means of classification. See H. L. Dreyfus, *Being-in-the-World: A Commentary on Heidegger's "Being and Time," Division 1;* and P. Ricoeur, *The Rule of Metaphor,* 18.

44. Lakoff and Johnson's argument may, however, support the artificial-intelligence paradigm of connectionism.

45. For some alternative conceptions of the line, see G. Deleuze, *The Deleuze Reader,* 165–72.

46. This includes chaotic, nonlinear, and complex systems, as well as connectionism.

47. Johnson, *The Body in the Mind,* 104. There have been other choices in the development of the computer that reflect other metaphorical preoccupations. Digital (numerical) processing has been favored over analog. Digital computing has been favored over neural (connectionist) computing. Raster display technology has been favored over vector display. We have generalized computer systems rather than specialized systems, distributed (personal) computing rather than mainframe (centralized). Computer drawings and models are described with orthogonal grids rather than polar coordinates. It is common to store the endpoints of lines rather than vectors or equations. Often objects rather than actions are stored. The emphasis in drawing descriptions is on precision, photorealism, and now virtual reality rather

than communication or expression. In each of these choices, and others, communities of researchers, inventors, designers, and systems developers have been led by certain metaphorical orientations. These metaphors have defined what is a necessity in a particular situation.

48. Note that such writers as Gadamer rehabilitate Aristotle's thought from such reductive interpretations. See H.-G. Gadamer, *Philosophical Hermeneutics.*

49. See J. Derrida, *Of Grammatology;* J. Culler, *On Deconstruction: Theory and Criticism after Structuralism;* and C. Norris, *Deconstruction: Theory and Practice.*

50. See J. Derrida, "*Geschlecht* II: Heidegger's hand," *Deconstruction and Philosophy: The Texts of Jacques Derrida,* 161–196.

51. Of course the idea of usefulness is not unproblematic. I am here contrasting the pragmatic view with that of deconstruction. Note that Derrida makes no such distinctions between the pragmatic/scientific domain and that of philosophy/literature. For example, Derrida is ruthless in his extended criticism of Austin's and Searle's language theories.

52. In presenting this argument, I am echoing Derrida's identification of the kind of writing that precedes ordinary writing. This is a protowriting, of which both speech and ordinary writing are examples.

53. See M. Heidegger, *Being and Time,* 93; and Dreyfus, *Being-In-The-World,* 89.

54. The counterview is that both the computer and science are products of technology.

55. See M. Hesse, "The explanatory function of metaphor," *Revolutions and Reconstructions in the Philosophy of Science,* 111–24.

56. Ricoeur, *The Ricoeur Reader,* 84.

57. Hesse, "The explanatory function of metaphor," 112.

58. The Turing machine is named after Alan Turing, one of the founders of modern computing, who first proposed such a universal algorithmic machine. I describe it briefly in chapter 6.

59. For a full explanation, see D. I. A. Cohen, *Introduction to Computer Theory.*

60. Hesse, "The explanatory function of metaphor," 114.

61. Ibid.

62. Ibid., 120.

63. Ibid., 123.

64. G. Basalla, *The Evolution of Technology.*

65. Ibid., 15.

66. See G. Ryle, *The Concept of Mind;* Schön, *Displacement of Concepts;* and R. J. Sternberg, *Metaphors of Mind: Conceptions of the Nature of Intelligence;* E. A. Havelock, *The Muse Learns to Write: Reflections on Orality and Literacy from Antiquity to the Present.*

67. See M. McLuhan, *The Gutenberg Galaxy: The Making of Typographic Man;* W. J. Ong, *Orality and Literacy: The Technologizing of the Word;* E. A. Havelock, *The Muse Learns to Write;* I. Illich and B. Sanders, *ABC: The Alphabetization of the Popular Mind;* and M. Heim, *Electric Language: A Philosophical Study of Word Processing.*

68. Ong, *Orality and Literacy,* 56–57.

69. Ibid., 131–132.

70. Schön, *Displacement of Concepts.*

71. For evidence of the prominence of information processing as metaphor, see C. Shannon and W. Weaver, *The Mathematical Theory of Communication;* A. Newell and H. A. Simon, *Human Problem Solving;* O. Akin, "How do architects design?" *Artificial Intelligence and Pattern Recognition in Computer-Aided Design,* 65–119; and R. D. Coyne, M. A. Rosenman, A. D. Radford, M. Balachandran, and J. S. Gero, *Knowledge-Based Design Systems.*

72. There is also a sense in which technologies create the problems they are designed to solve. It is often pointed out that designers and other professionals now have to cope with a great deal of information and need methods and machines to deal with this. In fact, it can be shown that the quantity of information is very much a product of the information-processing tools, rather than a need that is "objectively" recognizable and independent of the information-processing metaphor. For example, remote sensing and monitoring devices generate information. Electronic mail services and desktop publishing result in the broadcasting of vast amounts of information with little discrimination. Data, such as census results, can be manipulated in ways that produce even more information. Notwithstanding the usefulness of some of this information it can be said that the solution (computers) is also causing the problem (how do we handle all the information?).

73. Basalla, *The Evolution of Technology,* 107.

74. W. J. Mitchell and M. McCullough, *Digital Design Media: A Handbook for Architects, Landscape Architects, and Urban Designers.*

75. Heidegger's original German word, which we translate as "letting be," is *Gelassenheit.*

76. Heidegger, *Being and Time,* 190.

77. Ibid., 201.

78. Dreyfus, *Being-in-the-World,* 42.

79. Johnson, *The Body in the Mind,* 126.

80. Dreyfus, *Being-in-the-World,* 199; Heidegger, *Being and Time,* 191.

81. M. Heidegger, *The Principle of Reason*, 48.

82. D. Wood, *Philosophy at the Limit*.

83. M. Heidegger, *The Principle of Reason*, 47.

84. Wood, *Philosophy at the Limit*, 35.

85. L. Wittgenstein, *Philosophical Investigations*.

86. Wood, *Philosophy at the Limit*, 35.

87. M. Heidegger, "Letter on humanism," *Basic Writings: Martin Heidegger*, 217–65.

88. Ibid., 236–37. See also Wood, *Philosophy at the Limit*, 36.

89. But then, as Wood points out, there may be another, more-profound dimension to Heidegger's denial of metaphor. The concept of metaphor may be implicated in the concept of home itself. The subject matter of the particular statement in question (language as the home of being) actually bears on the matter of metaphor itself. I will return to this line of inquiry at the end of this essay.

90. This is explained in Norris, *Deconstruction: Theory and Practice*, 143.

91. This is explained in Wood, *Philosophy at the Limit*, 39.

92. See Snodgrass and Coyne, "Models, metaphors and the hermeneutics of designing."

93. P. Ricoeur, *The Ricoeur Reader*, 82.

94. Johnson, *The Body in the Mind*, 168.

95. Ibid., 169.

96. Ricoeur, *The Ricoeur Reader*, 82

97. Ibid., 80.

98. Ibid., 81.

99. Ibid., 82.

100. Ibid.

101. See Ryle, *Concept of Mind*; and C. M. Turbayne, *The Myth of Metaphor*.

102. Ricoeur, *The Ricoeur Reader*, 85.

103. Ibid.

104. Ricoeur, *Rule of Metaphor*, 313.

105. Ibid.

Chapter 8

1. M. Jay, *Adorno,* 14. These passages are also quoted in Bernstein, *The New Constellation,* 201.

2. Jay, *Adorno,* 14–15.

3. Ibid.

4. See A. Hodges, *Alan Turing: The Enigma of Intelligence.*

5. The supposed precursors to modern-day computers are legion. There were the calculating devices, such as the abacus, tables, slide rules of various kinds, and various calculating machines. There were also logic machines and automata for replicating thought processes and animal and human behavior. And there were devices for storing and replaying machine instructions and storing numerical information. But there were also graphical devices, commonly described as analog machines, for surveying, mapping, and plotting the courses of the planets and the tides. See W. Aspray, *Computing before Computers.*

6. M. Weiser, "The computer for the twenty-first century," *Scientific American* 265 (3): 66–75.

7. Weiser cites the example of the "vanishing" of electric motors at the turn of the century. The average automobile now contains many motors and solenoids, but the driver is largely unaware of them. Electric motors have become inconspicuous and ubiquitous, as will computers. Ibid., 66.

8. F. Duffy, *The Changing Workplace.*

9. R. D. Coyne, S. McLaughlin, and S. Newton, "Information technology and *praxis*: A survey of computers in design practice."

10. See H. L. Dreyfus, "On the ordering of things: Being and power in Heidegger and Foucault," *The Southern Journal of Philosophy,* 28 (supplement): 83–96.

11. See M. Foucault, *The Foucault Reader: An Introduction to Foucault's Thought.*

12. Dreyfus, "On the ordering of things," 90.

13. Ibid., 91.

14. Ibid.

15. Ibid.

16. Ibid., 93.

17. Ibid., 94.

18. Ibid., 95.

References

Adams, Paul. 1993. In TV: On 'nearness,' on Heidegger and on television. In *RUA/ TV?: Heidegger and the Televisual,* ed. Tony Fry, 45–66. Sydney, Australia: Power.

Adorno, Theodor W. 1992. How to look at television. In *Critical Theory: The Essential Readings,* ed. D. Ingram and J. Simon-Ingram, 69–83. New York: Paragon House.

Adorno, Theodor W., and Max Horkheimer. 1979. *Dialectic of Enlightenment,* trans. J. Cumming. London: Verso. First published in German in 1944.

Akin, O. 1978. How do architects design? In *Artificial Intelligence and Pattern Recognition in Computer-Aided Design,* ed. J.-C. Latombe, 65–119. Amsterdam: North Holland.

Alexander, Christopher. 1964. *Notes on the Synthesis of Form.* Cambridge, Mass.: Harvard University Press.

———. 1975. *Oregon Experiment.* New York: Oxford University Press.

———. 1977. *A Pattern Language.* London: Oxford University Press.

———. 1988. A city is not a tree. In *Design after Modernism,* ed. John Thackara, 67–84. London: Thames and Hudson.

Allen, Reginald E. 1966. *Greek Philosophy: Thales to Aristotle.* New York: Free Press.

Argyros, Alex. 1990. Narratives of the future: Heidegger and Derrida on technology. *New Orleans Review* 17 (2): 53–58.

Aronowitz, S., and H. Giroux. 1985. *Education under Siege: The Conservative, Liberal, and Radical Debate over Schooling.* South Hadley, Mass.: Bergin and Garvey.

Aspray, William. 1990. *Computing before Computers.* Ames, Iowa: Iowa State University Press.

Ayer, A. J. 1976. *The Central Questions of Philosophy.* Harmondsworth, Middlesex: Pelican.

References

————. 1990. *Language, Truth and Logic.* London: Penguin. First published in 1936.

Bachelard, Gaston. 1964. *The Poetics of Space,* trans. Etienne Gilson. Boston: Beacon Press. First published in French in 1958.

Bajura, M., H. Fuchs, and R. Ohbuchi. 1992. Merging virtual objects with the real world: Seeing ultrasound imagery within the patient. *Proc. Computer Graphics (Siggraph '92)* 26 (2): 203–10.

Barker, J., and R. N. Tucker. 1990. *The Interactive Learning Revolution: Multimedia in Education and Training.* London: Kogan Page.

Barnsley, Michael F. 1988. *Fractals Everywhere.* Boston: Academic Press.

Barr, Avron, and E. A. Feigenbaum, eds. 1981. *The Handbook of Artificial Intelligence.* Vol. 1. Los Angeles: William Kaufmann.

Bartky, Sandra Lee. 1969. Heidegger's philosophy of art. *British Journal of Aesthetics* 9:353–71.

Basalla, George. 1988. *The Evolution of Technology.* Cambridge, England: Cambridge University Press.

Baudrillard, Jean. 1988. *Revenge of the Crystal: Selected Writings on the Modern Object and Its Destiny, 1968–1983,* trans. Paul Foss and Julian Pefanis. Leichhardt, NSW, Australia: Pluto Press.

————. 1988. Simulacra and simulations, in *Jean Baudrillard: Selected Writings,* 166–84. Stanford, Calif.: Stanford University Press.

Baum, D. R., S. Mann, K. P. Smith, and J. M. Winget. 1991. Making radiosity usable: Automatic preprocessing and meshing techniques for the generation of accurate radiosity solutions. *Proc. Computer Graphics (Siggraph '91)* 25 (4): 51–60.

Bell, G., and C. Mead. 1992. How things really work: Two inventors on innovation. *Industry Leaders in Computer Science.* Videotape series. Stanford, Calif.: University Video Communications, Apple Computers.

Benedikt, Michael. 1991. Introduction. In *Cyberspace: First Steps,* ed. Michael Benedikt, 2–25. Cambridge, Mass.: MIT Press.

Benjamin, Walter. 1969. The work of art in the age of mechanical reproduction. In *Illumination,* 217–51. New York: Schocken. First published in the 1920s.

Berman, Bruce. 1989. The computer metaphor: Bureaucratizing the mind. *Science as Culture* 7:7–42.

Bernstein, Richard J. 1971. *Praxis and Action.* Philadelphia: University of Pennsylvania Press.

————. 1983. *Beyond Objectivism and Relativism.* Oxford: Basil Blackwell.

————. 1991. *The New Constellation: The Ethical-Political Horizon of Modernity/Postmodernity.* Cambridge: Polity.

References

———. 1991. Serious play: The ethical-political horizon of Derrida. In *The New Constellation: The Ethical-Political Horizon of Modernity/Postmodernity*, 172–98. Cambridge: Polity.

Bertalanffy, Ludwig von. 1956. General system theory. *General Systems, Yearbook of the Society for the Advancement of General System Theory*, ed. Ludwig von Bertalanffy and Anatol Rapaport. 1:1–10.

Black, Max. 1962. *Models and Metaphors*. Ithaca, N. Y.: Cornell University Press.

———. 1979. More about metaphor. In *Metaphor and Thought*, ed. A. Ortony, 19–43. Cambridge, England: Cambridge University Press.

Bloom, Allan. 1987. *The Closing of the American Mind*. New York: Simon and Schuster.

Boden, Margaret. 1977. *Artificial Intelligence and Natural Man*. Brighton, Sussex: Harvester.

———. 1990. *The Philosophy of Artificial Intelligence*. Oxford: Oxford University Press.

Bohm, David, and David Peat. 1989. *Science, Order and Creativity*. London: Routledge.

Borgman, Albert. 1984. *Technology and the Character of Contemporary Life: A Philosophical Inquiry*. Chicago: University of Chicago Press.

———. 1987. The question of Heidegger and technology: A critical review of the literature. *Philosophy Today* 31 (2/4): 97–194.

Bradie, Michael. 1984. The metaphorical character of science. *Philosophia Naturalis* 21:229–43.

Brakel, J. van, and J. P. M. Geurts. 1988. Pragmatic identity of meaning and metaphor. *International Studies in the Philosophy of Science* 2 (2): 205–26.

Brand, S. 1987. *Media Lab: Inventing the Future at MIT*. New York: Viking.

Brandom, R. 1992. Heidegger's categories in *Being and Time*. In *Heidegger: A Critical Reader*, ed. H. L. Dreyfus and H. Hall, 45–64. Oxford: Blackwell.

Broadbent, Geoffrey. 1988. *Design in Architecture: Architecture and the Human Sciences*. London: David Fulton.

Campbell, Norman Robert. 1957. *Foundations of Science: The Philosophy of Theory and Experiment*. New York: Dover.

Caputo, John D. 1985. From the primordiality of absence to the absence of primordiality: Heidegger's critique of Derrida. In *Hermeneutics and Deconstruction*, ed. Hugh J. Silverman and Don Ihde, 191–200. Albany, N. Y.: SUNY Press.

———. 1986. *The Mystical Element in Heidegger's Thought*. New York: Fordham University Press. First published in 1978.

———. 1987. *Radical Hermeneutics: Repetition, Deconstruction, and the Hermeneutical Project*. Bloomington: Indiana University Press.

————. 1993. *Demythologizing Heidegger.* Bloomington: Indiana University Press.

Carey, James W. 1989. *Communication as Culture: Essays on Media and Society.* London: Routledge.

Carpenter, Edmund, and M. McLuhan, eds. 1960. *Explorations in Communication.* Boston: Beacon Press.

Carter, Kathleen. 1992. Computer-aided design: Back to the drawing board. Working paper. EuroPARC, Rank Xerox, Cambridge, England.

Casenave, Gerald. 1982. Heidegger and metaphor. *Philosophy Today* 26 (2/4): 140–47.

Castells, Manuel. 1989. *The Informational City: Information Technology, Economic Restructuring and the Urban-Regional Process.* Oxford: Basil Blackwell.

Charles, Prince of Wales. 1989. *A Vision of Britain: A Personal View of Architecture.* London: Doubleday.

Churchman, C. West. 1967. Wicked problems. *Management Science* 4 (14): B-141 and B-142.

————. 1968. *The Systems Approach.* New York: Dell.

Clark, Andy. 1989. *Microcognition: Philosophy, Cognitive Science, and Parallel Distributed Processing.* Cambridge, Mass.: MIT Press.

Closkin, William F., and C. S. Mellish. 1981. *Programming in Prolog.* Berlin: Springer Verlag.

Cohen, Daniel I. A. 1986. *Introduction to Computer Theory.* New York: John Wiley.

Cohon, J. L. 1978. *Multiobjective Programming and Planning.* New York: Academic Press.

Cooper, D., and M. Clancy. 1985. *Oh! Pascal.* New York: Norton.

Cooper, David E. 1986. *Metaphor.* Oxford: Basil Blackwell.

Copleston, Frederick. 1985. *A History of Philosophy.* Vol. 4, *Descartes to Leibniz.* New York: Image Books.

Cornford, Francis M. 1945. *The Republic of Plato.* London: Oxford University Press.

Coyne, Richard D. 1988. *Logic Models of Design.* London: Pitman.

————. 1992. The role of metaphor in understanding computers in design. *Proc. Mission, Method, Madness.* ed. K. M. Kensek and D. Noble, 3–11. Los Angeles: Association for Computer-Aided Design in Architecture, University of Southern California.

Coyne, Richard D., S. McLaughlin, and S. Newton. 1995. Information technology and praxis: A survey of computers in design practice, *Environment and Planning B* (to appear).

Coyne, Richard D., and S. Newton. 1992. Metaphors, computers and architectural education. *Proc. ECAADE '92*, 307–18. Barcelona: Education in Computer Aided Architectural Design in Europe, Escola Técnica Superior d'Arquitectura.

Coyne, Richard D., S. Newton, and F. Sudweeks. 1993. A connectionist view of creative design reasoning. In *Modeling Creativity and Knowledge-Based Creative Design*. ed. J. S. Gero and M. L. Maher, 177–209. Hillsdale, N. J.: Lawrence Erlbaum.

Coyne, Richard D., M. A. Rosenman, A. D. Radford, M. Balachandran, and J. S. Gero. 1990. *Knowledge-Based Design Systems*. Reading, Mass.: Addison Wesley.

Coyne, Richard D., and A. B. Snodgrass. 1993. Cooperation and individualism in design. *Environment and Planning B: Planning and Design* 20:163–74.

Crowell, Steven. 1990. Text and technology. *Man and World* 23:419–40.

Culler, Jonathan. 1985. *On Deconstruction: Theory and Criticism after Structuralism*. London: Routledge.

Cunningham, Andrew, and N. Jardine, eds. 1990. *Romanticism and the Sciences*. Cambridge: Cambridge University Press.

Davidson, C. 1993. The man who made computers personal. *New Scientist* (June): 32–35.

Davidson, Donald. 1979. What metaphors mean. In *On Metaphor,* ed. Sheldon Sacks, 29–45. Chicago: University of Chicago Press.

Davies, Paul. 1985. *Superforce: The Search for the Grand Unified Theory of Nature*. London: Unwin.

de Kleer, Johan. 1986. An assumption-based truth maintenance system. *Artificial Intelligence* 28 (2): 127–62.

Deering, M. 1992. High resolution virtual reality. *Proc. Computer Graphics (Siggraph '92)* 26 (2): 195–202.

Deleuze, Gilles. 1993. *The Deleuze Reader,* ed. Constantin V. Boundas. New York: Columbia University Press.

Derrida, Jacques. 1976. *Of Grammatology,* trans. Gayatri Chakravorty Spivak. Baltimore: Johns Hopkins University Press.

———. 1977. Fors. *The Georgia Review* 31:64–116.

———. 1978. *Spurs: Nietzsche's Styles,* trans. Stefano Agosti. Chicago: University of Chicago Press.

———. 1978. Structure, sign and play in the discourse of the human sciences. *Writing and Difference,* trans. Alan Bass, 278–93. Chicago: University of Chicago Press.

———. 1981. *Positions,* trans. Alan Bass. London: Athlone Press.

————. 1982. Différance. In *Margins of Philosophy,* trans. Alan Bass, 1–27. Chicago: University of Chicago Press.

————. 1982. *Ousia* and *Gramme:* Note on a note from *Being and Time.* In *Margins of Philosophy,* trans. Alan Bass, 29–67. Chicago: University of Chicago Press.

————. 1982. The supplement of copula: Philosophy before linguistics. In *Margins of Philosophy,* trans. Alan Bass, 175–205. Chicago: University of Chicago Press.

————. 1982. White mythology: Metaphor in the text of philosophy, In *Margins of Philosophy,* trans. Alan Bass, 207–71. Chicago: University of Chicago Press.

————. 1983. The principle of reason: The university in the eyes of its pupils. *Diacritics* 13:3–20.

————. 1985. Racism's last word, trans. Peggy Kamuf. *Critical Inquiry.* 12:290–99.

————. 1986. *Glas,* trans. John P. Leavey and Richard Rand. Lincoln, Nebraska: University of Nebraska Press.

————. 1987. *Geschlecht* II: Heidegger's hand, trans. John P. Leavey. *Deconstruction and Philosophy: The Texts of Jacques Derrida,* ed. John Sallis, 161–96. Chicago: University of Chicago Press.

————. 1988. *Limited Inc,* trans. Samuel Weber, ed. Gerald Graff. Evanston, Ill.: Northwestern University Press.

————. 1989. Three questions to Hans-Georg Gadamer. In *Dialogue and Deconstruction: The Gadamer-Derrida Encounter,* ed. D. P. Michelfelder and R. E. Palmer, 52–54. Albany, N. Y.: SUNY Press.

Descartes, René. 1968. *Discourse on Method and the Meditations,* trans. F. E. Sutcliffe, Harmondsworth, Middlesex: Penguin.

Dewey, John. 1916. *Democracy and Education: An Introduction to the Philosophy of Education.* New York: Free Press.

————. 1916. *Essays in Experimental Logic.* Chicago: University of Chicago Press.

————. 1958. *Experience and Nature.* New York: Dover.

————. 1968. *Philosophy and Civilization.* Gloucester, Mass.: Peter Smith. First published in 1931.

————. 1980. *Art as Experience.* New York: Wideview Perigee.

————. 1984. The public and its problems. In *John Dewey: The Later Works, 1925–1953.* Vol. 2, *1925–1927,* ed. J. A. Boydston, 235–372. Carbondale: Southern Illinois University.

————. 1991. *The Public and Its Problems.* Athens: Ohio University Press. First published in 1927.

References

Dews, Peter. 1987. *Logics of Disintegration: Post-structuralist Thought and the Claims of Critical Theory.* London: Verso.

Dietrich, E. 1990. Programs in the search for intelligent machines: The mistaken foundations of AI. In *The Foundations of Artificial Intelligence: A Source Book,* ed. D. Partridge and Y. Wilks, 223–33. Cambridge: Cambridge University Press.

Dommermuth, W. P. 1974. How does the medium affect the message? *Journalism Quarterly* 51(3): 441–47.

Dreyfus, Hubert L. 1972. *What Computers Can't Do: The Limits of Artificial Intelligence.* New York: Harper and Row.

————. 1990. *Being-in-the-World: A Commentary on Heidegger's "Being and Time," Division I.* Cambridge, Mass.: MIT Press.

————. 1989. On the ordering of things: Being and power in Heidegger and Foucault. *The Southern Journal of Philosophy* 28 (supplement): 83–96.

————. 1992. *What Computers Still Can't Do: A Critique of Artificial Reason.* Cambridge, Mass.: MIT Press. First published in 1972 as *What Computers Can't Do.*

Dreyfus, Hubert L. and Stuart E. Dreyfus. 1985. *Mind Over Machine,* New York: Macmillan/The Free Press.

Dreyfus, Hubert L., and H. Hall. 1992. *Heidegger: A Critical Reader.* Oxford: Blackwell.

Dreyfus, Hubert L., and P. Rabinow, eds. 1982. *Michel Foucault: Beyond Structuralism and Hermeneutics.* New York: Harvester Press.

Duffy, Francis. 1992. *The Changing Workplace.* London: Phaidon.

Duhem, Pierre. 1954. *The Aim and Structure of Physical Theory,* trans. Philip P. Weiner. Princeton, N. J.: Princeton University Press. First published in French in 1914.

Eberts, R. E., and C. G. Eberts. 1989. Four approaches to human computer interaction. In *Intelligent Interfaces: Theory, Research and Design,* ed. P. A. Hancock and M. H. Chignell, 69–127. Amsterdam: Elsevier.

Eco, Umberto. 1984. *Semiotics and the Philosophy of Language.* London: Macmillan.

Edwards, Betty. 1979. *Drawing on the Right Side of the Brain.* Los Angeles: J. P. Tarcher.

Eisenberg, A. 1992. Metaphor in the language of science. *Scientific American* (May): 95.

Erickson, T. D. 1990. Working with interface metaphors. In *The Art of Human-Computer Interface Design,* ed. B. Laurel, 65–73. Reading, Mass.: Addison Wesley.

Falzon, P., ed. 1990. *Cognitive Ergonomics: Understanding, Learning and Designing Human-Computer Interaction.* London: Academic Press.

Feenberg, A. 1991. *Critical Theory of Technology.* New York: Oxford University Press.

References

Feibleman, James K. 1970. *An Introduction to the Philosophy of Charles S. Peirce.* Cambridge, Mass.: MIT Press.

Fell, J. P. 1992. The familiar and the strange: On the limits of praxis in the earlier Heidegger. In *Heidegger: A Critical Reader,* ed. H. L. Dreyfus and H. Hall, 65–80. Oxford: Blackwell.

Ferguson, M. 1991. Marshall McLuhan revisited: The 1960s zeitgeist victim or pioneer postmodernist. *Media, Culture and Society* 13:71–90.

Fish, Stanley. 1980. *Is There a Text in This Class?: The Authority of Interpretive Communities.* Cambridge, Mass.: Harvard University Press.

———. 1989. *Doing What Comes Naturally: Change, Rhetoric and the Practice of Theory in Literary and Legal Studies.* Durham, S. C.: Duke University Press.

Fisher, S. S. 1991. Virtual environments: Personal simulations and telepresence. In *Virtual Reality: Theory, Practice and Promise,* ed. S. K. Helsel and J. P. Roth, 101–10. Westport, Conn.: Meckler.

Fiske, John. 1990. *Introduction to Communication Studies.* London: Routledge.

Foley, James D., and A. Van Dam. 1983. *Fundamentals of Interactive Computer Graphics.* Reading, Mass.: Addison Wesley.

Foley, James D., A. Van Dam, S. K. Feiner, and J. F. Hughes. 1990. *Fundamentals of Interactive Computer Graphics.* 2d ed. Reading, Mass.: Addison Wesley.

Forester, Tom. 1989. *Computers in the Human Context: Information Technology, Productivity and People.* Oxford: Basil Blackwell.

Foucault, Michel. 1977. *Discipline and Punish: The Birth of the Prison.* London: Penguin.

———. 1982. Afterword: The subject and power. In *Michel Foucault: Beyond Structuralism and Hermeneutics,* ed. H. L. Dreyfus and P. Rabinow, 208–26. New York: Harvester.

———. 1984. *The Foucault Reader: An Introduction to Foucault's Thought,* ed. P. Rabinow. London: Penguin.

Fraassen, Bas C. van. 1970. *An Introduction to the Philosophy of Time and Space.* New York: Random House.

Freire, Paulo. 1972. *Pedagogy of the Oppressed,* trans. M. B. Ramos. New York: Herder and Herder.

Fry, Tony. 1994. *Remakings: Ecology, Design, Philosophy.* Sydney: Envirobook.

Fry, Tony, ed. 1993. *RUA TV? Heidegger and the Televisual.* Sydney: Power Publications, University of Sydney.

Furst, Lillian R. 1969. *Romanticism in Perspective: A Comparative Study of Aspects of the Romantic Movements in England, France and Germany.* London: Macmillan.

References

Gadamer, Hans-Georg. 1975. Hermeneutics and social science. *Cultural Hermeneutics* 2:307–16.

———. 1975. *Truth and Method*. London: Sheed Ward.

———. 1976. *Philosophical Hermeneutics*, trans. D. E. Linge. Berkeley: University of California Press.

———. 1989. Reply to Jacques Derrida. In *Dialogue and Deconstruction: The Gadamer-Derrida Encounter*, ed. D. P. Michelfelder and R. E. Palmer, 52–54. Albany, N. Y.: SUNY Press.

———. 1990. Reply to my critics. In *The Hermeneutic Tradition: From Ast to Ricoeur*, ed. G. L. Ormiston and A. D. Schrift, 273–97. Albany, N. Y.: SUNY Press.

Galegher, Jolene, Robert E. Kraut, and Carmen Egido. 1990. *Intellectual Teamwork: Social and Technological Foundations of Cooperative Work*. Hillsdale, N. J.: Lawrence Erlbaum.

Gallagher, Shaun. 1991. *Hermeneutics and Education*. Albany, N. Y.: SUNY Press.

Gambino, R. 1972. McLuhanism: A massage that muddles. *The Midwest Quarterly* 14 (1): 53–62.

Gardiner, M. M., and B. Christie. 1987. *Applying Cognitive Psychology to User-Interface Design*. Chichester, West Sussex: Wiley.

Gardner, Howard. 1976. *The Quest for Mind: Piaget, Lévi-Strauss and the Structuralist Movement*. London: Quartet Books.

Gentner, Dedre, B. Falkenhainer, and J. Skorstad. 1988. Viewing metaphor as analogy. In *Analogical Reasoning: Perspectives of Artificial Intelligence, Cognitive Science, and Philosophy*, ed. David H. Helman, 171–77. Dordrecht, The Netherlands: Kluwer Academic Publishers.

Gibson, James J. 1950. *The Perception of the Visual World*. Boston: Houghton Mifflin.

———. 1979. *The Ecological Approach to Visual Perception*. Boston: Houghton Mifflin.

Gibson, William. 1984. *Neuromancer*. New York: Ace Books.

Giddens, Anthony. 1990. *The Consequences of Modernity*. Cambridge: Polity Press.

Glassner, A. S., ed. 1989. *An Introduction to Ray Tracing*. London: Academic Press.

Gleick, James. 1987. *Chaos: Making a New Science*. London: Cardinal.

Globus, Gordon G. 1991. Deconstructing the Chinese room. *The Journal of Mind and Behaviour* 12 (3): 377–92.

Goldberg, A., and D. Robson. 1983. *SMALLTALK-80 The Language and Its Implementation*. Reading, Mass.: Addison-Wesley.

Goodman, Nelson. 1968. *Languages of Art.* Indianapolis: Bobbs-Merrill.

———. 1978. *Ways of Worldmaking.* Hassocks, England: Harvester Press.

Grossberg, L. 1979. Interpreting the "crisis" of culture in communication theory. *Journal of Communication* 29 (1): 56–68.

Habermas, Jürgen. 1987. *The Philosophical Discourse of Modernity: Twelve Lectures,* trans. F. G. Lawrence. Cambridge: Polity Press.

———. 1990. The hermeneutic claim to universality. In *The Hermeneutic Tradition: From Ast to Ricoeur,* ed. G. L. Ormiston and A. D. Schrift, 245–72. Albany, N. Y.: SUNY Press.

———. 1990. A review of Gadamer's *Truth and Method.* In *The Hermeneutic Tradition: From Ast to Ricoeur,* ed. G. L. Ormiston and A. D. Schrift, 213–44. Albany, N. Y.: SUNY Press.

Haeberli, P. 1990. Paint by numbers: Abstract image representations. *Proc. Computer Graphics (Siggraph '90)* 24 (4): 207–14.

Hagen, M. A. 1986. *Varieties of Realism: Geometries of Representational Art.* Cambridge: Cambridge University Press.

Hall, R. L. 1967. Heidegger and the space of art. *Journal of Existentialism* 8 (29): 91–108.

Hattinger, G., M. Russel, C. Schöpf, and P. Weibel, eds. 1990. *Ars Electronica 1990.* Vol. 2, Virtuelle Welten. Linz, Austria: Veritas-Verlag Linz.

Haugeland, J. 1992. Dasein's disclosedness. In *Heidegger: A Critical Reader,* ed. H. L. Dreyfus and H. Hall, 27–44. Oxford: Blackwell.

Havelock, Eric A. 1986. *The Muse Learns to Write: Reflections on Orality and Literacy from Antiquity to the Present.* New Haven, Conn.: Yale University Press.

Hawkes, Terence. 1977. *Structuralism and Semiotics.* London: Methuen.

Hawking, Stephen W. 1988. *A Brief History of Time: From the Big Bang to Black Holes.* New York: Bantam.

Hayes-Roth, Barbara, and F. Hayes-Roth. 1979. A cognitive model of planning. *Cognitive Science* 3 (4): 275–309.

Hayes-Roth, Frederick, D. A. Waterman, and D. B. Lenat, eds. 1983. *Building Expert Systems.* Reading, Mass.: Addison Wesley.

Heath, Tom. 1984. *Method in Architecture.* Chichester, West Sussex: Wiley.

Hegel, George W. F. 1969. *Hegel's Science of Logic,* trans. A. V. Miller, Atlantic Highlands, New Jersey: Humanities Press. First published in German in 1812.

Heidegger, Martin. 1962. *Being and Time,* trans. J. Macquarrie and E. Robinson. London: SCM Press. First published as *Zein und Zeit* in 1927.

References

———. 1962. *Die Technik und die Kehre*. Pfullingen, Germany: Verlag Günther Neske (translated as The turning, see below).

———. 1966. *Discourse on Thinking*, trans. J. M. Anderson and E. H. Freund. New York: Harper and Row.

———. 1968. *What Is Called Thinking?* trans. J. G. Gray and F. T. Wieck. New York: Harper and Row.

———. 1969. *Identity and Difference*, trans J. Stambaugh. New York: Harper and Row.

———. 1971. Building, dwelling, thinking. In *Poetry, Language, Thought*, trans. Albert Hofstadter, 143–61. New York: Harper and Row.

———. 1971. Letter on humanism, trans. E. Lohner. In *Philosophy in the Twentieth Century*, ed. W. Barrett and H. Aiken, 192–224. Vol. 3, *Contemporary European Thought*. New York: Harper and Row.

———. 1971. The origin of the work of art. In *Poetry, Language, Thought*, by M. Heidegger, trans. A. Hofstadter, 15–87. New York: Harper and Row.

———. 1971. The thing. In *Poetry, Language, Thought*, by M. Heidegger, trans. A. Hofstadter, 165–86. New York: Harper and Row.

———. 1971. The turning. *Research in Phenomenology*, trans. K. R. Maly, 1:3–16.

———. 1973. Art and space, trans. Charles H. Seibert. *Man and World* 6 (1): 3–8.

———. 1974. The principle of ground, trans. K. Hoeller. *Man and World* 7:207–22.

———. 1977. *The Question concerning Technology and Other Essays*, trans. W. Lovitt. New York: Harper and Row.

———. 1984. *Early Greek Thinking: The Dawn of Western Philosophy*, trans. D. F. Krell and F. A. Capuzzi. San Francisco: Harper and Row. Collection of essays first published in German between 1950 and 1954.

———. 1991. *The Principle of Reason*, trans. Reginald Lilly, Bloomington: Indiana University Press. First published in German in 1957.

———. 1992. *History of the Concept of Time*, trans. Theodore Kisiel. Bloomington: Indiana University Press. First published in German in 1979.

———. 1992. *Parmenides*, trans. Andre Schuwer and Richard Rojcewicz. Bloomington: Indiana University Press.

———. 1993. *Basic Writings*, ed. David Farrell Krell. London: Routledge.

———. 1993. Letter on humanism. In *Basic Writings: Martin Heidegger*, ed. David Farrel Krell, 217–65. London: Routledge.

———. 1993. What calls for thinking? In *Basic Writings: Martin Heidegger*, ed. David

References

Farrel Krell, 369–91. London: Routledge. Extracts from What is Called Thinking first published in 1954 as Was heisst Denken?

Heim, Michael. 1986. Humanistic discussion and the online conference. *Philosophy Today* 30:278–88.

———. 1987. *Electric Language: A Philosophical Study of Word Processing.* New Haven, Conn.: Yale University Press.

———. 1991. The metaphysics of virtual reality. In *Virtual Reality: Theory, Practice and Promise,* ed. S. K. Helsel and J. P. Roth, 27–34. Westport, Conn.: Meckler.

———. 1992. The computer as component: Heidegger and McLuhan. *Philosophy and Literature* 16 (2): 304–19.

———. 1993. *The Metaphysics of Virtual Reality.* New York: Oxford University Press.

Helsel, S. K, and J. P. Roth, eds. 1991. *Virtual Reality: Theory, Practice and Promise.* Westport, Conn.: Meckler.

Hesse, Mary. 1970. *Models and Analogies in Science.* Notre Dame, Ind.: University of Notre Dame Press.

———. 1980. The explanatory function of metaphor. In *Revolutions and Reconstructions in the Philosophy of Science,* by Mary Hesse, 111–24. Brighton, Sussex: Harvester.

———. 1987. Unfamiliar noises—tropical talk: The myth of the literal. *Journal of the Aristotelian Society* (July): 297–311.

Hickman, Larry A. 1992. *John Dewey's Pragmatic Technology.* Bloomington: Indiana University Press.

Hiltz, Starr Roxanne, and M. Turoff. 1993. *The Network Nation: Human Communication via Computer.* Cambridge, Mass.: MIT Press.

Hirsch, Eric D. 1987. *Cultural Literacy: What Every American Needs to Know.* Boston: Houghton Mifflin.

Hodges, Andrew. 1983. *Alan Turing: The Enigma of Intelligence.* London: Counterpoint/Unwin.

Hospers, John. 1967. *An Introduction to Philosophical Analysis.* London: Routledge and Kegan Paul.

Houlgate, Stephen. 1991. *Freedom, Truth and History: An Introduction to Hegel's Philosophy.* London: Routledge.

Hybs, Ivan. 1995. Beyond the interface. *Leonardo,* (to appear).

Ihde, Don. 1991. *Instrumental Realism: The Interface between Philosophy of Science and Philosophy of Technology.* Bloomington: Indiana University Press.

———. 1993. *Philosophy of Technology: An Introduction.* New York: Paragon.

References

Illich, Ivan. 1971. *Deschooling Society.* London: Calder and Boyars.

Illich, Ivan, and B. Sanders. 1988. *ABC: The Alphabetization of the Popular Mind.* San Franscisco: North Point Press.

Ingram, D., and J. Simon-Ingram, eds. 1992. *Critical Theory: The Essential Readings.* New York: Paragon House.

James, William. 1978. *Pragmatism, a New Name for Some Old Ways of Thinking.* Cambridge, Mass.: Harvard University Press.

Jantsche, E. 1980. *The Self-Organizing Universe.* Oxford: Pergamon Press.

Jay, Martin. 1984. *Adorno.* Cambridge, Mass.: Harvard University Press.

Johnson, Mark. 1987. *The Body in the Mind: The Bodily Basis of Meaning, Imagination, and Reason.* Chicago: University of Chicago Press.

Johnson-Laird, Philip N. 1988. *The Computer and the Mind: An Introduction to Cognitive Science.* London: Fontana.

Jones, Beverly. 1989. Computer imagery: Imitation and representation of realities. *Leonardo,* 31–38. Computer art in context supplemental issue. Oxford: Pergamon Press.

Jones, J. Christopher. 1970. *Design Methods: Seeds of Human Futures.* London: Wiley.

Kaelin, E. F. 1987. *Heidegger's "Being and Time": A Reading for Readers.* Tallahassee: Florida State University Press.

Kay, Alan. 1984. Computer software. *Scientific American* 251 (3): 41–47.

———. 1987. Doing with images makes symbols: Communicating with computers. *Industry Leaders in Computer Science.* Videotape series. Stanford, Calif.: Apple Computers, University Video Communications.

———. 1990. User interface: A personal view. In *The Art of Human-Computer Interface Design,* ed. B. Laurel, 191–207. Reading, Mass.: Addison-Wesley.

———. 1991. Computers, networks and education. *Scientific American* (September): 100–107.

Kockelmans, Joseph J. 1985. *Heidegger on Art and Art Works.* Dordrecht, The Netherlands: Martinus Nijhoff.

Kockelmans, Joseph J., ed. 1986. *A Companion to Martin Heidegger's "Being and Time."* Lanham, Md.: University Press of America.

Kolb, David. 1984. *Experiential Learning: Experience as the Source of Learning and Development.* Englewood Cliffs, N. J.: Prentice Hall.

Kramer, Nic J. T. A., and Jacob de Smit. 1977. *Systems Thinking.* Leiden, The Netherlands: Martinus Nijhoff.

References

Kroker, A. 1984. Processed world: Technology and culture in the thought of Marshall McLuhan. *Philosophy of the Social Sciences* 14:433–59.

Kuhn, Thomas. 1970. *The Structure of Scientific Revolutions.* Chicago: University of Chicago Press.

Kurtzman, Howard. 1987. Deconstruction and psychology: An introduction. *New Ideas in Psychology* 5 (1): 33–71.

———. 1987. Deconstructionist psychology and human liberation: A reply to Philip Wexler. *New Ideas in Psychology* 5 (1): 77–94.

Lakoff, George. 1987. *Women, Fire, and Dangerous Things: What Categories Reveal about the Mind.* Chicago: University of Chicago Press.

Lakoff, George, and M. Johnson. 1980. *Metaphors We Live By.* Chicago: University of Chicago Press.

Langton, C. G. 1988. Artificial life. In *Santa Fe Institute Studies in the Sciences of Complexity.* Vol. 6, *Artificial Life,* ed. C. Langton. Reading, Mass.: Addison-Wesley.

Latour, Bruno. 1987. *Science in Action.* Cambridge, Mass.: Harvard University Press.

Latour, Bruno, and S. Woolgar. 1979. *Laboratory Life: The Social Construction of Scientific Facts.* Beverly Hills, Calif.: Sage.

Laurel, Brenda. 1991. *Computers as Theatre.* Reading, Mass.: Addison Wesley.

Laurel, Brenda, ed. 1990. *The Art of Human-Computer Interface Design.* Reading, Mass.: Addison Wesley.

Leder, D. 1964. The rule of the device: Borgman's philosophy of technology. *Philosophy Today* 32 (spring): 17–29.

Lefebvre, Henri. 1991. *The Production of Space,* trans. Donald Nicholson-Smith, Oxford: Blackwell. First published in French in 1974.

Lévi-Strauss, Claud. 1977. *Structural Anthropology,* trans. C. Jacobson and B. G. Schoepf, London: Penguin.

Lloyd, Geoffrey E. R. 1966. *Polarity and Analogy: Two Types of Argumentation in Early Greek Thought.* Cambridge: Cambridge University Press.

Lucas, J. R. 1973. *A Treatise on Time and Space.* London: Methuen.

Lyotard, Jean-François. 1986. *The Postmodern Condition: A Report on Knowledge,* trans. A. Bennington and B. Massumi. Manchester: Manchester University Press.

McHarg, Ian L. 1969. *Design with Nature.* Garden City, N. Y.: Doubleday-Natural History Press.

McLaughlin, Sally. 1993. Practices and primordial understanding: Major implications of Heidegger's philosophy for computer-aided architectural design research.

References

Unpublished Ph.D. thesis. Department of Architectural and Design Science, University of Sydney, Sydney.

McLuhan, Marshall. 1962. *The Gutenberg Galaxy: The Making of Typographic Man*. Toronto: University of Toronto Press.

———. 1964. *Understanding Media: The Extensions of Man*. London: Routledge and Kegan Paul.

McLuhan, Marshall, and Q. Fiore. 1967. *The Medium is the Massage*. New York: Bantam Books.

McLuhan, Marshall, and Bruce R. Powers. 1989. *The Global Village: Transformations in World Life and Media in the Twenty-first Century*. New York: Oxford University Press.

Macro, A., and J. Buxton. 1987. *The Craft of Software Engineering*. Wokingham, England: Addison Wesley.

March, Lionel. 1976. The logic of design and the question of value. *The Architecture of Form*, ed. L. March, 1–40. Cambridge: Cambridge University Press.

Marcuse, Herbert. 1988. *One-Dimensional Man: Studies in the Ideology of Advanced Industrial Society*. London: Routledge.

Marías, Julián. 1967. *History of Philosophy*, trans. Stanley Applebaum and Clarence C. Stowbridge. New York: Dover.

Marx, G. T., and S. Sherizen. 1989. Monitoring on the job. In *Computers in the Human Context: Information Technology, Productivity and People*, ed. T. Forester. Oxford: Basil Blackwell.

Meadows, Donella H., N. L. Meadows, J. Randers, and W. W. Behrens. 1972. *The Limits of Growth, a Report for the Club of Rome's Project on the Predicament of Mankind*. London: Potomac.

Merleau-Ponty, Maurice. 1962. *Phenomenology of Perception*. London: Routledge and Kegan Paul.

Meyrowitz, Joshua. 1985. *No Sense of Place: The Impact of Electronic Media on Social Behaviour*. New York: Oxford University Press.

Minneman, Scott L. 1991. The social construction of a technical reality: Empirical studies of group engineering design practice. *Report SSL-91-22* [P91-00160]. Palo Alto, Calif.: Xerox, Palo Alto Research Centre.

Minsky, Marvin. 1987. *The Society of Mind*. London: Heineman.

———. 1991. Logical versus analogical or symbolic versus connectionist or neat versus scruffy. *AI Magazine* 12 (2): 34–51.

Mitchell, William J. 1977. *Computer-Aided Architectural Design*. New York: Van Nostrand Reinhold.

————. 1990. *The Logic of Architecture: Design, Computation, and Cognition.* Cambridge, Mass.: MIT Press.

————. 1992. Computer-aided design media: A comparative analysis. In *Computers in Architecture: Tools for Design,* ed. F. Penz, 53–62. Harlow, England: Longman.

————. 1992. *The Reconfigured Eye: Visual Truth in the Post-Photographic Era.* Cambridge, Mass.: MIT Press.

Mitchell, William J., and M. McCullough. 1992. *Digital Design Media: A Handbook for Architects, Landscape Architects, and Urban Designers.* Cambridge, Mass.: MIT Press.

Murphy, John P. 1990. *Pragmatism from Peirce to Davidson.* Boulder, Colo.: Westview Press.

Nelson, Theodor H. 1990. The right way to think about software design. In *The Art of Human-Computer Interface Design,* ed. B. Laurel, 235–43. Reading, Mass.: Addison Wesley.

Newell, Allan, and H. A. Simon. 1972. *Human Problem Solving.* Englewood Cliffs, N.J.: Prentice-Hall.

Newton, Isaac. 1952. *Opticks: or a Treatise of the Reflections, Refractions, Inflections and Colours of Light.* Book 3, part 1, 404. New York: Dover. Fourth edition first published in 1730.

Nietzsche, Friedrich. 1974. *The Complete Works of Friedrich Nietzsche.* Vol. 2, *Early Greek Philosophy and Other Essays,* ed. Oscar Levy. New York: Gordon Press.

————. 1977. *Beyond Good and Evil: Prelude to a Philosophy of the Future,* trans. Walter Kaufman. New York: Vintage Books. First published in 1886.

————. 1977. *A Nietzsche Reader,* trans. R. J. Hollingdale. London: Penguin.

Norman, Donald A. 1988. *The Psychology of Everyday Things.* New York: Basic Books.

Norris, Christopher. 1982. *Deconstruction: Theory and Practice.* London: Routledge.

Olson, Alan M. 1980. Myth, symbol, and metaphorical truth. In *Myth, Symbol, and Reality,* ed. Alan M. Olson, 99–125. Notre Dame, Ind.: University of Notre Dame Press.

Ong, Walter J. 1971. *Rhetoric, Romance, and Technology: Studies in the Interaction of Expression and Culture.* Ithaca, N. Y.: Cornell University Press.

————. 1972. *Ramus: Method, and the Decay of Dialogue from the Art of Discourse to the Art of Reason.* New York: Octagon.

————. 1982. *Orality and Literacy: the Technologizing of the Word.* London: Routledge.

Ormiston, G. L., and A. D. Schrift, eds. 1990. *The Hermeneutic Tradition: From Ast to Ricoeur.* Albany, N. Y.: SUNY Press.

References

Ortony, Andrew, ed. 1979. *Metaphor and Thought.* Cambridge: Cambridge University Press.

Peirce, Charles S. 1935. *Collected Papers of Charles Sanders Peirce.* Cambridge, Mass.: Belknap/Harvard University Press.

———. 1957. How to make our ideas clear. In *Charles S. Peirce: Essays in the Philosophy of Science,* ed. V. Tomas, 31–56. New York: Liberal Arts Press. First published in 1878.

———. 1984. Some consequences of four incapacities. In *Writings of C. S. Peirce: A Chronological Edition,* ed. E. C. Moore, 211–42. Bloomington: Indiana University Press.

Pinkard, T. 1991. The successor to metaphysics: Absolute idea and absolute spirit. *The Monist* 74 (3): 295–328.

Polanyi, Michael. 1967. *The Tacit Dimension.* London: Routledge and Kegan Paul.

Popper, Karl. 1972. *Objective Knowledge: An Evolutionary Approach.* London: Oxford University Press.

Radford, Antony D., and J. S. Gero. 1988. *Design by Optimization in Architecture, Building and Construction.* New York: Van Nostrand Reinhold.

Rafaeli, Sheizaf, and R. J. LaRose. 1993. Electronic bulletin boards and "public goods" explanations of collaborative mass media. *Communications Research* 20 (2): 277–97.

Rand, Ayn. 1972. *The Fountainhead.* London: Grafton.

Ray, Christopher. 1991. *Time, Space and Philosophy.* London: Routledge.

Redding, Paul. 1991. Hegel's logic of being and the polarities of Presocratic thought. *The Monist* 74 (3): 438–56.

Reddy, Michael. 1979. The conduit metaphor—a case of frame conflict in our language about language. In *Metaphor and Thought,* ed. Andrew Ortony, 284–324. Cambridge: Cambridge University Press.

Reisman, R. 1990. A brief introduction to the art of flight simulation. In *Ars Electronica 1990.* Vol. 2, *Virtuelle Welten,* ed. G. Hattinger, M. Russel, C. Schöpf, and P. Weibel, 159–69. Linz, Austria: Veritas-Verlag.

Relph, Edward. 1985. Geographical experiences and being-in-the-world: The phenomenological origins of geography. In *Dwelling, Place and Environment: Towards a Phenomenology of Person and World,* ed. David Seamon and Robert Mugerauer, 15–31. Dordrecht, The Netherlands: Nijhoff.

Rheingold, Howard. 1991. *Virtual Reality.* New York: Summit Books.

———. 1993. *The Virtual Community: Homesteading on the Electronic Frontier.* Reading, Mass.: Addison Wesley.

References

Richards, Ivor A. 1936. *The Philosophy of Rhetoric,* London: Oxford University Press.

Ricoeur, Paul. 1977. *The Rule of Metaphor,* trans. R. Czerny with K. McLaughlin and J. Costello. London: Routledge and Kegan Paul.

———. 1981. *Hermeneutics and the Human Sciences,* trans. J. B. Thompson. Cambridge: Cambridge University Press.

———. 1991. *The Ricoeur Reader: Reflection and Imagination,* ed. Mario J. Valdes. Hemel Hempstead: Harvester Wheatsheaf.

Rittel, Horst W. J., and M. M. Webber. 1974. Wicked Problems. In *Man-Made Futures,* ed. N. Cross, D. Elliott, and R. Roy, 272–80. London: Hutchinson.

Rockefeller, Steven C. 1991. *John Dewey: Religious Faith and Democratic Humanism.* New York: Columbia University Press.

Rorty, Richard. 1980. *Philosophy and the Mirror of Nature.* Oxford: Basil Blackwell.

———. 1982. Overcoming the tradition: Heidegger and Dewey. In *Consequences of Pragmatism (Essays: 1972–1980),* 37–59. Minneapolis: University of Minnesota Press.

———. 1987. Unfamiliar noises: Hesse and Davidson on Metaphor. *Journal of the Aristotelian Society* (July): 283–96.

———. 1989. *Contingency, Irony and Solidarity.* Cambridge: Cambridge University Press.

———. 1991. Philosophy as science, as metaphor, and as politics. In *Essays on Heidegger and Others: Philosophical Papers,* by Richard Rorty, 9–26. Vol. 2. Cambridge: Cambridge University Press.

———. 1992. Heidegger, contingency and pragmatism. In *Heidegger: A Critical Reader,* ed. H. Dreyfus and H. Hall, 209–30. Cambridge, Mass.: Basil Blackwell.

Rosch, Eleanor. 1981. Categorization of natural objects. *Annual Review of Psychology* 32:89–115.

Ross, W. D., ed. 1924. *The Works of Aristotle.* Vol. 11. Oxford: Clarendon Press.

Roszak, Theodore. 1986. *The Cult of Information: The Folklore of Computers and the True Art of Thinking.* New York: Pantheon.

Rothbart, Daniel. 1984. The semantics of metaphor and the structure of science. *Philosophy of Science* 51:595–615.

Rumelhart, David E., P. Smolensky, J. L. McClelland, and G. E. Hinton. 1987. Schemata and sequential thought processes in PDP models. In *Parallel Distributed Processing: Explorations in the Microstructure of Cognition,* ed. D. E. Rumelhart and J. L. McClelland, 7–57. Vol.1, *Foundations.* Cambridge, Mass.: MIT Press.

Ryle, Gilbert. 1963. *The Concept of Mind.* Harmondsworth, Middlesex: Penguin.

Saito, T., and T. Takahashi. 1990. Comprehensible rendering of three-dimensional shapes. *Proc. Computer Graphics (Siggraph '90)* 24 (4): 197–206.

Sallis, John. 1986. The origins of Heidegger's thought. In *A Companion to Martin Heidegger's "Being and Time,"* ed. Joseph J. Kockelmans, 89–103. Lanham, Md.: University Press of America.

Salner, Marcia. 1988. Introduction: Metaphor and human understanding. *Saybrook Review* 7:1–19.

Saussure, Ferdinand de. 1983. *Course in General Linguistics,* trans. Roy Harris. London: Duckworth. First published as *Cours de Linguistique Générale* in 1916 (Paris: Payot).

Schank, Roger. 1990. What is AI anyway? In *The Foundations of Artificial Intelligence: A Source Book,* ed. D. Partridge and Y. Wilks, 3–13. Cambridge: Cambridge University Press.

———. 1982. *Dynamic Memory: A Theory of Reminding and Learning in Computers and People.* Cambridge: Cambridge University Press.

Schank, Roger C. and R. Abelson. 1977. *Scripts, Plans, Goals and Understanding.* Hillsdale, N. J.: Lawrence Erlbaum.

Schofield, Simon. 1993. A general approach to interpretive (non-photorealistic) rendering. Unpublished Ph.D. thesis. University of Middlesex, Cat Hill, Hertfordshire.

Schön, Donald. 1963. *Displacement of Concepts.* London: Tavistock.

———. 1979. Generative metaphor: A perspective on problem-setting in social policy. In *Metaphor and Thought,* ed. Andrew Ortony, 254–83. Cambridge: Cambridge University Press.

———. 1982. *The Reflective Practitioner.* Cambridge, Mass.: MIT Press.

Schumacher, Ernst F. 1974. *Small Is Beautiful: A Study of Economics as if People Mattered.* London: Abacus.

Scruton, Roger. 1983. Photography and representation. In *The Aesthetic Understanding,* 102–26. Manchester: Carcanet New Press.

Seamon, David, and Robert Mugerauer. 1985. *Dwelling, Place and Environment: Towards a Phenomenology of Person and World.* Dordrecht, The Netherlands: Nijhoff.

Sefler, George F. 1973. Heidegger's philosophy of space. *Philosophy Today* 17:246–59.

Shannon, Claud, and W. Weaver. 1971. *The Mathematical Theory of Communication.* Urbana: University of Illinois Press.

Sheehan, Thomas. 1985. Derrida and Heidegger. In *Hermeneutics and Deconstruction,* ed. Hugh J. Silverman and Don Ihde, 201–18. Albany, N. Y.: SUNY Press.

Shortliffe, Edward H., and B. G. Buchanan. 1975. A model of inexact reasoning in medicine. *Mathematical Biosciences* 23:351–79.

Shriver, D. W. 1972. Man and his machines: Four angles of vision. *Technology and Culture* 13 (1): 531–55.

Simon, Herbert. 1969. *The Sciences of the Artificial.* Cambridge, Mass.: MIT Press.

Snodgrass, Adrian B. 1990. *Architecture, Time and Eternity,* Satapitika Series, No. 162, New Delhi, India: Aditya.

———. 1991. Asian studies and the fusion of horizons. *Proc. Gadamer, Action and Reason,* 35–42. Faculty of Architecture, University of Sydney, Sydney.

———. 1991. Design evaluation. Working paper. Faculty of Architecture, University of Sydney, Sydney.

———. 1993. Hermeneutics, the university and the letting-be of technology. *Proc. Universities as Interpretive Communities,* 75–94. University of Sydney, Sydney.

Snodgrass, Adrian B., and R. D. Coyne. 1992. Models, metaphors and the hermeneutics of designing. *Design Issues* 9 (1): 56–74.

Sontag, Susan. 1978. *On Photography.* London: Allen Lane.

Spivak, Gayatri Chakravorty. 1976. Translator's preface. In *Of Grammatology,* by Jacques Derrida, ix–lxxxvii. Baltimore, Md.: Johns Hopkins University Press.

Spring, M. B. 1991. Informating with virtual reality. In *Virtual Reality: Theory, Practice and Promise,* ed. S. K. Helsel and J. P. Roth, 3–17. Westport, Conn.: Meckler.

Stanfill, C., and D. Waltz. 1986. Toward memory-based reasoning. *Communications of the ACM* 29 (12): 1213–28.

Steadman, Philip. 1979. *The Evolution of Designs: Biological Analogy in Architecture and the Applied Arts.* Cambridge: Cambridge University Press.

Stefik, Mark J. 1987. Book reviews: Understanding computers and cognition—a new foundation for design. Four reviews and a response. *Artificial Intelligence* 31:213–61.

Sternberg, R. J. 1990. *Metaphors of Mind: Conceptions of the Nature of Intelligence.* Cambridge: Cambridge University Press.

Stiny, George. 1975. *Pictorial and Formal Aspects of Shape Grammars.* Basel, Switzerland: Birkhauser Verlag.

———. 1980. Introduction to shape and shape grammars. *Environment and Planning B* 7:342–51.

———. 1986. A new line on drafting systems. *Design Computing* 1:5–19.

Stults, Robert. 1988. Experimental uses of video to support design activities. *Report SSL-89-19 [P89-00019].* Palo Alto, Calif.: Xerox, Palo Alto Research Center.

References

Suchman, Lucille A. 1987. *Plans and Situated Actions: The Problem of Human-Machine Communication.* Cambridge: Cambridge University Press.

Swinburne, Richard. 1968. *Space and Time.* London: Macmillan.

Tavistock Institute. 1966. *Interdependence and Uncertainty: A Study of the Building Industry.* London: Tavistock.

Taylor, Charles. 1980. Understanding in human science. *Review of Metaphysics* 34:3–23.

Teller, S. J., and C. H. Séquin. 1991. Visibility preprocessing for interactive walkthroughs. *Proc. Computer Graphics (Siggraph '91)* 25 (4): 61–69.

Turbayne, Colin M. 1970. *The Myth of Metaphor.* Columbia: University of South Carolina Press.

Turkle, Sherry. 1980. Computer as Rorschach. *Society* (January/February): 15–24.

———. 1984. *The Second Self: Computers and the Human Spirit.* New York: Simon and Schuster.

Turner, Mark. 1988. Categories and analogies. In *Analogical Reasoning: Perspectives of Artificial Intelligence, Cognitive Science, and Philosophy,* ed. David H. Helman, 3–24. Dordrecht, The Netherlands: Kluwer Academic Publishers.

Upstill, S. 1989. *The Renderman™ Companion: A Programmer's Guide to Realistic Computer Graphics.* Reading, Mass.: Addison-Wesley.

Vesely, Dalibor. 1992. The nature of creativity in the age of production. *Scroope Cambridge Architecture Journal* 4:25–30. Department of Architecture, University of Cambridge, Cambridge.

———. 1992. The question of technology. Working paper. Department of Architecture, University of Cambridge, Cambridge.

Wasson, R. 1972. Marshall McLuhan and the politics of modernism. *Massachusetts Review* 13 (4): 567–80.

Weinsheimer, Joel C. 1985. *Gadamer's Hermeneutics: A Reading of "Truth and Method."* New Haven, Conn.: Yale University Press.

Weiser, Mark. 1991. The computer for the twenty-first century. *Scientific American* 265 (3): 66–75.

Weizenbaum, Joseph. 1984. *Computer Power and Human Reason: From Judgement to Calculation.* Harmondsworth, Middlesex: Penguin.

Wexler, Philip. 1987. And now for a little deconstruction: A response to Kurtzman. *New Ideas in Psychology* 5 (1): 73–76.

Wilks, Y. 1990. One small head: Models and theories. In *The Foundations of Artificial*

Intelligence: A Source Book, ed. D. Partridge and Y. Wilks, 121–34. Cambridge: Cambridge University Press.

Winner, Langdon. 1986. *The Whale and the Reactor*. Chicago: University of Chicago Press.

Winograd, Terry. 1990. Thinking machines: Can there be? are we? In *The Foundations of Artificial Intelligence: A Source Book*, D. ed. Partridge and Y. Wilks, 167–89. Cambridge: Cambridge University Press.

———. 1972. Understanding natural language. *Cognitive Psychology*, 8–11. No. 3. New York: Academic Press.

Winograd, Terry, and F. Flores. 1986. *Understanding Computers and Cognition: A New Foundation for Design*. Reading, Mass.: Addison-Wesley.

Wittgenstein, Ludwig. 1953. *Philosophical Investigations*. Oxford: Basil Blackwell.

Wood, David. 1990. *Philosophy at the Limit*. London: Unwin Hyman.

Wright, Kathleen. 1984. The place of the work of art in the age of technology. *Southern Journal of Philosophy* 22:565–83.

Wrigley, E. A. 1967. Demographic models in geography. In *Models in Geography*, ed. R. J. Chorley and P. Haggett, 189–215. London: Methuen.

Zadeh, Lofti A. 1983. The role of fuzzy logic in the management of uncertainty in expert systems. *Fuzzy Sets and Systems* 11 (3): 199–228.

Zavarzadeh, Mas'ud, and D. Morton. 1986–87. Theory pedagogy politics: The crisis of the subject in the humanities. *Boundary* 2 (15): 1–22.

Zimmerman, Michael E. 1990. *Heidegger's Confrontation with Modernity: Technology, Politics, Art*. Bloomington: Indiana University Press.

Index

Index

Index